AGENTS OF INFLUENCE

Aaron Edwards is a Senior Lecturer in Defence and International Affairs at the Royal Military Academy Sandhurst and an Honorary Research Fellow in the School of History, Politics and International Relations at the University of Leicester. Born in Belfast in 1980, he obtained his PhD in Politics from Queen's University Belfast in 2006 and was appointed a Fellow of the Royal Historical Society in 2012. He is the author of several acclaimed books, and his work has appeared in *Fortnight, The Irish Times, Belfast Telegraph, Irish News, Belfast News Letter* and *The Dublin Review of Books.*

Also by Aaron Edwards:

UVF: Behind the Mask

Strategy in War and Peace: A Critical Introduction

War: A Beginner's Guide

Mad Mitch's Tribal Law: Aden and the End of Empire

Defending the Realm? The Politics of Britain's Small Wars since 1945

The Northern Ireland Troubles: Operation Banner, 1969–2007

The Northern Ireland Conflict: A Beginner's Guide
(with Cillian McGrattan)

*A History of the Northern Ireland Labour Party:
Democratic Socialism and Sectarianism*

*Transforming the Peace Process in Northern Ireland: From
Terrorism to Democratic Politics* (edited with Stephen Bloomer)

AGENTS OF INFLUENCE

BRITAIN'S SECRET INTELLIGENCE WAR AGAINST THE IRA

Aaron Edwards

MERRION
PRESS

First published in 2021 by
Merrion Press
10 George's Street
Newbridge
Co. Kildare
Ireland
www.merrionpress.ie

© Aaron Edwards, 2021

978-1-78537-341-1 (Paper)
978-1-78537-342-8 (Kindle)
978-1-78537-343-5 (Epub)

A CIP catalogue record for this book
is available from the British Library.

Typeset in Minion Pro 11/14 pt

Front cover image: Alfredo 'Freddie' Scappaticci (extreme left, in colour)
pictured at the 1988 funeral of IRA man Brendan Davison. Gerry Adams
is pictured carrying the coffin. Scappaticci was otherwise known as
'Stakeknife' the Army's top informer inside the IRA. Photo courtesy
of Pacemaker Press.
Back cover image: Graffiti in Derry referring to RUC Special Branch
agent Raymond Gilmour. Photo courtesy of Alamy.

Merrion Press is a member of Publishing Ireland.

CONTENTS

AUTHOR'S NOTE

As with my previous book on the Ulster Volunteer Force (UVF), it has been necessary for security reasons to protect the identities of many of the people who helped me with my research. Although the vast majority of the information contained in this book was obtained from publicly available sources, including an array of now-declassified files obtained under the UK's Freedom of Information Act (2000), some of it comes from eyewitness accounts. To avoid disclosing sensitive information, the manuscript has had to be read by legal professionals. It has long been the policy of Her Majesty's Government to Neither Confirm, Nor Deny (NCND) issues relating to national security, including the identity of agents. Therefore, it must be emphasised that the views and opinions expressed are those of the author alone and should not be taken to represent those of Her Majesty's Government, the Ministry of Defence, Her Majesty's Armed Forces or any government agency. I am solely responsible for the interpretation of historical events scrutinised herein. While every effort has been made to ensure *Agents of Influence* is accurate, I am happy to correct any errors in future editions.

DRAMATIS PERSONAE

British Security and Intelligence Officials

Michael Bettaney aka 'Ben', MI5 officer/agent runner who handled Agent 3007

John Deverell, MI5 officer and Director and Coordinator of Intelligence at Stormont

Harold 'Hal' Doyne-Ditmas, MI5 officer and Director and Coordinator of Intelligence at Stormont

Michael Oatley, MI6 officer who held secret talks with the IRA

Sir Maurice Oldfield, former Chief of SIS and Intelligence and Security Co-ordinator at Stormont

David Ranson, MI5 officer and Director and Coordinator of Intelligence at Stormont

'Alan Rees-Morgan', MI5 officer who recruited Agent 3007

Sir Brooks Richards, former SOE Operations Officer and Intelligence and Security Coordinator at Stormont

Dame Stella Rimington, Director General of MI5

Sir Patrick Walker, Director General of MI5

Northern Ireland Office (NIO)

Humphrey Atkins, Secretary of State for Northern Ireland, 1979–81

Jim Prior, Secretary of State for Northern Ireland, 1981–84

Douglas Hurd, Secretary of State for Northern Ireland, 1984–85

Tom King, Secretary of State for Northern Ireland, 1985–89

Peter Brooke, Secretary of State for Northern Ireland, 1989–92

Sir Patrick Mayhew, Secretary of State for Northern Ireland, 1992–97

Sir John Blelloch, Permanent Under Secretary, 1988–90

Sir John Chilcot, Permanent Under Secretary, 1990–97

British Army

Lieutenant Colonel David Benest, Commanding Officer, 2 PARA, 1994–97

Major General Sir Jimmy Glover, Commander Land Forces, Northern Ireland, 1979–81

Major General Sir James 'Jimmy' Glover, Commander Land Forces, Northern Ireland, 1979–81

Lieutenant General Sir Timothy Creasey, GOC, Northern Ireland, 1978–80

Lieutenant General Sir Richard Lawson, GOC, Northern Ireland, 1980–82

Brigadier David Ramsbotham, Commander of 39 (Infantry) Brigade, 1979–81

Lieutenant General Sir Robert Richardson, GOC Northern Ireland, 1982–85

Lieutenant General Sir Roger Wheeler, GOC Northern Ireland, 1993–96

Royal Ulster Constabulary (RUC)

Sir John Hermon, Chief Constable, 1980–89
Jack, E4 HMSU officer
Jimmy B., E4 HMSU commander
Frank 'FT' Murray, Regional Head of Special Branch
Peter, Regional Head of Special Branch
Ronnie, E4 HMSU officer
Toby, Special Branch officer

Irish Republican Movement

Gerry Adams, Sinn Féin President
Ivor Bell, PIRA Chief of Staff
Gerry 'Whitey' Bradley, PIRA leader in the Ardoyne area of Belfast
Brendan 'Ruby' Davison, PIRA leader in the Markets area of Belfast
John Joe 'The Hawk' Haughey, PIRA GHQ
Jim Lynagh, East Tyrone PIRA
Seamus McElwain, Monaghan PIRA commander
Bernard McGinn, South Armagh PIRA
Martin McGuinness, PIRA Chief of Staff and later OC Northern Command
Kevin McKenna, PIRA Chief of Staff
John Joe Magee, PIRA Internal Security
Danny Morrison, Director of Publicity for Sinn Féin
Seán Savage, PIRA Explosives Officer
Freddie Scappaticci, PIRA Internal Security

Agents of Influence

Willie Carlin, Derry Sinn Féin and MI5/FRU agent of influence
'Síomón', IRA member and MI5/FRU agent of influence
'Tony', MI5 agent of influence

Intermediaries

Brendan Duddy, Derry businessman and link between the IRA and British
   Intelligence

LIST OF ABBREVIATIONS

ACC	Assistant Chief Constable
ARF	Airborne Reaction Force
ASU	Active Service Unit
CAT	Civil Administration Team
CGS	Chief of the General Staff (British Army)
CID	Criminal Investigation Department
CLF	Commander Land Forces
CO	Commanding Officer
COP	Close Observation Platoon
CTR	Close Target Reconnaissance
CWIED	Command Wire Improvised Explosive Device
DC	Detective Constable
DCI	Director and Coordinator of Intelligence
FRU	Force Research Unit
GAA	Gaelic Athletic Association
GHQ	General Headquarters (the IRA's authority for operations)
GCHQ	Government Communications Headquarters
GOC (NI)	General Officer Commanding (Northern Ireland)
GPMG	General Purpose Machine Gun
HIAI	Historical Institutional Abuse Inquiry
HMSU E4	Headquarters Mobile Support Unit, Special Branch specialist firearms unit
HQNI	British Army Headquarters Northern Ireland (Thiepval Barracks)
HSB	Head of Special Branch
HUMINT	Human Intelligence
IJS	Irish Joint Section (MI5/SIS)
INLA	Irish National Liberation Army
IRA	Irish Republican Army (can refer to Provisional IRA or Official IRA)

JIC	Joint Intelligence Committee
MI5	Military Intelligence, Section 5 (Security Service)
MI6	Military Intelligence, Section 6 (Secret Intelligence Service)
MISR	Military Intelligence Source Report
MoD	Ministry of Defence
MRF	Military Reconnaissance Force
NCO	Non-commissioned Officer
NIO	Northern Ireland Office
OC	Officer Commanding
Op	Operation
PAC	Provisional Army Council
PARA	Parachute Regiment
PEC	Province Executive Committee
PIRA	Provisional Irish Republican Army
PRONI	Public Record Office of Northern Ireland
PSNI	Police Service of Northern Ireland
PVCP	Permanent Vehicle Checkpoint
RCIED	Remote Controlled Improvised Explosive Device
RUC	Royal Ulster Constabulary
SAS	Special Air Service (British Army Special Forces)
SB	Special Branch (RUC)
SB50	Special Branch Form 50 (RUC intelligence report)
SIS	Secret Intelligence Service
SPG	Special Patrol Group (RUC)
SPM	Security Policy Meeting
TAOR	Tactical Area of Responsibility
TCG	Tasking and Coordination Group
TTP	Tactics, Techniques and Procedures
UDA	Ulster Defence Association
UDR	Ulster Defence Regiment
UVF	Ulster Volunteer Force
VCP	Vehicle Checkpoint

PREFACE

'The job of CID is to investigate this morning's murder. The job of Special Branch is to prevent this evening's murder,' said 'Toby', a former Royal Ulster Constabulary (RUC) officer who had agreed to meet me 'off the record', meaning that I would have to disguise his identity. A veteran of RUC Special Branch in the 1980s and 1990s, Toby was eager to make the case that he and his colleagues were all about 'saving lives' during the events that have become euphemistically known as the 'Troubles'. As the local police force, the RUC was charged by the government with protecting life and property, preserving the peace and preventing and detecting crime. Special Branch, the RUC's intelligence unit, served a vital purpose in helping the police carry out these functions. Toby's initial observations mirrored those of Patrick Walker, a senior member of the Security Service, MI5, who conducted a major review of intelligence sharing inside the Northern Irish constabulary in 1980.[1] At the time, a firm division of labour within the RUC saw 'the Branch' concerned primarily with the 'collection, collation and dissemination of intelligence on terrorist individuals and organisations', with the Criminal Investigation Department (CID) concentrating on the 'investigation of major crimes', including 'interviewing witnesses, interrogating suspects and [the] collection of evidence'.[2]

The Walker Report consolidated Special Branch primacy on all intelligence matters in Northern Ireland.[3] Importantly, it also helped focus the minds of police officers on the use of human intelligence, known to RUC officers as 'two-legged agents' and to the military as 'HUMINT'. As far as Walker was concerned, an agent was 'an individual recruited (and usually controlled by SB on regular payments) to provide information on the activities of a subversive organisation'.[4] As another senior MI5 officer would later disclose to the Bloody Sunday Inquiry, twenty years after the Walker Report, the Security Service drew an important distinction between agents and informers. 'Agents are not the same as informants,' Officer A told Lord Saville. 'Though they are not employed by the Service in the normal sense, they are subject to control and direction, and the relationship is an established one.'[5] As I learned during my meeting with Toby, agents were the primary means by which the RUC, Military

Intelligence and MI5 collated secret information on terrorist organisations during the Troubles.

Nowadays, Irish republicans see Special Branch as being responsible for prolonging the conflict, rather than helping to end it. I have always believed in giving people a fair hearing, so I offered Toby the benefit of the doubt. That lunchtime, in a café in the shadows of the towering yellow cranes of Harland and Wolff, which represent Belfast's famous industrial heritage and dominate the city's skyline, I felt a little jaded by Toby's tendency to see everything through rose-tinted glasses. Like most members of the Security Forces I have met over the years, he seemed to be of the opinion that everything he and his colleagues did was morally and ethically right. I do have some sympathy with that position. These were people who risked their lives to defend the community from the scourge of terrorism. In objective terms, the British state, one of the world's oldest liberal democracies, had an obligation to protect its population.

However, my contacts right across the political spectrum, including former members of the IRA, cast the methods employed by the British government and its armed forces, law enforcement and intelligence agencies in a different light. In their eyes, there is a serious question mark over how the British state ran its counter-terrorism campaign. For the professional historian, it is important to keep in mind that there are always differing perspectives on the past. Although it would be easy to allow my own personal biases to colour my research, I have always endeavoured to be as balanced as possible. Therefore, I felt obliged to ask Toby some awkward questions. And he offered me the perfect opportunity to do so.

'You must have questions,' he said.

We were surrounded by people who were oblivious to our secret liaison. I did have questions. I had lots of them. Perhaps the most important of these was: how did Special Branch run agents against their principal enemies in the Provisional IRA (PIRA)? Did he and his colleagues follow a strategy for combatting violent republicanism?

'Well,' said Toby. 'If there was a strategy, it wasn't happening in the Branch.'

Then he began to lead me down a narrow tunnel into the past, every twist and turn of which seemed to suggest that the Branch improvised its response to the IRA on a day-to-day basis. In Toby's mind it was all a game of cat and mouse – or cops and robbers – in which brave Branch officers made personal sacrifices for the collective security of all the people of Northern Ireland. This sounded plausible, if somewhat romantic, but it didn't explain who was pulling the strings. Were those in charge to be found in RUC Special Branch headquarters in Belfast or elsewhere, perhaps in MI5? Toby was sceptical. He wanted to impress upon me that the Branch led the way: 'When you went to Thames House, or Curzon Street before it, you were greeted by people who were inherently soft. Anyone you found who would have been up for a few pints or a game of rugby was obviously on secondment from the MoD or former Army.' He seemed sceptical of those from Great Britain, especially members of the Security Service, who were casually dismissed by the 'hard men' of the Branch as 'the rich cousins'. This is a view I have come across many times when interviewing former RUC officers.

As a student of Britain's small wars of the twentieth century, I was intrigued by Toby's reluctance to talk about the influence of strategic thinking on his actions and those of his colleagues. This was especially surprising given that Toby had risen up through the ranks of this world-renowned intelligence organisation and would have been responsible for following orders and issuing them at one time or another. Having a deliberate, well-thought-through plan seemed essential to me, especially since I had been told by several senior Special Branch officers a decade earlier that it had been 'an intelligence-led war from the 1980s' onwards.[6]

Toby spoke glowingly of tight time frames for operational decision-making and executive action in one of the world's premier counter-terrorism units: 'At 4 p.m. on a Friday anyone in [MI]5 was heading for a train in Waterloo. The Branch wasn't like that. We were back planning, trying to assemble a jigsaw puzzle of intelligence that didn't come with an accompanying box cover to aid assembly. Sometimes you had only a few pieces. Saving lives was time-sensitive.' I listened patiently and attentively as he painted a picture of a small band of idealistic crime fighters battling hardened criminals against the odds. I was reminded of the team of desperadoes led by FBI Special Agent Eliot Ness that eventually took down the infamous Chicago mobster Al Capone in the interwar years.

Toby was clearly enjoying himself as he regaled me with boys' own tales of derring-do. I wished to talk to this former shadow warrior about how secret intelligence was gathered and disseminated, but he was intent on talking up the superiority of the Branch. Where were the spymasters in all of this? Who was deciding on the plan of action, the strategy for taking down the IRA? Was there even a strategy? Alas, Toby remained tight-lipped.

He had his own perspective to share with me and would not be deterred. It was obvious that our conversation had run its course. I would not get any further answers to my questions that afternoon.

On my journey back to the anonymity of the city centre, I wondered whether British Intelligence followed a deliberate strategy in combatting IRA terrorism. If Special Branch couldn't tell me, then who could?

Perhaps the British Army had the answers I was seeking?

According to the Army's now-declassified report on Operation (Op) Banner, which constituted thirty-eight years of continuous military operations in support of the police, 'almost all the military structures which eventually defeated PIRA were in place' by 1980, yet it would take another fourteen years to bring about a ceasefire. The Army blamed this on there being 'no single authority in overall charge of the direction of the campaign, but rather three agencies, often poorly-coordinated'.[7] According to the Army's own analysis of the longest-lasting troop deployment in British military history, there was no overarching strategy or vision for ending the violence. This makes Army activity in Northern Ireland seem rather uncomplicated and, like the police perspective, plays down the tactical and operational efforts to end the conflict. It also obscures the intellectual challenges and moral and ethical dilemmas faced by members of the Security Forces during one of the world's most protracted terrorist campaigns.

A year after meeting Toby in Belfast, I met another former Intelligence Officer in the Midlands. 'Bob' had served in Military Intelligence during Op Banner. He was eager to explain that the Army gained considerable insight into the PIRA via HUMINT. 'While there was technological penetration of terrorist organisations, the vast majority of intelligence came from human sources,' Bob said. 'It was so sophisticated that we were reading the minutes of the IRA's General Army Convention before they were disseminated to their senior membership.' Fascinated though I was by this revelation, I was also sceptical. However, as I have learned in the course of writing this book, these claims can be substantiated by the historical record. As a result of the UK's Freedom of Information Act (2000), we have proof that the British government had access to an extraordinary amount of source reporting of high-level IRA and Sinn Féin meetings.

In Bob's view, obtaining such secret information was not without its challenges. He emphasised that persistent competition between the RUC, the Army and MI5 made combatting the IRA more difficult than it needed to be. I had heard this before. A few years ago, at an event I had organised examining the security lessons learned in Northern Ireland, I listened attentively as a former RUC Special Branch officer complained about the lack of coordination between the different security and intelligence agencies in the fight against the IRA.[8] It appeared that each of these agencies prized their own agents and informers above those of the other agencies. The British counter-insurgency expert Sir Robert Thompson cautioned against this in his 1972 book detailing his experiences in Malaya and Vietnam in the 1950s and 1960s. 'Mutual suspicion and jealousies will arise,' he wrote, 'quite likely with the result that the separate organisations merely end up spying on each other.'[9] Respected journalist David McKittrick reported as early as 1980 that the competition was 'immensely damaging to the overall intelligence effort'; each agency believed it 'should be running the show'.[10] There is some evidence, however, that such competition had subsided by the 1990s. Several former Special Branch officers have even boasted that Britain's intelligence war had become 'a Rolls Royce of an operation by then'.[11]

Like his RUC colleagues, Bob believed that relations between the various intelligence agencies did eventually improve. Interestingly, the rationale given for the division between the agencies had previously been outlined by Major (later General Sir) Frank Kitson in his book *Gangs and Counter-gangs*, in which he insisted that the military should always maintain its own intelligence-gathering capabilities.[12] Kitson is generally credited with the formation of the Military Reconnaissance Force (MRF) in Northern Ireland, which is considered to have been a disaster by most accounts. However, the MRF was born at a time when the military led counter-terrorism operations, a time when the attitude was 'have a go'.[13] With the advent of police primacy in the mid-1970s, however, the Army was forced to play second fiddle to the RUC. By the end of the decade, it had fallen not to Kitson, but to Major General Jimmy Glover, a fellow Royal Green Jackets officer who served as Commander of Land Forces in Northern Ireland from 15 February 1979 to 22 October 1980, to establish an intelligence organisation that would continue to provide the Army with a seat at the decision-making table.

Importantly, at a joint Army–RUC study day on agent handling in May 1979 – convened by Glover – the Head of Special Branch criticised the military on two grounds. 'The first was their tendency to gallop off without consultation,' he said. 'The second was the use by Army handlers of other people's intelligence in tasking sources.'[14] As 'Peter', a former Regional Head of RUC Special Branch, later reflected, "The British Army was given to improvisation. They had the men and the resources. The GOC had a point. He had 20,000 troops at his disposal whereas the Chief Constable had 4,000–5,000 officers. In the Army mindset, if you are at war with an enemy, you will push the envelope.'[15]

It was in this spirit of improvisation that the Force Research Unit (FRU) was created by Glover as the Army's premier agent-running organisation. The FRU remains shrouded in mystery. What we do know has been gleaned from public inquiries and reviews. Set up under the direction of the Intelligence Corps, it was commanded by a lieutenant colonel, with a second in command, and based in the Army's headquarters in Lisburn. The FRU had four regional detachments in the north, south, east and west of Northern Ireland, all commanded by junior officers holding the rank of captain.[16] In a statement to the Stevens Inquiry in 1990, a former FRU Commanding Officer (CO) outlined his unit's mission:

> The secret role of the FRU is to obtain intelligence from secretly penetrating terrorist organisations in Northern Ireland by recruiting and running agents and informants. This role is vital to counter terrorist operations because only the 'inside knowledge' provided by agents can lead to a true understanding of the terrorists and their intention.[17]

As I learned from Toby, some Branch officers remain dismissive of the FRU. 'Over 95% of sources were handled by the Branch,' he told me. Although he downplayed the military's handling of agents, it is generally believed that the FRU played an important role in the intelligence war against the IRA.[18] As the Army admitted in its study of Op Banner, the importance of intelligence gathering 'is hard to understate', for the 'insurgency could not have been broken, and the terrorist structure could not have been engaged and finally driven into politics without the intelligence organisations and processes that were developed'.[19]

Apart from Special Branch and the FRU, secret information was also obtained by MI5. For MI5, 'agents have helped us to stop many terrorist plots and attacks in the last decade. Although we are not able to publicly recognise individuals who help, it is no exaggeration to say that they really are unsung heroes.'[20] MI5 has become more open about its efforts to combat terrorism, particularly since the terrorist attacks in the United States on 11 September 2001 and in the United Kingdom in 2005 and 2017. Indeed, it is now possible to read about MI5's intelligence-led operations against the IRA in the Service's official history.[21] Additionally, MI5 have released original source reports into the public domain for various inquiries. Since they were officially acknowledged thirty years ago, British Intelligence agencies have been subjected to more scrutiny than ever before. In an era of Islamist terrorism, their failures have been paraded for all to see. Their successes, however, are less well known. This book constitutes an attempt to highlight both their successes and their failures in Northern Ireland and was written in the context of Sir John Chilcot's examination of Britain's intervention in Iraq, which recommended that we learn lessons from the episode. 'Identifying lessons learned is not new,' Rob Dover and Mike Goodman, respected scholars of Intelligence Studies, suggest. 'In the intelligence world it is, however, a new approach. Various attempts to extract the wider lessons have been utilised at various points in the past, but their common problem is that they are forgotten as fast as they appear.'[22]

Agents of Influence is chiefly concerned with learning the lessons of our secret past in Northern Ireland. It is also about the extraordinary measures that have been taken to protect liberal democracy. In liberal democracies, intelligence agencies report directly to government to give ministers the information they need to make better decisions.[23] The book explores the decisions made by people who disagreed with each other about how to deal with the pernicious challenge posed by terrorism. Many of these people had been schooled in three opposing world views. There were those who had served in colonial hotspots, such as Malaya, Kenya, Cyprus and Aden, and had witnessed first-hand violent rebellions against British rule. These people saw the secret war against the PIRA in colonial terms and believed that they were at war with terrorism. Often they were soldiers, but not always. Another group of Intelligence Officers had been schooled in the broader clash between Western liberal democracies and Soviet communism. The thinking of these Cold War warriors was shaped by an international struggle waged principally against subversion and espionage targeting the British state. They were principally found in the ranks of MI5 and MI6. The third group of Intelligence Officers, found mainly in the RUC, saw the PIRA as an existential threat to the lives of the people of Northern Ireland. Above all, however, this book is about the men and women who were asked by these Intelligence Officers to put their lives at risk in order to obtain secret information. In the course of the research for *Agents of Influence*, I have met several of these individuals and discovered how they were recruited, handled and, eventually, 'retired'. This is the story of the risks they took, some of which can now be revealed for the first time.

Prologue

IN THE ZONE

'The first duty of an underground worker is to perfect not only his cover story but also his cover personality.'

– Kim Philby, former SIS/KGB double agent[1]

London Waterloo, Lunchtime, Mid-September 2018

It is a sunny day in London, one of the last before more autumnal weather sets in, and I am in Waterloo to meet a former soldier who has agreed to act as my guide through the secret world of Northern Ireland's intelligence war. It is a murky world, characterised by double-crossing, controversy and death. The vast majority of secret intelligence and covert action operations remain top secret. This comes as no surprise considering the nature of the conflict: the smoke and mirrors, the lies and half-truths that surround it and influence any retelling of what happened in the past.

I am about to meet a man who claims to have been one of Britain's most secret agents. His name is Willie Carlin and he says he was recruited by the Security Service, MI5, and inserted into the heart of the Irish Republican Movement, a term used throughout this book to refer to the PIRA and their political associates in Sinn Féin. His mission was to establish and maintain a cover personality so he could feed information on the Provisionals' political strategy to his handlers in British Intelligence. Having heard a little about him from journalist contacts, I expected him to overplay his role in the secret intelligence struggle against the IRA. I recall reading a punchy article in *The Blanket* by former IRA prisoner Anthony McIntyre at the time of the breaking of the 'Stakeknife' affair in which he, correctly in my view, warned us to treat with scepticism the word of 'barroom braggers' who seemed 'more concerned with inflating their own standing in the eyes of journalists as men at the epicentre of great system shaking events rather than being the purveyors of mess hall tittle-tattle'.[2] I have met my fair share of these types, who are desperate to reinvent themselves to anyone who will listen. As I ventured into central London that morning, I anticipated more of the same. However, what I would hear that day challenged my scepticism and sent me on a fascinating journey into the shadowy recesses of contemporary British and Irish history.

Moments after entering the building in which our secret liaison would take place, I detect the dulcet tones of a Northern Irish accent to my left and spot a small, wiry man perched on the edge of a sofa, engrossed in animated conversation with a group of tourists. He is well dressed, but otherwise unremarkable. His codename as an agent was 3007 and was given to him by his handlers in the covert Military Intelligence outfit known as the FRU. Unlike Ian Fleming's famous character James Bond, 3007 was a secret agent, not an Intelligence Officer. This distinction is lost on most people because of how little is known about this hidden world. 3007 was directed and run by an agent handler, but it was the agent who took all the risks. His handlers merely debriefed him, often from the relative safety of a military camp or safe house.

Today, Agent 3007 is wearing a suit and is well groomed. His tie is straight. His shoes are polished. He is every inch the old soldier. He spots me, stands up straight, approaches and shakes my hand. A few minutes later, I'm ordering us coffee. 'It's great to meet you,' he says. We begin by chatting about two friends we have in common. This is how Northern Irish people tend to break the ice when they meet a person for the first time. Northern Ireland used to be likened to a village by British soldiers who served there and it's true that everybody has mutual acquaintances. We take a seat in the corner, away from prying eyes. I start by telling him about myself. I need to reassure him of my scholarly credentials. I give him a gift of two of my books, so he can get a sense of how I approach my research.

Agent 3007 then begins to regale me with extraordinary tales of the secret intelligence he gathered on the IRA in Derry, where he was born; of clandestine debriefs along Northern Ireland's breathtaking northern coastline and in the much less salubrious surroundings of Ebrington Barracks in the Waterside area of the city. He tells me, too, of his cover being blown and the bravery of his handlers in extracting him from the dangerous arena of paramilitary politics, of his meeting with Margaret Thatcher and her words of thanks to him and his family in Downing Street in the mid-1980s, and of his many moves from safe house to safe house. He even talks about the threat of death that hangs over him. Members of the Republican Movement call such people informers or 'touts' and many have been murdered with a bullet to the back of the head, their bodies casually dumped in lonely country lanes. One academic has estimated that the IRA killed some seventy-one suspected informers during the Troubles.[3] As 3007 reminds me, death sentences remain extant and can still be enacted many years after the betrayal.

This is what I'm here to learn from Agent 3007. As far as I'm concerned, he is the quintessential 'agent of influence': a man recruited by British Intelligence to infiltrate the ranks of the Republican Movement. As one leading expert on this form of deep-cover intelligence gathering wrote:

> Agents of influence are allies in the councils of a foreign power. It is misleading to think of agents of influence as mere creatures of a foreign power, mercenaries, or robots carrying out orders. Because such people exercise influence – indeed this is why they are cultivated – their sympathies cannot be wholly secret. (But the degree to which they coordinate their activities with a foreign power is likely to be secret.) So for a government to maintain or increase the influence of its agents abroad, it must provide them the 'cover' that only a certain ambiguous kind of success can bring.[4]

It's impossible to know how many agents of influence operated inside the Republican Movement. Official recognition of spies is rare; disavowal is routine. 'We Neither Confirm Nor Deny,' runs the government's mantra.

I once heard a former high-ranking Intelligence Officer explain Britain's three-pronged strategy to a largely foreign audience in the context of an open forum. The first prong, he said, was to 'recruit' former soldiers to infiltrate the terrorist group and their political associates. The second prong was to 'turn' terrorists. And the third prong was to build up a more complete picture of known 'players' through the tireless patrolling and surveillance work of uniformed police officers and soldiers.[5] 'Toby', a former RUC Special Branch officer, once described this to me as an 'intelligence pyramid', with uniformed Security Forces at the bottom and 'two-legged agents', like Agent 3007, at the top. Such agents may have been at the forefront of Britain's secret war against the IRA, but the intelligence they provided was only useful when all the cogs of the counter-terrorism machinery operated in sync. But how was this intelligence collected, collated, assessed and disseminated? What impact did it have in persuading the IRA to abandon armed struggle? And, most importantly, what lessons does the intelligence war have for future conflicts?

I'm eager to discover how Agent 3007 was recruited:

I was in the office one day ... I was organising something ... and the phone rang ...

'Can I speak to Sergeant Carlin?'

'Speaking.'

He called me 'Sergeant'. I was only a Corporal at the time. I was acting, unpaid and unwanted.

'My name is Captain Thorpe.'

Anyway, he wanted to meet me. 'Can you skip off tomorrow afternoon?'

I could, so he arranged to meet me in Cloud's Hill at the back of Bovington Camp, which is where Lawrence of Arabia's cottage is. So, that's where we met.

And he said to me, 'There's somebody that wants to meet you.' He had a wee Mini Morris Countryman – you know, with the green paint and wooden frame. So, he drove off and he says, 'I'm going to park up here.' And this Merc[edes] came along – now, compared to today's Mercs it was a big car then. This man got out. Beautifully dressed, wearing gloves. He took off his gloves and shook my hand.

'Let's walk.'

And that's when he said, 'You've been brought to our notice.'

And I says, 'Who's we?'

'Well, I'm not in the Army and I'm not a politician,' he says. 'Colleagues of mine have been looking for someone to go to Derry and get involved in the early stages of politics. Not the IRA. Absolutely not. This is safe. And nobody will know about you.'

It strikes me that MI5's recruitment pitch could only have worked on someone who belonged to the close-knit community that gave birth to and nurtured the city's Republican Movement. It soon becomes clear that Carlin was a distant relation of Martin McGuinness, the IRA's long-serving chieftain. He's also related to known players who surrounded McGuinness on a day-to-day basis. If ever there was someone with the credibility to infiltrate the 'closed shop' of Derry republicanism, it's Carlin.

'I'm in the zone,' he says. 'I knew when I spoke to you on the phone that I had entered this place.'

I ask him what he means and he informs me that it's what he says whenever his mind drifts back to his time as an agent of influence.

'"James" [a former FRU commander] took me to the side and said, "I am worried about you. I'm unsure where your loyalties lie."'

This is common amongst agents of influence. How they managed to conceal their true intentions is a mystery. Even their closest family members aren't always aware of their betrayal. Carlin opens his briefcase, takes out a Zippo lighter and hands it to me. On one side is an Irish tricolour and on the other is the Union flag. He then shows me a wallet made by legendary IRA hunger striker Bobby Sands.

'It was given to me by Bobby's mother in appreciation for a poem I'd composed about the hunger strikes.'

The fact that Agent 3007 was suspected of divided loyalties is probably more indicative of his abilities as a double agent than his political convictions. I'm beginning to understand the psyche of this man who risked everything to report news to the British establishment from the front line of this dirty little war.

We've been talking about his exploits all day, but I get the sense he has more to tell me.

'Did you ever have a final debrief?' I ask him.

'No,' he replies.

A wave of surprise washes over me as it occurs to me that perhaps he thinks I'm debriefing him. He is remarkably candid. Agent 3007 believes he helped move the IRA towards peace. It is an intriguing claim. I tell him that I'd like to test it against the publicly available evidence.

As well as his telling me of long strolls along windswept beaches and through picturesque forests with his handlers, clandestine pick-ups in blacked-out vans and his rapid exfiltration from the danger zone, he made other observations too. Rather than describing the life of a man at the centre of the action, he gave me a vivid picture of the psychology and organisation of the Republican Movement from the point of view of a long-term secret agent. His account was more 'fly on the wall' than 'man in the big picture', as we say in Belfast.

What follows is the story of how the secret information provided by Agent 3007 and others not only helped the Security Forces prevent terrorist attacks, but also, perhaps more importantly, ultimately informed political decision-making in Belfast and London and altered the course of a centuries-old conflict forever.

1

THE WAR AGAINST TERRORISM

'It is the Government's firm policy that we should continue in Northern Ireland to do our utmost to defeat terrorism.'

– Sir Humphrey Atkins, Secretary of State for
Northern Ireland, 2 July 1979[1]

Narrow Water, Warrenpoint, County Down, 4.40 p.m., 27 August 1979

It was a blistering hot Bank Holiday Monday in Narrow Water, a picturesque townland on Carlingford Lough, which straddles the border between Northern Ireland and the Irish Republic. On the main A2 dual carriageway, soldiers from A Company of the Parachute Regiment's 2nd Battalion were making their way in a convoy from their base in Ballykinlar to relieve their comrades in Newry RUC station. As the rear vehicle, a four-tonne truck, rumbled along, the driver noticed a trailer loaded with hay bales parked in a nearby lay-by. The bales concealed a 700lb fertiliser-based bomb, packed tightly into milk churns and surrounded by petrol cans. The bomb exploded, sending a massive fireball into the back of the vehicle that burnt through the flesh of the soldiers piled into it. Six soldiers were killed immediately.[2] Two civilians who had pulled into the lay-by for a picnic on the shoreline felt the initial shockwave pass through them and heard the loud bang that followed. 'I looked up and saw a large cloud of smoke where the lorry used to be,' one of them recalled. 'I saw soldiers running back to the explosion. I thought the bomb had been meant for the soldiers and that they had got away.'[3] The scene was one of utter devastation.

Twenty-eight-year-old Captain Tom Schwartz from Farnborough in Hampshire was among the young Parachute Regiment officers in an accompanying Land Rover. He described what he saw after the explosion: 'I have never seen such a sight in my life and never wish to see it again. Bits and pieces of people were scattered all over the place.'[4] He said he was hit by a 'great rushing wind', though he managed to escape with his life. After the initial blast, he raised his head and saw that everything was completely enveloped in thick dust. As the survivors began to pick themselves up and brush themselves off, it was clear that some of the young soldiers were wracked with fear, but trying not to show it.

A patrol of Royal Marines from 40 Commando were in nearby Warrenpoint when they heard the explosion. They lost no time in radioing in a 'contact report'. The senior officer who came over the net was 34-year-old Major Barry Rogan. He immediately rushed out the door of Newry RUC station with reinforcements, arriving at the scene of the bomb blast within minutes. He was accompanied by Major Pete Fursman, also in his mid-30s, whose soldiers had been targeted in the explosion and who had arrived ahead of his men. Back in the Army's regional Operations Room at Bessbrook Mill, deep inside South Armagh, commanders mobilised an Airborne Reaction Force (ARF). At that time, Bessbrook was the busiest helipad in Europe and the first port of call for the deployment of air support in the southern border region. The ARF was tasked with swiftly responding to incidents and so always included a medic on-board to deal with any casualties. The unfortunate reality was that casualties were a common occurrence in this part of the world. The principal objective of the soldiers rushing to the scene was to preserve life and establish what had happened.

Meanwhile, 40-year-old Lieutenant Colonel David Blair, the CO of the Queen's Own Highlanders, was in a Gazelle helicopter hovering 3,000 feet overhead. Colonel Blair had been on a separate mission when he received a radio report about the attack at Narrow Water. He immediately directed the pilot to the incident. As the helicopter prepared to land in the grounds of the Narrow Water Castle country estate, just opposite where the explosion had taken place, Blair spotted the smouldering military vehicles on the dual carriageway. Along with his signaller, 24-year-old Lance Corporal Victor MacLeod, Blair jumped out of the aircraft and ran towards the scene to begin coordinating the response. As the two Highlanders reached the gateway lodge of the estate, a pair of IRA men lying on a grassy bank on the Irish Republic side of Carlingford Lough flicked a switch on their handheld radio-controlled firing device, initiating a second charge. Colonel Blair and Corporal MacLeod were killed instantly, along with ten other soldiers. 'I will always remember the chilling silence after that second explosion,' recalled Tom Schwartz, 'and the total lack of noise of any type.'[5] A police officer who arrived soon afterwards recalled seeing 'bodies scattered around the area', which were 'blackened and some were mutilated'.[6] A fireman who had been busy putting out the raging fires was struck by shrapnel that had been hidden beside the keep of Narrow Water Castle to maximise casualties. Most of the soldiers killed in the IRA attack had only been in Northern Ireland a matter of weeks.

Back at Bessbrook, 35-year-old Major Mike Jackson was enjoying a tea break in the Officers' Mess when he got a call from the Ops Room about the first explosion. Jackson was the Officer Commanding (OC) of B Company of 2 PARA. He and his men had only just returned to barracks after having been out on operations. As his company replenished their ammunition and sorted their kit, he hurried to the Ops Room, where he was joined by Brigadier David Thorne, the commander of 3rd (Infantry) Brigade, who had flown in from his headquarters in Dungannon to take control of the situation. Thorne told Jackson to 'get down to Warrenpoint and sort it out'. Jackson immediately roused his company and organised an airborne move to Narrow Water. No sooner had his helicopter lifted off than word came over the net of a second explosion. As Jackson neared the scene, he peered down. 'There was human debris everywhere – in the trees, on the grass verge and in the water,' he later recalled. 'Mostly unidentifiable lumps of red flesh, but among them torsos, limbs, heads, hands and ears. I had seen the effect of bombs before but never carnage on this scale.'[7]

Pathologist Arthur Orr, who arrived an hour later, also said that he had 'never seen such carnage'. He stated that it was 'the most distressing incident' he had ever encountered in his twenty-five years as a coroner. Presiding over the inquests in July 1980, Orr described the deaths as 'the most abhorrent and gruesome that I have ever had to deal with, and I have no doubt that no other deaths have caused greater public grief in this province'.[8] He reserved much of his opprobrium for those responsible: 'These villains with their lookouts, their signallers and their activator lay in wait and, not satisfied with one death-dealing explosion, they knew that the army would rush to the rescue and they were ready to set off a second and more massive explosion.'[9]

Two IRA volunteers, Brendan Burns and Joe Brennan, both in their early twenties, were stopped by An Garda Síochána (Irish police) while riding a motorbike in the vicinity. Despite reportedly finding traces of gunshot residue and explosives on their hands and clothing, the Gardaí could not conclusively tie either of the men to the scene and so released them soon afterwards.[10]

In an interview given by a representative of the IRA's ruling Army Council at the time, the group commented on its success in ambushing the troops: 'The first bomb was 1,100lb, the second 800lb. It was the second one which caused most of the deaths. Both were remote-detonated. The British Army has been very, very fortunate in escaping major losses since the sophisticated remote was developed – very, very lucky.'[11]

In claiming responsibility for the attack on the paratroopers, the Provisionals referred to the regiment's involvement in the killing of thirteen civilians in Derry seven years earlier. 'Without apology we republicans are proud of the battle being fought and we unreservedly support the methods,' the IRA told its newspaper, An Phoblacht/Republican News. 'The Paras had their Bloody Sunday and they sowed, and now, they have reaped their Bloody Monday.'[12]

One former RUC Special Branch officer who policed these borderlands characterised the region as being 'lawless and lacking in any sustained intelligence coverage.'[13] The IRA's ability to cultivate sources inside the Gardaí hindered cross-border cooperation aimed at defeating the terrorists and created difficulties for law enforcement agencies in the North. 'When I was down with the Crime Squad, working on the murder of four policemen at Bessbrook, [I was] temporarily redirected to Warrenpoint to the murder of the paratroopers,' recalled CID officer Roy Cairns. 'We were warned by a uniformed Sergeant in the Garda down there, if we were coming down, not to tell anybody we were coming down. To tell him and tell no one else. And [Officer X] was identified to us as giving information to the IRA.'[14] Such leakage inside the Gardaí was compounded by another, perhaps more corrosive problem: the lack of coordination between the RUC and the Army, which made it easier for the IRA to act with impunity along the porous border.

★ ★ ★

British Prime Minister Margaret Thatcher was working on official correspondence at her private residence in Chequers in Buckinghamshire when a member of her staff broke the news about Narrow Water to her.[15] She had already been informed earlier that day of the assassination of the former Chief of Defence Staff Lord Louis Mountbatten, his 14-year-old grandson and a local teenager at Mullaghmore in County Sligo. Reports of the deaths touched a raw nerve in her. As soon as she had finished composing a letter to the Royal Family expressing her condolences on Mountbatten's death, she asked her Private Secretary, Sir Clive Whitmore, to furnish her with the addresses of the next of kin of the eighteen dead soldiers. Thatcher was eager to write to their families personally.[16] She then asked Whitmore to arrange her return to Downing Street before assisting her with the drafting of a statement on the day's dramatic developments. The language in her statement was uncompromising: 'The Government will spare no effort to ensure that those responsible for these and for all other acts of terrorism are brought to justice. The people of the United Kingdom will wage the war against terrorism with relentless determination until it is won.'[17]

Thatcher arrived back in London the next morning to convene a high-level meeting with her Cabinet colleagues to discuss the government's response. In attendance were Home Secretary Willie Whitelaw, the Lord Privy Seal, Sir Ian Gilmour, and Defence Secretary Francis Pym, all of whom returned later that evening for a second crisis meeting to decide on what steps to take. Further cooperation with the Irish government was seen as a top priority, along with, perhaps, 'more vigorous use of the SAS [Special Air Service]'. Thatcher, however, felt that the best step forward for longer-term success against the terrorists was to improve cooperation between the RUC and the Army, particularly in the intelligence field. It was clear to everyone, from Thatcher in Downing Street to senior military commanders in Lisburn, that there was 'distressing evidence of mutual distrust at the highest levels of the RUC and the Army'.[18] Thatcher considered the appointment of an overall Director of Operations to 'exercise control of operations both by the Police and the Army', an essential first step in dealing with the breakdown in police–Army relations.[19] She made arrangements to visit the front line herself in order to obtain an overview of how precarious the security situation was on the ground.

The next day, Thatcher travelled to Belfast aboard her personal RAF jet. Upon arrival, she was driven to Musgrave Park Hospital to meet the survivors of the Narrow Water attack. After speaking with the injured soldiers, she visited Belfast city centre to meet the public. 'I shall never forget the reception I received,' she later wrote. 'It is peculiarly moving to receive good wishes from people who are suffering. One never knows quite how to respond. But I formed then an impression I have never had reason to revise that the people of Ulster will never bow to violence.'[20] Her next stop was Mahon Road Barracks in Portadown, where she received a briefing from Brigadier Thorne, who informed her of a 'deterioration of the situation, the level of casualties, the number of incidents'. There was 'nothing new in what I was saying', he later recalled.[21] To emphasise his exasperation, Thorne placed David Blair's rank epaulette, the only trace of the late colonel that remained at the scene, on the table beside Thatcher.[22]

Emboldened by what she had been told, Thatcher donned military fatigues and boarded a short helicopter flight to South Armagh to experience for herself the challenges facing the Security Forces. 'I saw the bomb-battered Crossmaglen RUC station – the most attacked RUC–Army post in Northern Ireland – before running back to the helicopter,' she confided in her memoirs. 'It is too dangerous for either security force personnel or helicopters to remain stationary in these parts,' she added.[23] After visiting senior RUC officers in Gough Barracks in Armagh, Thatcher returned to London. There was a considerable amount of work to do.

Over the next few weeks, Whitmore and Thatcher's incoming Cabinet Secretary, Robert Armstrong, were shortlisting suitable candidates for the role of Director of Operations. Several names crossed their desks, including the former Permanent Under Secretary at the Department of Education and Science, Sir William Pile, and Sir Donald Maitland, Britain's former Ambassador to Libya. Neither man seemed right for the position. Thatcher's senior advisers agonised over the right person, though they were entirely in agreement on the terms of reference for the appointment. Whoever got the job needed to have a 'strong personality, able to operate by persuasion and in a style appropriate to dealing with both police officers and soldiers', as well as having 'planning and operational experience and ingenuity', though they did not want someone with a 'command' style or a public figure.[24] The job description outlined that the person chosen for the role would be responsible for 'advising and assisting SSNI [Secretary of State for Northern Ireland] in the formulation of security policy objectives', giving guidance to the Security Forces, and helping coordinate across all departments and agencies to 'support the total security effort'.[25] The dispatch of a leading personality from London to the spot where trouble had broken out was a course of action that had been taken by previous British governments whenever they faced similar challenges in their disengagement from empire.

By late September, Thatcher's advisers were expressing their preference for a senior official who had experience managing tricky international matters. Sir John Killick, an old hand in the Foreign Office who had served as British Ambassador to Moscow in 1971–73 and the North Atlantic Treaty

Organisation (NATO) in 1975–79, was renowned for 'being somewhat robust', believed in 'calling a spade a spade' and was just the sort of tough-minded career diplomat needed for this important mission.[26] However, Killick declined the offer because he felt that his wife had already been 'dragged around to some unpleasant places over 30 years' as a result of his work and also because he did not feel he had the knowledge or skills necessary for the role. Intriguingly, Killick drew a comparison between the situation in Northern Ireland and British counter-insurgency efforts in Malaya two decades earlier. He thanked Downing Street for the opportunity and said that he believed Thatcher had been right to focus on appointing someone with the 'impact of personality and ability to inject a new sense of purpose' into the situation.[27] After further deliberation, Downing Street officials settled on one person who now seemed to stand out among all others.

On 24 September, they decided to approach Sir Maurice Oldfield, the recently retired Chief of the Secret Intelligence Service (SIS), MI6, to invite him for interview at Downing Street. Oldfield had known Thatcher from her time as Leader of the Opposition and readily agreed to a meeting with her.[28] Oldfield had left MI6 in 1978 for an academic position at All Souls College in Oxford, where he began researching the role of the clergy in medieval times.[29] Some of his contemporaries believed that he had grown bored and frustrated since leaving the Service as he spent more time reading newspapers and enjoying sumptuous lunches than engaging in serious scholarly work. Indeed, much of his retirement was spent at his family's farm at Bakewell in Derbyshire. Oldfield telephoned Whitmore thirty-six hours after his meeting at Number 10 to accept the offer. Whitmore promptly convened a meeting with outgoing Cabinet Secretary Sir John Hunt, the Permanent Secretary at the MoD, Frank Cooper, his opposite number at the Northern Ireland Office (NIO), Brian Cubbon, the Director General of MI5, Sir Howard Smith, and the new Chief of MI6, Sir Dickie Franks, to discuss the new role with Oldfield. They decided to publicly announce Oldfield's appointment after the departure of the Pope, who was in the UK on a state visit.[30]

Thatcher believed that the appointment of a Security Coordinator in Belfast was vital. In discussions regarding the next step, two major questions preoccupied her: 'How were we to improve the direction and co-ordination of our security operations in the province? And how were we to get more co-operation in security matters from the Irish Republic?' Thatcher and her senior ministers, advisors and intelligence chiefs believed that the first question could be answered only if the difficulties of coordination between the Army and the police were resolved by way of a 'new high-level security directorate'.[31] The Prime Minister was confident that Oldfield could deliver on these objectives.

Now aged 63, Oldfield was a 'small tubby man' with thick-rimmed glasses. He often carried an umbrella, wore 'ginger shoes' and 'flashy cuff links' and had 'dark nicotine stains on his fingers'.[32] However, Oldfield possessed a formidable mind. He had served in Military Intelligence in the Middle East and North Africa during the Second World War. He joined MI6 in 1947 and rose through the ranks, becoming head of station in Singapore a decade later. This was a crucial time in the struggle against communist terrorists in the British colony of Malaya. Having directed considerable resources towards winning the violent contest in South-east Asia, Oldfield was rewarded with a promotion and made a special envoy to Washington as the key British Intelligence representative in the United States in the early 1960s. A decade later, after two abortive attempts to lead MI6, he was finally appointed Sir John Rennie's successor as Chief in January 1973.[33] In Downing Street's press release confirming Oldfield's appointment as Director of Operations, no mention was made of Oldfield's distinguished intelligence career: 'Sir Maurice Oldfield was born in 1915 and served in the army during the 1939–45 war. He joined the Foreign Office in 1947 and served in Singapore and Washington as well as in London. He retired in 1978 and for the past year has been Visiting Fellow at All Souls College, Oxford. He is unmarried.'[34]

The government press officers took a 'defensive line' with the media as they sought to play down Oldfield's almost forty-year-long professional career as an Intelligence Officer and, instead, emphasise his personal qualities. The press responded by filling in the gaps in Oldfield's curriculum vitae. Within a week of his appointment, *The Daily Telegraph* was talking up how Oldfield had been the inspiration for Ian Fleming's character 'M' and John Le Carré's 'George Smiley'.[35] Indeed, the media frenzy surrounding his appointment was fuelled by Le Carré's admission that he had previously invited Oldfield to lunch with him and actor Alec Guinness, who was playing Smiley in a BBC drama series that had been airing since 10 September.[36] Although the *Telegraph* welcomed the appointment, it added a caveat: 'Better intelligence in itself cannot be a substitute. The police, with the advantage of permanence and local knowledge, already have excellent intelligence; the dilemma is how to convert this information into evidence acceptable to the courts.' Beyond Oldfield's personal expertise, the newspaper cautioned that 'his task is the far broader one of equipping the Security Forces with a strategy and seeing that this strategy is pursued in unison by the army and the police'.[37] It was in this climate of mystique and expectation that Oldfield was sent to Belfast, having allegedly never previously served in Northern Ireland.[38]

★ ★ ★

On Monday, 8 October 1979, an Andover military airplane landed at RAF Aldergrove, close to the shores of Lough Neagh. On-board were the Secretary of State Humphrey Atkins and his new security supremo Sir Maurice Oldfield. Atkins quickly boarded a military helicopter and was flown the 27 miles to Stormont Castle, while Oldfield travelled separately to the same location in an unmarked police car.[39] Before his flight to Belfast, Oldfield had admitted to a friend that he was worried about his new role, particularly the danger in which he was putting himself and his wider family back in England.[40] As he took in the scenic views of Belfast from the M2 motorway, Oldfield was mindful of the challenges that lay ahead. He was keenly aware of the hostility he might face from the tough-talking, no-nonsense General Officer Commanding (GOC), Sir Timothy Creasey, a man who was said to have 'freaked out' in the wake of the Narrow Water ambush and who craved a return to military control of the security situation.[41] There was also the RUC Chief Constable Ken Newman, who had cut his teeth as a Special Branch detective in Palestine in the late 1940s.[42] The imposing nineteenth-century Stormont Castle would act as an austere backdrop for these strong characters. This dark, looming building nestled in the east Belfast skyline was home to the Security Service, MI5, which ran its intelligence operations from the grand ballroom, the oak-panelled rooms and the surrounding beautifully manicured gardens and conservatory. The Head of MI5 in Northern Ireland saw Oldfield's arrival as a slight and he and his officers greeted the retired MI6 Chief with a high degree of scepticism. Several of them personally blamed Oldfield for alerting former Prime Minister Harold Wilson to the right-wing plot against him in the mid-1970s, an episode which had allegedly involved some of their officers.[43]

Until he was sent to Belfast, Oldfield had divided his time between his flat in Marsham Court in central London, a handful of exclusive restaurants, and his family home in Derbyshire, a place of sanctuary where he could enjoy the anonymity of rural life.[44] Now, he was entering a more alien and inhospitable place than any he had experienced overseas. For years, friction between the GOC and the Chief Constable had poisoned relations between the Army and the police. Behind the scenes, their respective Intelligence Officers were making slow progress: they 'could not claim to be getting at [IRA] "Brigade" Staffs, and if by a miracle we did charge them, they would be replaced immediately'. The Security Forces believed that the IRA was 'scraping the barrel by the end of 1974', particularly as the '[p]olice were making progress with reasonably significant people at the "battalion" level'.[45] Creasey and Newman may have harboured doubts about Oldfield's appointment, but they had been promoted and were scheduled to move on in the new year. It was during this period of transition that Oldfield made his initial observations to Atkins. He reported a competitive edge to relations between the various agencies and departments tasked with defeating terrorism. He informed the Secretary of State that '[o]ur personal relations are very good' and that there was 'no difficulty agreeing at operational level but there are matters of higher policy'.[46] Much would need to be done to improve the situation.

2

INSIDE THE STORMONT KGB

'[T]he strong invader can only conquer his elusive antagonists by learning their methods, studying the country, and matching them in mobility and cunning.'

– Erskine Childers, *The Riddle of the Sands* (1903)[1]

On 3 March 1980, a few months after Sir Maurice Oldfield's appointment, Margaret Thatcher was preparing to deliver the inaugural Airey Neave Lecture at the Quaker Meeting House on Saville Row in London. Neave's assassination by members of the Irish National Liberation Army (INLA) during the 1979 General Election campaign had touched the British Prime Minister in a deeply personal way. Tipped to become a future Secretary of State for Northern Ireland, Neave had served as a Military Intelligence Officer during the Second World War and had even escaped from the Nazi prisoner-of-war camp at Colditz Castle. Neave pressed for a 'freer hand for the army, greater use of the SAS and longer prison sentences', which is how he came to the attention of the INLA. After his murder, the group justified having killed Neave by branding him a 'militarist' who 'supported the present order and increased repression against the Catholic people in the six counties'.[2] As he drove his car out of the House of Commons car park on 30 March 1979, Neave was killed by a bomb that had been placed beneath the front seat. A year after his death, Thatcher was eager to express her contempt for the scourge of terrorism. In her view, by killing Neave, the terrorists had struck 'in the homeland of Britain itself'. This transgression would not go unpunished, she told her audience. Instead, there would be a 'united response from a nation which has shown once more that, when faced by a clearly identifiable menace, it can respond with wisdom and fortitude'.[3] She clearly also had the assassination of Lord Mountbatten and the killing of eighteen soldiers at Narrow Water in mind as she outlined the merits of her war against terrorism.

In praising the contributions of all Irish people, both North and South, to the cause of defending democracy, she namechecked famous generals of Irish lineage, including Alanbrooke, Montgomery and Templer. Thatcher may have been strongly committed to her unionism, but she was even more committed to facing down the threat posed by terrorism. In talking up the positive relations between Britain and Ireland, as two sovereign states, she reiterated her position on the question of Northern Ireland's position within the United Kingdom:

> Despite these years of bloodshed in Ulster, the IRA are no closer to achieving their aims. It is recognised in the Irish Republic and elsewhere that there has always been a clear majority of the population of Northern Ireland which continues to want to remain part of the United Kingdom. A survey carried out in 1978 and published by the Economic and Social Research Institute of Dublin clearly showed that three-quarters of all the people of Northern Ireland, including nearly half the Catholics, wished to retain their links with the United Kingdom. The moral of those findings is worth pondering very seriously. No democratic country can voluntarily abandon its responsibilities in a part of its territory against the will of the majority of the population there. We do not intend to create any precedent of that kind.[4]

Thatcher was firm on what would later be called the principle of consent. A few days after her speech, Humphrey Atkins rose to address MPs from the Dispatch Box to reiterate the government's counter-terrorism policy:

> Any death by terrorist activity is one too many. We continually strive to reduce the number of deaths. I know that the Hon. Gentleman realises that it is impossible to provide round-the-clock protection for everyone in Northern Ireland. I know that the efforts that we are making will bring about a gradual decrease in terrorist activity. I hope that one day those activities will be reduced to such a level that they will no longer be a menace to anyone.[5]

In his regular briefings for Atkins, Oldfield made the Secretary of State aware of the difficulties associated with linking the government's policy of defeating terrorism with the security tactics being utilised. He knew that the only way of really attacking the IRA and the INLA was by way of an intelligence-led strategy that prioritised human sources.

Sir Antony Acland had only been in the role of chairman of the Joint Intelligence Committee (JIC) a matter of months when he received directions from Thatcher that more resources needed to be invested in Oldfield's intelligence-led strategy. As a former Principal Private Secretary to Foreign Secretary Sir Alec Douglas-Home and then James Callaghan during the period 1972–75, Acland would have been well acquainted with Oldfield during his tenure as Chief of MI6. Acland's predecessor, Sir Antony Duff, had moved into the more senior role of Intelligence and Security Coordinator in the Cabinet Office. The two men greatly respected Oldfield. Indeed, they had hosted Thatcher at a JIC meeting at the end of February 1980 and so they were well aware of her personal backing of Oldfield. Writing to Acland afterwards, she said she was 'very glad to have had the opportunity on Friday of sitting in at a meeting of the Joint Intelligence Committee. I found the occasion both thoroughly enjoyable in its own right and of value in the longer term in that it will help me to see your weekly product in its context.'[6] At the time, the JIC was creaking under the 'incessant time pressure' placed on it by ministers and senior civil servants seeking intelligence. Acland's position gave him considerable influence over government policymaking.[7]

Housed in the Cabinet Office in Whitehall, the JIC sat at the apex of the intelligence hierarchy as it received intelligence from all of the various agencies charged with its collection.[8] The JIC was 'responsible for making assessments for Ministers and officials of a wide range of external situations and developments', drawing on 'all relevant information: diplomatic reports and telegrams, the views of Government departments and publicly available information, as well as secret intelligence reports'.[9] It also played a coordinating role in the work of the security and intelligence agencies, including MI5, MI6, Government Communications Headquarters (GCHQ), and Defence Intelligence.[10] Additionally, through its assessments branch, the JIC sought to turn secret intelligence into briefings for the Prime Minister and her senior ministers. In assessing intelligence, the JIC was charged with sounding out threats to the UK homeland and overseas territories and dependencies.[11]

A number of key national security concerns preoccupied the JIC throughout 1980, including PIRA and INLA violence. The JIC noted how both groups had 'stated that it is their intention to attack British targets outside the United Kingdom; and PIRA has mounted attacks on BAOR

[British Army of the Rhine]'.[12] This danger was later underscored by the assassination of a middle-ranking British Army officer on 16 February 1980 in Bielefeld, West Germany. According to eyewitnesses, 44-year-old Army officer Colonel Mark Coe was getting out of his car, after having reversed into the garage outside his married quarters, when a man and a woman ran towards him and shot him three times in the chest and stomach.[13] Colonel Coe staggered into his house, where his wife was putting their young children to bed. Despite the efforts of a local doctor who arrived on the scene immediately after the shooting, Colonel Coe died of his wounds. 'He didn't have a chance. It looks like a very professional attack,' a West German police chief told a press conference. The police offered 50,000 Deutschmarks for any information that might lead to the capture of the colonel's killer.[14]

The IRA had been involved in violence on the Continent before, of course. The group's European Active Service Unit (ASU) was responsible for a number of bombings in July 1978, as well as the assassination of the British Ambassador to Holland, Sir Richard Sykes, on 22 March 1979.[15] They were closely linked to what remained of the left-wing Red Army Faction, also known as the Baader-Meinhof group, and, according to one source, German terrorists provided accommodation, documents, guns and ammunition for the IRA assassins who had arrived in the guise of migrant workers.[16] The IRA subsequently issued a statement taking responsibility for the murder of Colonel Coe, who had been targeted because he had served in Northern Ireland and was 'an administrator in an army suppressing nationalist people'.[17] The group proceeded to warn other British troops 'lounging about their German bases' that there was no safe refuge from the Irish front line. The Provisionals were well aware of the propaganda value of striking at British interests in Germany, as evidenced by a piece in the Republican movement's newspaper, *An Phoblacht*: 'Overseas attacks also have a prestige value and internationalise the war in Ireland. The British government has been successful in suppressing news about the struggle in the North ... But we have kept Ireland in the world headlines.' The IRA believed they were on track to foment an 'expression of discontentment, probably from the English people rather than from the army', which would 'snowball and the British government's ability and will to stay which we are sapping, will completely snap'.[18] It was an effective strategy and opened up a new front in the IRA's armed struggle.

Despite the public opprobrium generated by the IRA's napalm attack on the La Mon House Hotel in North Down on 17 February 1978, in which twelve Protestant civilians were murdered, to say nothing of Mountbatten's assassination and the Narrow Water massacre, the IRA was experiencing a resurgence.[19] The NIO had noted how the 'PIRA have shown themselves still highly sensitive to the risk of informers as [they were] to the reaction by public opinion throughou the community to their operations [sic]'.[20] According to British assessments, careful scrutiny of targets meant that the IRA's campaign now fluctuated 'sharply both in level and in type of violence'.[21] Three days after Colonel Coe's murder in West Germany, the JIC noted the 'risk that the United Kingdom will again be the venue for terrorism activity against non-British targets, which, at present, was greater than the risk of action against British targets'. Intriguingly, the JIC emphasised that it had 'no evidence to disprove assurances given by Colonel Qadhafi since 1975 that Libya no longer provides PIRA with material support'. Ironically, the JIC remained silent on emerging armed reactions to the imposition of a new revolutionary regime in Iran. Several opponents of the Tehran regime were in London and planned to take hostages in the country's embassy. Such oversights demonstrate the highly speculative nature of JIC assessments, which tended to downplay the threat posed by international links between terrorist groups:

> In the period under review, international links have developed significantly in the area of Irish Republican terrorism. These links are more in the nature of psychological support than operational collaboration and it is unlikely that any collaboration would extend to terrorist activity in Great Britain. The Provisional Sinn Féin (PSF) have continued to develop their traditional links with Basque and Breton separatist extremists but a comparatively new phenomenon has been the growth of Irish Republican solidarity groups and contacts with terrorist support groups elsewhere in Western Europe particularly in West Germany and Holland.[22]

In order to gain greater insight into these Irish Republican solidarity groups, JIC staff authorised MI6 to conduct an 'offensive penetration operation' codenamed SCREAM in West Germany.[23] Simultaneously, the top-secret Section 28 unit of the British Army's Intelligence Corps began its own agent-running programme within the Irish expatriate community in West Germany, on the assumption that the community provided a support network for the organisation's European ASU. Additionally, MI5, under the direction of 'the head of MI5's F5 Section, which deals with Irish terrorism, John Deverell, began its own operation'.[24] Another organisation, known as the British Services Security Organisation (BSSO), consisting of civil servants from the Ministry of Defence who had been working in the area since earlier Cold War days, also began to fish in the same pond.[25] Inevitably, as in Northern Ireland during the 1970s, competition between the various agencies grew.[26]

The threat level was also deemed to have increased. Within eight weeks of Colonel Coe's assassination, the JIC was sounding an alarm bell about the IRA threat on the Continent: 'It [the IRA] would prefer to concentrate on "prestige" targets (e.g. the murders of Lord Mountbatten and of the British Ambassador to The Hague), but recent attacks against British military personnel in West Germany indicate that "softer" targets can present better opportunities, and further indiscriminate attacks cannot be ruled out'.[27]

With dire warnings of increasing IRA activity against British interests, all eyes now turned to Sir Maurice Oldfield and his intelligence-led strategy.

★ ★ ★

3 Brigade HQ, Mahon Road Barracks, Portadown, Morning, 29 March 1980

Sir Maurice Oldfield and his Planning Staff had come to 3 Brigade's headquarters at Mahon Road Barracks in Portadown to hear for themselves the measures that were being taken to combat the IRA in East Tyrone. Along with West Belfast and South Armagh, East Tyrone posed perhaps the greatest threat to British interests.[28] A month after the Narrow Water massacre, twenty IRA volunteers took over the village of Carrickmore in County Tyrone, only 15 miles from the Irish border, and effectively sealed it off, openly carrying weapons and questioning drivers.[29] Mahon Road was home to specialist units, including G Squadron of the SAS, which was charged with dealing with one of the region's most ruthless IRA squads. Seated around the conference table were the senior military commander for the region, Brigadier John Waters, his counterpart in the RUC, Assistant Chief Constable for South Region Charlie Rodgers, and over a dozen of their best officers, who were responsible for delivering briefings on ongoing operations.

Oldfield was pleased with what he heard that morning. He had been a key supporter of the Tasking and Coordination Group (TCG), which was initially set up in Castlereagh on 1 May 1978 and was rolled out to RUC stations in Gough Barracks in Armagh in 1979 and on the Strand Road in Derry (later moved to Ballykelly) soon afterwards.[30] Oldfield succeeded in breathing new life into the concept and ensuring that RUC–Army operations at a lower divisional/battalion level were more fully integrated into Britain's overall efforts to combat terrorism.[31] He named these new structures the 'Joint Planning Committee', which, according to one source, comprised 'the SPG (Special Patrol Group, RUC) Bronze Section, HQ Company (14 Company), Special Branch, RUC, MI5 and MI6, SAS (including a Special Tasks' team in Belfast called "Whiskey")'.[32] The new operational structures were unofficially referred to by those who served in them as 'The Oldfield System'; to their enemies in the PIRA they were known as 'The Stormont KGB'.[33]

Oldfield sensed the unanimity of purpose as he entered the conference room that morning in late March. Soldiers and policemen mixed with each other harmoniously. In an earlier briefing to Humphrey Atkins, Oldfield had observed that this was 'largely a matter of personalities', though he felt that it was characterised by a 'new atmosphere of co-operation rather than competition', as well as a 'sense of direction in that the people on the ground see some progress'.[34] 'Peter', who was steadily climbing the ranks of RUC Special Branch at the time, recalled how Oldfield was appointed 'really just to hold people's hands' as the new coordinating processes were established.[35] Despite there being no 'tangible successes' against the terrorists in the area, Oldfield nevertheless felt that there had been a general improvement in the system he had introduced to defeat them. During the proceedings, he asked those around the conference table one simple question: 'Are we winning?'

Emotions in the room were mixed. The RUC officers knew better than anyone how seriously the IRA's 'soft-target' strategy was beginning to hurt, especially under the direction of Jim Lynagh and his Monaghan-based gang.[36] The killings of 62-year-old Clifford Lundy in Kingsmills and 60-year-old Robert Crilly, an off-duty RUC Reservist, in Newtownbutler demonstrated that the IRA had perfected the implementation of their close-quarter shootings tactics. Lynagh's boss was a young IRA volunteer called Seamus McElwain, who had led the squad that killed three Ulster Defence Regiment (UDR) men in a landmine attack and shot dead 44-year-old off-duty UDR man Aubrey Abercromie in Kinawley on 5 February 1980. A week later, McElwain's squad blew up an RUC patrol in Rosslea, killing two officers:

21-year-old Joseph Rose and 35-year-old Winston Howe. On 7 March, they murdered 38-year-old Harry Livingstone, a former member of the UDR, at his farm near Tynan.[37]

It would take time for the Oldfield System to prevent attacks like these and the IRA knew it. On the basis of reports received from an informer who had spotted Oldfield visiting St George's church in Belfast city centre, the group's General Headquarters (GHQ) decided to assassinate the security supremo. In a meeting between one Special Branch handler and his source on 30 April, the source told him he had overheard IRA volunteers talking about their plot to assassinate Oldfield. The handler quickly filed an SB50 form, detailing what his source had told him:

> X had been contacted by a person who had close ties with P.I.R.A. in the Andersonstown area. This person stated the P.I.R.A. had ascertained that Mr OLDFIELD regularly attended the Sunday morning Service held at St. George's Church, High Street, Belfast. The P.I.R.A. are aware that on these occasions Mr OLDFIELD is accompanied by 3–4 bodyguards, but they believe that a well-placed sniper could still assassinate him and successfully escape.[38]

This was not the first time that Oldfield had found himself on an IRA hit list. GHQ's Intelligence Officer had been tracking Oldfield's movements ever since his time as MI6 Chief and had even ordered that a bomb be placed in the toilet of a restaurant beneath his flat in London back in October 1975. Newspaper cuttings relating to the spy chief were subsequently recovered from an IRA safe house in the city a few weeks later.[39] Now that Oldfield was established in his new post at Stormont, the Provisionals, emboldened by recent successes at home and abroad, were contemplating an even more audacious assassination plan. Oldfield's death would send a clear statement to the heart of the British establishment. However, the plot was disrupted by Special Branch before it could be executed. Although he may not have been fully aware of it at the time, Oldfield owed his life to the very intelligence system he was putting in place.

Despite being the IRA's number-one target, the group hadn't quite made up its mind about Oldfield. This was reflected in contemporary republican writings. 'We saw Oldfield as second rate,' recalled Danny Morrison, Sinn Féin's Director of Publicity and editor of *An Phoblacht* at the time.[40] Morrison had even commissioned a series of articles by journalist

John McGuffin, who parodied Oldfield throughout his time as Security Coordinator. McGuffin took aim at the spymaster, to whom he referred as 'Maurice the Mole', and the British establishment.[41] In denigrating Oldfield and viewing him as mediocre, however, republicans underestimated him.[42] Respected journalist David McKittrick was more circumspect: he believed that the Provisionals were 'still not quite sure what to make of him',[43] but he surmised that Oldfield's performance would be judged by 'cold statistical tables' and, within a year or so, 'everyone will know' if he had been a 'success or failure'.[44] Only time would tell.

3

OPERATION ARTICHOKE

'Special Forces patrols popped up where the enemy least expected to find them, behind their own lines.'

– Henry Gow, former member of 22 SAS[1]

371 Antrim Road, North Belfast, Late Morning, 2 May 1980

Answering the front door of her home, Rosemary Comerford was startled by the sight of four men. 'We are from the Irish Republican Army,' one of them said, drawing a pistol from his waistband. The men gestured her inside and informed her that she was under 'house arrest'. Two hours later, there was another knock on the door. This time it was Rosemary's sister Ann. She was quickly bundled into the living room, where she found her sister in tears. Forty minutes later, Rosemary's husband, Gerard, arrived home from work for his lunch. He was ushered into the living room at gunpoint by 28-year-old Joe Doherty, 27-year-old Robert 'Fats' Campbell, 33-year-old Paul 'Dingus' Magee and 24-year-old Angelo Fusco. Doherty was a member of the North Belfast IRA and the others were part of an IRA squad from Ballymurphy in West Belfast. Campbell, who is believed to have been on the IRA's GHQ staff, and Magee had already gained something akin to legendary status within the organisation.[2] Recognised by police as 'a dangerous gunman', Campbell was very much in charge of the situation.[3] This was a classic house takeover tactic used by the IRA prior to ambushing the Security Forces. The Comerfords were the latest in a long line of members of the Catholic community to be taken hostage by republicans and used as human shields.

The IRA squad loaded and checked an M60 general purpose machine gun (GPMG) they had brought with them. The M60 was one of six such weapons stolen by a criminal gang known as the 'Roxbury Rats' from a US National Guard base in Danvers, near Boston, and smuggled into Ireland by US arms dealer George Harrison.[4] Weighing 31.3lb, with an effective range of 1,000 metres, and firing up to 1,000 rounds per minute from belt-fed rounds held in an ammunition box, the M60 was the American Army's primary heavy machine gun. It had been used extensively in the Vietnam War and made a distinctive *chug-chug* sound when it was fired, making it easy to distinguish from other weapons, such as handguns and assault rifles, commonly used by Irish terrorists. The bullets – or rounds – fired from the M60 were 7.62mm in diameter, exactly the same as the Self-Loading Rifle (SLR) carried by British troops on the streets. The M60 was the American equivalent of the British Army's GPMG, which was rarely carried in urban areas because of its devastating killing potential. By introducing the M60 onto the streets of Belfast, the IRA was making a bold statement to its enemies in the Security Forces. Not only did the weapon pack a heavy punch, it was also a propaganda tool of immense value for the Provisionals. On the day that the IRA's 'M60 gang' called at the Comerford home, they had one mission in mind: 'to ambush a security force patrol'.[5]

At 2.07 p.m., the IRA men were startled by the screech of brakes outside. It dawned on them that they were about to be ambushed themselves. Members of the elite SAS regiment had come to arrest the gang. The operation, codenamed ARTICHOKE, was the latest attempt by the Security Forces to neutralise this dangerous IRA gang. Leading the SAS operation was 28-year-old Captain Richard Westmacott, who had travelled with his team from the nearby Girdwood Army Barracks, where he had briefed his men on his plan for capturing the M60 gang.[6] As part of the plan, Special Forces operators had allegedly 'jarked' (bugged) the heavy machine gun when it lay in a hide, apparently also rendering it inert and unable to fire.[7] As the SAS team pulled up in their Morris Marina car, the soldiers spotted a balding man rubbing his head. He was a classic spotter or 'dicker', whose job it was to signal to watching IRA gunmen. As soon as Westmacott and his men climbed out of the vehicle, they came under high-velocity gunfire: the IRA gang fired two bursts of seventy rounds at the soldiers. Evidently, the gun had not been disabled.[8] The soldiers returned fire while they dashed for cover in the doorway of 369 Antrim Road. The Staff Sergeant glanced back to see that Westmacott had been shot in the head and neck. He died instantly. 'A number of shots were fired,' Doherty later recalled. 'Split seconds later we fired back. A British soldier was struck. He seemed to fall.'[9] Meanwhile, another three soldiers at the rear of the property came under gunfire from an upstairs window. They spotted one IRA man, Dingus Magee, exiting the building and running towards a car the gang had hijacked earlier that morning. He was promptly arrested. A cursory search of the vehicle yielded a carrier bag containing a pistol and a loaded rifle magazine.[10]

Meanwhile, 500 miles away, in central London, members of A Squadron's sister unit, B Squadron, were preparing to storm another building. Terrorists from the Arabistan People's Political Organisation had seized control of the Iranian Embassy at Princes Gate and were holding a number of hostages. The terrorist leader, 27-year-old Awn Ali Mohammed, codenamed 'Salim' by the police and soldiers, had earlier threatened to shoot a hostage. The SAS checked their kit and familiarised themselves with the layout of the fifty-four-room building, with some watching the World Snooker Championships on a small television.[11] Robin Horsfall, a member of B Squadron, remembered the news of Richard Westmacott's death filtering in from Belfast:

> Richard Westmacott was highly regarded by his men. The error of assaulting the wrong building gave time for the IRA to ready themselves. He led the assault from the front which was brave but not necessarily correct for a Troop Commander. He should have been outside coordinating the attack. I am not sure whose recce error created the problem.[12]

A secret Headquarters Northern Ireland (HQNI) report later found that the interval between the arrival of the terrorists and the approach of the SAS team could be 'accounted for by the time needed by the Security Forces for operational planning'. The soldiers had initially been briefed by RUC Special Branch officers, which indicated the presence of a heavily armed IRA squad on the Antrim Road. The authority for mounting Special Forces raids in Belfast was typically given by the local Army commander, in this case Brigadier David Ramsbotham. Ramsbotham recalled personally approving Captain Westmacott's plan, trusting the Troop Leader's judgement that he would be able to accomplish the ambitious mission he had set himself: 'Richard was in my office before he went out. I told him to do a recce then tell me how he wanted to do it. "I think we need a five and three," he told me.'[13]

A subsequent HQNI report confirmed the involvement of 'SAS covert operations' and indicated that 'the movement of particular individuals and weapons ... [remained] under surveillance'.[14] Support for the technical aspects of the operation, including the jarking of the M60, would have been provided by Special Branch under the direction of the TCG in Castlereagh, essentially the 'nerve centre' and clearing house for all intelligence-led operations mounted against terrorism in the city.[15] Henry Gow, a member of Air Troop, A Squadron, recalled how most covert action undertaken during the three months leading up to Op ARTICHOKE had been 'lacklustre' and poorly executed: 'Ops were frequent although most, mounted on Special Branch information, were little more than speculative. There was a general feeling in the unit that a certain amount of these were carried out to placate Special Branch before you got a really good job.'[16] Gow's view of this period is contested by 'Toby', a former RUC Special Branch officer, who said that he was involved in debriefing all of the soldiers involved in the operation: 'His troop Sergeant was off on leave, leaving Captain Westmacott with a poor plan unchecked by the ranking NCO in the team.'[17]

The IRA's M60 gang had been operating in the city relatively unimpeded since the killing of a British soldier in 1978. This was made possible by the IRA's reorganisation into cells, which operated independently of a geographic chain of command. Before his arrest in 1978, Tommy Gorman was a member of the IRA's D Company on the Falls Road. He recalled that in the early 1970s the IRA had 'independent groups moving about in our companies and companies within the First Battalion'. IRA volunteers referred to such activity as being 'out on floats' where 'nothing was pre-planned'. By 1977–78, all operations went 'through the leadership', who would 'tell you the targets'. Gorman said, 'You'd have engineers in [each cell]. Snipers in it. People who could handle guns. People who could make explosives. Wire explosives up and stuff like that. Drivers, everything, in one group. They could be from several areas. And they acted independently.' In order to enhance the protective security of IRA operations, the local IRA commander would be told, 'Right, stand down for a week or two or a couple of days.' This system of democratic centralism in military operations was key to how IRA squads now operated.[18]

When independent groups like the M60 gang carried out attacks, the attacks were promptly claimed by the IRA leadership through *An Phoblacht*. In April 1980, the newspaper reported that the gang had created 'havoc' when it shot up an RUC Land Rover in West Belfast. 'In a daring and carefully planned ambush in West Belfast on Wednesday morning,' one article read, 'IRA Volunteers manning an M60 machine-gun hit every member of the RUC mobile patrol.' In reality, however, the IRA squad had lured the police officers into the area by tricking a civilian into reporting a burglary at Suffolk Library. The M60 gang opened fire on the RUC patrol as they dismounted from their Hotspur Land Rover. The attack killed 24-year-old Constable Stephen Magill and wounded three of his colleagues.[19] 'Despite being adjacent to a major Brit barracks, the IRA active service unit safely withdrew from its ambush position,'[20] the article read.

In the face of such attacks, the SAS had to adapt its own Tactics, Techniques and Procedures (TTPs) in a way that was proportionate to neutralise the threat posed by the M60 gang.[21] As Robin Horsfall explained:

> Rural ops were more aggressive. Recces of PIRA homes at close range and ambushes. Tracking the movement of suspects. Urban ops were mostly about recce and observation posts. Undercover ops in the community were the remit of 14 Int, not SAS. Our role was to find them, and, if possible, kill them in the act.[22]

The morning the SAS sprang into action on the Antrim Road, Special Branch notified soldiers of a particularly ruthless IRA gang that would not be taken without a fight. Joe Doherty later explained how his M60 gang operated:

> Of course you act independently. I haven't the time to turn round to Volunteer Campbell and ask for permission to shoot. Of course we were soldiers. The armed services are told to use their own discretion on immediate crisis which is about to appear. You don't keep asking your subordinate: 'Can I pop me rifle over me shoulder or can I do something else?'[23]

Doherty also explained that 'no one volunteer takes responsibility for "a kill" or admits who used the murder weapon'. He did, however, admit that Fats Campbell gave the orders to 'Get the hell outa here!'[24] A few minutes later, the house was completely surrounded. Regular uniformed troops from the 'Green Army' had arrived in force to bolster the SAS team. As was typical of IRA operations at the time, the gunmen opted to surrender because they believed they were 'more valuable in a prison cell than in a cemetery'.[25]

Dozens more soldiers and police officers soon swarmed the house. Brigadier Ramsbotham arrived and took charge of the operation. As he dismounted from his vehicle, he saw the body of the young SAS officer lying on the ground outside the Comerford home, covered in a blanket.[26] A few moments later, Ramsbotham saw that the IRA men had tied white sheets around the barrels of their guns and poked them out of an upstairs window. As police officers moved towards Number 371, the IRA men surrendered, shouting defiantly, 'Up the Provos!', as they were taken into custody.[27] Ramsbotham watched two of the city's most wanted terrorists, Fats Campbell and Joe Doherty, being led out of the house in handcuffs. He was under no illusion that their capture was little more than a pyrrhic victory for the Security Forces. His men may have arrested one of the most dangerous IRA squads in Belfast, but they had lost one of their most promising young military commanders in the process. Nevertheless, the operation offered Secretary of State Humphrey Atkins the opportunity to stand at the dispatch box and inform the country that the deadly M60 machine gun, 'used in Belfast on a number of occasions in attacks on security forces', had now been taken out of circulation. 'The seizure of this weapon,' he said, was 'therefore, particularly significant.'[28] Inside the MoD, a covert operation like ARTICHOKE was 'very attractive because it "put the fear of God into the terrorists"' as they 'could never be sure whether they were conducting their activities under observation'.[29] However, covert action was by no means universally supported inside the British government, with the NIO reportedly apprehensive about the use of force.[30]

Despite the death of Captain Westmacott, Op ARTICHOKE had achieved its objective. It was among the first of twelve operations mounted by British Security Forces in the course of a few months. One of the most significant of these was the prelude to Op ARTICHOKE, known as Op DEERSTALKER, which saw Intelligence Officers from the RUC's E4A unit, the Army and MI5 work together for the first time to track down the M60 gang.[31] However, like most covert action mounted at the time, both DEERSTALKER and ARTICHOKE were mainly reactive ops. RUC Special Branch officers obtained intelligence from their sources in the IRA and fed it to the TCG in consultation with MI5, which requested that the Commander Land Forces (CLF), Major General James Glover, task the SAS with neutralising the threat. These operations built on an earlier surveillance operation codenamed HAWK, which led to the arrest of the IRA's quartermaster, Brian Keenan, in March 1979.[32]

However, there were also failures. Over the twelve months leading up to Op ARTICHOKE, the Belfast TCG had been tracking an IRA bomb team led by a young republican known as Mr X in an operation referred to as Operation BLUB. This was a joint police–Army operation designed to capture Mr X and his bomb squad red-handed. It had little success and Mr X continued to evade arrest for several months. Shortly after the completion of Op ARTICHOKE, David Ramsbotham reported the following to his boss Jimmy Glover:

> [W]e are close to the bombing organisation, but there is little that the framework operation can do except when specifically tasked. This operation has grown out of much patient work by many people and there have been a number of successes against the bombers, either pre-planned, resulting from coordinated anti-bombing operations, or self-induced of the own goal variety.[33]

Despite the tendency of junior SAS soldiers, such as Henry Gow, to bemoan the poor quality of Special Branch intelligence, the truth was that these operations were reasonably successful in that they helped to build trust and good working relationships between the RUC, the Army and MI5.

The foundations for such joint working practices had been established the previous summer in a top-secret conference held at HQNI. James Glover chaired the meeting, which was attended by all three of his brigade commanders: David Ramsbotham, Colin Shortis and John Waters. They were joined by the Army's top Military Intelligence Officer, the RUC's Assistant Chief Constable in charge of all Special Branch operations, Mick Slevin, and MI5's Director and Coordinator of Intelligence (DCI). It was clear from the tone of the conference that intelligence-led operations were characterised by 'strict need to know rules concerning the identity of sources', which meant that even the Head of Special Branch did not know the identity of his men's sources, 'except in occasional cases'.[34] The one person who knew the identities of agents, however, was his deputy, who was 'responsible for controlling all SB operations'. Importantly, Slevin flagged the 'increasing need to control the operational exploitation of intelligence very carefully in order to protect key assets'.

In his address to the conference, Slevin's deputy began by reminding his military colleagues that 'there was no text book on agent handling which was a matter essentially of dealing pragmatically with human beings'.[35] He believed in the superiority of human sources over technical sources: 'Technical sources – which often originated because of intelligence gained from human sources – could not be tasked or questioned and were, moreover, open to misinterpretation.'[36] Those at the conference were well aware of the difficulty of penetrating 'target organisations', as David Ramsbotham noted: 'The all-important process of turning intelligence into operations has long been a problem area, not just in Belfast, but everywhere in Northern Ireland.'[37] After a year of intense intelligence-led operations against the IRA, there was an even greater recognition that the only way to defeat the terrorists was to gather more intelligence through human sources.

Recruiting agents inside the IRA was by no means an easy task. Special Branch classified its contacts into two categories. The first was 'the casual contact', who was not registered and whose information was 'restricted largely to local atmosphere and low level reporting'.[38] Although these sources could be tasked with attending a Sinn Féin meeting, they were 'not really conscious of the real purpose behind the relationship' with their handler. Casual contacts were always seen as potential agents, according to Special Branch. The second category was the 'genuine agent', who was defined as 'someone who had been reporting accurately for at least three months from within a target organisation'. These agents were registered and 'given a number'. The recruitment of both kinds of sources happened by way of a 'pitch', that is, an approach at a time and place decided upon by the Branch. Many pitches occurred after suspects had been arrested and taken to a place of detention.

Only some of these pitches were successful as most republicans were so ideologically committed that they would not betray their comrades. One such republican was 24-year-old former prisoner Gerard McMahon, who was arrested on 27 May 1980 by the RUC under Section 11 of the Prevention of Terrorism Act and taken to the interrogation cells at Castlereagh. As he told *An Phoblacht*, he was woken up just after 6 a.m. by the RUC banging on the door, warning occupants of the house that the building was about to be raided. After searching the house for half an hour, McMahon was taken away. 'About 10am I was taken for the first interview by two Special Branch men,' he recalled. 'They explained that they were not CID men and were not trying to charge me but were interested in getting information from me. They asked me who I knew in the Sticks [Official IRA], the IRSPs [Irish Republican Socialist Party, aligned to the Irish National Liberation Army] and the Provos. I said I did not know anyone.' McMahon said that one of the officers told him, 'We are out to get you', and even threatened to plant 'gear' in his home. The Special Branch officers were primarily interested in the names of people and the locations of arms caches. After an hour, two more Special Branch officers entered the interview room. One promptly left, returning moments later with a sheet of paper which stated that McMahon had been released from prison on licence until 1984. The officer allegedly produced a gun and told McMahon, 'If I put this in your house, you are going away for ten years.' Another officer turned to him aggressively and said, 'We are going to sink you.' A third officer entered the interrogation room and said, 'You have a lot of information and we want it.' McMahon was asked if he would 'hang around the street corners and see what people get up to. He offered me money: one hundred pounds for every gun I got for them.' When McMahon refused to cooperate, the officers resorted to more coercive techniques. 'If we can't set you up the IRA will do it,' he recalled one of the officers telling him. In one final plea for information, an officer told him that 'if anything went wrong, they would get me out of the country'. McMahon still refused to budge. The interrogation ended and McMahon was told that if he changed his mind, he should phone '51444 on Saturday morning and ask for Newell'. Apparently, the officers even gave him the codename 'Pipes'. They were so confident that he would turn that they arranged a meeting for Monday night. McMahon alleged that one of the officers told him that if he thought they were being set up, 'they would shoot me'. As he was leaving, McMahon was told, 'We are letting you out now, let's see what the Provos do with you.'

Immediately after his release, McMahon reported the episode to *An Phoblacht*, which carried the story as a warning to others who might find themselves in a similar situation.[39] Although this particular pitch had been unsuccessful, these coercive techniques did sometimes yield results. In the summer of 1979, the Deputy Head of Special Branch reckoned that the Branch had a fifty-fifty success rate.[40] Maurice Oldfield was a big fan of this strategy. He knew better than anyone that the only way to defeat terrorist organisations was to turn their own members against them. As he confided to a close friend, Tony Cavendish:

> You can infiltrate rogues as agents in Northern Ireland and you can pay the price by being shown up as the employer of rogues. It is a risk with some doubtful promises of success. Or you can try to win

over some of the terrorists, which offers no easy solution, but a rather better chance of success, though it can still be misinterpreted by the PIRA as concocting evidence. There is absolutely no safe and sure way to defeat terrorism, but on balance I prefer to win informers.[41]

Oldfield would continue to promote 'win[ning] over some of the terrorists', rather than 'infiltrat[ing] rogues' into the heart of their organisation. He believed that this approach would pay dividends because of the deep divisions and paranoia it would create inside the IRA.

4

THE OLDFIELD SYSTEM

'We are not looking for somebody to change the system but to keep the newly established Oldfield system going.'

– Sir Robert Armstrong to Margaret Thatcher,
14 May 1980[1]

Sir Maurice Oldfield's stomach was causing him constant trouble and painful flare-ups interfered with his plans to travel the short distance from Stormont to Castlereagh to see first-hand how RUC detectives were turning IRA members into informers. Castlereagh was infamous. Several Special Branch officers believed that its reputation had a profound psychological effect on terrorist suspects when they found out where they were being taken.[2] Oldfield understood the edge that this gave interrogators, for he had used the same technique in Palestine during the Second World War.[3] Many of Britain's post-war detention centres, from Kokkinotrimithia in Cyprus to Fort Morbut in Aden in South Yemen, had been intimately involved in the ill-treatment of selected prisoners.[4] Although Oldfield supported the RUC's interrogation of suspects as a means of producing valuable intelligence, he was distracted from his work by an increasingly painful personal medical complaint. His physician subsequently diagnosed it as diverticulitis.[5] This ailment was aggravated by stress. Shortly before he chaired the Joint Planning Session at Mahon Road Barracks in late March, Downing Street had received information that outed Oldfield as a homosexual.[6] The allegation undermined Oldfield's integrity, suggesting that he may have lied during his Positive Vetting interviews about sexual encounters with men.

At the request of the Cabinet Secretary, Sir Robert Armstrong, MI5 initiated an investigation. Ironically, the method of interrogation used in Belfast and fully supported by Oldfield was now used against him on a return visit to London. At first, the former MI6 Chief denied that he was gay. The Security Service was keen to know whether Oldfield 'may have been compromised in his role in a way that would damage national security'.[7] A cloud of suspicion descended upon him and made his position as Security Coordinator untenable. Armstrong invited him to resign, which he did under the pretext of his pre-existing medical compliant. In a letter to the Prime Minister, Oldfield reflected on his six months at Stormont: 'As you say, some things have been done, but there remains a lot to be achieved. I'm certain the tasks are clearly understood and the framework is right. I only wish I could have done more myself.'[8]

Despite his untimely resignation, Oldfield had achieved a considerable amount during his tenure. He had supported rolling out the TCG concept in Belfast, Armagh and Derry, and the meshing together of 'the four competing intelligence-gathering and security organisations – MI5, MI6, the RUC Special Branch and Army Intelligence – into a cohesive security machine, steering them away from the infighting which was prevalent before his appointment'.[9] He had also ensured that the intelligence cycle operated in a way that connected government policymakers in Downing Street to the efforts of the Security Forces on the ground.

Upon learning of his imminent departure, the IRA turned to satire to express its satisfaction. For six months, the organisation had poked fun at Oldfield as 'Maurice the Mole', a pompous caricature of the revered spymaster who was always battling to obfuscate the heavy-handedness of the Army or the police. John McGuffin's final article on Oldfield in *An Phoblacht* read: 'This elderly gangster, normally a recluse and shy with the media, is not a bit shy when it comes to the clinical planning of repressing the nationalist people in the North.' Emphasising that their struggle continued unabated, the IRA repeated an assertion made by an unnamed source in *Hibernia* magazine that Oldfield had told Security Force chiefs upon his appointment that he would 'have the IRA sorted out within six months'. It had never been Oldfield's intention to defeat the IRA overnight, for he knew better than anyone the difficulties inherent in dealing with terrorism. The IRA also claimed that the British establishment knew 'that their present strategy has made no dent in republican morale or operational ability since Narrow Water and Mountbatten'. *An Phoblacht* held that Oldfield had indulged in little more than 'self-preservation', stating that he would have 'the humiliation of failure' to look back on after he left his post.[10] The organisation remained oblivious to Oldfield's talents as a spymaster. He was, above all, 'an ordinary man, gifted with a natural simplicity',[11] who had put in place a system that would have a persistent corrosive effect on the IRA as the decade wore on.[12]

For every detractor, Oldfield had a champion. His biggest fans were to be found in the Army. The military's top brass in HQNI strongly supported the continuation of the Security Coordinator post after Oldfield's departure. Sir Robert Armstrong noted that there was now 'good order' in the so-called 'Oldfield System'. Oldfield himself believed that he did 'not need to be replaced' as he had 'established the new system on a secure footing' and that it would 'go along perfectly well without him'.[13] For political reasons, however, Armstrong declared that it was necessary to appoint someone new who would not change the system already in place.[14] Sir Anthony Duff was initially touted as the 'best replacement', but it was quickly decided that Sir Brooks Richards, Duff's successor at the Cabinet Office, would be the better choice.

Richards had served with the Special Operations Executive (SOE) in the Second World War. A Royal Navy Lieutenant Commander, he was an experienced wartime operations officer and agent runner in occupied France.[15] He was charged with liaising with the French Resistance during the war and headed up the French Section of the SOE in German-occupied Algiers. Assignments for the Foreign Office in Athens, Bahrain, Bonn and, finally, as British Ambassador in Saigon between 1972–74 and Greece in 1974–78 resulted in his appointment as Intelligence Coordinator in the Cabinet Office in 1978. Richards officially took over from Oldfield on 18 June 1980.

Richards decided early on that his Planning Staff should be reinforced by a senior figure from the MoD. He chose 50-year-old John Blelloch, who had served as an Assistant Under Secretary of State at the MoD for four years. The key task now was to recruit people to penetrate the IRA and loyalist groupings at all levels.

* * *

Headquarters Northern Ireland, Thiepval Barracks, Lisburn, 15 July 1980

HQNI, as it was known to soldiers stationed in Northern Ireland, was an austere-looking building situated a couple of hundred yards from the front gates of Thiepval Barracks, the Army's major military base in the market town of Lisburn. Constructed in the 1970s, when most government buildings were designed in such a way that they looked like comprehensive schools, HQNI had a green façade, single-paned windows and was considered one of the coldest places to work in Britain's sprawling defence estate. As British Military Intelligence's headquarters, it was a round-the-clock hive of activity.

Located in one of the larger offices at the end of one of the building's narrow, warren-like corridors was Brigadier David Ramsbotham. A tall and imposing man of 45 years of age, Ramsbotham had been in command of all Army operations in Belfast since 1978. As one of the so-called 'G3 ops guys', he was first and foremost an infantry officer.[16] Alongside the cavalry or artillery, the infantry tended to send the very best officers to command soldiers in its three operational fighting brigades in Northern Ireland. By this stage in his career, Ramsbotham already had experience of theatres of conflict as diverse as Kenya and Borneo in the 1960s. Following a stint as a staff officer in West Germany, he commanded his regiment, the 2nd Battalion of the Royal Green Jackets (2 RGJ), from 1972 to 1974. At that time, 2 RGJ were on a two-year residential tour based in Shackleton Barracks in Ballykelly on the north coast. At the end of their tour, they were posted back to Catterick in North Yorkshire, deploying briefly to South Armagh on an Emergency Tour in April–May 1974 and then to Ballymurphy, Springfield and Whiterock in West Belfast for a five-month tour of duty in the winter of 1974–75. Therefore, 2 RGJ was one of the most operationally experienced units in the British Army and David Ramsbotham one of the most experienced commanders.

Despite his infantry pedigree and operational experience, David Ramsbotham was atypical of most infantry officers. He combined tough-minded soldiering skills with a fierce intellect and, significantly, was driven to learn about the social, political and strategic context in which he found himself. As he himself used to say, there was 'nothing more important than knowing the enemy'.[17] Ramsbotham was fully prepared to take the risks necessary to build relationships with the RUC and other government and civilian agencies in the fight against terrorism. In seeking the 'ground truth' of the security situation, he found himself frequently joining patrols with those troops deployed onto the streets of West Belfast, one of the most dangerous parts of Northern Ireland. Consequently, he was in a position to establish good relationships with local community leaders, including independent Labour councillor Paddy Devlin.[18] It was undoubtedly his willingness to listen to moderate and pragmatic voices like Devlin's that afforded Ramsbotham in-depth insight into the security situation in Belfast.

By the summer of 1980, Ramsbotham's tenure as the top Army officer in Belfast was coming to an end. In his final report to Jimmy Glover, Ramsbotham identified one of the key successes during his time in charge of 39 Brigade: 'Whatever lessons may or may not have been learned during the Army's involvement in the current troubles in Northern Ireland since 1969, one stands out above all others – the crucial importance of relationships with the RUC.'[19] Joint operations were to be a firm foundation upon which the Security Forces, law and order could combat terrorism. In this, Ramsbotham proved an advocate of the Oldfield System.

Ramsbotham had taken over command of 39 Brigade at a time when the GOC, Lieutenant General Sir Timothy Creasey, was midway through his tenure. Nicknamed 'The Bull' by his men, Creasey had begun his military career in the Baluch Regiment of the Indian Army in 1942 and served in the Far East, Italy and Greece during the Second World War. He transferred to the Royal Norfolk Regiment after the war and became the Brigade Major of 39 Brigade in 1955–56. He later commanded 1 Royal Anglian on operations in 1965–66 in Aden and South Arabia.[20] Later, he was posted as a Loan Service officer in command of the Sultan of Oman's Armed Forces during the People's Front for the Liberation of Oman and the Arabian Gulf (PFLOAG) insurgency of 1972–75.[21] Thereafter, he returned to Britain, where he briefly served as Director of Infantry before being promoted to GOC Northern Ireland in 1977.

As GOC, Creasey had a reputation as a tough, no-nonsense Army officer who believed strongly that the defeat of terrorism was 'not only possible but inevitable.'[22] After the attack in Narrow Water, Creasey's bruising relationship with the RUC and the NIO drew criticism. While civil servants in the NIO and the MoD plotted against him, Creasey used the occasion of a speech at the Army Staff College in Camberley in 1979 to reiterate his preference for a more coercive strategy:

> I feel it vital for success to draw together the different strands, namely the Army, the Police, Intelligence, PR/IP [Public Relations/Information Protocol], and Civil Administration where it impacts on the security situation. Maurice Oldfield is the person who has both the staff, the authority under SSNI, and the continual presence in the Province to do this. I believe his appointment is possibly the most positive step taken in the whole campaign. As a result, I am most optimistic about the future.[23]

During his earlier deployment in South Arabia, Creasey had met Major General Richard Trant, who would later serve as his deputy in Northern Ireland. Trant had formerly filled the role of operations officer with the Federal Regular Army (FRA) in the Arabian Peninsula in 1965–66. Despite Creasey's preference for muscular operations, it was Trant who would ensure that the Army worked closely with the locally recruited RUC and UDR. Trant was a firm proponent of the need to build up an indigenous intelligence network managed by the police. The groundwork laid by Trant enabled his successor, Major General James Glover, to begin the long process of improving relations between the police and the Army from mid-February 1979 onwards.

Born in India in 1947, Glover served as a Company Commander with the 3rd Battalion of the Royal Green Jackets and an officer in the Royal Tank Regiment. He also served in South Arabia as Chief of Staff of the newly renamed South Arabian Army (formerly the FRA) in the last days of British rule. Having been at the forefront of operations against the National Liberation Front, he knew the value of intelligence operations, particularly those that blended Special Branch interrogations of suspects and the use of informers and military operations in support of the police when required.

Under Creasey, Trant, Glover, Lawson and Ramsbotham, the Oldfield System flourished.

For much of Ramsbotham's final year in command of 39 Infantry Brigade, he and Jimmy Glover walked the short distance from their houses in Thiepval Barracks to their respective offices in HQNI together. They talked about the security situation, much to the annoyance of Glover's staff, who believed it was their job to brief the CLF on ongoing operations across Northern Ireland. 'Jimmy learned about intelligence matters in Cyprus,' Ramsbotham recalled. 'He had a good political instinct.' That is to say that he understood the role of the military in assisting the RUC in the discharge of its duties to enforce law and order. 'His report on how we should be taking the IRA seriously, was ahead of its time,' Ramsbotham said. 'I was very impressed to learn how much the IRA had developed.'[24] Ramsbotham's knowledge of West Belfast, gleaned from having soldiered there a decade earlier, had been decisive in his leadership during the previous twenty-four months. On 15 July, after one of his final morning walks with Glover, Ramsbotham sat down to put the finishing touches to his end-of-tour report:

The events of 3 May 1980 on the Antrim Road, when the SAS finally came to grips with the team, showed just how right our assessment that you cannot put 18-year-old soldiers up against these people had been. This operation continues against the remaining members, and must do so until they are eliminated. However, no one should be in any doubt that the specialists are in the lead, and must be, with everyone else in support, not just to ensure that the killers are hunted down, but to prevent the loss of more unskilled lives.[25]

Ramsbotham was aware of the danger posed by the IRA. Although his G2 officers[26] had informed him that the number of terrorists who could be called upon to carry out shooting and bomb attacks was at an all-time low, this was partly intentional on the part of the IRA's Northern Command. Gerry Bradley, one of the IRA's leading gunmen at the time, noted that recruitment had contracted due to the reorganisation into cells and the tightening of internal security.[27] Based on the intelligence briefings he received, Ramsbotham believed that there would be no major changes inside the Belfast IRA as a result of such restructuring. He wrote: 'Rather there has been a gradual contraction, not entirely voluntary, and refining of the operational pattern with a shooting ASU in West Belfast under the control of the Belfast brigade in the person of [Mr V], and a bombing group under the control of [Mr W] receiving his instructions direct from Northern Command.'[28]

In light of the changing nature of the IRA threat, the Oldfield System necessitated better working relations between the Army, the police, MI5 and the NIO, but the sticking point appeared to be the NIO, in which, Ramsbotham believed, ministers were badly served by 'out-of-touch' civil servants. The Security Coordinator's Planning Staff, he said, had 'injected another filter into the system, rather than heal the breach.'[29] Ramsbotham had experienced the same frustrations five years earlier when he commanded his own regiment in West Belfast, when Special Branch refused to share intelligence. He felt that too much information was being sent upwards and very little was coming back down. 'I am fully aware of the requirements of the "need-to-know" principle, but I do also feel that there is a grave danger of this principle being over-applied,' he told Glover. The need for secrecy was well understood outside of the police, but Ramsbotham believed that soldiers were being kept in the dark by Branchmen preciously guarding their sources. The need-to-know principle inside the RUC was so rigid that the new Chief Constable, John Hermon, had to turn to MI5 to compile a report on the matter and make recommendations for an improvement in intelligence sharing. MI5's most senior officer in Northern Ireland at the time was David Ranson, who asked his deputy, Patrick Walker, to take on the task.[30] Walker's findings were illuminating: 'The whole system of intelligence and intelligence-based operations will only work properly if those who need to know are informed and they are all confident that security will be maintained.'[31]

Ramsbotham accepted that the IRA would only be defeated if the RUC took the lead in all intelligence operations. Indeed, this was one of the fundamental components of the Oldfield System. 'It makes no sense to conduct parallel operations when the size of the terrorist organisation is diminishing,' Ramsbotham told Glover, 'and a refined attack by using all resources to the best of their different abilities is a much more effective operation.'[32] With the difficulties in sharing intelligence, Ramsbotham remained cautious: 'We are still faced by a determined and professional enemy, and it was foolish to talk in terms of their imminent defeat.'[33] He did, however, believe that the Army had something to offer. Earlier that year, he had been privy to the establishment of the Army's own agent-running section, known as the FRU, which had 'benefited from the tasking and advice of Special Branch'. Indeed, the Head of Special Branch in Belfast freely admitted to Ramsbotham how he had 'gained from many aspects of the military operation, not least the production of records and the cross-fertilisation of ideas that is now possible'.[34] The FRU would enable the Army to maintain a network of sources 'behind enemy lines', in places where the RUC and MI5 often found it difficult to operate. Much would depend on whether Special Branch was prepared to work as part of this system.

★ ★ ★

Highfield Estate, West Belfast, Late Evening, 14 November 1980

On the evening of 14 November, uniformed RUC officers responded to reports of a body found on waste ground on the edge of the mainly Protestant Highfield estate, nestled between North and West Belfast. The dead man was identified as 33-year-old Peter Valente, an IRA volunteer from Stanhope Drive in the Unity Flats area of North Belfast.[35] Valente had been recruited by RUC Special Branch after the leader of his IRA squad, Martin Meehan, sent him to meet with a rogue RUC officer who promised to pass on sensitive information. It seems he was spotted by a police surveillance team and earmarked for arrest and interrogation.[36] 'Jack', a fellow RUC officer, recalled that the rogue officer's motivations were 'strange'. He was a full-time Reservist with the elite undercover Bronze Section, but he had been 'pulled off the ground before being put into the stores. Later he was moved into an Int. job where he worked for Martin Meehan.'[37] The RUC was alerted to the leak by one of their sources inside Meehan's gang. Jack recalled that '[h]ow they got him was they fed different information to each member of the unit and then waited for the information to be passed on to the source. When it was, they knew who had leaked it.'[38] The officer was promptly arrested and questioned by detectives in Castlereagh, who suspected him of being the source of a leak that had caused the 'inexplicable failure of a number of operations'.[39] Although a case was prepared for the DPP, the officer was never prosecuted. He was reportedly forced to resign by Detective Inspector Ronnie Flanagan, who had recently moved from a staff role to an operational position within Special Branch.[40] Valente was arrested around the same time and taken to Castlereagh, where he was interrogated by detectives and pressured into working for the police.[41]

Over the next twelve months, the Branch turned the tide on Meehan's gang. However, all did not go according to plan. Valente was spotted meeting with a police officer in a restaurant and this information was passed on to the IRA by North Belfast commander Gerry Bradley.[42] North Belfast OC Martin Meehan quickly ordered his abduction and interrogation on 12 November. 'I'm not a tout; I'm a British agent,' he said before he was shot.[43] Valente's body was dumped in Highfield estate in an attempt to frame loyalists. A £20 note was enclosed in his hand as a subtle message to the Branch that the IRA was aware of his treachery. Although Valente's meeting with the rogue RUC officer fatally compromised him, his fate also demonstrated the IRA's ruthlessness in weeding out informers in their ranks.

* * *

Months after receiving the Walker Report, John Hermon had yet to implement its recommendations. On the streets, Special Branch handlers continued to make approaches to recruit casual sources and agents. These officers were well aware of the value of two-legged sources who could tell them more in a five-minute debrief than five or six weeks of technical surveillance by E4A. However, surveillance operators in this clandestine unit, which had been formed in 1977, were getting better at following suspects and mounting observation posts.[44] Working closely with MI5's watchers and the Army's reconnaissance experts from the Det (the Army's 14th Intelligence Company, a secretive surveillance unit), they sought to fill gaps in intelligence reporting from two-legged sources. The quality of surveillance was greatly augmented in 1980 by the formation of E4's Special Support Unit (SSU), known more popularly by its cover name, the Headquarters Mobile Support Unit (HMSU). The 'Unit', as it was known to its members, provided a 'dedicated Quick Reaction Force to surveillance teams', enabling E4A operators to push the envelope in tracking terrorist suspects.[45] In meeting an agent the handler had to 'blend in and scan the area at the same time as listening to what the agent was saying', recalled former E4A officer William Matchett.[46] This posed huge risks to handlers, who worked in a high-pressure environment.

Ian Phoenix was one such E4A operator. After playing a leading role apprehending those behind the IRA's counter-espionage operation against the RUC, he was transferred to the TCG at Castlereagh. He often started his day in the TCG with the question, 'What's happening and what the fuck are you doing about it?' A former soldier, Phoenix soon surrounded himself with a team of police officers who were more willing to take greater risks. This was just the sort of teamwork John Hermon was encouraging amongst his subordinates as he attempted to militarise the police response to terrorism.

5

THE SPY WHO CAME IN
FROM THE COLD

'On balance it appears that the best agents for deception on a high
level are long-distance agents, who have been carefully built up, and
who have served a long apprenticeship before any major deception is
attempted through them.'

– J.C. Masterman, *The Double-Cross System in
the War of 1939 to 1945* (1972)[1]

The Whispering Gallery, St Paul's Cathedral, London, 5 December 1980

Temperatures in England plunged to lows of -5 degrees Celsius during
the first week of December.[2] In London, just after midday, Margaret
Thatcher was visited in Downing Street by *Sunday Telegraph* journalist
Peter Simmonds, who had come to interview her about her government's
major policies, including those relating to Ireland. Simmonds was eager to
ascertain her views on the IRA's demand that their imprisoned members be
given the status of political prisoners. This issue had contributed to prison
agitation since 1976. The IRA had resorted to their traditional hunger-strike
strategy by 1980 in an attempt to extract further concessions. Thatcher was
in a typically combative mood:

> Murder is murder ... To carry explosives is to carry explosives. To
> be prepared to risk the lives of innocent men, women and children
> is a terrible thing to do, for which you take personal responsibility. It
> has nothing to do with political status. It is a crime against humanity
> for which the person who did it is personally responsible. We can do
> nothing on political status whatever.[3]

There would be no compromising with the Provisionals, at least not publicly.
Later that day, Thatcher paid a visit to MI5's headquarters on Curzon Street

to be briefed on the latest security threat posed by the IRA.[4] Although she had been personally briefed by the DCI, David Ranson, and the Security Coordinator, Sir Brooks Richards, in Downing Street a week earlier,[5] some of the intelligence she heard on 5 December would have almost certainly drawn on reporting from MI5's deep-cover agents inside the Republican Movement.

One such agent was Willie Carlin, who had been recruited by MI5 in 1974 during his time as a serving soldier in the Queen's Royal Irish Hussars, a British Army cavalry regiment then based in Bovington Camp in Dorset. Carlin had spent the past six years reporting on political developments within the Republican Movement in his home city of Derry. To maintain his cover and earn extra money while collecting unemployment benefits, Carlin pursued his musical ambition and became a well-known singer on Ireland's thriving showband circuit. In 1978, he even formed his own band, named Rhinestone in homage to Glen Campbell's chart-topping song. Carlin performed all over Ireland, sharing a stage with Stella Mae Parton, sister of the iconic country-and-western singer Dolly, and played to sell-out crowds at the King's Hall in Belfast. He rubbed shoulders with the likes of Bill Monroe and the Bluegrass Boys. Later, Carlin played in a band with Omagh-born guitarist Arty McGlynn, who came from a traditional Irish music background. Carlin frequently appeared in the newspapers, lauded by music critics for his lyrical dexterity. Beneath his popular stage persona, however, he was a politically attuned man from a well-known republican family in Derry. Carlin's sister Doreen was a member of Cumann na mBan, the women's section of the IRA, and lived in the Waterside area of the city. It was MI5's interest in Doreen Carlin's activities that afforded the Service the perfect opportunity to recruit her brother.

Willie Carlin met with his handlers regularly, often providing information on the thinking and movements of key players in the PIRA and Sinn Féin. Carlin was particularly important to British Intelligence as he was part of one of the city's 'Five Families', which controlled the Derry Brigade of the IRA. This brought him into frequent contact with its chief, Martin McGuinness. Carlin first became aware of British Intelligence's interest in McGuinness in November 1980, when he was driving past the British safe house in Limavady and spotted a car pull out onto the main road and drive off in the direction of Derry:

> As I was heading up the hill, the gates opened to the driveway to the house. And this car came out. It was a blue Renault.[6] And it came

towards me. I don't know who the driver was, but Martin McGuinness was sitting in the passenger seat. And he was looking down at something. I don't know if he was reading something or looking at something. I've no idea but he drove past me. Jesus, did that scare me.

Carlin's nerves got the better of him and he took his foot off the accelerator, causing the car to jump. He worried that McGuinness had seen him. Carlin also wondered why the IRA leader was secretly meeting with British Intelligence Officers. Carlin did not know that McGuinness had begun a dialogue with Michael Oatley, the MI6 officer operating a back channel between the British government and the IRA during the first hunger strike. McGuinness had been appointed to represent the Provisional Army Council (PAC) in a secret liaison aimed at defusing tensions surrounding IRA prisoners' demands for political status. The person facilitating the meetings was Derry businessman Brendan Duddy, who had played a key role in helping to broker an earlier IRA ceasefire in 1975.[7]

On the day on which he spotted McGuinness leaving the safe house, Carlin had been instructed to meet his MI5 handler Michael Bettaney at the Londonderry Arms Hotel on the shores of Carnlough in the Glens of Antrim. He recalled: 'And I thought to myself, "Do you think are they telling him about me? Maybe I'm going to get shot?"' Carlin parked his car and wandered into the bar to find Bettaney drinking heavily. He was swaying and his speech was slurred. Bettaney's drinking had been a serious problem for some time. An MI5 report later revealed that he was a 'loner, unhappy and unstable', with an unhealthy penchant for Nazism, who had 'changed his northern accent to an upper-class drawl'. It noted that Bettaney was 'a man with a considerable sense of inferiority and insecurity' who harboured fantasies of defecting to the Soviet Union.[8] For Carlin, Bettaney was:

> an unusual character. A wee small guy [with] glasses, [who] smoked a pipe, [wore a] tweed jacket, check shirt, corduroy trousers … [He] just didn't look the part [of an MI5 officer]. Actually, he did, if you thought about it. He was perfect because you would never have thought in a million years he was what he was.[9]

Bettaney became an alcoholic after two traumatic experiences in Belfast. In one incident he narrowly escaped being killed by an IRA car bomb, and in another the Provisionals meted out a punishment beating to one of his sources, during which Bettaney reportedly cowered under a bed with his fingers over his mouth, watching the drama unfold.[10] Although his drinking clearly posed a security risk, Bettaney's bosses at MI5 did nothing about it.[11]

Towards the end of 1980, Carlin was becoming concerned for his own safety. His anxiety only grew after spotting McGuinness emerge from the safe house and so he decided he would contact the man who had recruited him, a man he knew only by the name Alan Rees-Morgan: 'I phoned London and I said, "You have to get this guy out of here. He's going to get me killed."' Rees-Morgan travelled across to Northern Ireland and met with Carlin at the Killyhevlin Hotel in Enniskillen. Bettaney accompanied him but spent most of the time drinking. Rees-Morgan asked Carlin to continue to spy on the Five Families, but he refused. At a further meeting, at the Ballygally Castle Hotel north of Larne on the Antrim coast, Rees-Morgan arranged for Carlin to take an all-expenses-paid trip to London. During his visit, Carlin stayed in the Penta Hotel, and he recalls having around six meetings with Rees-Morgan and someone introduced to him only as 'Paula', who Rees-Morgan said was his 'secretary'.[12] 'Paula' was none other than Stella Rimington, one of his deputies. Rees-Morgan had invited Rimington along to his meetings with Carlin to bring her up to speed on developments inside the Republican Movement. Carlin was cross-examined by Rimington on recent developments in the city, though she appeared 'more interested in Martin McGuinness and his views on things' than anything else.[13]

MI5 had been involved in Northern Ireland since 1969. Their role was to obtain political information from a range of technical and human sources. A small agent-running section operated from two Irish Joint Section (IJS) safe houses – one in Laneside in County Down and another in Limavady in County Derry.[14] One MI5 officer who operated from the safe houses explained how the agent-running section operated:

> An agent handler will be briefed by intelligence desks on any topics on which they believe the agent may be able to provide useful reporting. Once the agent handler has met and debriefed the agent, he will write up the meeting in the form of a contact note. This will give all the details of the meeting (location, duration, issues covered) and any non-intelligence matters discussed (payments made to the agent,

welfare issues etc.) Contact notes have a very limited distribution. The agent handler will also write up any intelligence provided. These would usually be in the form of source reports, and there would usually be a separate report for each topic, but there might be a composite report of a number of items if the intelligence on them was brief ... The source reports are drafted in such a way as to disguise the identity of the agent. These are sent to intelligence desks, who will grade the intelligence according to its value and provide comments in the way I have outlined above. These comments might highlight how the latest intelligence fits with previous material, seek permission to pass the intelligence, suitably disguised, to another agency or pose supplementary questions for the agent. Each desk officer would only see reports relating to his/her area of responsibility. Unless there are particular arrangements, source reports will not be passed outside the Security Service except to SIS and GCHQ. Reports on Irish Terrorism are sent to other organisations and government departments (including the Army) in Northern Ireland Intelligence Report (NIIR) format ... and or as Security Service Reports.[15]

As MI5's focus was on gathering and exploiting secret political information, it was left to the RUC Special Branch and the FRU to run agents who could provide the Security Forces with access to the IRA's operations at the lower, tactical levels.

Carlin returned from his London debrief suitably reinvigorated. Both Rees-Morgan and Rimington had given him assurances that his work was vital in the quest to end the conflict in Northern Ireland. After being summoned to a meeting with McGuinness, Carlin recalled driving into the narrow working-class street in the Brandywell and spotting Michael Bettaney, drunk and boisterous, not far from the IRA chief's home. He immediately pulled up onto the pavement and jumped out of the car. 'You're going to get killed. And you're going to talk about me,' he told Bettaney. 'I'd love to meet McGuinness and I'll tell him what's going on behind his back,' Bettaney replied, swaying as he spoke. 'He'd often said that to me,' Carlin recalled. 'He wanted to be able to prove to MI5 that he wasn't crazy, and he wasn't a drunk ... And they were worried about him.' Carlin managed to persuade Bettaney to move on, though later that evening he called Rees-Morgan and reported his handler's erratic behaviour. With Christmas fast approaching, Carlin was called to the Limavady safe house. He was nervous. He worried about his personal safety and about whether Rees-Morgan would move Bettaney on. He met Bettaney in the kitchen of the house. After a quick conversation, Carlin was handed a paper bag containing £2,500. It was his pay-off to settle his affairs.[16] Although Bettaney had become a problem for MI5, it was Carlin who would be retired, not his handler. MI5 bosses had other plans for Bettaney. He was moved to the Russia desk to work on counter-espionage. Carlin accepted the money and made his way home to Derry. He was now officially retired as an MI5 agent.

★ ★ ★

The new year ushered in new possibilities for the spymasters at Stormont Castle. IRA leader Brendan Hughes had called off the hunger strike in the Maze Prison in December 1980. The Intelligence Officers operating out of the IJS safe house in Limavady had successfully averted a major political storm over the matter. It was an opportune moment, therefore, for a review of the Oldfield System. Sir Brooks Richards began to compile a new report for Downing Street, in which he recorded how 'Intelligence operations are the key element in the attack on the terrorist organisations.' Recalling the 'dissension' between the Army and the RUC in late 1979, he stated that he felt that such tensions had significantly diminished: 'There is now full recognition of the need for co-ordination and all Army intelligence effort is committed in support of the Special Branch – on the one hand to supplement the RUC effort where necessary and on the other to provide specialist skills and forms of support not available within the police force.' Richards impressed upon the intelligence and security chiefs in London that they must make certain that their local representatives continued to 'ensure that the agreed policy is put into practice'. As terrorist organisations had become much 'more reduced and refined', he believed that the counter-terrorism response should be 'more considered, precise and co-ordinated from the intelligence agencies'.[17]

Over the previous eighteen months, Britain had gone from having a badly stovepiped intelligence apparatus in Northern Ireland to one that was much better coordinated.[18] At the top was the newly reinvigorated post of DCI, held at the time by MI5 officer David Ranson.[19] The DCI's job was to provide advice to the Secretary of State for Northern Ireland on all intelligence matters. This earned him a seat at the Security Policy Meeting (SPM), which was chaired by the Secretary of State and attended by the

Chief Constable and the GOC. Below the SPM there were the TCGs, which, in theory at least, represented the fusion of all operational and tactical intelligence. The TCGs, Richards noted, were 'a major advance' that ensured 'all useable intelligence is better exploited'.[20] He also wrote that the TCG concept now needed to be rolled out in other parts of Northern Ireland. 'As "normality" returns,' he noted, 'it is right that Army involvement in intelligence acquisition should reduce', though he believed it 'essential that the Army remain fully briefed on available intelligence and involved in the assessment process'. Richards advocated that any Army 'redeployment … be done in a sensitive and informed manner'. As far as he was concerned, the military should continue to occupy a key position in the intelligence pyramid. In comparing his time at Stormont Castle with his time as Intelligence Coordinator in the Cabinet Office in London, Richards stated that he was suitably impressed by what he had seen in Northern Ireland.[21]

As Richards penned his report to London, he was mindful of the foundations laid by Sir Maurice Oldfield. The old spymaster had envisioned a unified effort to combat the IRA, which drew on his long service around the world. As *Irish Times* journalist David McKittrick observed at the time, Oldfield was probably appointed to 'tinker with the police, tailor the Intelligence Services, soldier with the Army, or spy on the whole lot of them'.[22] Richards knew that the Oldfield System was designed to do all of these things. By strengthening the links between the security and intelligence agencies on both sides of the border, Oldfield wanted to woo influential 'sections of the Catholic community', while also seeking 'the cultivation of the "deep cover" informer' inside that community.[23] Oldfield believed that only by building up a more comprehensive understanding of the community hinterland context in which the IRA operated could the organisation be properly neutralised. Richards understood this and helped to reinforce Oldfield's vision of a lasting penetration of the IRA, which would ultimately lead to the defeat of the group's military campaign.

However, not everything could be as tightly controlled, as the Security Forces were soon to discover. On 1 March 1981, a 26-year-old IRA prisoner called Bobby Sands refused food inside the Maze Prison. Over the coming weeks, other republican prisoners followed Sands' lead. The heady political atmosphere generated by the hunger strikes threatened to undermine the Oldfield System as the IRA prisoners elicited sympathy and support from the wider nationalist community in both the Republic of Ireland and Northern Ireland, and in the United States. Seeking to exploit this new set of circumstances, the IRA decided to pursue a twin-track approach, increasing the tempo of its armed campaign on the one hand, while exploiting the hunger strike for international support on the other. On 19 March, the IRA's South Armagh Brigade shot dead 40-year-old Catholic civilian Gerry Rowland, who had accepted a lift from a local off-duty UDR member. Later that month in Belfast, the Markets-based IRA squad shot dead 25-year-old UDR soldier John Smith, who was on his way to work. A week later, the South Armagh IRA killed an RUC officer as he left Bessbrook Mill. Despite the efforts of the Security Forces, the intelligence needed to prevent such attacks became harder to gather as attitudes within the Catholic community hardened in support of the hunger strikers.

In a speech to the Belfast Rotary Club on 6 April, GOC Sir Richard Lawson heaped praise on Chief Constable John Hermon, reiterated his commitment to 'give the police whatever military support they require to maintain law and order, preserve life and protect property' and assured those gathered of 'the closely coordinated police/army strategy and our joint efforts to preserve law and order'.[24] For the time being, the operational coordination between the Security Forces remained unshakable, despite the opprobrium evoked by the hunger strike.

★ ★ ★

Anderson Crescent, Gobnascale, Derry, 7 April 1981

'There's a girl coming down them steps and she's crying,' said 67-year-old Mary Carlin, who was having a cup of tea with her son Willie in the front room of her home.[25] Mrs Carlin let 29-year-old Protestant student Joanne Mathers in and told Willie to fetch her a glass of water from the kitchen. Mathers was badly shaken and wept as she spoke. 'I'm a census collector,' she said. 'Now, love, sit down here and tell me what happened,' Mary Carlin told her calmly. 'I went up to that house at the end of the street and the guy there came out and said he would kill me.' Willie Carlin immediately recognised that she was in danger. 'Listen, love,' he told her, 'there's a couple of people in this street who would fill out the forms, but this is mainly a "don't-go-there street".' Willie advised her to leave the area as quickly as possible. Carlin, unlike Mathers, knew that there were eight or nine people closely associated with the IRA living on that one street in Derry. Willie called them 'the fuck-up squad' because they had a tendency to kill people who, in his words, 'didn't deserve to die'. He alleged, 'They were involved in murder, fuck sake, outside my door. It was embarrassing.'[26] Mathers asked if he would see her out of the house. 'I said yeah. She was looking at a picture of my daughter. She said she was from a farm and that she had a wee boy the same age as [my daughter] Maria. I took a look up the steps and said go on down there.'[27]

As they moved quickly along the street, Willie Carlin pointed out what he called 'friendly houses'. Mathers felt reassured by the kindness of the strangers she had encountered. 'As she came up the steps she did this wave, with a lovely smile on her face. She went up the stairs to Betty Kearns' house. And she knocked on the door and a guy came round the corner and shot her.'[28] The man of the house opened the door and Joanne Mathers fell into the hallway. Startled, the man closed the inner glass door but the gunman ran through it 'like he was on cocaine'. He shot Joanne twice in the head before trying to grab the clipboard from her lifeless body. He couldn't loosen her grip. He gave up and ran away back down Anderson Crescent towards Trench Road.[29]

Willie Carlin couldn't believe what he had seen. He ran up to the house. 'She was lying on the floor, blood on the walls. Frank said to me, "Jesus, this wee girl's dead."' There was a terrible commotion in the street. One woman across the street turned to Carlin and shouted, 'You're nothing but a pack of murdering bastards.'[30] 'And she was right,' he said. Carlin alleged Mitchel McLaughlin, along with Keenan, had tried to persuade the local residents of the area not to participate in the census. Going one step further, in a statement released to the *Derry Journal*, the IRA stated that those who sought to 'profile republican communities, by official or unofficial means, would be summarily executed'. Carlin said republicans believed the census was 'designed to collect intelligence. One night we collected them and burnt hundreds of them.'[31] Mathers' murder had a huge effect on Carlin. He was 'devastated' and 'angry', and he made the decision there and then to return to work for MI5.[32] 'Something said to me, "Ah, fuck it, I'm getting in touch again. I need to phone Alan."'[33]

★ ★ ★

Over the coming weeks, Carlin wrestled with his conscience over the murder of Joanne Mathers. Outwardly he was a committed IRA supporter who spent much of his time out canvassing for Bobby Sands, who was running as a candidate in the Fermanagh and South Tyrone by-election, and he was a fanatical proponent of the Provisional Republican Movement's world view, even engaging in large-scale personation to ensure Sands' victory, which was achieved on 9 April 1981 when he was elected as an MP. Sands died on 5 May, after sixty-six days on hunger strike. As a mark of respect, 415 republican prisoners in the Maze refused to work, take exercise or wear prison clothing.[34] A week later, Bellaghy IRA man Francis Hughes died after fifty-nine days on hunger strike. Riots promptly flared up across nationalist areas and two days later, on 14 May, the IRA orchestrated a rally in Gobnascale, during which black flags were hung from the windows of almost every house. Women beat dustbin lids and blew whistles, and young people carried cardboard coffins in honour of Sands and Hughes. Despite the surge in support, the IRA was short of confident public speakers. Someone proposed that Willie Carlin read out a poem he had composed about the hunger strike. As he climbed onto the back of a flatbed coal lorry in Gobnascale, Carlin looked around to see a crowd of around 100 people staring back at him in the tiny working-class housing estate. A little nervous, Carlin began to speak:

> In the month of May in the year '81
> Irish history was made but not with a gun
> Two young Irishmen who'd never really met
> Died peacefully and the world was upset
> People said of Sands and Hughes,
> They didn't have to die; they had a right to choose
> They were right
> But when they left us,
> It was their choice that became daily news[35]

As he looked around him, he could see that some of the crowd was moved to tears. He ended the poem with the words:

> But when this war is over
> And Irish freedom is daily news
> They'll build great big monuments to volunteers
> like Bobby Sands and Francis Hughes.[36]

Carlin was greeted by a stunned silence. 'You could hear a pin drop,' he said. Then it came. Rapturous applause. 'It was the biggest round of applause I ever got in my life.'[37] Afterwards, Carlin was approached by a man in a brown duffel coat who asked him if he would be prepared to read out his poem to a larger rally in the city centre a week later. The man was none other than Mitchel McLaughlin, a leading member of Derry Sinn Féin.[38]

Outwardly, Carlin was enjoying the adulation of those who had heard his defiant republican eulogy in Gobnascale. Inwardly, however, he had already made the decision to return to the MI5 fold. Only thus could he truly relieve himself of the burden he had carried since Joanne Mathers' death. He decided to contact his MI5 handlers in an attempt to come in from the cold.

He tried to telephone the number he had been given by Rees-Morgan, but the line was dead. He decided to take the most obvious course of action open to him and rang the Army's Operations Room at Ebrington Barracks.

'My name is Sean,' he said, giving his MI5 codename. 'And I would like to speak to the Company Intelligence Officer.'

'I won't be able to contact him until tomorrow. Is there anything I can do?' replied the soldier on the other end.

'No, that's fine,' replied Carlin. 'Just pass the message on and say that I'll ring tomorrow at 3 p.m.'

At the time, very few soldiers would have heard of MI5, so it is not surprising that the soldier who took the call did not appreciate its importance and merely reported the message up the chain of command. When Carlin rang the next day, he asked the Company Intelligence Officer if he could get in touch with Alan Rees-Morgan.

'We need to meet you,' replied the Army officer. 'You could be anyone. So how about we meet? And come in and have a chat.'

Carlin was unsure. He didn't know what 'come in' meant; however, he agreed and was given instructions to go to the car park of his local doctors' surgery in the Waterside.

'This Hiace van pulled in and these guys got out and I thought "fuck me", but it was me they were looking for. "Jump in," they said. I knew by the white trainers and the jeans and the leather jackets these guys weren't fucking MI5. You just knew. And the white socks. And I thought, "Fucking Brits."'[39]

There were two undercover soldiers in the back of the van who introduced themselves only as 'Eddie' and 'John'. Carlin complied with their instructions. The van was driven at speed along the narrow roads of the Waterside and out towards Ebrington, where it eventually came to a halt. Carlin was led into an interview room in Ebrington Barracks. He had come in from the cold.

6

THE DERRY FALANGE

'Our school education was governed by and run by the church, by our priests ... We were indoctrinated. We were brainwashed. Call it what you like. About Jesus. About God. And we learned all our prayers in Gaelic ... Our school education; our religious education, dictated our politics ... We were always like that and then young volunteers, pre-McGuinness becoming Chief of Staff ... always carried wee bits and pieces [of prayer cards and other symbols]. The one that any volunteer had to have was the St Joseph's Prayer. And if you've got a St Joseph's Prayer, turn it over and on the back you'll see that this used to be carried by soldiers in the Crusades. And they carried it because the prayer, said regularly, would allow you never to fall into the hands of the enemy, nor would poison ever pass your lips.'

– Willie Carlin, agent of influence inside
Derry Sinn Féin, 1980s[1]

Derry/Londonderry is one of the oldest cities in Ireland. By the seventeenth century, it had grown from a small market town into a thriving mercantile hub. Thick walls were erected to protect the economic centre from the native Gaels who lived beyond its walls. In December 1688, thirteen Protestant apprentices shut the gates of the city upon seeing a detachment of Jacobite redcoats approach on a ferry across the River Foyle, thus involving Derry in the wider Williamite Wars being fought to depose the Catholic king, James II. By April 1689, James had travelled from France to Ireland to take personal command of the siege, which was only broken 105 days later, when ships carrying food breached the Jacobite lines. This defiant act of rebellion would be commemorated in 1814 by the formation of a cultural organisation known as the Apprentice Boys of Derry. Violence was common between the Apprentice Boys and the Catholic community. In 1871, for instance, the annual ritual of shutting the gates ended in serious rioting, during which, as one newspaper reported, 'some heads have been broken'. Six hundred soldiers and police were deployed by the Lord Lieutenant to break up the 'provoking Orangemen and sensitive Papists'. To onlookers, it was a scene of tribal skirmishing. 'Guns were fired, the usual effigy of Lundy was burned, and the wildest excitement prevailed.'[2] For the next half-century, trouble periodically flared between the two communities. In August 1913, following annual commemorations to mark the relief of the city, Catholic gunmen shot and killed a Protestant who was watching a riot from his bedroom window in Old Hill. A further escalation of violence was only narrowly averted when unionist politicians appealed for restraint.[3] Seven and a half years later, trouble again broke out, with *The Daily Telegraph* reporting 'a state of wild turmoil' as 'Sinn Féiners' opened fire on a soldier and several loyalists.[4] Sectarian violence was never far from the surface and would flare up again in the 1960s.

Derry's historic walls have traditionally offered the best vantage point from which to view the entire city. Bishop Street and its gate, next to the central Diamond precinct, separate the Protestant Fountain Estate from the Catholic Bogside. Bishop Street also affords a commanding view of the city cemetery, which is nestled alongside the Creggan estate to the north-west and Rosemount and Shantallow to the east. To the south runs the River Foyle, which slices the city in two, with the city walls on one bank and the Waterside on the other. Although locals are divided regarding the official name of the city, they do agree on its designation as the Maiden City. Between the seventeenth and nineteenth centuries, Derry was the biggest centre for commerce and trade in Ireland. The city thrived into the twentieth century, despite being eclipsed by Belfast and Dublin. However, economic prosperity was unevenly spread among its people. A powerful elite within the local Unionist Party protected the interests of middle-class and aristocratic families, with the so-called 'Faceless Men' dominating political, economic, social and cultural life in the city to the detriment of working-class Catholics and Protestants. With inequality rife across the city, it is not surprising that Derry became the focus of the nascent Northern Ireland Civil Rights Association in the late 1960s.

Serious violence broke out in Derry on 5 October 1968, when the RUC baton-charged a crowd of civil rights protestors in Duke Street on the Waterside. However, it was the beating of 42-year-old family man Samuel Devenny by the RUC a few months later, on 19 April 1969, that ignited the anger of the city's Catholic community. Devenny had been watching the rioting from his home when local youths, chased by police officers, ran into the Devenny home in a bid to escape. Officers who entered the home beat Sammy Devenny, two of his children and a family friend. Sammy died on 17 July 1969.

Within the space of a few weeks, Derry became a battleground. Eamonn McCann was one of the leaders of the civil rights movement in Derry at the time of Devenny's death. He recalled that there was 'something quite distinctive about Derry, which is to do with geography, demography, perhaps related to the border', which contrasted sharply with Belfast. 'Derry was always distinctive,' he said. 'It wasn't just to do with parochial pride. The makeup of the city is different, and its history is different.'[5] Politically, Derry was divided along nationalist or unionist lines, with republicans concentrated in areas of the Waterside like Gobnascale, and the Bogside on the West Bank, and loyalists in the Nelson Drive, Irish Street and Fountain estates. McCann blamed the Catholic Church for fostering division, citing the hostility of the clerical hierarchy towards the idea of Catholic–Protestant unity until the rise of ecumenicalism and the Second Vatican Council of 1962–65. 'They didn't want Catholics contaminated with Presbyterian radicalism,' McCann said, which, in republican terms, meant 'a whole rejection of the tradition of [Wolfe] Tone'.[6] With the outbreak of the Troubles, the Church remained tethered to the cause of constitutional nationalism in the form of the Social Democratic and Labour Party (SDLP). While the Church did much to stem the flow of young men into the IRA, the British Army's killing of thirteen unarmed Catholic civilians in the Bogside on 30 January 1972 turned a steady trickle into a fast-flowing river of new recruits. Such was the anger in the community that even parish priests were drawn into the ranks of the IRA, with Father James Chesney and Father Patrick Ryan becoming actively involved in bomb attacks.[7] Other priests, like the Bishop of Derry, Edward Daly, strongly opposed violence, but nonetheless expressed sympathy for IRA hunger strikers.[8]

Sympathy aroused by the hunger strikes led many young men towards the republican cause. In Derry, the Republican Movement came to resemble an armed militia akin to one of the Falangist groups active during the Spanish Civil War in the 1930s. Willie Carlin, a member of the movement, explained how the rank and file sought to emulate their leader, Martin McGuinness:

> These younger volunteers who were now in the movement, they seen [sic] McGuinness as their man ... They didn't have any doubts like

the other guys [who asked] 'Why are we doing this political stuff?' They were used to it. Martin's a politician [they thought] … They still joined the IRA and they weren't against what he was doing because he was their leader. And because McGuinness influenced people in Derry, by going to Mass, by going to Confession, by meeting Bishop Daly all the time, and, on occasion me and Seamus [Keenan] writing stuff that kind of led into that religious way of life. They were quite happy to follow his path militarily, to a greater extent, politically, to a lesser extent, and religiously, definitely … We all went to Mass … We all believed. We all had St Joseph Prayers [on our person]. And then when we were introduced to other prayers and other people, and we all had these symbols on us. And you wouldn't leave home without them … And you were like the mafia family in Derry. I mean you had the McGuinnesses, the McLaughlins and the McFaddens, we are all Catholics. We all believed in God. We all went to Mass … I mean, you couldn't bury a volunteer without fucking Mass. All over the world, terrorists, allegedly or otherwise, they're buried. There's no religious ceremony for a lot of them. In Derry, there's no way that a volunteer is getting buried without a Requiem Mass. No way. And we had riots outside the church door to be let in … You won't find a Derry volunteer who is buried without Mass. You won't find one …[9]

The 'Derry Falange' reached a turning point on 28 May 1981, when several of its volunteers were involved in a firefight with British Special Forces in the Creggan Estate. Two men, 21-year-old Charles 'Pop' Maguire and 24-year-old George McBrearty, were killed. Another volunteer, John 'Stylo' Curran, who was badly wounded, was spirited across the border to receive medical treatment.[10] It was during the funerals of the two volunteers a few days later that Mitchel McLaughlin invited Willie Carlin to join Sinn Féin.[11]

Two weeks after the deaths of its volunteers, the 'Derry Falange' organised a mass rally in support of the hunger strikers. Tensions were running high. Seven years after moving home to Derry to spy for the British, Carlin took to the stage to address the crowd. As a devout Catholic and a committed republican, he bought into the idea of martyrdom. Sands and Hughes, to say nothing of Maguire and McBrearty, were his heroes. As he climbed onto a makeshift stage, flanked by the movement's leading lights, Gerry Adams, Martin McGuinness, Seán Keenan and Barney McFadden, Carlin felt a sense of pride wash over him. The crowd, numbering hundreds, had been whipped into a frenzy. 'Speech. Speech. Speech. Speech,' they chanted as they whooped and cheered. 'I was standing at this microphone and Seán Keenan was standing behind me,' Carlin recalled. 'He was a fantastic old-time republican. And he had heard the monologue before and he said, "Go ahead!"' Although Carlin had previously read his poem to the gathering in Gobnascale, this time he was facing a much bigger audience. He felt nervous. Adams and the others looked on in silence as he began to speak. The Security Forces stayed well back and watched proceedings from a distance.

The local FRU detachment commander, 'Dessie', was covertly monitoring Carlin. FRU operations were centrally directed by the unit's CO and his second in command, who were based at HQNI, but they had a number of outstations, known as Force Research Offices (FRO), which were scattered across Northern Ireland. As one former member of the unit recalled:

> The FRO(N) was one of two sub divisions of HQ West Detachment which was part of the Force Research Unit (FRU). The Officer Commanding (OC) of HQ West Detachment was (then) Captain XX. I worked for him at FRO(North). During my time at FRO(N) I had 6 people working for me and HQ West Detachment had 4 people – the OC, the second in command and two clerks.[12]

The tiny FRO(N) office was housed inside Ebrington Barracks. It was here that the Army mounted its covert operations against the IRA in the north-west. Established in 1980, the FRU was relatively new to the agent-running business compared to the RUC and MI5. However, by the summer of 1981, source reporting from inside the IRA was starting to dry up for all three agencies as the mass mobilisation of republicans onto the streets in support of the hunger strikes was hindering agent-running operations.[13] Willie Carlin's decision to return to the fold, therefore, offered British Intelligence an unprecedented opportunity to resume its coverage of the politics of the resurgent IRA. It was in this context that Carlin believed the Army would move quickly to recruit him. However, it seems that the FRU's interest in recruiting him as an agent, rather than as a casual contact, was frustrated by MI5. Carlin was certain that this could be attributed to his poor relationship with his former handler, Michael Bettaney, who:

coloured their view of me. On the one hand he told them I wasn't to be trusted. I had become a republican and he wasn't sure of my politics. And I was protected, as he said, by 'the powers that be'. I had seven volunteers around me to protect me … Ben was still active. He didn't have a very nice word [to say] about me.[14]

Despite Bettaney's best attempts to dissuade the FRU from recruiting Carlin, a decision was made to reactivate him and he was given the unique codename 3007. 'They couldn't get that information [secret intelligence on the IRA's strategy and operations]. Derry was a closed shop. Nobody was getting in,' Carlin recalled. 'The Army was drawing a blank.'[15] Carlin was offering the FRU not only privileged access to the Republican Movement, but also valuable information on the IRA's Chief of Staff, Martin McGuinness.

★ ★ ★

Two weeks after Bobby Sands began his hunger strike, Derry businessman Brendan Duddy received a postcard from Pretoria in South Africa. It was sent to him by his friend Michael Oatley, an MI6 officer who had earlier been seconded to the IJS, which brought together officers from MI5 and MI6 at a safe house in Laneside.[16] Both men had worked to secure a peaceful end to the first hunger strike in December 1980. Duddy was interested in resurrecting the process during Sands' fast, but Oatley was sanguine:

I'm told there can't possibly be any service of the pipeline at the mainland end, or any thought of it, while the weather looks so black. I don't suppose this worries you at all and I don't see why (and have said) it should affect your own personal position. This is accepted. But it still makes things a bit difficult just now.[17]

Oatley had hoped to return in a week or two to discuss these matters with Duddy, hinting that he was part of a broader push for secret diplomacy between the British and the IRA. In the meantime, it was left to the DCI at Stormont, David Ranson,[18] to brief Margaret Thatcher on the latest thinking within the IRA, which, he assured her, 'recognised they could not win through terrorism. Their thinking was concentrated on the need to find a way to win back the support of the Catholic community which they had lost in recent years.'[19] Drawing on reporting from MI5's own network of spies in the Northern Ireland, Ranson concluded:

They saw the hunger strike, about the launching of which they had grave doubts, as a way to drive a wedge between the Catholic community and the Government. They knew that the situation was delicately balanced and that their effort might already have peaked in PR terms. There might be an opportunity in the next few weeks for the Government to attempt to reassure the Catholic community.[20]

Three weeks later, Ranson produced a more comprehensive briefing note for Thatcher based on his privileged access to all available source reporting:

We have tended to regard the involvement of the Provisionals in political activity as a development to be encouraged. But it is a development that requires a response from Government, as their terrorist activities receive a response. There is very general agreement that the Catholic community has been disturbed by the hunger strikers' deaths, that it blames Government, that there is a degree of alienation and that the Provisionals are getting more support. Unless their political exploitation of the hunger strike situation – and the resulting recrudescence of support for PIRA – can be countered, then the Provisionals 'going political' can succeed, where their terrorist activity has failed, in reversing the progress of recent years towards 'normality' and renewing for them a base from which a revitalised terrorist campaign could be launched.[21]

That response would soon come in the form of an offer from the British government.[22]

In the eyes of high-ranking republicans involved in liaising with the hunger strikers, the security and intelligence officials inside the NIO were fast becoming an obstacle to a resolution of the whole episode. Danny Morrison, the Sinn Féin Publicity Director at the time, recalled:

So, it wasn't a Third World country but it was still a situation where you had a tiny oligarchy, especially when it came to Direct Rule, dictating the pace to everyone in the north, including the unionists who were pro-state and who had little say in the situation except at senior civil service level. An area that has never been forensically examined is the disproportionate power wielded by the NIO ... Increasingly ... it appears to me that there is a possibility that Thatcher, for pragmatic reasons, was interested in around July '81 of just getting shot of the hunger strike but she was prevented from doing so by Atkins and Allison, who were overwhelmingly influenced by NIO unionist-type figures. And that, I can substantiate ... In my visit to the jail on 5 July 1981 when senior Prison Officers said, 'This is a fucking sell out. What's that bastard doing here?' And then when I'm thrown out of the jail two hours later, it was as if there was a power struggle between the Foreign Office in England and the NIO, and the NIO eventually won. But they were blind, they were stupid, all they could see was 'nil to the republicans, one up for us', without realising that dead republicans was building [support and sympathy] and they were going to reap a whirlwind for what they were sowing.[23]

In the battle for public sympathy and support over the hunger strikes, the Provisionals were indeed winning. Following further consideration of Ranson's recommendations, Downing Street moved to end the strike. On 5 July, the British offered concessions, which were rejected by Sinn Féin. However, over the course of the death march during the summer months, many nationalists drifted away from all-out support of the hunger strike and the SDLP openly repudiated it on 21 September. The following afternoon, Richard Lawson confidently reported to Humphrey Atkins that support for the hunger strikers and the level of public disorder were beginning to diminish. A number of 'good finds of arms, ammunition and explosives' were made by the Security Forces, Lawson said. Of even greater significance was the arrest of senior Belfast IRA man Bobby Storey in Andersonstown.[24] According to one of the prisoners on hunger strike, Tommy McKearney, the IRA's decision to give its stamp of authority to the mass protest and emerging political movement reflected its desire to be in control of the protest action on the streets.[25]

★ ★ ★

Ness Wood, Oughtagh Road, County Derry, October 1981

Sources and their handlers took serious risks in meeting to exchange secret information. The risks were even greater in areas where the IRA and the INLA held sway. Even in more anonymous public spaces, such as towns and cities, there was a danger that the clandestine liaison would be discovered. Derry IRA member Raymond Gilmour became an RUC Special Branch agent aged 16, often making contact with his handlers by way of public phone boxes. Communications between agents and their handlers were 'notoriously problematic' and handlers would only risk meeting an agent in person if the information being shared was judged important enough.[26] On such occasions, Gilmour would be 'constantly checking reflections in cars and windows and even doubling back on my tracks'. Typically, he would be picked up in Derry city centre and driven to the other side of the River Foyle, where he would be debriefed.[27] Handlers would vary their routines when planning 'meets' with sources to avoid being double-crossed. RUC Standard Operating Procedures (SOPs) – known as tradecraft in the Branch – recommended that four detectives should attend a 'meet' between a handler and a source: two to meet the source and at least another two to provide cover.[28]

RUC officers opted to meet their sources in the city, whereas MI5 and FRU handlers chose to meet them outside the city's limits. Carlin owned his own car, so he often met his handlers farther away. Many of his debriefings in the early 1980s took place in the leafy surroundings of Ness Wood Country Park, some 10 miles from Derry city centre. Situated close to the Glenshane Pass, the main arterial route between Dungiven and Drumahoe on the approach road to Derry, Ness Wood lies along the banks of the Burntollet River. On most occasions, Carlin would park in the visitors' car park and make his way along a sandy path to a bridge, where he would find his handler waiting. 'I always got there on time. I was never followed. My favourite trick was to drive round a roundabout three times and drive back in the opposite direction,' Carlin recalled.[29]

The information Carlin shared about the Derry Falange was largely political in nature. Although he was now being handled by the FRU, he kept at the forefront of his mind his initial brief from MI5, which had been to collect secret political information.[30] In a matter of months, Carlin had been transformed from a lowly Sinn Féin canvasser in Derry to one of its most prominent members. Mitchel McLaughlin and Martin McGuinness were so impressed by his performance on stage at the hunger strike rallies that they asked him to take control of the Waterside branch. Having demonstrated his proficiency as a public speaker, he set his mind to writing. Beginning with low-level press releases, Carlin went on to write grant applications and liaise with statutory bodies, including the Northern Ireland Housing Executive.

The more Carlin became involved in Sinn Féin political activism, the more he found himself in rooms in which IRA Civil Administration Team (CAT) activities were being discussed. Although precluded from 'Army business', he was nevertheless privy to general discussions of republican strategy. This would prove invaluable to his handlers in British Intelligence, who wished to exploit the opportunity to control the party machine now emerging.

7

AN HONOURABLE COURSE

'No matter what happened, the agent had to feel that he was pursuing an honourable course even if this involved money changing hands.'

– Deputy Head of RUC Special Branch, 24 May 1979[1]

Finaghy Community Centre, South Belfast, 14 November 1981

Forty-year-old Robert Bradford was feeling pugnacious as he sat in his constituency surgery in the community centre in Finaghy in South Belfast. He had been elected as an MP for the right-wing Ulster Vanguard Movement, which he left for the Ulster Unionist Party (UUP) in 1978. Prior to becoming involved in politics, Bradford had been a Methodist minister in the Suffolk area of West Belfast. First elected in February 1974, he successfully defended his seat eight months later in a snap election and again in 1979. Born in Limavady, to where his family had been evacuated during the Blitz of 1941, Bradford returned to Belfast in later life.

As a politician, Bradford could be bruising in his analyses of the security situation, particularly in relation to the IRA. In a hard-hitting speech in the House of Commons on 2 July 1981, he recommended that those on the government benches bring back capital punishment for convicted IRA terrorists, whom he accused of treason.[2] He stated:

> We need to destroy the morale of the IRA, which, when it eventually evaporates in the face of United Kingdom courage and resolution, will render emergency provisions unnecessary. We must destroy the morale of the IRA. We must put its objective beyond its reach, its touch and its attainment. That will not happen through the statement made by the Secretary of State on 30 June about the Maze prison. It will have the opposite effect to eroding the morale of the IRA. It will encourage the IRA to extract more concessions from the Government.[3]

The speech was widely reported in the press and sparked opprobrium amongst IRA members. During what remained of the summer, the group's GHQ staff put in motion a plan to assassinate the unionist MP, which they finally enacted in November. A former member of the FRU claimed that a source inside the IRA's ranks had warned that Bradford's life was in imminent danger. 'This was not a general warning,' said the soldier. 'We had someone in the IRA giving us information on the planned attack. I know for a fact that Special Branch also had someone inside giving them the same information.'[4] However, this information does not seem to have been acted upon.[5]

On the morning that the IRA came to murder the South Belfast MP, he was holding a constituency surgery in a local community centre in Finaghy. The centre was alive with people, including over 100 children attending a youth disco. As Bradford's RUC bodyguard stood chatting to the centre's caretaker, Ken Campbell, by the front door, he noticed two men in white, paint-spattered boiler suits carrying a plank of wood into the centre. He sensed that there was something suspicious about the men, but before he could do anything to stop them, they produced guns and shouted, 'Freeze!' The bodyguard reached for his gun, but he was overpowered by one of the gunmen, who tackled him to the floor and pinned him down. The other gunman fired a shot at Campbell and a third terrorist, who had followed the two men into the centre, kept watch. Two of the gunmen made their way into a back office, where Bradford was sitting behind a desk talking to an older man and woman. They opened fire on him with a handgun and a machine gun, hitting him seven times. The bullets struck him in the eye, ear, neck and chest at close range.[6] One eyewitness, Eyewitness A, recalled what happened next:

> I heard a bang outside. And it was like a firework going off. Well it was actually quite loud. I didn't really think anything of it and then a couple of seconds later these guys came rushing in. One was quite tall with a pock-marked face. The other one was stockier, smaller, behind him. The first one had a – I could see – had a revolver in his hand. There was somebody else came in and knelt down. It looked like he had a Thompson sub-machine gun. Of course, everybody started to run to different places, scream, shout. All the rest of it. And the guy, I remember, raised the gun towards where I was standing – and the door was open for – I think it was – the gents' toilets. And, so, I

pushed somebody else and a couple of other people and we went in there and closed the door. Then there was a flurry of gunfire. A lot of screaming and shouting and what have you. When I came out, I don't think they'd actually left when I came out because I could see the backs of them. And I don't know what it was, I walked into the room where Bradford was and seen he'd been shot somewhere about the face, in the chest and, I think, in the eye because his glasses were sitting, you know, at the bottom of his nose. And I remember coming out and I lifted the stock – the handle – of a Thompson sub-machine gun, which had come off in the melee.[7]

After the gunfire had subsided, Eyewitness A walked outside and saw Ken Campbell lying on the ground, mortally wounded. A couple of people were trying their best to save him.

The gunmen climbed into a waiting getaway car and drove off at speed. Meanwhile, the police bodyguard had drawn his pistol, but seemed paralysed by the shock of what had just happened. By now, the place was swarming with people, including the children attending the disco. One 15-year-old boy, Eyewitness B, told reporters that the terrorists were wearing Halloween masks to hide their faces. 'I was helping run the disco,' he said. 'I was doing the records when I heard the shooting. I heard five shots and then another one. The kids in the disco just went wild, they were running about all over the place.'[8] However, Eyewitness A described the gunmen acting in the following way:

The guys who came in, if I remember rightly, weren't wearing any masks. There was no attempt to hide their identities. The police told me afterwards that they could have been wearing wigs, could have been wearing makeup or false moustaches. But it didn't look like that. It looked pretty natural looking, if anything a little bit of wax on their faces or a wee bit of Vaseline or something … I think the idea was that they were coming in dressed as if they were workmen. Because I think there was work getting done to the community centre at the time … One definitely had a boiler suit on or a type of boiler suit. The first one I seen, the taller of the three, he seemed to have a very tight-fitting suit on. And a detective afterwards said he might have been wearing a flak jacket or a bulletproof jacket or something. But they were actually quite – I wouldn't say the word – professional but they knew exactly what they were about to do. You know, there was no nerves by it … They seemed to know exactly where to go and what positions to take up. They seemed to be well rehearsed or something … I got the sense that the second guy [who] came in was making sure Bradford was dead. They were quite cool and focused. It looked like nothing was going to stop them. It was well planned. They seemed to know that nothing was going to stop them. They had all their bases covered. They seemed to have been there before.[9]

Eyewitness A described the men quite accurately, though, oddly, he was never asked by the RUC to give a statement. The first gunman, he said, 'had a revolver in his hand. Something like a .38 or a 357 magnum. He was quite tall. He might have been about six foot. He'd a very pock-marked face like bad skin or scarred on the face.' The second gunman, he recalled, 'was dark … tanned. Darker skin.' Even more curiously, despite having picked up the Thompson sub-machine gun stock, Eyewitness A was never fingerprinted to eliminate him from inquiries. 'There was no interest in following it up,' he said.[10]

The gunman carrying the Thompson sub-machine gun was 29-year-old John Joseph 'The Hawk' Haughey, known as 'Joe Buck' to his IRA comrades.[11] Originally from Carrick Hill on the fringes of Belfast city centre, he lived in the Unity Flats area of North Belfast and was one of the Belfast IRA's most active gunmen. A married man with children, it was said that Haughey was related by marriage to the wife of UDA commander James Pratt Craig. Some said Haughey was more in love with the IRA than he was with his wife. He even adopted the motto, 'I'm the hawk from the walk but I don't squawk.'[12] A trusted member of the IRA's GHQ staff at the time, he had been acquitted of murdering Constable Stephen Magill and Captain Westmacott a year earlier. In an attempt to capitalise on the outpouring of grief over the hunger strikers, he and his small squad, which allegedly included 35-year-old Freddie Scappaticci, a republican from the Markets area of East Belfast,[13] initiated the assassination plot against Bradford. Despite his fingerprints being found on the butt of the Thompson, Haughey was never arrested for the attack.[14] This was strange as his fingerprints would have been on file since his first arrest in 1972 for armed robbery and the possession of illegal weapons.[15] He escaped justice on at least two other occasions, including for the M60 gun attacks, which resulted in the deaths of Constable Magill and Captain Westmacott.[16] Either Joe Buck had luck on his side or someone was watching out for his well-being.[17] In the immediate aftermath of the murder, the IRA issued a statement to the press:

> Belfast Brigade IRA claims responsibility for the execution of Robert Bradford MP, one of the key people responsible for winding up the loyalist paramilitary sectarian machine in the North. Let Mr Tyrie (UDA leader) and the UDA know well the cost of killing innocent nationalist people.[18]

Earlier in the year, two-legged sources inside the IRA were reporting 'a growing feeling in the movement that the time has come to call a halt – at any rate for a time'.[19] However, the boost in mass protest action and support arising from the hunger strikes enabled the IRA to assert its control over the popular movement, thereby enabling it to build up a nascent Sinn Féin.[20] Killing unionist politicians like Robert Bradford was an essential part of this new twin-track approach.

* * *

Security Coordinator's Office, Stormont Castle, Belfast, Mid-November 1981

Sir Brooks Richards was sitting quietly at his desk, putting the finishing touches to his review of the security situation in Northern Ireland. Like his predecessor, Maurice Oldfield, Richards found his job challenging. He had been briefed regularly by Intelligence Officers and had, on occasion, even ventured outside the heavily protected grounds of Stormont Castle to visit those men and women running agents, collating intelligence and providing covert tactical support. In his view:

> The hunger strike had little lasting impact on the available coverage. During the rioting it was often impossible to meet and obtain information from agents and the surveillance teams found it difficult to operate within Republican areas. Once the streets were cleared and life returned to normal intelligence again became available. In the summer PIRA instigated a rigorous 'tout' hunt following the Security Forces successes in Belfast. Many members of PIRA were interrogated and a few murdered as alleged informers. Although this

had an inhibiting effect on some potential agents it also resulted in disaffection among PIRA activists and has not significantly stemmed the flow of information. Nevertheless, good intelligence remains hard to come by. As far as Loyalist terrorism is concerned there has been good preventive intelligence.[21]

Richards now judged there to be little appetite within the IRA for ending its armed struggle. The regenerative effect of the hunger strikes would make the embryonic 'ballot box and Armalite' strategy much more appealing.[22] As his Liaison Staff made clear in a widely circulated threat assessment, 'both PIRA and INLA have the capacity and the will to sustain indefinitely the pattern of activity of recent months'.[23] In the meantime, their targeting of off-duty members of the Security Forces, cross-border attacks and the bombing of commercial properties would continue. Richards wrote:

> The terrorist organisations have now been refined into relatively small and secure groups. The successful attack on the terrorist organisations comes from intelligence-based covert operations. Such methods result in the conviction of key terrorists following 'red-handed' arrests and may achieve local, short-term reductions in violence but they do not often result in a lasting cessation of terrorism in an area.[24]

It was a frustrating set of circumstances, he thought. Nobody knew this better than RUC detectives working round the clock to recruit more informers inside the IRA.

★ ★ ★

Boyhill, Maguiresbridge, Fermanagh, Evening, 17 November 1981

On a windswept evening in deepest Fermanagh, a squad of IRA gunmen made the short car journey from Lisnaskea to a farm at Boyhill in the Maguiresbridge area. After being dropped off close to the farm, the IRA men made their way across a moonlit field to their target. They had been stalking him for some weeks, methodically building up a picture of his every movement and working out when would be the best time to kill him. Despite the pre-existing enmity between local Protestant and Catholic communities, the IRA had managed to gather information regarding their target's routine. For instance, they were able to ascertain that 44-year-old Corporal Albert Beacom, a married man with five children, would, that evening, be dropping off two of his sons at a neighbouring church hall in Brookeborough, where they would be attending their local Boys' Brigade evening. They also knew that he would be returning to his farm shortly afterwards and that he would likely be home alone. As the IRA squad neared the Beacoms' farm, they spotted the headlights of Albert's car turning in from the main road. After parking, he got out of his car and walked a few feet to an outbuilding to switch on a pump. Two gunmen crept up behind him and shot him five times in the back. His wife, Essie, who had been inside the farmhouse, heard the shots and ran outside to find her husband covered in blood. She quickly telephoned 999 before returning to comfort him. Meanwhile, the IRA squad succeeded in escaping. As the gunmen disappeared into the pitch-black night, their victim was taken to Erne Hospital, where he was pronounced dead on arrival.

RUC officers wasted little time in making an arrest. They went to the home of a local man, Patrick Pearse O'Neill, and promptly took him to the RUC station in Enniskillen for interrogation.[25] Detective Inspector Brendan Hart confronted O'Neill with evidence of tyre tracks and footprints from the murder scene, as well as some of O'Neill's clothing, including muddy shoes. 'I didn't shoot anybody,' he told Hart. He then became visibly distressed, resting his head in his hands and shaking nervously. He didn't deny that he had been present at the Beacom farm that evening, but he refused to reveal why he had been there. The next morning, O'Neill was interviewed for a second time, this time in Gough Barracks in Armagh. Again, he refused to cooperate.

Later that afternoon, he was interviewed for a third time, by 36-year-old Detective Chief Inspector Frank Murray. O'Neill told Murray that he had left a local shop around 6 p.m. and driven a friend's red Hillman Avenger to Lisnaskea, where, he said, he was stopped by two men whom he believed to be police officers standing in the middle of the road. Oddly, he said that both men were wearing masks and he couldn't make out their identities.

'We know you were at the lane in the car close to where the firing point was and that you were driving when a Security Forces patrol stopped you 7–8 minutes later about 3.5 miles away,' Murray told O'Neill. Murray then confronted O'Neill about his involvement in the murder.

'I'm not saying I wasn't there,' he replied, shaking.

'What was your role?' Murray asked.

'I said I'll tell you the full story about last night when I see my solicitor.'

'Why can't you tell us now?'

'I don't want to say the wrong thing.'

'What kind of education do you have?'

'Six O Levels,' replied O'Neill.

'Why can you not give us an account of your movements last night?'

'I told you I want to talk it over with the solicitor first.'

'Why, you're not a stupid person.'

'You need to say the right thing when you're in my position.'

'You agree that you are in a serious position,' Murray told him. 'We know you were at the scene of that murder.'

'I didn't shoot that man.'

'You were there.'

Silence.

'I said I will tell the whole truth when I talk it over with my solicitor.'

'Are you going to tell the whole truth?'

'As far as I can remember. There may be things I can't remember.'

'What about the guns that were used?'

'I know nothing about them.'

'Now, that's not true. You saw them in the car before the two gunmen got out.'

'But I don't know anything about them now.'

'You know where the gunmen got out of the car.'

'I'm not talking any more about it.'

Murray talked to O'Neill about his employment status and family life, attempting to build up a rapport with his suspect. The Lisnaskea man was unemployed and in receipt of benefits, but he admitted to 'doing the double' as a casual labourer laying concrete in Carrybridge. The Hillman Avenger car, he said, had been borrowed from a workmate. A former bank worker in Cookstown and Galway, O'Neill had dropped out of employment some months previously.

'Did you know the gunmen?' Murray inquired again.

'I'm not saying.'

'Why not?'

'I won't be naming any names when I make the statement. I will give you an account of my movements.'

'So you know the men who murdered the UDR man last night.'

O'Neill remained silent.

'Is that right?'

'I will give you an account of my movements when I get advice from my solicitor.'[26]

Chief Inspector Murray interviewed O'Neill one further time, on the morning of 20 November, this time with the explicit intention of persuading him to provide information on the weapons used in the attack. Early reports from Beacom's autopsy suggested that the murder weapons were an Armalite and a Carbine, which Murray was eager to take out of circulation in order to prevent further bloodshed. O'Neill refused to cooperate any further. Murray and his team referred his case to the Director of Public Prosecutions. A week after Albert Beacom's funeral, Pearse O'Neill appeared in court charged with his murder. He pleaded not guilty.

In the wake of Beacom's murder, *Guardian* journalist John Cunningham travelled to Fermanagh to cover the killing. What he found horrified him: 'There are as many solicitors' nameplates glinting along the main street of Enniskillen as there must have been undertakers in a cowboy town. It is a mean place which the lawmen, at least, have sewn up.'[27] Enniskillen sits on a hill, like a fort on a plain, Cunningham reflected, and there was a real risk of vigilantism if the government did not act quickly.

The Reverend Ian Paisley and his sinister, red-beret-sporting 'Third Force' were the most palpable manifestation of fear amongst rural Protestants. One of Paisley's followers, Reverend Ivan Foster, expressed the feelings of many of these people when he told Cunningham: 'My family came from England 300 years ago and we've been fighting them Indians ever since. Ulster Protestants, by virtue of centuries of toil and hard work, have earned the right to call Ulster their land and to preserve it.' Foster's words echoed those of another Fermanagh Protestant, Lord Ernest Hamilton, a former cavalry officer, a novelist and a former MP for North Tyrone, who wrote in his book *The Soul of Ulster* (1917) that every nation had its 'bad men': 'The soul of the native Irish has not at the present day changed by the width of a hair from what it was in 1641 and again in 1798.'[28] As Hamilton reminded his readers, 'to the native Irish mind' these one million Protestants represented 'the one unspeakable evil, that is to say the British Usurper.'[29] Almost two centuries later, little had changed. Northern Irish Protestants living along the frontier interpreted the IRA's terrorism as an existential threat to their way of life. The IRA's sectarian campaign along the border did little to dispel this myth.[30]

The British government announced the deployment of a new regiment to the area in the wake of the murders of Albert Beacom and other part-time members of the Security Forces. The changeover of the Armagh Roulement Battalion was announced on 11 December 1981. The red berets of Paisley's Third Force would be replaced by the maroon berets of the British Army's elite Parachute Regiment. As Northern Ireland's emergency spearhead battalion, the PARAs were to deploy imminently to Forward Operating Bases along the border under the reorganised brigade system.[31] 1 PARA replaced the Royal Hampshire Regiment, who departed for Belfast by helicopter, the first time RAF Chinooks had flown in Operation Banner.[32]

★ ★ ★

Despite the best efforts of detectives like Frank Murray, rural IRA squads were proving tough opponents. Sir Brooks Richards' careful assessment of the difficulties facing the Security Forces was based on an acute insight into the challenges of agent handling that he had gained during his time as an SOE officer in wartime Europe. However, he was prepared to follow the guidance of his predecessor, Sir Maurice Oldfield, who preferred informers to agents. Oldfield's belief that, on balance, it was probably best to 'turn' paramilitaries would soon be validated.

On 21 November 1981, the RUC arrested several men mounting an illegal roadblock in the Ardoyne area of North Belfast, including 29-year-old Christopher Black.[33] Recently paroled, Black had been a member of the IRA's 3rd Battalion based in the Ardoyne area for several years and was 'well known as a quiet but committed IRA man'. He had recently been released from a ten-year prison sentence, having served half of his full term for armed robbery and IRA membership. A naïve, short man, he was slightly built and sported a wispy moustache. He had been recruited into the IRA in 1975. He later stated that he had joined simply 'to be a somebody, to gain local status and impress young women'. His initial role was in a unit known locally as 'The Sweeney', which settled the IRA's accounts with local hoods, dealing out punishment beatings, including kneecappings. He later graduated from bank robberies to more serious activities, such as targeting, assassinations and bombings, though in his evidence to police he admitted to being a bit of a 'bungler'.[34] Typically, IRA volunteers who had graduated from the group's so-called 'punishment squads' were regarded with suspicion.

Black hadn't been out of prison long when he was arrested again. Faced with the prospect of returning to prison to serve out the remainder of his sentence, he decided to turn Queen's evidence.[35] Within days he had divulged information regarding a number of IRA men across Belfast. The Security Forces netted some twenty suspects, while the RUC arrived at Black's home with several Land Rovers and a removal van to escort his wife, mother-in-law and four children out of the area.[36] The information Black gave the RUC was invaluable. He explained that the IRA continued to organise itself in brigades, battalions, companies and squads. His information even led to a Garda raid of an IRA training camp in Donegal, where eleven Armalite rifles, a shotgun and 4,000 rounds of ammunition were found.[37] The information he shared also helped Security Forces capture Michael McKee, one of the M60 gang who had escaped from the Crumlin Road prison the previous summer. In an interview in *The Observer*, unionist MP Harold McCusker voiced the opinion of many in the wider community about sources like Black when he said, 'Immunity is a terrible price to pay. On the other hand the Security Forces are caught between the vice of wanting to extinguish terrorism and the cellular system of the IRA.'[38]

Thanks to Black's information, the RUC had the Belfast IRA on the ropes. RUC headquarters at Knock in East Belfast began to capitalise on the intense media speculation around the Black case, releasing statistics to illustrate the progress that had been made against terrorism. By now, the Security Forces had recovered some 356 rifles, handguns, machine guns and rocket launchers, twice as many as the previous year; 1,506lb more explosives had also been uncovered and the number of charges being brought for terrorist offences rose by 70 per cent to 861 by the end of November,[39] suggesting that the cellular structure was not entirely effective. In December alone, the RUC arrested some twenty-six people, mostly as a result of the information Black had given them.

This new 'supergrass' strategy caused internal strife in the IRA, which was becoming increasingly paranoid about informers. Over the festive period, the GHQ-appointed Internal Security Unit (known colloquially as 'The Nutting Squad') killed five men accused of being informers. Early in the new year, Dickie Lawson reported to new Secretary of State Jim Prior that he did not 'think that the security situation had fundamentally changed in the period since the end of hunger strike'. There had been little terrorist activity in Belfast, though there were two IRA squads 'capable of committing murders and imposing violent punishments'. As far as the Security Forces were concerned, 'PIRA in the area had been fairly effectively disrupted for the time being'. Lawson was dismissive of 'the activities of Gerry Adams or, for example, Bobby Sands', which he believed had not 'achieved much'.[40] In his view, the one factor that appeared to be driving the success of current operations was the 'continuing good relations between the NIO, the RUC and the Army', with the NIO 'respected for being honest and straightforward in the dealings with the security forces'.[41]

Further swoops by the Security Forces in the Markets area of Belfast in early February 1982 were the direct result of information given by informers.[42] Outside Belfast, Detective Chief Inspector Frank Murray and his team had turned an IRA member in the Mid Ulster area. Paddy McGurk had given them information on several of his comrades, including 24-year-old Paddy Kelly, an IRA member from Dungannon.[43] It was a major coup for Murray and led to him being noticed by senior Special Branch officer Trevor Forbes. 'Tip-offs, and a more elaborate and prolonged supply of information,' reported *The Daily Telegraph*, 'played a major role in a widespread security operation in Ulster during the past few days which resulted in the detention of 43 people, all of whom were still being questioned.'[44]

The Provos claimed to have murdered six members who were believed to be informers in the preceding fourteen months. In an unprecedented move, they announced a fourteen-day amnesty during which informers who came forward would be spared execution. In a desperate bid to disrupt the new supergrass system, the IRA targeted Lord Chief Justice Lowry, who visited Queen's University Belfast to give a lecture on 2 March 1982. IRA gunmen opened fire on him as he was arriving at the venue, but missed their target. A member of the academic staff, Professor Robert Perks, was injured in the attack. It was later alleged that the information about Lowry's visit would only have been known to a select few people and must have been leaked by a mole inside the university, though this has never been proven. In other parts of the city, soldiers on patrol were fired upon. Three were killed in an ambush near Springfield Road police station on 25

March. The gunmen responsible had been armed with two rifles and an M60 machine gun, which police suspected had been smuggled into the area from South Armagh.[45] One soldier and nine civilians were also wounded in the attack.[46] Despite the damages it had suffered as a result of the Security Forces intelligence attack on its operations, the IRA nonetheless remained a persistent threat.

8

PROJECT 3702

'Larger company areas covered by less bricks have made the detailed targeting of addresses and personalities a difficult task. It has also led to the downgrading of the reliability and value of the 3702 facility. Police information gathering from neighbourhood patrols is minimal and so far uncollated, and is seldom passed on. This further limits the low level intelligence effort through company intelligence cells ... Special Branch were always quick to ensure the military were aware of any threats and made sure they disseminated any intelligence which troops on the ground needed to know.'

– 2nd Battalion, Royal Green Jackets, Post Operational Tour Report (1982)[1]

Security Policy Meeting, Stormont Castle, 29 March 1982

Fifty-five-year-old Sir John Hermon arrived at the SPM on the afternoon of 29 March 1982, having just told the press that the PIRA had been left 'reeling' by the influx of secret information now being passed on to his force by informers and supergrasses.[2] However, behind closed doors, Hermon was more circumspect. The minutes of the SPM record that he was 'well aware that informers needed to be handled carefully', given 'the traditional stigma attached to touting, especially when money was involved'. He insisted that these 'supergrasses' 'had not been offered large sums of cash, but the police clearly had to ensure the future safety of those who gave information'. Secretary of State for Northern Ireland Jim Prior reminded Hermon of the 'need to request Government assistance in resettling informers in other countries'.[3] Prior always chaired the SPM and, in addition to the Chief Constable, the high-level forum was also attended by the Permanent Under Secretary at the NIO, 58-year-old Philip Woodfield, the GOC, 56-year-old Lieutenant General Sir Richard Lawson, and the recently appointed DCI, 52-year-old Harold 'Hal' Granville Terence Payne Doyne-Ditmas, MI5's top spymaster in Northern Ireland.[4]

Doyne-Ditmas perhaps knew better than anyone else in the room the true extent of the penetration of loyalist and republican terrorist groups.[5]

Recruited by the Security Service in the 1950s, Doyne-Ditmas' tenure with MI5 took him overseas to Malaya and later to Russia, where he learned Cold War tradecraft combatting the KGB. He had been appointed DCI in late 1981 and had previously worked under Sir Brooks Richards when he was Intelligence Coordinator in the Cabinet Office.[6] Armed with a highly imaginative and deeply analytical understanding of terrorism and insurgency, he was keen to increase the predictive capabilities of intelligence operations.

The post of DCI had been established by the first Secretary of State Willie Whitelaw on 31 October 1972. Whitelaw stipulated that the post-holder should 'act as both his personal security adviser and his main link with the senior army general and the RUC Chief Constable'. The position of DCI had initially been offered to MI5, but there was 'no one of sufficient seniority [who] was willing to fill it', so it initially went to MI6.[7] However, by the early 1980s, the post had switched from MI6 to MI5. In reality, the title DCI was regarded by senior Intelligence Officers as a 'misnomer'. The DCI never directed intelligence operations and the post-holder's 'main function was intelligence liaison and co-ordination' in order to deliver 'high-level policy direction and advice relating to intelligence activity in Northern Ireland'.[8] Although he had no operational responsibilities, the DCI was the principal link between the intelligence machinery in London and Belfast. The role earned Doyne-Ditmas his privileged place at the top table of the SPM.[9]

By the early 1980s, the RUC was very much in the driving seat of operational security, with MI5 and the military playing supporting roles. Doyne-Ditmas considered gathering information, both secret and open source, in a manner that supported the RUC to be part of his role. He brought a vast amount of experience to the table. One of the techniques he introduced in Northern Ireland was known as 'Movements Analysis'.[10] This built on technical assets available to Intelligence Officers, including Signals Intelligence (or SIGINT), which drew on the bulk data capability of the GCHQ, which spent much of its time intercepting telephone conversations. Doyne-Ditmas combined such interception with analysis of the movements of known terrorists. In this, he was greatly aided by the British Army, which had developed a vast person identification system known as 'P Checks', as well as a vehicle number plate recognition system that enabled soldiers on the ground to run 'traces' of vehicles at checkpoints.[11] The hardware utilised to crunch the huge amount of information was known as Automatic Data Processing (ADP) or by its military codename 'Project 3702'.[12] The ADP system gave the Army an edge over the RUC because the police did not have a comparable computerised database, though Special Branch did possess a computer system. However, John Hermon did 'not feel able to allow Army access to SB information stored on computer'.[13] As a result of inadequate cooperation between the Army and the police, the military built up its own database of suspected terrorists 'secretly, without the RUC's knowledge'.[14]

Project 3702 was a first-generation intelligence collation system that had been in use since 1976.[15] 'The purpose of the system,' one government official reported, 'is to eliminate the inconsistencies and duplication of effort in the manual system previously in operation, and to speed research and dissemination.' The system was in widespread use at HQNI, at brigade and unit level, and 'among the Force intelligence units',[16] and allowed its operators to confirm links between suspected terrorists, their families and friends, as well as offering an overview of their everyday movements on foot and in vehicles. Crucially, the ADP system afforded Intelligence Officers the ability to predict terrorist attacks. This technique 'had first been developed by the Canadians and was used extensively by MI5 to track the movements of Soviet intelligence officers in London'.[17] In Northern Ireland, information was 'fed into the system from the numerous computer terminals in the province at roadblocks and from general intelligence gathering'.[18] However, as officials recognised at the time, 'the collection of data is focussed much more sharply upon known or suspected terrorists'. Although collated by battalions on the ground, 'it is principally exploited by the Force Intelligence units and the assessment staff at HQNI, in countering an increasingly sophisticated and security-conscious enemy'.[19]

Doyne-Ditmas was aided in his mass surveillance of the IRA by the muscle provided by Military Intelligence Officers based at HQNI. The Army's main analysis unit was 12 Intelligence Company's 1st Intelligence Section. Its junior NCOs worked around the clock hoovering up vast amounts of information, which they stored in twenty-five four-drawer filing cabinets in a huge storeroom. According to one soldier who served with the unit, their day-to-day activities involved 'the collation of information and intelligence, the analysis of data to identify patterns and trends and the dissemination of the final product through oral and written briefs'.[20] Most of the intelligence they handled came in the form of RUC Intelligence

Reports and Comments (known to the Military as RIRAC and to the RUC as SB50s) and Military Intelligence Source Reports (MISRs) – effectively hard-copy summaries of pertinent reporting – with a 'lesser amount of other intelligence product' in the form of intelligence reports, which were to be collated and assessed before being fed back down to brigades and battalions on the ground.[21] The soldiers in 121 Intelligence Section were very busy, particularly in 1981 when the hunger strikes were on and in the aftermath throughout 1982, secretly inputting SB50s into the 3702 system 'without the RUC's knowledge'.[22] Most collators in 121 Section were young and inexperienced, but what they lacked in experience they more than made up for in energy and commitment. Some enterprising individuals, such as Intelligence Corps analyst Ian Hurst, compiled files on significant players and incidents on their own initiative.[23] Hurst held Level 1 clearance and had oversight of much of the top-secret information held in the Intelligence Registry at HQNI.

In practice, 121 Intelligence Section was a huge bureaucratic conveyor belt for raw information. It was manned twenty-four hours a day, seven days a week, and sat at the apex of intelligence processing in Northern Ireland. Most of the product it handled was marked SECRET, with the additional caveat of 'No Downward Dissemination' (NDD), meaning that it could not be passed down to the operational brigades. One smaller team known as 3 Special Collation Team (3SCT) loaded as much of the material as they could onto the 3702 system, enabling MI5 to undertake rudimentary analysis of the movements of individuals.[24] MI5 Liaison Officers co-located at HQNI ensured that questions relating to specific operational matters could be answered quickly and efficiently. However, the NDD protocol tended to reflect the institutional silos that characterised the collection and collation aspects of the intelligence cycle.[25]

* * *

The presence of institutional silos would have devastating consequences for the British in more fundamental ways beyond Northern Ireland. The Argentine invasion of the Falkland Islands, a Crown dependency in the South Atlantic, took the British completely by surprise. Margaret Thatcher had learned of the movement of Argentine naval forces less than forty-eight hours before they landed at Port Stanley, when it was too late to do anything to prevent it. She now faced one of the UK's worst intelligence failures in modern history. Outraged, she told her Secretary of State, John Nott, 'If they are invaded, we have got to get them back.'[26] She authorised Nott to deploy a task force to recapture the islands. Due to the gravity of the situation, the MoD mobilised its high-readiness forces, 3 Commando Brigade, augmented by two Parachute Regiment battalions. As senior defence planners drew up their Order of Battle, they knew they would be short one Parachute battalion, as the 1st Battalion was well on its way to Fermanagh.

For the soldiers in 1 PARA, whose CO was Lieutenant Colonel Ian McLeod, a veteran of operations in the Middle East and Northern Ireland, there was a sense of disappointment. The men had been informed well in advance that they would take over responsibility for the Tactical Area of Responsibility (TAOR) in Fermanagh from the 1st Battalion of the Hampshire Regiment. Their mission was to defeat terrorism while also supporting normal policing throughout their TAOR. Many of the 1 PARA soldiers had completed Northern Ireland tours before and the unit had been present on Bloody Sunday a decade earlier. 1 PARA had, therefore, a notorious reputation in Northern Ireland, particularly in republican communities. Some of the battalion's senior soldiers and officers had even served in South Yemen in the 1960s. When Colonel McLeod and his men arrived at St Angelo Barracks to take over from the Hampshires, the outgoing CO noted 'a certain reluctance on the part of their advance party to engage in the handover presuming that they would be joining their 2nd and 3rd Battalions then on their way to the Falklands'.[27] Much of the Hampshires' tour had been uneventful, with the notable exception of the murder of 21-year-old Drummer Colin Clifford, who was killed in a landmine explosion near Belleek on 30 April.[28]

In the month leading up to Clifford's murder, Special Branch intelligence had led the Hampshires to discover illegal ammunition in Relagh and bomb-making materials in Trillick, and to arrest an IRA suspect in Lisnaskea. Ten days prior to Drummer Clifford's death, the Hampshires had readied themselves for a concerted IRA attack after bombs exploded in Strabane, Derry, Bessbrook, Armagh, Ballymena and Magherafelt, and a patrol of soldiers came under fire from an IRA squad at Lackey Bridge. The principal task of the Hampshires and their successors in 1 PARA was to conduct 'framework patrols', the aim of which was to catch terrorists red-handed, if possible, deter terrorist activity, and reassure the local population, a significant proportion of which consisted of Protestant farmers in isolated areas. Additional duties included protecting vulnerable points, such as bridges and border Permanent Vehicle Checkpoints (PVCPs), as well as 'soft targets', such as part-time UDR members who lived in the border county.

The primary threats to 1 PARA in their TAOR were three IRA units. The first was the Donegal IRA, which Security Forces believed was responsible for the murder of Drummer Clifford. The second, arguably more deadly IRA squad was the Monaghan IRA. The Army knew that IRA volunteers in these squads were not tied to the groups and instead 'floated' between them. Two of the leading members of both groups were Jim Lynagh and Seamus McElwain. The day that Ian McLeod and his troops took over command of the TAOR, IRA members Kevin Lynch and Gerard Mulligan received lengthy prison sentences for a radio-controlled car bombing in Enniskillen in October 1980. That day, news also broke of the escape of Monaghan IRA member Aiden McGurk, who had previously been arrested by the Gardaí on 25 October 1981 after he was found sitting at the firing point of a Command Wire Improvised Explosive Device (CWIED). Perhaps the biggest success, however, was the sentencing of McElwain's squad, the members of which had been arrested on 14 March 1981. Each man was handed down a lengthy sentence, with the most severe sentence of thirty years awarded to McElwain, who was convicted of the murders of 44-year-old UDR man Aubrey Abercrombie and 36-year-old Reserve RUC officer Ernest Johnson. The third IRA squad was based in Donagh around the Knox Hills area.

When they took over from the Hampshires, 1 PARA was provided with a reasonably accurate intelligence picture of their opposition. One Army intelligence report made it clear that they should expect the IRA to be involved in the following violent activities:

(a) Soft target murders of UDR, RUC and RUC(R) members or ex members by shooting or booby trap devices on cars. Off duty Regular Army personnel are similarly at risk.

(b) Culvert bombs, particularly in south east Fermanagh. These devices may be either CWIEDs or RCIEDs and most vulnerable routes are those which lead to SF [Security Forces] bases, RUC stations or PVCPs.

(c) Mortar attacks against SF bases, RUC stations and PVCPs.

(d) Shooting attacks which can take the form of snipes against PVCPs, SF bases or border patrols which expose themselves unnecessarily.

(e) Proxy or car bombs at PVCPs, SF bases, RUC stations or in urban areas.[29]

The IRA was thought more dangerous because of their acquisition of sophisticated intercept (jamming) capability. As the 3 Brigade intelligence report informed McLeod:

> South East FERMANAGH has been quiet for several months. An incident here is long overdue. This is particularly the case considering the success of the BALLYSHANNON/BUNDORAN PIRA with CWIED on 30 April. MONAGHAN PIRA have been quiet for a long time and are clearly suffering resupply and leadership problems. They will be keen to overcome the problems and emulate the success of the grouping in DONEGAL.[30]

Much of the intelligence received by Colonel McLeod and his men was speculative. It tended to focus on the intent of local IRA squads and their likely intended targets. One such target was the PVCP at Mullen Bridge, which had previously been attacked with a car bomb on 26 November 1981. Local IRA leader J.J. McGirl issued a public statement threatening an attack, which he then ordered the Ballyconnell/Swalinbar IRA to carry out. Worryingly, some intelligence pointed to the creation of a new IRA unit in Cavan and Leitrim, which now had the Mullen Bridge PVCP in its crosshairs. Military Intelligence believed, on the basis of previous attacks, that the IRA would attack the PVCP either with a proxy bomb hidden in a vehicle or with home-made mortars.

The day-to-day responsibility for protecting the PVCP was handed over to 1 PARA's Close Observation Platoon (COP), which consisted of the battalion's toughest and most physically agile soldiers. The COP worked directly with RUC Special Branch commanders in the local TCG.[31] It was the COP, for example, that watched two leading terrorists meet in a pub in the Drumsloe Salient on 24 May 1982, a notorious haunt for IRA planning meetings. Such information was invaluable for Special Branch, as well as Military Intelligence and MI5, which could track the movements of known terrorists using Project 3702. One of the benefits of plotting the movements of terrorist players was the ability to work out who had replaced IRA leaders Jim Lynagh and Seamus McElwain, who were now languishing in prison. In this case, COP soldiers recorded a spike in the movements of 33-year-old Philip McDonald, the Monaghan IRA's quartermaster, whom Special Branch suspected was beginning to assume a more important role in the absence of Lynagh and McElwain. A native of the Fermanagh/Monaghan borderlands and a married man with nine children, McDonald joined the IRA in the early 1970s. Regarded as having an 'immense knowledge of the contours of the border', he became one of the IRA's key Intelligence Officers for the region.[32] By the early 1980s, he was dividing his time between Clones in the Irish Republic and Fermanagh in the north.

As well as watching McDonald, 1 PARA's COP was tasked with keeping an eye out for 30-year-old IRA suspect John Anthony Downey. On 4 June 1982, intelligence reports shared by the Gardaí stated that Downey hadn't been seen in County Donegal recently and had, perhaps, slipped into 1 PARA's TAOR. Special Branch was well aware that he spent time in Ballyconnell and Swalinbar, and that he did not go to these places for 'purely social reasons'.[33] It later transpired that Downey had, in fact, been dispatched by Northern Command to England, where he became 'an active participant' in a planned attack in Great Britain.[34]

Throughout their tour, 1 PARA continued to watch IRA suspects in their TAOR, as a secret intelligence report confirmed:

> The value of int[elligence] and information gathering cannot be overestimated. All tasks are to have an int gathering purpose to them. In addition, all ops [operations] are to be planned and executed with a view to defeating the terrorist int[elligence] org[anisation]. Ops are to be unpredictable and are to avoid any 'pattern'.[35]

As well as shadowing IRA suspects, 1 PARA had to deal with a deterioration in community relations between Protestants and Catholics in the Fermanagh area, with reports of intimidation and a number of sectarian slogans daubed on people's homes. McLeod believed this was 'likely to incur some form of violent reaction from PIRA'. Interestingly, Philip McDonald was proving less ruthless than his boss Jim Lynagh, preferring to focus on attacks on soft targets. Through vigorous framework patrolling and the round-the-clock efforts of their COP, 1 PARA severely curtailed McDonald's operations in their area. He grew so frustrated that he directed Owen Carron, Bobby Sands' replacement as the local MP for the area, to complain to the NIO about the behaviour of the paratroopers in the Kinawley area. Carron said the soldiers were 'somewhat over-enthusiastic about their duties', alleging that they were deliberately holding up drivers at PVCPs for 2–3 hours. Oddly, Carron admitted that relations between the locals and the Hampshires had been 'good'. But, he claimed that 1 PARA's 'provocative attitude' was spoiling relations with the local community.[36] The real issue, however, was that 1 PARA had succeeded in disrupting McDonald's operations. This had been achieved through good tactics, good working relations with Special Branch and good intelligence provided by the 3702 system. The IRA's inability to kill Parachute Regiment soldiers would leave a lasting impression on McDonald and his squads for many months.

9

A SOLDIER'S MENTALITY

'You may tell the Brits to look out – the boys intend to get a couple of them this weekend.'[1]

– Threat received on the Confidential Telephone
on 17 September 1982

Central London, 10.30 a.m., 20 July 1982

Sixteen soldiers from the Household Cavalry were making their way from Knightsbridge Barracks to Buckingham Palace to perform the world-famous Changing of the Guard ceremony. As the soldiers and two police officers passed Hyde Park, a bomb exploded. Four soldiers – 23-year-old Lieutenant Anthony Daly, 19-year-old Trooper Simon Tipper, 19-year-old Lance Corporal Jeffrey Young and 36-year-old Squadron Quartermaster Corporal Roy Bright – were killed. Thirty-one other people were wounded and seven horses also died as a result of the attack. The IRA squad responsible for the attack had detonated a Remote Controlled Improvised Explosive Device (RCIED), consisting of 20–25lb of commercial high explosive packed with nails, which they had placed in the boot of a Morris Marina car. Two hours later, the same IRA squad exploded another bomb, this time under the bandstand in Regent's Park, where soldiers from the Royal Green Jackets were performing a lunchtime concert. Seven bandsmen were killed. While the emergency services were dealing with the casualties at the scene, officers at HQNI were feeding their telex machines in order to break the news to the Army's brigade HQs: 'London bombings were anticipated spectacular. Remains to be seen if attacks continue in NI. Coord[ination] to be done with RUC to see if precautions can be improved on Mil[itary] bases and prestige trgts [targets] might happen but no hard evidence ...'[2] The Security Forces braced themselves for further attacks in different parts of the Northern Ireland.

A few hundred yards away, in Gower Street in Mayfair, MI5's directors had been holding a meeting when they heard the first explosion. The Director of F Branch hastily informed those gathered that the IJS 'expected for some time that PIRA would launch a new bombing campaign in London.[3] They expected the IRA squad to return to the Irish Republic by fishing boat later that day, but it was likely that the mastermind behind the two bombs would remain to plan further attacks in Britain.[4]

The explosions at Hyde Park and Regent's Park were the latest in a series of coordinated attacks that had rocked the English capital, including the bombing of Chelsea Barracks on 10 October 1981, when two civilians were killed and a number of soldiers were injured, and the attempted murders of the Attorney General Sir Michael Havers and the Commandant of the Royal Marines, Lieutenant General Sir Steuart Pringle.[5] In the aftermath of the Hyde Park and Regent's Park explosions, William Hucklesby, the Met's Anti-Terrorist Branch commander, urged everybody to 'be on the alert from now on'. He intimated that the police were expecting an attack based on the discovery of weapons and explosives in Northern Ireland and London.[6] Despite initiating one of the biggest manhunts in its history, the Met Police failed to capture the bombers or the mastermind of the attacks, a member of the IRA's South Armagh Brigade.

The IRA had learned a lot since it first bombed London in the early 1970s, including the necessity of maintaining a network of sleeper agents in the city. At the time of its attacks on 20 July 1982, the IRA's England Department consisted of several people who lived and worked in London, kept a low profile and consciously avoided other Irish people. On the political front, the IRA placed a 'rigid hierarchical structure' in control of Sinn Féin, which mirrored the democratic centralism of the army.[7]

A concerted intelligence attack against its cellular structure, not to mention the publicity surrounding the Falklands War, led the IRA to open up a new front in Britain. However, Britain's closer cooperation with the Irish authorities was beginning to pay dividends. The arrest of five IRA men and the seizure of half a tonne of explosives, seven primed rockets and a rocket launcher in Castlefin, County Donegal, in July 1982 brought an end to the IRA's elaborate plan to launch a series of coordinated attacks on British Army patrol bases along the border.[8] Journalists observing events from Fleet Street in London believed that the IRA was settling in for a long war of attrition. One reporter wrote that the IRA knew that 'attacks in mainland Britain have far more impact than those in Northern Ireland', but the operational difficulties of such attacks prevented them being carried out more frequently.[9]

* * *

By the autumn, the IRA was ramping up its attacks, particularly in its West Belfast heartland. Its volunteers were turning their attention to the soldiers of the 1st Battalion of the Worcestershire and Sherwood Foresters, a hardened infantry regiment that recruited its soldiers from Derbyshire, Nottinghamshire and Worcestershire. Formed in 1970 when the Worcestershire Regiment and Sherwood Foresters, two regiments with a long history of fighting in India and Ireland, were amalgamated, the regiment had first deployed to Northern Ireland on a tour of Derry in 1972. One of the rising stars in the regiment was 26-year-old Patrick Mercer, who had commissioned from Sandhurst in 1975. Mercer's first tour of Northern Ireland occurred in the spring of 1977, during which he spent time in the company of Robert Nairac, a young Guards officer who had previously served with 14th Intelligence Company on a tour a few years earlier. Mercer recalls Nairac telling him that 'if you can raise a source then there are ways for us to handle that source'. Mercer and his men 'talent spotted' for Nairac. Mercer enjoyed the thrill of assisting with undercover work. He was even successful at recruiting a local woman as a casual source with the codename 'Winter's Night'. However, Mercer took a mixed view of intelligence operations, which he saw as ineffective, particularly in the border areas.[10]

By the time Mercer's regiment returned to Northern Ireland in September 1982, he had attained the same rank Nairac had held when they first met. Given his interest in intelligence work, Mercer's CO appointed him as his Intelligence Officer for their four-month roulement tour of West Belfast. It was a particularly busy tour, as Mercer recalled:

> We had our arses shot off. We really did. It was a terribly violent and extremely exciting tour where we had three killed [the number was actually two] and five wounded, which was quite a lot of action really for West Belfast. And we subsequently discovered that there had been a directive gone out [from] the IRA [which] said don't let the British public forget that just because the Falklands is going on and they're doing great things ... that we're killing British soldiers over here. And they did. They gave us a right good run for our money ... I spent the whole of my tour in plain clothes. Other than for the odd 'walk in' as we called them – in other words, just people coming off the street and volunteering [information] – I didn't get involved in any source handling at all on that tour, which was a shame because it was

something I thought I was rather good at. But I acted as essentially a 'post box' between the fast-developing Force Research Unit, elements of 14 Intelligence and Security Company, which had come into being at that time ... and the conventional intelligence organisations in 39 Brigade and the Special Branch. I spent a lot of time with Special Branch ... They were very good men. Very brave men ...[11]

Mercer said that the RUC was under constant attack from republicans throughout his time in West Belfast:

I remember they had an armoured taxi, literally, that used to run from the Oaks, which is a little police station just on the Shankill, from there through to Howard Street through to Springfield Road ... It was driven by a couple of Full Time Reserve Officers. They were frequently attacked ... several times with RPGs. They were predictable but these men were no more used to being RPG'd than I was dancing a ballet. They were very, very frightened by it. Who wouldn't be? They didn't want to be shot at whereas our lot did want to be shot at ... It was difficult times ...[12]

The regiment lost two soldiers during their tour: 19-year-old Private Martin Jessop, killed by the IRA on 20 September, and 22-year-old Corporal Leon Bush, killed by the INLA on 27 September. Jessop's murder, however, would be the last IRA killing for a few months because of the PAC's narrow vote in favour of supporting Gerry Adams and Martin McGuinness in the forthcoming Assembly elections.[13]

The decision by Adams and McGuinness to run in the elections did not enjoy unanimous support from the PAC. Even McGuinness was in two minds about stepping down from his role as IRA Chief of Staff. As a committed militarist, politics didn't really interest him. In Derry, Mitchel McLaughlin sought to reassure him by giving Willie Carlin the task of developing Sinn Féin support right across the city. Carlin recalled:

As time went on, I managed to get a house, we bought a house and we turned it into a Sinn Féin advice centre and even Martin said, 'Fuck me, how'd youse do it?' But it was all done with government money. So, there's a certain amount of truth in saying there was no Sinn Féin so I started one. I mean, you could debate it ... I now found myself going from the Sinn Féin meeting to the *Comhairle Ceantair* [Area] meeting and now round the table with Mary Nellis, Barney McFadden, Willie McGuinness, McBrearty, Des McCreggan, round the table getting things done.[14]

In the run-up to the Assembly elections on 20 October 1982, Carlin was visited by a man from London who went by the name 'Alec': 'And he said to me. "There's a view amongst us" – whoever us is – "that the nationalists and, to a lesser extent, republicans have a case and it's imperative that you do what you can to get McGuinness elected."' Carlin drew breath. 'Even if that means breaking the law?' he inquired. Alec leant forward and told Carlin; 'Listen. Whatever it takes. Whatever it takes.'[15] Alec explained the rationale for his request:

> 'There's a view amongst unionists that your man speaks for nobody. He's a terrorist and he holds the people of Derry to ransom, and they're afraid.' He says, 'Now we need to change that,' and I says, 'Who's we?' 'Let's put it this way ' [Alec replied]. 'We'll still be here when people who are in government in London are long gone. We will always be here ... We're trying to do things to bring peace to this Province ...' I think Martin [McGuinness] got 8,207 votes in the first count. Now, I'm not really sure if he would have made it without our efforts. Maybe a hundred votes out but he would have got elected on the second vote. Cathal Crumley's vote would have went to him.[16] The interesting thing was that Gregory Campbell, that was his first vote out as well, and he had often said the same thing: 'Martin McGuinness speaks for nobody. He's a bigot ...' What he [Campbell] never tells people is that in the 1982 Assembly Election he never reached the quota. He never got even half-way near the quota.[17] Gregory Campbell was elected as the last man standing ...[18]

Based on a PAC ruling earlier in the summer, McGuinness finally stepped down as IRA Chief of Staff after his electoral win, allegedly passing the torch to Belfast republican Ivor Bell. Not long after the election, in a dramatic turn of events, Gerry Adams sent an emissary to Bell to sound him out on the prospect of a ceasefire in November. 'The Chief of Staff said, well, no, it would split the IRA. We would consider it, but it would split the IRA ... That's when the approach was made, and the Chief of Staff knew who had sent the emissary.'[19] Despite Adams' approach, the IRA maintained its war footing. It was not alone. The Security Forces were becoming more proactive in their own use of lethal force.

★ ★ ★

Tullygally East Road, Lurgan, Evening, 11 November 1982

It was a cold, dark and wet November night. Three IRA volunteers were making their way along Tullygally Road East near Lurgan in a Ford Escort. Driving the car was 31-year-old Gervaise McKerr. In the passenger seat next to him was his friend and comrade 21-year-old Eugene Toman and in the back seat was 21-year-old Sean Burns. All three men had been personally responsible for multiple attacks across County Armagh, including a massive landmine attack that killed three RUC officers on the Kinnego Embankment, Oxford Island, near Lurgan, on the southern shores of Lough Neagh two weeks earlier.[20] The explosion was so big that it left a 15-foot-deep and 40-foot-wide crater, and was apparently so loud that it was heard by Chief Constable John Hermon, who was returning from a nearby school where he had delivered a speech.[21] An informer inside the ranks of the Lurgan IRA later confirmed the involvement of the three men in a debriefing with his handler, who passed the information to the RUC Source Unit for wider dissemination.[22] The information was then, presumably, shared with the TCG in Armagh, which, in turn, would have tasked members of the E4 HMSU with intercepting the squad.[23]

The five RUC officers of the E4 SSU/HMSU patrol who set up the VCP that evening had been told by their superiors that the three IRA men were on their way to carry out a murder and were probably armed.[24] As the headlights drew closer, the RUC officers opened fire on the car. Their volley of shots pinged the vehicle, causing sparks, which, one RUC officer familiar with the incident argued, gave the officers the impression that those inside the car were returning fire.[25] In all, the officers discharged a total of 109 rounds, killing all three men. After cordoning off the area, Scenes of Crime officers examined the bodies and took photographs. They also took possession of the police patrol's rifles, a machine gun and a pistol, all of which had been fired in the incident. As part of the investigation, CID detectives interviewed the RUC officers involved, three of whom were invited to give written statements. None of the officers admitted to being privy to intelligence about the IRA squad.[26] It later emerged that the HMSU officers had been directed by the TCG not to disclose anything about the 'advance intelligence' to prevent it from 'becoming public knowledge and hampering efforts to fight terrorism'.[27] As members of the RUC's new elite armed response unit, which was the equivalent of the famed Los Angeles Special Weapons and Tactics (SWAT) detachment, these men had been highly trained in aggressive tactics. They were also subject to the Official Secrets Act, which prevented them from publicly divulging anything about the operations in which they were involved. Their job was to follow orders, not to question them.

'We slept on old sofas in a makeshift headquarters at Lisnasharragh,' recalled 'Jack', a former member of the E4 HMSU. 'We each had a locker for our kit and equipment. We were clearing 300 hours overtime every month.'[28] From their headquarters, they responded to incidents throughout Northern Ireland. Jack was in his late twenties and a four-year veteran of the Special Patrol Group when he volunteered to undertake what the RUC euphemistically termed 'The Assessment' for admittance into its specialist counter-terrorism outfit. The incoming Chief Constable, John Hermon, had recognised that the RUC needed a specialist armed response capability to deal with hostage sieges, as well as other high-profile threats. The unit would be the RUC equivalent of the military's Quick Reaction Force (QRF) and would be central to Hermon's plans for developing the RUC's new in-house counter-terrorism capability.[29]

Those in the Operational Training Unit (OTU) were the RUC's experts in building the capability. They established a tough selection course in Ballykinlar, the British Army's sprawling training base on the County Down coast. Jack recalled how the first stage of the assessment was about 'beasting' candidates, running them through military-style training to put them under intense psychological and physical pressure. The initial group of twenty-five officers was soon whittled down as those more used to dealing with everyday policing activity elected to leave the course. 'There was no shame in doing so,' Jack said. The course was designed to weed out those who couldn't hack the unique demands of Northern Ireland. 'We were fortunate,' he said, 'in that we had the right men, at the right time in the right place.' He continued:

We were presented with weapons, including an SLR and a Sterling [sub-machine gun] and told to run up to Flagstaff Hill and back. I picked the SLR so I could rest it on my shoulders and put my arms over it. It was tough going. We were police officers, not soldiers, though we needed to have a soldier's mentality. Some of us were better suited to the training than others.[30]

Another member of the unit, 'Ronnie', a former agent handler, was on the very first assessment. He recalled how candidates were plastic-cuffed, had bags placed over their heads and were bundled into a prison van and driven to a remote location:

> We were taken away in the van for what seemed like an hour or so and then frogmarched into an old derelict cottage. The bags and cuffs were taken off and we saw the training staff in front of us. They asked us if we wanted anything. One guy said he wanted sandwiches, another said he needed the toilet. As soon as they walked through the door that was them off the course.[31]

The OTU's training regime was deliberately tough. Jack and Ronnie said that SPG members were more likely to pass the course, whereas others, including ordinary uniformed officers, were more likely to fail.

News of the unit's highly classified training soon leaked to the press. *Irish Times* journalist Ed Moloney spoke to one officer who told him that the unit had originally been the brainchild of an RUC inspector in South Armagh and that it was designed as a way for the police to gain re-entry into a contested region:

> Meanwhile, preparations for training and selection of members went ahead and those who had answered the circular were asked to turn up at Ballykinlar army barracks, some 25 miles from Newry, for assessment. Over 100 South Armagh policemen turned up but within two weeks the unfit had been weeded out and the number was down to 34. A week later the unit reached its operational strength of 28; throughout its year of life the unit's strength never went below 25 and only rarely were new members allowed to join.[32]

However, the unit was a Northern Ireland-wide organisation that was not limited to South Armagh and there were several assessments, not just one. Those who passed the first and second assessments found themselves formed up after the Christmas leave period to hear an address by John Hermon.

'The Chief Constable addressed us and said, "the people of Northern Ireland demand bacon. It is time to slice up the pig", Jack recalled.[33]

In his Chief Constable's Report for 1980, Hermon recorded how other, newly created Divisional Mobile Support Units (DMSUs) would complement the pre-existing SPG sections in North and South Regions, ultimately increasing the number of units to over a dozen. 'The units are extremely effective in anti-terrorist operations, discovering arms and explosives and capturing active terrorists,' Hermon wrote. 'They are also successfully deployed in the organised searching of houses and land, extended observation exercises and in escorting high-risk prisoners and valuable property.' SPGs would bolster RUC efforts guarding prisoners, on escort duties, performing searches, maintaining public order and carrying out security patrols.[34] This reorganisation of tactical response units would give Special Branch a dedicated back-up unit in the form of E4 SSU/HMSU.

Hermon's tough-talking briefing to the founding members of the unit, resonated with those officers who had undertaken 'The Assessment'.[35] Jack was sanguine regarding the unit's name change from E4 SSU to HMSU. 'We didn't think of ourselves as special,' he recalled. 'Jimmy B. [the unit's first commander] hated the name and so it was changed to HMSU.' Soon, the HMSU was training under the watchful eye of the Army. They practised Close Quarter Battle (CQB) drills, including how to storm houses and rescue hostages, as part of a wider government drive to ensure that all of the UK's constabularies received training in Close Target Reconnaissance (CTR) and CQB drills. Jack explained:

The instructors thought they would have people who didn't know what they were doing. We got into it. We were a different breed. We were up for it ... I think a few of those softer men from English country constabularies were close to taking heart attacks [due to the intensity of the training]. I recall when we went through the 'Kill House' and we were instructed not to shoot the TV. One of the lads shot the TV and then the control room came over the Tannoy to stop us from progressing through.

Jack recalls being equipped with a variety of different firearms, including M1 carbines and, later, Heckler and Koch MP5s, favoured by Special Forces. The unit's senior officers even paid a visit to Germany to source new weapons and learn about tactics from their counterparts in the elite GSG9.[36] In taking on a more paramilitary-style role, the RUC were fulfilling John Hermon's vision for growing its own specialist counter-terrorism capability. Yet, by inculcating a 'soldier's mentality' in his police officers, he was inadvertently raising the stakes in the arena of covert action.

★ ★ ★

Droppin' Well Pub, Ballykelly, Evening, 6 December 1982

Soldiers based at Shackleton Barracks were enjoying a typically uneventful day in Ballykelly, relaxing in the Navy, Army and Air Force Institute (NAAFI) or making their way a mile down the road to the Droppin' Well pub for a few pints. Although there was a feeling of slight apprehension whenever they stepped outside the gates of the camp, most soldiers felt safe in the village. Located 14 miles from Derry city, Ballykelly was a quiet village of 500 people, many of whom enjoyed close links to the military garrison. The village itself consisted of only a handful of shops, a hotel, two pubs and a couple of interdenominational schools. Most of the soldiers based in Shackleton Barracks were from the 1st Battalion of the Cheshire Regiment, which had originally been raised by the 7th Duke of Norfolk in 1689 to quell an Irish rebellion. The regiment later distinguished itself in the Boer War, as well as the First and Second World Wars. It was a battle-hardened infantry regiment that had previously completed a tour of Northern Ireland in the 1970s and returned for an extended period in 1982. As the resident battalion, each of the Cheshire's four companies rotated through a cycle of conducting operations in Derry city, followed by a spell as Brigade Reserve, training, leave and guard duties. The CO believed that the tour promised to 'offer the soldiers an interesting variety of operational and recreational activity' and he told his soldiers that they should 'resist allowing "the situation" to dominate our lives to the exclusion of any form of recreation, amusement, and the quality of life'.[37]

It was in this spirit, three weeks before Christmas, that soldiers began to fill the Droppin' Well pub. Shortly after 10 p.m., a bomb went off, causing the building to collapse. One young girl remembered that '[w]e had just walked on to the dance floor after getting supper. Suddenly there was a flash and the next thing I knew I was struggling to get out of the debris. The whole scene was chaos. It was horrifying.'[38] Bodies were strewn everywhere. Eyewitnesses reported seeing people with blood pouring from their wounds walking around dazed, confused and screaming. There was carnage everywhere: a man without a foot, his legs sticking out from under the rubble; a girl with burns covering her entire body and a huge hole in her leg. Lifeless bodies lay crushed underneath the rubble. One girl had her legs blown off; another had lost an arm. 'The people responsible for this must be psychopaths,' one survivor told reporters. Harry Bennett was one of the first medics on the scene. 'Our first job was to assess each casualty to see what their chances were,' he said. 'The ones with the best chance went first and then other serious cases. It was heart-breaking. For the first time I felt tears. A lot of the nurses were crying too. I can't find words to describe how I feel about the bombers.' Twenty-year-old Clinton Collins from Stockport was a clerk celebrating his promotion to Lance Corporal after having successfully completed the Potential NCO's course. He had been married only a few months. When his mother heard the news, she said, fighting back tears, 'He was going out with his new wife Tina to celebrate. If it had not been for that he would not have been in the pub. They are murdering savages. The Army was my boy's life. He was just doing his job. He didn't have a chance.'[39]

The attack was devastating for the regiment and the wider Army. Military Intelligence recorded that:

> PIRA had threatened to resume a campaign of commercial bombing in the weeks that led up to Christmas. The fact that the threat never really materialised can be attributed in part to pre-emptive action by the Security Forces in finding and neutralising the devices, and in part to the current strategy of Martin McGuinness and Gerry Adams in holding back from indiscriminate attacks, lest they should harm their political campaign. The same cannot be applied to INLA, who claimed responsibility for the Ballykelly bomb at the Droppin' Well Inn on 6 December. In that incident 11 soldiers and 6 civilians died. The device containing 2–3 kilograms of commercial explosive caused the collapse of the concrete roof of the crowded discotheque. In addition to the fatal injuries, a further 25 soldiers and 14 civilians were admitted to hospital, 20 of them with serious injuries.[40]

Flags were flown at half-mast over Chester Castle and every other town in the regiment's home county.[41] Colonel Dick Peel, the Regimental Secretary, told reporters that the Droppin' Well massacre was 'the worst peacetime disaster to affect us in modern times.'[42]

Not long after the attack on the off-duty soldiers, an E4 HMSU patrol in Lurgan, in response to intelligence provided by a former Sinn Féin member working for the RUC, was tracking the movements of two of the INLA's most active members in Mid Armagh, Seamus Grew and Roddy Carroll, and their Chief of Staff, Dominic 'Mad Dog' McGlinchey.[43] One E4A surveillance officer believed that Grew and Carroll were escorting McGlinchey to Grew's home.[44] The police officers were then directed to mount a VCP on a route the men were known to use frequently. As Grew and Carroll drove into Armagh along their usual route, they came upon a road traffic accident involving a plain-clothes soldier and an RUC vehicle. One of the RUC officers, John Robinson, spotted the men and gave chase. He managed to overtake them and block them off. He then fired fifteen shots into the car, killing both men.[45] McGlinchey was not in the car, having been dropped off earlier. He was furious and wanted revenge. It would take some time to track down the man he blamed for leaking information regarding his movements: 43-year-old Eric Dale. A married man from Armagh, he was abducted and murdered a few months later, his body dumped in Killeen on the Irish border.[46] The repercussions of the Grew and Carroll shootings were immense, especially when linked to the earlier shootings of McKerr, Toman and Burns, and the killing of 17-year-old Michael Tighe and the wounding of his 19-year-old friend Martin McCauley elsewhere in Armagh on 24 November. Allegations of a 'shoot-to-kill' policy on the part of the British government began to circulate in the press. Militant republicans responded to these allegations by taking the war to the RUC.

10

CHAMPIONING THE BULLET AND BALLOT BOX

'Man is a political animal admittedly
But, politics being incalculable, I shall
With your permission pour myself another; I see
Nothing for it but to be animal.'

– Louis MacNeice, 'Obituary' (May 1940)[1]

The Square, Rostrevor, County Down, 11 a.m., 6 January 1983

Forty-one-year-old Sergeant Eric Brown, a married father of three, and 23-year-old Reserve Constable Brian Quinn, a single officer from Bangor, were in an unmarked police car, watching the entrance to the post office in Rostrevor from across the town square. Sergeant Brown had been on the beat in the town for many years. That morning, he had received a tip-off from his colleagues in the CID that the IRA was planning to rob the post office.[2] Around 11 a.m., the RUC officers spotted a suspicious vehicle pull up on Bridge Street, close to the post office. One of their colleagues, who had been in the front passenger seat, climbed out of the car. He made his way over to the vehicle. Before he had time to react, a gunman jumped out of the suspect car and opened fire, wounding him in the shoulder. As he crawled to take cover in a nearby doorway, the gunman closed in on Sergeant Brown and Constable Quinn and began firing again, hitting both of them with a volley of shots. The gunman then got back into his vehicle and sped off. The IRA later claimed responsibility.[3] At Sergeant Brown's funeral two days later, the Bishop of Down and Dromore, Dr Robin Eames, blamed the attack on the climate of 'concentrated condemnation of the RUC', which, he said, 'presented a real and devastating danger to society'. Bishop Eames' sermon was couched in language that emphasised the timeless struggle between good and evil. 'Every right-thinking person in the community recognises the appalling dilemma facing the police,' he told mourners. Sergeant Brown and Constable Quinn had been the latest in a long line of RUC officers to be murdered by the IRA.

Despite being one of the most dangerous professions in Northern Ireland, the RUC saw its manpower surge to 5,000 for the first time in the opening months of 1983. It was, perhaps, an opportune moment for senior officers to expand Special Branch. 'Following manpower increases and decentralisation of E4(A) units', one highly classified report read, 'relocation of teams in the North and South regions, introduction of selected Headquarters Mobile Support Units to this type of duty has identified a need for additional equipment ...'[4] The increase in personnel and new orders for kit and equipment led to a demand for more sophisticated training. The eighty-four members of E4 HMSU were soon enrolled in courses on 'emergency medical procedures, firearms, driving and map reading',[5] with support coming directly from the Army's new GOC, Lieutenant General Sir Robert Richardson. Richardson was a Scots Guardsman who had seen combat in Aden in 1967 and in West Belfast in the early 1970s. In his first public address at a lunch of the Belfast Chamber of Commerce on 23 March, he reaffirmed the Army's commitment to support the RUC in 'overt and covert ways to help defeat terrorism. If terrorist organisations thought they could outlast the efforts of the Security Forces to defeat them,' he told business leaders, 'then they were making a mistake.'[6]

★ ★ ★

Sinn Féin/IRA Headquarters, Cable Street, Derry, Mid-April 1983

The Sinn Féin advice centre on Cable Street was situated deep in the heart of the republican Bogside. An old, red-brick, terraced house bought by Mitchel McLaughlin in the early 1970s, it had fallen into disrepair in the intervening decade. The first thing people noticed upon entering the premises was the smell of damp. Furniture was sparse and the threadbare carpet had seen better days. An old battered sofa sat under the window, flanked by a couple of three-drawer desks on which sat two old Olivetti typewriters. Two telephones were manned constantly by two women, Bernie and Briege, who also drafted letters and typed up the minutes of meetings. There was a small kitchen with a linoleum floor and an adjoining toilet. Both were immaculately clean. A flight of stairs led up to the first floor, where there were three offices, one on the left and one on the right, with another at the back. The one at the back was used by Mitchel McLaughlin and the one on the right was used by Martin McGuinness for IRA meetings. This latter room was as ramshackle as the rest of the building, though it contained more modern furnishings. Seamus Keenan sat at a desk in the room on the left, hastily scribbling the statements of the Republican Movement before handing them to reporters at the *Derry Journal*. All of the telephones in the building had been connected by Joe McColgan, McGuinness' brother-in-law and a BT engineer.[7]

Around Easter 1983, the old, damp advice centre was transformed into something altogether more 'spic and span'. One visiting journalist, Patrick Bishop, remarked that the front waiting area smelt of fresh paint and was adorned with a new typewriter and a row of filing cabinets. Bishop said a small army of 'clean-cut young people' were manning the phones and filling the filing cabinets with copious council forms. These community activists 'battl[ed] against the oppressive forces of damp and blocked drains when less than two years ago they were coordinating the macabre theatre that accompanied the deaths of 10 hunger strikers'.[8] The Cable Street advice centre had become a metaphor for the transformation now underway within the Provisional Republican Movement. The successes at the 1982 Assembly Election had given Sinn Féin a new-found purpose.

Dressed in his trademark tweed jacket, cords and sensible brown shoes, McGuinness was settling into his new public persona as an elected official. Away from the prying eyes of the press, he was struggling to reconcile himself to the loss of power he had experienced since stepping down as Chief of Staff and he began to slip into a deep depression.[9] The Derry IRA chief was plagued by conflicting thoughts about what the new Sinn Féin strategy meant for the armed struggle. Until the announcement of his candidacy in October 1982, McGuinness had 'never been in a polling station'. As Mitchel McLaughlin recalled at the time, the election had been 'a major breakthrough for us and a significant set-back for the SDLP', but McGuinness, especially, was finding it difficult to accustom himself to not having the role of Chief of Staff.[10]

Younger republicans who voted for Sinn Féin were perfectly content with following their hero in whatever direction he wished to take them. They saw the SDLP as middle class and somewhat detached from their own working-class lives.[11] Within months of his election, McGuinness' attention turned to the question of how Sinn Féin might fare in future polls. 'Nationalists voted for you because you were Sinn Féin. Republicans voted for you because you were Chief of Staff,' Willie Carlin told McGuinness at the time.[12] Carlin did his best to assuage McGuinness' fears. 'Martin wasn't a fan of PR,' Carlin added. 'He was beginning to get his head round it. He regarded a second preference as a loss.'[13]

Although he may have relinquished the role of Chief of Staff, McGuinness was now OC Northern Command, a role which effectively placed him much closer to the action. The presence of agents of influence around him arguably resulted in British Intelligence gaining even greater insight into the IRA. As Military Intelligence reported at the time:

> Various indications point to further coordinated attacks by PIRA across the Province. There have been a series of meetings amongst leading Provisionals which it is thought might herald a determined effort by them to launch simultaneous attacks in the near future. The timing of such activity is not surprising. Speculating on the possibility of an early General Election PIRA will want to make its terrorist mark before fine-tuning their campaign in any pre-election period. They may therefore be planning to concentrate attacks into a short timeframe to gain maximum effect. Although targets will be primarily members of the SF [Security Forces] prestige attacks against leading figures are possible. A spectacular effort to mark the ending of the Christopher Black trial or the anniversary of Bobby Sands' death on 5 May cannot be excluded.[14]

Within weeks, the IRA was indeed planning a series of coordinated attacks, though these were 'foiled by pre-emptive intelligence',[15] which led to the arrest of a seven-man IRA squad in West Belfast:

> In another successful operation a well-known terrorist gunman, XX was apprehended before he and his associates were able to carry out a shooting attack against a policeman. XX had been armed with a .38 revolver and his arrest will have unnerved other members of the Belfast shooting team. He is known to have been responsible in part for several murders the most recent of which was the shooting of a police reservist on 16 May.[16]

Alongside military activity, the Republican Movement launched a subversive campaign against their opponents in the SDLP, which included a coordinated plan of intimidation to force John Hume's party to withdraw its support for the candidacy of UUP Deputy Mayor Jim Guy as the next Mayor of Derry City.[17] Later in the summer, SDLP Mayor Len Green expressed private misgivings that the party 'would continue to lose electoral ground to Sinn Féin because of electoral abuses'.[18] Despite the NIO giving assurances to the SDLP, the British government did not take a unified stance on the matter. In his meetings with his handlers, Carlin was actively encouraged to help Sinn Féin win more votes 'by any means necessary'.[19] There were also allegations that the NIO's Security Department was ignoring reports from Special Branch officers about the level of personation and intimidation.[20]

★ ★ ★

As the autumn approached, RUC detectives in Belfast were eager to score a success against the PIRA. The arrest of 37-year-old Robert 'Beano' Lean, an aide to Gerry Adams, offered them a prime opportunity. Lean was alleged to have been the adjutant of the Belfast Brigade Staff and was well placed to give up the secrets of the organisation.[21] When enterprising CID officers managed to turn him, he incriminated IRA Chief of Staff Ivor Bell and twenty-seven other senior people. This would have far-reaching consequences for the organisation, as former IRA volunteer Anthony McIntyre observed:

> I think, perhaps, a more crucial year is 1983 when there's a change in the composition of the leadership and the Chief of Staff was replaced and the balance of power within the Army Council shifted to the people who favoured Adams' more political strategy from those who favoured Bell's more military strategy ... And I think this is where the role of the intelligence agencies is crucial. That happened as a result of the arrest of Ivor Bell in September 1983 on the evidence of Bobby Lean. Bobby Lean did not work with Ivor Bell in the IRA. Bobby Lean's contacts were with Gerry Adams, yet the British got Bobby Lean to take Ivor Bell out of the equation. Ivor Bell, because he was the Chief of Staff at the time – this is public knowledge – was replaced by a new Chief of Staff. And, by the end of 1983, the Army Council were backing Adams, rather than backing Bell.[22]

The new Chief of Staff was 38-year-old Tyrone republican Kevin McKenna. McKenna had an established pedigree as an IRA man, having joined the organisation in the 1960s before emigrating to Canada for a few years, then returning to Ireland in 1971.[23] He had only been in his new role a matter of days when he presided over one of the IRA's most daring operations: a prison break from the Maze. The escape plan had been in the works for several weeks.

One prisoner eager to break out was Brendan 'Bik' McFarlane, the West Belfast republican who had carried out a sectarian gun and bomb attack on the Bayardo Bar on the Shankill Road in 1975. McFarlane had been captured by paratroopers stationed in Ardoyne. 'It was almost as if the Commanding Officer had been expecting them,' one young PARA officer recalled.[24] Other IRA volunteers who would take part in the escape included Gerry Kelly, Hugh Corey, Harry Murray, Marcus Murray, Seamus Campbell and Seamus McElwain. The official investigation into the escape detailed what happened:

At 1445 hours yesterday all wings in H7 were taken over simultaneously by armed prisoners. 38 prisoners tied up staff and blindfolded them. When attempting to take over the Block Control Room Office [redacted] was shot twice in the head and is critically ill. The prisoners destroyed their security photographs and papers relating to themselves in the Control Room before leaving. Some of the prisoners put on Officers' uniforms. When the van arrived to deliver the evening meal at approximately 1540 hours to the driver everything appeared to be normal but the vehicle was immediately hijacked by the prisoners. The driver was ordered at gunpoint to go through the H7 gate which had been taken over by prisoners and through 2 more gates to the tally lodge. At 1600 hours when staff in the block heard everything go quiet they realised the prisoners had gone and began to release themselves. Meanwhile at the tally lodge a fight had ensued between staff and escaping inmates. One officer received a bullet wound in the leg and 8 others were severely beaten or stabbed. Officer [redacted] later died of stab wounds. Two prisoner officers attempted to block the main gate of the Cellular prison but most of the prisoners escaped across the fields. 3 prisoners were re-captured at the gates; one inmate, XX, was shot and wounded. Of the 35 prisoners who escaped 7 were quickly apprehended in the immediate vicinity of the prison. Police in

Lisburn caught another one prisoner, while a further 4 were captured during the night. Latest information is that another 2 inmates have been captured in Castlewellan leaving a total of 21 prisoners still at large.[25]

The IRA later dubbed their prisoners' exploits 'The Great Escape' in homage to the popular 1960s Steve McQueen movie:

We perceived the escape as a military operation from beginning to end. It could not have been achieved in any other way, and the Active Service Unit – as Volunteers of the Irish Republican Army – were under strict orders throughout from an operations officer whose judgement was crucial and whose every order had to be obeyed.[26]

The escape gave a huge boost to IRA morale and would be capitalised upon at the Sinn Féin *Ard Fheis* at the end of November 1983.

For the British, the escape was an embarrassment, with one intelligence report noting that:

Following several months of disruption and setbacks, the breakout from the Maze on 25 September came as a most welcome and timely respite for the Provisionals. The escape had been planned at a high level and its success proved to be a considerable fillip for the newly reconstituted Provisional leadership, which in Ivor Bell's absence, has been headed by Kevin McKenna. Although only half of the escapees evaded capture, the fact is that so many were able to defy the tight security of the prison [which] was a major boost to their morale. However, the escape will do little in itself to counteract the operational and logistical difficulties that PIRA have been experiencing.[27]

The escape also did little to prevent the continuing leakage of information from supergrasses and other casual contacts and agents who were damaging the IRA from Derry to Dungannon. Special Branch believed that many of the escapees would return to active service and promptly issued a general warning to the bodyguards of VIPs and other high-profile figures to be vigilant because of the expected IRA resurgence. Attacks on such figures would be a central part of McKenna's strategy to escalate his group's campaign. 'Renewed attacks on the mainland would certainly strengthen

Adams' position within the leadership and might placate critics of his joint political/military strategy,' one British Intelligence summary reported.[28] It was perhaps a sign of how well the British had penetrated the IRA that Intelligence Officers now believed that two factions were beginning to emerge inside the Republican Movement:

> The PSF annual party conference (*Ard Fheis*) was held in Dublin and the Old Guard led by Rory O'Brady were finally defeated by the Northerners led by Gerry Adams who was elected President of PSF. Adams, who with Morrison, champions the Bullet and Ballot Box strategy must now balance the military and political campaigns of the PIRA and PSF and thus endeavour to keep 2 opposing factors in a state of equality. Additionally he must expect hostility from the Old Guard as well as mistrust from those members of PIRA who view political action as meaningless.[29]

With Adams in control of the political wing of the IRA, McKenna began to refine his strategy of striking high-value targets and issued an order to one of his squads in South Belfast under the command of 'Mr V' to seek out new targets.[30]

★ ★ ★

College Square, Queen's University Belfast, Morning, 7 December 1983

On a wintry morning in early December 1983, 29-year-old law lecturer and Unionist Assembly member Edgar Graham had just walked into University Square when he was confronted by two gunmen who shot him at point-blank range. As he fell to the ground, one of the gunmen fired a further three bullets into his body. The IRA's decision to assassinate Graham was part of an operational imperative to eliminate high-profile unionist politicians who opposed them publicly. It was also the latest in a series of attacks by an active IRA cell in South Belfast that centred on Mr V, an IRA veteran, who could call on IRA members and sympathisers at Queen's at the time. The same South Belfast-based gang had also killed another politician, Robert Bradford, in November 1981. Secretary of State Jim Prior now faced a barrage of criticism from MPs in Parliament, with unionist representatives accusing him of failing to adequately protect elected representatives. In his defence, Prior acknowledged that '[t]he RUC's problem is that it receives information from the public about specific threats and targets each day'. He added, 'It then has to form a judgment on how much protection it is able to give. It is not possible to protect everyone in these circumstances.'[31] Although Prior downplayed the threat assessment issued by Special Branch in late October, he would have been well aware of a follow-up intelligence assessment, which stated:

> The most important of their attacks was the murder of Edgar Graham. Knowledge of the operation would have been restricted within PIRA and cleared at the highest level, almost certainly by Adams.[32] The murder exacerbated the tensions caused by the Darkley murders and the OUP [Official Unionist Party] withdrawal from the Assembly, as well as dramatically removing from the scene a member of the Protestant establishment who was an outspoken opponent of terrorism.[33]

Slowly but surely, the British revised their analysis of the IRA's planned offensive, particularly in light of the group's bombing of Harrods, which resulted in the deaths of six people, including an American tourist:

> It is possible that the Harrods bomb was planted without authorisation as the IRA claim. Intelligence pointed towards carefully targeted attacks rather than indiscriminate ones and Adams is clearly aware of how counter-productive politically such operations can be. Whether the bomb was the result of a failure in communications or a deliberate attempt by the supporters of the Southern Old Guard to discredit Adams and his policies is unclear. The weekend of 16–18 December will have been a setback for PIRA/PSF.[34]

By the new year, the British had a firmer grasp of who was responsible for Edgar Graham's assassination. 'The attack was almost certainly carried out by the West Belfast ASU led by XX,' one Military Intelligence report read. 'Graham was an outspoken opponent of terrorism and as a prominent loyalist politician was always a vulnerable and likely target.'[35] The IRA's murder of individual unionist politicians did not go unnoticed by loyalist paramilitaries; however, they were powerless to react as so many of their commanders were in prison awaiting trial on the word of supergrasses.[36]

Graham's murder demonstrates how effective the IRA could be, especially on a much smaller budget than the British who recognised they could only minimise terrorism not eradicate it completely. Estimates vary, but some analysts have suggested that the IRA had an annual operating budget in 1978 of around £1 million, which increased steadily to around £5.3 million by the end of the decade.[37] Under McKenna, the IRA also began to change its focus to targeting England, which worried high-ranking civil servants. As one senior civil servant told the Cabinet Office, 'Over the years Irish terrorist organisations have become more sophisticated and our own intelligence effort has had to adapt to the changes in tactics. For terrorist activity in Great Britain, liaison with the security authorities in Northern Ireland and in the Republic of Ireland is central to our strategy.'[38] Beyond cross-border liaison, the British looked to the IRA's support networks overseas. Following his release after the collapse of the Lean case, Ivor Bell was 'given the task of liaising with Libyan intelligence', a new relationship that would prove highly significant in the coming months.[39] Bell's replacement as Chief of Staff, however, eroded his support base and confined him to opposing electoralism from the sidelines. A new trajectory was being mapped out for the IRA, one that saw senior IRA figures champion the Armalite and the ballot box.

11

FIGHTING BRITAIN IN HER OWN HOME

'Contemporary national liberation movements are themselves social movements. They will not come to an end before every group is liberated from the domination of another group.'

– Muhammad Al Gaddafi, *The Green Book* (1976)

Libyan People's Bureau, St James's Square, London, Late Morning, 17 April 1984

At 5 foot 2½ inches, 25-year-old Yvonne Fletcher was probably the smallest police officer in England. In fact, she was a little under the standard height requirement for a Metropolitan Police officer. It was mostly due to her determination, drive, intelligence and suitability that Scotland Yard made an exception and admitted her into the police training programme.[1] Fletcher was based at Bow Street station, which had become something of a second home in her seven years as a Woman Police Constable (WPC). She was among the first officers to respond to reports of serious civil disturbances outside the Libyan embassy. Fletcher and her colleagues struggled to keep the peace in what was becoming an increasingly fraught situation. As the officers jostled with protestors, a series of shots were fired from inside the embassy, hitting up to a dozen of the people outside.[2] Fletcher fell to the ground, fatally wounded by a bullet to the stomach. Her fiancé and colleague, PC Michael Liddle, immediately ran to her aid. He cradled her head in his arms until paramedics arrived and rushed her to Westminster Hospital. Despite the best efforts of the most skilled surgeons in the country, WPC Yvonne Fletcher died on the operating table.

News of the killing soon travelled to the Libyan capital, Tripoli, where British Ambassador Oliver Miles was trying to contain a similar demonstration outside his country's embassy. Miles and his staff were being prevented from leaving the building by 'a group of revolutionaries who are issuing orders to the police.[3] After telegramming London, Miles rang the office of Libyan Foreign Minister, Ali Traiki. Traiki told Miles that he would try to find a way to de-escalate the situation.[4] Meanwhile, back in London, the diplomatic fallout from the murder of WPC Fletcher was beginning to be picked up by the international media. Senior civil servants in the Foreign Office were debating whether the UK should break off diplomatic relations with Libya altogether. As Thatcher was in Lisbon on an official visit and her Foreign Secretary Geoffrey Howe was in Brussels, Miles telegrammed Home Secretary Leon Brittan seeking direction. The Foreign Office view was that the UK should break off ties. Thatcher believed that the aim must be to 'show this not as a confrontational act, but as a way of de-escalating tension and resolving the issue'.[5] The British Prime Minister even 'wondered whether a solution could be devised, short of breaking off diplomatic relations, which embodied effectively exchanging the two Embassy staffs'.[6] The next day, under Brittan's chairmanship, the Cabinet Officer Briefing Room Alpha (COBR(A)) decided that 'at some stage we should break diplomatic relations', but it was left to Metropolitan Police Commissioner, former RUC Chief Constable Sir Kenneth Newman, to urge caution. He thought that breaking off diplomatic relations might inflame the situation and could be interpreted by the Libyans as a 'hostile act', leading to 'an escalation of the situation'.[7]

Meanwhile, back in Tripoli, matters were coming to a head. Oliver Miles watched from the embassy roof as demonstrators continued to gather below. He was joined by his Security Officer, who told him, 'Oh good. We will be alright. They've brought the water cannon.' Miles relaxed slightly. 'We were very worried that they'd try and burn down the embassy. They'd done it before in Tehran,' he recalled. He was worried for the safety of his staff.

'Are you scared?' he asked the Security Officer.

'No,' he replied.

'Why are there police around the embassy?'

'Because I've asked them to be there.'

'Then I realised. They were facing outwards, protecting the embassy.'[8]

Miles relaxed a little more and allowed his mind to return to everyday matters. He and his family had just arrived in Tripoli, but as the crowd swelled outside, Miles thought he might have to leave again before long. Libya was proving to be one of his toughest overseas assignments yet.[9]

As a career Arabist, Miles knew how to deal with Middle Eastern and North African rulers. Miles found Gaddafi very 'mercurial', a man, he recalled, who tended to 'overestimate Britain's role as a Great Power while also overestimating Libya's importance as a regional power'. Gaddafi held 'a very Iranian outlook' in that he saw Britain as being 'all powerful'. Miles' impression of the Libyan dictator was that he was 'bright, though he had no formal education'. Gaddafi had periodically supplied the IRA with weapons and explosives from the early 1970s. In one of his infamous speeches on his Irish connection, Gaddafi told Libyan Radio on 11 June 1972:

> We support the revolutionaries of Ireland, who oppose Britain and who are motivated by nationalism and religion. The Libyan Arab Republic has stood by the revolutionaries of Ireland. It maintains strong links with the Irish revolutionaries. There are arms and there is support for the revolutionaries of Ireland ... We have decided to move to the offensive. We have decided to fight Britain in her own home. We have decided to create a problem for Britain and to drive a thorn in her side so as to make life difficult for Britain ... She will pay a double price. She will pay dearly. We will give her two blows for one received.[10]

Yet, Gaddafi's support for the IRA vacillated under the influence of international sanctions. Miles recalled meetings with his Libyan counterparts, who would frequently mention arms:

> Libyans were absolutely obsessed with weapons and wanting to buy weapons. They wanted, in particular, Rapier surface to air missiles but the British refused to supply them. Every single meeting in London and Tripoli – and in engagements behind the scenes – Libyans wanted those weapons. They had more military grade explosives than the entire US Army. It was just extravagant.[11]

Despite sanctions, the Libyans successfully imported weapons and explosives. CIA officer-turned-contractor Edwin Wilson had been hired by the Libyan regime to train its 'cross-eyed army'.[12]

A decade after telling Britain that he would fight them in their own home, Gaddafi again reiterated his support for the IRA, arguing that providing support to armed groups permitted Libya to achieve three objectives simultaneously:

> It helps us to entrench ourselves in the line of support for all liberation movements. It helps us to prove to the whole world that the Arab

revolution is capable of moving from a position of defence to that of attack. Finally, it helps us to pay Britain back for a small part of the harm it caused and causes to our Arab nation.[13]

As a result of the Libyan regime's declaration of support for Argentina during the Falklands War and its shielding of WPC Fletcher's killer, Anglo–Libyan relations sank to an all-time low. With a major diplomatic crisis brewing between the UK and Libya, the Derry IRA sought to exploit the international turmoil further by launching a bold attack on the British Army.

★ ★ ★

Derry City, Evening, 21 April 1984

Two masked men who claimed to represent the Derry IRA arrived at the door of a family home. 'It'll spoil the whole thing if I have to blow your leg away,' one of them said to a startled family member. 'There'll be blood everywhere if you can't get this man to calm down,' the second man said. It soon became apparent to the occupants of the house that the masked gang had come for the van parked in the driveway. 'I want the keys,' said the younger man. 'If you just give me the keys no harm will come to you or any of your family.' The family were frightened. They knew the reputation of the Derry IRA and quickly handed over the keys. After starting the vehicle, one of the men returned to the house. 'If you want to report this to the Police don't do it for 2 hours after we have left,' he told the occupants. 'Goodnight,' he said as he ran out of the house, calling back, 'Sorry for your trouble.'[14] The Ford Escort van was driven to another part of the city, where it was promptly loaded with a 45-gallon incendiary drum and packed with several concrete breeze blocks, thus enhancing its killing potential. The IRA squad drove the van into the heart of the city centre and parked it in the car park beside the main bus station on Foyle Street. The men fixed a command wire to the bomb and gave 20-year-old Richard Quigley explicit instructions to detonate the bomb once he spotted a passing Security Forces patrol.

Quigley was one of the Derry IRA's newest recruits.[15] He was dressed in a green leather jacket, a white shirt, blue jeans and burgundy shoes, wore gold-rimmed glasses and had a small moustache. He was from Lisfannon Park in the Bogside. Like so many other young men in the city, Quigley was unemployed. He carried his house keys, a car key, a silver crucifix on a silver chain, a wristwatch, two £5 notes, a St Gerard Holy Mascot, a St Joseph prayer card and an accompanying medal.[16] From his vantage point behind the flat-roofed public toilets opposite the Hungry Horse bar, Quigley could see a dozen or so cars in the car park. Eventually, he spotted two British Army Land Rovers making their way across the bottom deck of the Craigavon Bridge. They turned right onto the expressway by the bus station. The military Land Rovers stopped at the traffic lights at the junction with Water Street and were overtaken by a police Hotspur, which passed them in the outside lane. When the convoy continued along Foyle Street, Quigley flicked the switch on the command wire, exploding the bomb and engulfing the second Army Land Rover in flames. All of the soldiers inside were badly burnt. The soldiers piled out of the back of the vehicle and quickly dropped to the ground in a bid to extinguish the flames.[17] Quigley, who had stuck his head round the corner of the toilets out of morbid curiosity, was hit by a concrete breeze block. He died instantly.[18]

Although the IRA had lost one of its own volunteers, the group was undeterred. IRA volunteers came together with their supporters and sympathisers on Easter Sunday in an annual pilgrimage to the city cemetery next to the Creggan Estate against the backdrop of an upsurge in violence. An attack on an RUC foot patrol on 9 January 1984 signalled the beginning of one of the Derry Brigade's most active years. In another attack, a CWIED containing 10kg of high explosives was placed at Stephen's Bakery on Great James Street close to the Bogside in order to kill police officers.[19] The IRA in Gobnascale then planted incendiary devices around the city centre and undertook an armed robbery of the Ardmore post office, stealing £700 in cash and £700 in stamps on 3 March.[20] Significant IRA-orchestrated violence occurred on 21 March when a military foot patrol came under sustained attack from fifty youths in Abbey Park. Buses were set on fire and baton rounds discharged. No one was killed. However, on 27 March, the IRA succeeded in killing a soldier, 31-year-old David Ross, who was caught in a bomb attack as he drove a minibus past Gransha Hospital. The explosion narrowly missed causing death or serious injury to schoolchildren, nurses and psychiatric patients close to the scene.[21]

The remaining members of the 'Derry Young Hooligans' were back on the streets on Easter Monday. A riot ensued and petrol bombs were thrown at soldiers on a routine patrol on the city walls. As a Land Rover passed through the area, young republicans threw a petrol bomb onto the vehicle.

Upon catching fire, Private Neil Clarke kicked open the rear doors and was immediately shot dead by an IRA gunman.[22] While Private Clarke lay on a mortuary slab, the IRA was burying one of its own. Volunteer Richard Quigley was laid to rest in the Republican Plot in the city's cemetery. Three armed and masked members of the Derry IRA stood to attention at his grave and fired thirty shots in his honour. More than 2,000 people turned out for the funeral, with Father James Shiels telling those gathered that Quigley was 'good, kind, considerate and one who was a shining example to others'.[23] Shiels added, 'as we mourn and grieve and express our sorrow, we must remember that he is one of the many young men who have taken a path that, whether we like it or not, is part of what is happening in this city of ours today'.[24] Celebrated and eulogised by McGuinness and others, Quigley's sacrifice would be used to recruit other young men, replenishing the ranks of an organisation that demonstrated remarkable resilience in the face of overwhelming odds.

On the same day, Oliver Miles was finally instructed by the Foreign Office to break off Britain's diplomatic relations with Libya. Miles said that he went into their foreign ministry and announced that the UK was expelling its mission from London. The Voice of the Arab Homeland radio station told its listeners that the 'people's committees will form an alliance with the secret IRA' in order to liberate 'the Irish nation from the tyranny of British colonialism'.[25] A few days later, Gaddafi formally announced that he would resume his cooperation with the IRA in retaliation for Britain having harboured what he called 'masked terrorists and stray dogs escaping justice and law'.[26] The Foreign Office took a balanced view of Libyan rhetoric, suggesting that since the Irish Navy, in March 1973, captured the *Claudia*, a 298-tonne West German-owned ship carrying 5 tonnes of arms and ammunition from Libya to the IRA, evidence of direct arms supplies remained 'circumstantial'. They did, however, note that the 'possibility of a new arms supply arranged through clandestine contacts cannot be ruled out'.[27]

The violence in Derry caused some former agents to rekindle their relationships with their handlers. Unlike Willie Carlin, an MI5 agent codenamed INFLICTION had been a leading member of the IRA. His MI5 handler later recalled that INFLICTION was 'a reliable agent', though at the time it was 'not always possible to judge immediately the accuracy of the information supplied'.[28] In the spring of 1984, INFLICTION was 'providing information, which was potentially of great value, but much of it could not be verified at the time'. The MI5 handler admitted that INFLICTION often withheld information. He recalled that some of their conversations 'would be formal, with an agenda and I would make notes that I would write up afterwards'. On other occasions, they would be informal, 'with neither of us having any particular topic we wanted or needed to discuss. In these cases I would make up my notes within a short time (no more than a few days later).'[29] After the murder of Private Clarke, INFLICTION claimed that he had important new information for the British based on a conversation with Martin McGuinness. The source reported to his handler that the Northern Commander felt 'as responsible as the British' for the deaths on Bloody Sunday. He went on to claim that 'McGuinness seems to be Mr Nice Guy, although really "he" was a pretty hard terrorist'.[30] However, this chink in McGuinness' armour was enough for MI5 to want to more closely examine the IRA chief's psychology, a better understanding of which could prove useful in trying to work out what he was likely to do next. It was decided to draw on agent source reporting about McGuinness in a more concerted manner in order to obtain a more rounded insight into his intentions in Derry and elsewhere in the context of resurgent IRA violence.

★ ★ ★

Willie Carlin was now meeting the FRU on a weekly basis. Sometimes the Hiace van arrived to pick him up; the door would slide open and he would climb in with a supermarket bag of documents tucked under his arm. The van took him directly to Ebrington Barracks, where Agent 3007 would sit through hours of debriefings with his handlers. Carlin tried to stick as closely to his original brief from MI5 as he could. However, the FRU wanted more detailed information on the IRA's operations. They were becoming desperate:

> And all these guys wanted to know was who shot who, "where's the gear," "who's he?", "do you know this guy?," "do you know where he's from?" Do you know these photographs?'" All this kinda stuff. Now, did I give them any information? Yes. But only what the dogs in the street already knew. What I didn't know was that they couldn't get that information. I didn't know that they'd spent years trying to get into somewhere. And what frustrated me was that on one particular occasion, I brought in political stuff. Sinn Féin meetings and minutes, and the sort of stuff that I was asked to do originally. And I brought it

in a Kelly's supermarket bag and I gave it to Eddie and I said, 'Look, Eddie, you need to tell Rees-Morgan.' Two weeks later I was back in the room with more stuff and the Kelly's supermarket bag was still lying in behind the radiator where he'd put it. He never gave it to anybody. Now, I spent two years from '81 to '83 bringing in political information. All the time Sinn Féin was growing and growing and growing. We were no longer paper sellers. We were no longer collecting money for the PDF, we were on the rise and, to an extent, the tail was now waggin' the dog, in Derry anyway.[31]

Carlin was part of a long lineage of agents tasked with gaining access to secret political intelligence that stretched back to the early days of the British Secret Service. One senior Intelligence Officer at the time, Michael Herman, reflected on how:

The most valuable modern Humint asset is the long-serving agent in place, undramatically copying documents, and drawing a regular supplementary income as part of an apparently normal life. He or she may be an ideologue or patriot, or have begun as one; or may have been moved by the accidents and mixed motives that create other criminals.[32]

Thus, Carlin played a vital role. He was well placed to subtly move Sinn Féin towards a space where it could engage with the British on a political level.

However, such lofty political insights did not help the FRU, which, like Special Branch, was under increasing pressure from its own chain of command to get results in the form of arrests or seizures of weapons. According to one FRU officer, the unit 'decided to preserve the cover' of one of their agents at all costs.[33] The agent in question, Frank Hegarty, codenamed 3018, had, like Carlin, built up trust with McGuinness and was now in a position to inflict damage on the Derry IRA if he chose to do so. Hegarty's knowledge of the locations of IRA arms dumps in the city proved invaluable.[34] However, if the FRU were to seize these weapons, they would have blown Hegarty's cover. Likewise, the 'jarking' of the weapons would have alerted the IRA to the presence of an agent in its ranks. According to journalists Liam Clarke and Kathryn Johnston, the FRU's commander in the city, 31-year-old Captain John Tobias, decided on an alternative course of action: he would recover the weapons, record their serial numbers and return them to the hide.[35] Ian Hurst was a young Corporal serving in the FRU in Derry at the time.[36] As Hegarty's co-handler, he recalled that he was 'a wonderful man, a typical working class Derry man. Not bright, yet streetwise. A gambler by instinct.'[37] By leaving Frank Hegarty in place, the FRU had an influential agent in the ranks of the IRA who would complement Willie Carlin's infiltration of Sinn Féin. The net soon began to close around Martin McGuinness, who became increasingly paranoid about treachery.

★ ★ ★

Sinn Féin/IRA Headquarters, Cable Street, Derry, Early June 1984

One of the ladies who helped out at the advice centre of the Sinn Féin headquarters in Derry had been tapping on a typewriter when she glanced up to see Carlin standing over her. Carlin looked at the clock. It was fast approaching 3 p.m. It would be impossible for him to leave the high-level meeting he was having with Martin McGuinness and Mitchel McLaughlin. Upon realising that he would miss the meeting with his handler, he placed a call to Ebrington Barracks directly from Sinn Féin's Cable Street offices.[38] A few weeks later, Carlin was asked by a fellow Sinn Féin activist what he thought of a statement they had issued to the *Derry Journal*, which reported that a young man had been approached by British Intelligence and asked to ring a number that had also been rung in the Sinn Féin office. Carlin claimed that Joe McColgan, a BT engineer and Martin McGuinness' brother-in-law, had been monitoring calls in and out of the Cable Street HQ and had noticed that someone inside the building had telephoned the barracks.[39] Carlin could not believe he had taken such a chance, but he was audacious enough to deny any knowledge of the call and make light of the matter. The truth was that he was taking more risks, which would greatly limit his 'shelf life' as an agent of influence inside the Republican Movement.

'Most agents and informers have a limited shelf life,' another agent inside the Derry IRA at the time observed. 'It was mainly down to luck that I'd escaped detection by the Provies,' claimed Raymond Gilmour. Gilmour's luck had finally run out in mid-August 1982, when he finally admitted his treachery to his wife. For months, Gilmour had been drinking heavily, becoming more and more paranoid that the IRA's Nutting Squad were on to him, especially since many of the operations he was involved in had been fatally compromised, which he felt too obviously implicated him. He made a decision to ask for exfiltration.

A little over a week later, the RUC, supported by British troops, raided the homes of scores of suspected members of the Derry IRA. Despite charging thirty-five suspects, the city's IRA squads remained a force to be reckoned with. Their continued use of violence was so intense that it placed considerable strain on the Security Forces. In some of his debriefs, Carlin's handlers had turned to him to plug the gap left by Gilmour, pressuring him into giving military-related information, which went against his initial briefing by MI5 to only report on political intelligence.[40] The upsurge in violence led to an increase in the number of debriefings by his handlers, probably placing him in even greater danger as he became part of a tighter group of activists with intimate knowledge of the locations of arms caches and financial transactions between Sinn Féin and the IRA.[41] Little did he know that the information he was sharing was creating a trail that would eventually lead the IRA to his door. And it was none other than his former handler, Michael Bettaney, who finally set the IRA on that trail.

Bettaney was an unlikely spy. Intelligent and irreverent, he thought differently to many of his fellow spooks. When he was transferred from agent-running duties in Northern Ireland to the Soviet desk in London, he began to betray secrets to the Russians by pushing intelligence documents through the letterbox of the Second Secretary of the Soviet Embassy in London on Easter Sunday 1983.[42] Bettaney was later apprehended when an MI6 agent inside the embassy, 46-year-old KGB officer Oleg Gordievsky, told his own handlers of the betrayal.[43] Bettaney became the thirty-third person convicted of breaching the Official Secrets Act (1911) under the espionage clause.[44] Although he had clearly attempted to pass information to the Soviets, it was said that he had not leaked information regarding operations in Northern Ireland. This was a lie. Once Bettaney found himself on remand in Brixton Prison, he began to strike up conversations with former IRA quartermaster Brian Keenan during Mass in the prison chapel. According to Carlin, Bettaney willingly gave details of British agents reporting on the IRA, as well as their handlers:

> He did speak to a volunteer in prison. Because he was a Catholic, he was allowed to go to Mass. And this IRA volunteer who was in prison

for a very short amount of time … The guy thought he was a nutcase. Word went back out and was returned, [proving] that he was who he said he was. He said to this guy. 'There's a guy in Derry who's an ex-soldier – his name is Willie – and he has given MI5 some of the most vital information on republican political thinking.'[45]

Unsurprisingly, these reports soon found their way back to Martin McGuinness. 'Martin, I'm told, said, "Listen, you're talking nonsense. He's just a community worker in the Waterside. Leave him alone,"' Carlin recalled.[46] Nevertheless, the allegation lingered and re-emerged a few months later.

12

THE McGUINNESS HALF HOUR

'Londonderry PIRA have continued to be the most active group of terrorists in the Province ... [T]he threat of spectacular attacks by PIRA remains high, both in Northern Ireland and on the mainland.'

– Army Intelligence Summary (1984)[1]

Security Policy Meeting, Castle Buildings, Stormont, 9 July 1984

Jim Prior was in a good mood as he congratulated his top team for the way they had handled the security surrounding the European elections, stating that even though the RUC and Army continued to take casualties, 'he had heard much remark on the achievements of the security forces from quite unexpected quarters recently'. John Hermon had personally visited the families of several of his slain officers, but he, too, seemed upbeat, emphasising to those gathered around the top table that intelligence was now pointing to 'strains in the Northern Command leadership of PIRA', whose 'operations had been significantly inhibited by the extent to which they had suffered paranoia about informers'.[2] Turning to a discussion of the IRA's military capability, Hermon commented that '[i]ndividual PIRA members on the run continued to cause concern and there were particular worries about PIRA groups in the Armagh/Lurgan and East Tyrone areas'. He also had reason to celebrate. Two high-ranking terrorists had been captured. Dominic McGlinchey, the INLA's Chief of Staff, had been arrested by the Gardaí, which 'severely dislocated' the group and left it facing 'continuing difficulties over leadership'. In the United States, the FBI, working in conjunction with MI5, arrested PAC member Joe Cahill. Cahill was the group's chief fundraiser and his arrest coincided with successful operations being mounted by the RUC's anti-racketeering unit, which slowed the flow of money into the IRA's coffers. While this was positive news, Hermon warned that the Derry unit was 'still the most threatening' and would need to be tackled by the security and intelligence officials gathered around the table.[3] Jim Prior agreed with Hermon's assessment, remarking that the situation in the city had been 'worrisome for a little while'.[4]

Joining the top table for the first time was a senior civil servant, John Bourn, who had transferred from the MoD to the NIO. Bourn had been given lead responsibility for conducting a new security review, which was soon christened 'Bourn Again'. Bourn was more familiar than anyone with the resources the government had at its disposal in its war against the IRA. One report he received from a middle-ranking Army officer at HQNI estimated that some 4.6 per cent of its deployed troops were dedicated to the secret intelligence war against the IRA:

> Covert operations are the cutting edge of the attack against the terrorist. These operations include the acquisition of intelligence and the exploitation of this intelligence by covert action. Usually these 2 functions are intimately interconnected. Some 600 servicemen are involved in covert operations, ranging from the in-Province SAS detachment to the regular battalion Close Observation Platoons (COPs). The main source of intelligence is from informers. Both the RUC and Army run these human sources: The Army does so through the Force Research Unit (FRU). The greater part of such intelligence is gained by the RUC agencies, who have the advantage of local knowledge and background, and who have a higher number of personnel involved. But a significant proportion of the intelligence comes from the FRU, which is able to attract sources who feel safer working to handlers who are not resident Ulstermen, and who can work incognito in the more hostile areas within the framework of routine Army operations.[5]

Prior judged the Derry IRA to be the biggest security threat facing the British, so he turned to Hermon, Richardson and Doyne-Ditmas in the hope of prompting a security response. All eyes now turned to Derry IRA chief and OC Northern Command, Martin McGuinness.

★ ★ ★

In Martin McGuinness, the PIRA had its very own enigma machine.[6] McGuinness knew all of the organisation's secrets, from the number of weapons and explosives held in its arms dumps to the number of volunteers in each squad. Originally from the staunchly nationalist Bogside area, he had joined the Official IRA in 1969 before crossing over to the ranks of the Provisionals. By 1972, he was second in command of the Derry Brigade of the IRA. McGuinness had witnessed British troops march up Shipquay Street first-hand and was present on 30 January 1972 when Parachute Regiment soldiers opened fire on protestors. By the mid-1970s, he was sitting on the PAC. He stepped down in October 1982 to serve in an operational capacity as OC of Northern Command. Over the years, McGuinness had earned a reputation based on his personal participation in IRA operations, though not all IRA men were convinced that he risked his own life as much as he risked the lives of others. It was believed by some that he held back 'from the worst of the action'.[7] He was one of the first IRA leaders to engage in talks with British Intelligence and government officials in the early years of the Troubles. He accompanied Dáithí Ó Conaill and Brian Keenan to meet Billy Mitchell and other senior members of the Ulster Volunteer Force (UVF) on the banks of Lough Sheelin in County Cavan in 1974.[8] By the end of the decade, McGuinness had replaced both men on the PAC.

By the early 1980s, McGuinness' reputation as a militant IRA man drew a lot of younger men into the ranks of the IRA. In Willie Carlin's view:

These guys would have went anywhere with him to be truthful. Martin himself would have come in and sat in meetings and sometimes you'd wonder why he was there because he never spoke. Then he got up and left. He was a listener. He listened to everything. He said very little sometimes and then sometimes he would speak. And what he would say would be quite profound, you know. But all I can tell you is that when he was in the room, people didn't free up. They weren't as forthcoming as they would have been if he wasn't there. Sometimes we used to speak about him when he wasn't there, like 'How does Martin feel about this?' And Mitchel [McLaughlin] would have to say, 'This is what he's thinking. This is what he says.' And we didn't always discuss military stuff at *comhairle ceantair* [area] meetings. In fact, it was quite frowned upon. You only spoke about military stuff outside, maybe walking along the road or something. But it's hard to explain. These guys loved McGuinness. They knew he had power. They knew he wouldn't let them down.[9]

In those front-line IRA squads from the Bogside, Creggan, Shantallow and Gobnascale, Martin McGuinness was considered a 'God'. 'McGuinness had a reputation,' one IRA member said. 'He would have scared you.'[10] For McGuinness' opponents in Special Branch, he was a 'psychopath' – 'cold', 'unemotional' and 'ruthless'.[11]

McGuinness' ruthlessness would soon manifest itself in the wake of the capture of the *Marita Ann*, which was intercepted by the Irish Navy on 29 September 1984. After boarding the ship, sailors detained five crew. A search of the ship yielded some 70,000 rounds of ammunition, ninety-one rifles, eight sub-machine guns, rocket warheads and police-issue bulletproof vests supplied by serving members of the Boston Police Department.[12] It was the largest illegal arms shipment seized since 1973, when the Irish Navy intercepted the *Claudia*. The capture of the *Marita Ann* was part of what was believed to have been a massive multi-national intelligence operation involving a United States KH-11 spy satellite, an RAF Nimrod reconnaissance aircraft and the 792-tonne Irish Navy cutter *Emer* and its sister ship *Aisling*.[13] Irish Taoiseach Garret FitzGerald issued an angry press statement in which he made it clear that the weapons were destined for Ireland to 'murder Irish people, north or south' and that their seizure would save many lives. He told reporters, 'There are still people in the United States who are failing to comprehend the situation in this country and are willing to give aid for the purpose of sending arms and ammunition to murder people, including members of our Security Forces here.'[14] FitzGerald said the Irish government remained 'vigilant all the time' and was determined to prevent any further arms from being spirited onto the island. One of those arrested on-board the *Marita Ann* was 34-year-old Martin Ferris, OC of the IRA's Southern Command. He later gave a defiant interview to *An Phoblacht*:

> We tried to get the *Marita Ann* away but the navy vessels opened up with gunfire. Members of the navy, Gardaí and detectives boarded us and we were arrested and towed to the naval base at Cobh. We were later driven to the Bridewell in Cork. It was obviously a setback for the IRA – not that we were apprehended but because the arms and ammunition were badly needed to counteract the British occupation of our country. Three of us got ten years.[15]

It would later transpire that information about the shipment had been leaked by IRA Southern Command officer Sean O'Callaghan.[16] Despite

American press speculation that US Intelligence had been involved, MI5 claimed the 'Americans were not involved at any stage, and indeed are rather annoyed at the press speculation that they were'.[17]

Shortly after news of the *Marita Ann* broke, Willie Carlin drove Martin McGuinness to the Killyhevlin Hotel in Enniskillen, where he allegedly met with two high-ranking members of the IRA from South Armagh. This was Carlin's third visit to the hotel; his first had been when he played a gig there in the 1970s and his second had been when he met his handlers from MI5 in the closing months of 1980. During the return journey, McGuinness revealed something cryptic to Carlin:

> And he said, 'You've no idea, the challenge.' He says, 'You cast off. You've got this fly bobbing on the top of the water. It attracts the trout. The trout will look at it a couple of times and then it will take a bite. As soon as it does, you start reeling it in. Then it stops struggling, and then when it stops struggling, you let it go again. Let it out, let it go. And it'll swim away, and it'll stop, still caught, but it doesn't know that. And just when it feels safe, you bring it in again. Only closer this time. And it'll start struggling again and then you let it go again. And eventually you bring it in. And you've now got it because this thing will never give up. And you take the hook out and you put it back in the water for another day.' And I said, 'That sounds a bit like the boys, attracting foot patrols and, you know.' And he says, 'Aye, I know, except for one thing, we are the trout and we are not letting go.'[18]

Carlin relayed the conversation to his handlers in a debrief a few days later, during what Carlin called 'The McGuinness Half Hour'. This was a specially allotted time when Intelligence Officers talked to Carlin in great detail about the IRA's Northern Commander. The next time Carlin visited Ebrington Barracks, he noticed that soup, coffee, tea and sandwiches had been laid out. He was also surprised by the presence of a 'very nice, well-dressed woman who introduced herself as a psychologist'. The woman was there to talk to him about the fishing story:

> Somewhere along the line, in the back room somewhere, people must have been thinking, they are about to do peace. And then we have the Chief of Staff saying, 'We aren't giving up.' It was odd ... The only

thing is, Martin was a fisherman and the FRU's mantra was 'Fishers of Men', you couldn't make it up. You couldn't make it up.[19]

Based on Carlin's report, the British may have surmised that McGuinness was unlikely to take the capture of the *Marita Ann* lying down. After all, the shipment had been destined for Northern Command.[20]

McGuinness had a coterie of trusted republican supporters to whom he routinely turned when he needed advice. One member of this coterie was 48-year-old Derry businessman Brendan Duddy. Around the time of his birthday in June 1984, Duddy wrote a strategic policy paper for Sinn Féin in which he argued that McGuinness and Adams should build on their 'ghetto vote' by expanding their support base to include voters in what he called 'Middle Ireland'. It was astute political advice. However, Duddy was not satisfied with commenting purely on the ballot box; he also offered McGuinness his thoughts on the use of violence:

The retargeting of the Military conflict towards British executives and away from protestant Northern Irish serving in the Security Forces will gradually lessen the fear of civil war. As well as clarifying aims for the Republican Movement it will reassure both Ireland and Britain that violence is not self perpetuating. Alongside this should run an ongoing campaign in Britain aimed at alerting and converting the British public and establishment to the justness of the nationalist claim to constituting the majority in the island of Ireland. This, in effect, means sustained and clever lobbying of British politicians and media perhaps accompanied by repeated large scale publicity campaigns. It is counterproductive and sterile in this day and age to advocate and indulge in boycotts. Any forum which sells Sinn Féin's policies should be used and Sinn Féin does not have to agree or give consent to an existing 'position' to work within that 'position's' existing boundary.[21]

Duddy's ideas resonated with the Northern Command OC. 'Armed resistance coupled with the present level of political protest may continue for the next 25 years or more,' he informed McGuinness, 'but even if success comes from this struggle the victory will go or be given to the moderate alternative which will emerge as the war develops and continues.'[22] Duddy judged the next twelve months 'vital in the history of Sinn Féin' and he believed that the council elections on the horizon offered 'an opportunity to come forward with constructive, far seeing and attractive policies'. While Duddy believed the 'price of change' would be 'high' and, perhaps, 'unwelcomed by many in the Republican Movement', his argument regarding IRA violence was pragmatic, for there was a 'price of remaining where we are'. Duddy likened the choice to the one faced by United Irishmen at the Battle of Vinegar Hill in 1798, which was a turning point in their rebellion against English rule; a time, Duddy recalled, 'where honest and brave men died charging English muskets with pikes and swords'.[23] McGuinness had much to mull over after reading Duddy's document. By the autumn, he had made up his mind about what to do next.

★ ★ ★

Room 629, The Grand Hotel, Brighton, 3 a.m., 12 October 1984

In September, 33-year-old IRA man Pat Magee had been dispatched from Belfast to augment the technical proficiency of the IRA's England Department. He was on a secret mission personally authorised by Martin McGuinness, which, if successful, would change the course of the armed struggle. Magee slipped the Special Branch net with ease as he made his way to the seaside resort of Brighton, where he checked into the Grand Hotel on the seafront. He was in position two weeks prior to the anticipated arrival of Thatcher and her Cabinet for the annual Conservative Party Conference. Magee stayed long enough to construct a suitcase bomb and hide it behind the bath panelling in his room.[24] Over the following two weeks, the timer on the bomb in Room 629 gradually wound its way down. At 3 a.m. on 12 October 1984, the timer clicked, sending an electrical pulse into a home-made circuit board, which detonated 100lb of high explosives. The force of the explosion shattered the bathroom tiles into thousands of tiny pieces and sent a 'searing ball of flame' ripping through the hotel, causing the centre of the hotel to collapse in on itself. Sleeping in the room next door was Jeanne Shattock, who was married to the chairman of the Conservative Party's West of England branch. She was killed instantly in the blast by the thousands of fragments of bathroom tiles that were 'driven like bullets' into her body.[25] 'I heard this terrible bang and I knew immediately it was a bomb. I felt as if I was falling. I thought I was going to die,' recalled Lady Berry. She had just switched sides on the twin bed with her husband, Sir

Antony Berry, who was killed immediately. Jennifer Taylor, whose husband Eric was the chairman of the Conservative Party's North West branch, recalled: 'There was a big bang. I was lifted up and then there was a sense of falling and falling. When I finished falling, I opened my eyes believing I had been dreaming.'[26]

The explosion sent debris and heavy concrete crashing down on guests sleeping in the rooms below, killing a total of five people and wounding thirty others. In the wake of this audacious operation to target a sitting Prime Minister and her Cabinet, the IRA issued a statement claiming, 'Today we were unlucky, but remember, we only have to be lucky once; you will have to be lucky always.' The day after the atrocity, *The Times* newspaper carried a leader in which it argued that the bomb represented 'the most destructive single assault on the organs of the state since the attempt to blow up parliament 380 years ago.' For the editors of *The Times*, security was ultimately 'a state of mind and not a situation on the ground' and society now had to 'reconcile the challenge posed by terrorism with the need to preserve its liberal democratic values'. The IRA's *modus operandi* appeared to revolve around so-called 'sleepers' who 'spend long periods working and living normally, and staying away from obvious Irish haunts'. The IRA would send someone from Ireland to carry out the attack with the sleepers as 'backup'.[27]

On the face of it, the Brighton attack seemed to strengthen the hand of those IRA members in favour of escalating the military campaign at the expense of the political project. It came several months after the poor performance of Danny Morrison in the European elections: he had polled 91,000 votes, trailing behind SDLP leader John Hume's 147,000 votes. 'At Brighton, the IRA got closer to the centre of British political life than ever before,' Brendan Keenan wrote in the *Financial Times*. 'It was an undoubted military coup for them, but at a time when Dublin and London are working more closely together than ever in the search for a political settlement it could in the long run prove a costly mistake.'[28] Seen from another angle, the attack was a clear instance of Martin McGuinness following the strategic advice of one of his confidants, Brendan Duddy.

So severe was the political effect of the bomb that the JIC began to re-prioritise its intelligence requirements. In practice, the JIC set the requirements for agencies like MI5, MI6 and Defence Intelligence every two years. Spy chiefs looked to these requirements in order to organise their own methods of collection. They could draw on the JIC's designation of threats as being of First, Second and Third orders of importance. 'The most readily recognisable threat, and the most complex' posed to UK national security, wrote the JIC's outgoing chairman Sir Antony Duff, was the Soviet Union and its Warsaw Pact allies. Under Duff, the JIC asked for intelligence on their 'political and military intentions' and their capabilities. Next on the list came other sources of political violence, sabotage and subversion, and espionage. Lastly, came:

> all aspects of the threat to the security and the political stability of Northern Ireland from Republican and Loyalist extremist groups, both political and para-military, especially the Provisionals and the Irish National Liberation Army (INLA), and including relevant political developments in the Republic of Ireland. There is a particular need for timely tactical intelligence for the Security Forces.[29]

★ ★ ★

According to the recently appointed Secretary of State, Douglas Hurd, the 'Provisional IRA could be held in check, but neither the Army, the RUC nor the intelligence services believed they could be crushed out of existence without a marked increase of cooperation from the Irish Republic'.[30] Until that happened, the IRA would continue to make life difficult for the Security Forces in Derry. On 13 November, a squad took over a house in the Creggan area and held a man and his family hostage, before firing sixty rounds at a passing Army patrol, which returned fire, hitting the house twenty-two times, but causing no injuries. As the terrorists made good their escape, another gunman opened fire at the Security Forces. A subsequent search revealed a Beretta 9mm SMG and thirty-one empty cases in the garden of a nearby house.[31] Two weeks after the incident, Lieutenant General Sir James Glover was back in Northern Ireland to evaluate the situation for himself.[32] Much had changed in the four years since he had left, though the IRA was no closer to being defeated. During his visit, four sawn-off-shotgun-toting terrorists held one of the city's elderly postmistresses hostage until she handed over £13,000 from the safe. Later that evening, an IRA squad took over a house in Ardmore in their quest to find a child who had picked up a sub-machine gun belonging to them. In Strabane, the IRA took over yet another house and stole a family car, which would later be used in another attack. Not everything went according to plan. On 2 December,

Maze escapee Antoine Mac Giolla Bhrighde and four other IRA men were digging in a huge 1,000lb landmine near Kesh when they were ambushed by the SAS.[33] In the exchange of gunfire, both Mac Giolla Bhrighde and Trooper Al Slater were killed. Another man, 26-year-old IRA member Kieran Fleming, drowned in the Bannagh River as he tried to escape the firefight.[34] Four days later, his 19-year-old brother Willie was killed, along with his friend, 23-year-old Danny Doherty, by SAS troops in the grounds of Gransha Hospital. The two men had been on their way to murder an off-duty UDR man who worked as a hospital porter. Carlin had just buried his father when he heard the news of their deaths. He was furious. 'To my mind,' he said, 'I still believe this was a revenge killing.'[35] Doherty had been hit nineteen times and Fleming had been hit four times.[36] Doherty had been wearing a helmet, but Carlin said that the soldiers had removed it before shooting him twice behind the ear.[37] The incidents in Kesh and Derry 'resulted from the exploitation of informer intelligence.'[38]

Reflecting on this period, GOC, Lieutenant General Sir Robert Richardson, recalled, 'Covert operations became our cutting edge, closely coordinated with the RUC, SAS as the need arose ... Our goal was to shoot terrorists dead, within the rules, staying close to the Yellow Card, using minimum force.'[39] On the concept of 'minimum force', Richardson added:

> Yes, there were anxieties about Special Forces, like E4A in the RUC's case. But all of these episodes happened fast. It was dark. There was fear and there was adrenalin pumping too. I had my anxieties about them but when it came to it, it came down to basics: Kill or be killed. I wanted the rules observed. Minimum force, etc, and I believed in accountability too – but ask yourself how many terrorists of all kinds were arrested and convicted on my watch. There were 464 of them, compared to 11 killed. How many of them were trapped and arrested at stakeouts, given the choice to drop their weapons?[40]

An experienced commander of troops, Richardson knew both the value and limitations of employing Special Forces soldiers in such intelligence-led operations:

> I saw no military solution working on its own but we had to find a balance between civil liberty and the protection of life and property in a society plagued by terrorism. On my watch terrorist activity fell

by 70% and there was a 60% drop in attacks with incendiary devices, which to me felt [like] we had made progress, even given that, according to all evidence, 75% of those jailed, then released, went back into terrorist involvement. And police primacy was working.[41]

Like Dickie Lawson, Richardson's relationship with Hermon was so good that he was confident the Chief Constable 'didn't keep secrets' from him. Hermon, he said, insisted on briefing the Army's top commander on imminent operations, especially if he knew that Army back-up would be required. Ironically, despite being in overall charge of military operations, Richardson himself was only briefed on a 'need-to-know' basis. He admitted that the names of sources never crossed his desk because they were principally handled by 'specialist units and agents … needed to be kept secret, protected, so names … wouldn't have come to me.'[42] So sacrosanct was the 'need-to-know' principle within the intelligence system that even if the British had wanted to curtail the Derry IRA's operations even further, they could not have done so. Douglas Hurd had inherited this reality when he took over from Jim Prior on 27 September 1984.

Martin McGuinness may not have been an early convert to the Armalite and ballot box strategy, but he had grown to become one of its chief proponents. It was said that he had flown into a rage whenever Danny Morrison first floated the idea at the 1981 *Ard Fheis*. As Chief of Staff and then as OC Northern Command, McGuinness found himself charged with reconciling both elements of the twin-track strategy on the ground. By ambushing several IRA volunteers in McGuinness' own personal power base, the British were opting to box him in so he would place more emphasis on the IRA's political ambitions. PAC member Ivor Bell suspected as much when he travelled to Derry in the new year to confront McGuinness about his recent decision to direct more money towards Sinn Féin. Carlin was at the foot of the stairs and overheard the ensuing row between the two men:

'You!' I heard him roar, 'Aye, you! Who was it that covered for you, eh? Me, that's who. I went out on a limb for you. It took fucking weeks to get Gerry Adams to come around. Such was the outrage caused by those deaths that we were forced to admit that it hadn't been authorised [the bombing of Harrods].' This was the first time I'd ever heard Martin McGuinness in a full-blown rage.[43]

It was clear from the row that the two men profoundly disagreed over how best to effectively implement the Armalite and ballot box strategy. McGuinness remained confident of Brendan Duddy's analysis. As far as Bell was concerned, Duddy's approach was wrong-headed. Shortly after returning from his meeting on Cable Street, Bell was court-martialled and expelled from the organisation. McGuinness and Adams' other close confidant, Kevin McKenna, were now in control of the Republican Movement.

13

THE FRANK MURRAY SHOW

'To recruit a terrorist source, you have to have a strong lever on him one way or another.'

– Former RUC Special Branch source handler (2018)[1]

Forty-year-old Frank Murray joined the force as a police cadet in the mid-1960s and rose through the ranks to become a key figure in Special Branch twenty years later. He cut his teeth as a CID officer in Derry, Portadown and Armagh. 'Peter', a fellow officer, first met Murray in 1974 when they were both Detective Inspectors in J Division. 'He was a good CID officer,' recalled Peter. 'He had his faults, he wasn't perfect. The CID office in Lurgan was split into those in Frank's camp and those deemed not worthy to be in Frank's camp.' Soldiers who later worked with Murray in South Region recall a man of considerable integrity and boundless energy.[2] His reputation was well deserved, but it almost cost Murray his life. 'He could be extremely guarded about intelligence and information generally,' Peter recalled. He went on to explain:

> Frank enjoyed the opportunity to make a contact or two and he got himself a source. The source promised Frank he could get him the weapon, an Armalite. The source went to the 'RA or was of a sufficient position to decide himself that he didn't want recruited. Frank thought he could put pressure on the guy.[3]

Another one of Murray's colleagues recalled that 'Frank was one for touts' and liked to turn IRA volunteers whenever he could – as he demonstrated, albeit unsuccessfully, in his attempts to recruit Pearse O'Neill in November 1981. Nevertheless, Murray's tenacity almost cost him his life.

In order to enhance his standing with the Army, Murray would carry out reconnaissance of IRA hides.[4] He is said to have visited several such hides and counted the rounds of ammunition contained therein, which he would then report in his briefs to his Security Forces colleagues. Murray's intelligence was so specific that when the soldiers searched hides he had visited, they found exactly the number of rounds he had said were there. Murray's determination to squeeze information out of IRA suspects during interrogations before venturing out of the station to confirm the veracity of the information backfired catastrophically in 1976. Accompanied by his Detective Sergeant, Murray travelled to the location of a hide in the Kilwilkie estate in Lurgan. As the two men pulled away the stones from the front of the hide, they unwittingly tripped a booby-trap bomb. 'The explosion could be heard by police officers in Lurgan RUC station,' Peter remembered.[5] Reports of a man staggering about on the road next to the railway line in Lurgan soon flooded the RUC's switchboard. The man, Murray, was said to be disorientated and suffering from considerable shock. A passing police patrol immediately rushed Murray and his colleague to Craigavon Area Hospital, where they were stabilised.

Murray had suffered severe, life-changing injuries in the blast: he had lost a leg, an arm and an eye. 'They didn't think he was going to pull through in the hospital so to give him hope they told him he would "get back [into the RUC]",' 'Jim', an RUC officer in CID and then in Special Branch, recalled. Meanwhile, as he recovered from his horrific injuries, Murray was visited by RUC Assistant Chief Constable Davy Rodgers, who made him a promise that he would not be invalided out of the police force. Murray was determined to get back into full-time duties, which he did within a year of the explosion. Murray was awarded an MBE during the 1977 Queen's Birthday Honours and earned a promotion to the rank of Detective Chief Inspector the same year.[6] 'The funny thing was he got promoted quicker after he was blown up, than he had before,' said Jim. 'He was incredibly driven and decisive.'[7] Highly respected by most police and Army officers who came to know him, Murray soon earned a reputation as one of the RUC's most experienced intelligence practitioners.

Although the IRA scored a huge success by almost killing such a senior CID officer, the group would suffer significant setbacks over the next few years. Peter recalls how he and a number of officers were sent in to shake things up and get the IRA out of Lurgan. Following the killings of Seamus Grew and Rodney Carroll in late 1982, John Hermon moved to replace Mick Slevin with Trevor Forbes as Head of Special Branch.[8] Forbes soon initiated a wholesale clear-out of the Branch old guard, replacing them with CID officers, and, crucially, appointing Frank Murray as Head of

Special Branch (HSB) in South Region in 1984.[9] Based at Gough Barracks in Armagh and later Mahon Road Barracks in Portadown, Murray was responsible for the towns of Cookstown, Enniskillen and Dungannon in the south-west, Portadown and Lurgan in Mid Ulster, Crossmaglen in the south and Newcastle in the south-east. These were the most active regions for the PIRA and the group's South Armagh Brigade remained virtually impenetrable to British Intelligence.[10] 'Frank ran the show,' Jim recalled. 'There was him and a Chief Inspector who acted as his driver and that was it. Everything went through Frank.'[11]

An Army Intelligence Officer who worked in the South Region TCG at the time said, 'Frank kept everything in his head. He couldn't write because of his injuries. He would have called people in, including the TCG, and said, "This is what's happening," and sent us out to do it. He had the source handlers report directly to him.'[12] Murray quickly earned a reputation as an all-powerful figure in Northern Ireland's covert arena. He even persuaded MI5 to step up its technical support to the RUC in the South Armagh area, perhaps another indication of the lack of human intelligence assets at the time.[13] Nicknamed the 'bionic man' after the 1970s television series *The Six Million Dollar Man* starring Lee Majors, Murray never complained about the injuries he had sustained in the bomb blast that had almost killed him. Those who worked with him closely, however, knew that he was driven to 'get the terrorists', as he used to say. 'I don't know if that was more out of revenge for what happened to him, or not,' Jim said.[14] Murray was so fixated on disrupting and preventing attacks that he immersed himself in intelligence work. 'He galvanised people,' recalled 'Jimmy B.', 'bringing all the source handlers in and threatening to cut their "danger money"[15] if they didn't get out and recruit more sources.'[16] He was one of the IRA's most formidable opponents.

The IRA's mortar attack on Newry RUC Station on 28 February 1985, which killed nine RUC officers, reminded Murray of his immense responsibility for keeping his colleagues safe from harm. It was an incident that haunted him and motivated him, like many of his colleagues, to ensure it never happened again. Jimmy B. was handpicked by John Hermon to run the E4 HMSU. He observed that Murray often preferred to bypass the system put in place several years earlier by Oldfield:

> Even amongst the agent handlers … If they trusted the person in charge's judgement, they'd have told you more … In theory, the TCG

was in charge but some of the regional heads, if you take somebody like Frank Murray, they would have bypassed that even to go straight up to the top man if they thought it was sensitive enough ... Frank Murray did that all the time, even as a Chief Super[intendent]. He bypassed everybody ... Always ...[17]

Murray was one of a handful of high-ranking Special Branch officers who presided over an organisation that was spending over £500,000 a year on informers.[18] The main slush fund used by the police to pay sources was known as the Chief Constable's 'B Account'. On average, the NIO was transferring between £15,000 and £30,000 per month in bulk payments to this account. For instance, in August 1984, they made a monthly payment of £45,000 and in December the transferred funds had risen to £69,000, a sign that informers were being rewarded annually for their information with a Christmas bonus.[19]

Money was only one of a range of reasons why people passed on information about terrorism in Northern Ireland. Other reasons included 'threats, blackmail, revenge, or even the thrill, and occasionally the desire to defeat terrorism'.[20] Some handlers likened their trade to fishing, with bait used to attract potential sources, which were hooked and reeled in. The circumstances giving rise to the cultivation of a source differed from handler to handler. The men chosen to handle sources were usually experienced police officers with several years of service under their belts. Above the source handlers were the Detective Inspectors and Detective Sergeants who directed Special Branch activities locally, often through a process of trial and error. Depending on the operational circumstances, certain handlers would meet their sources on a daily basis. Most regional Special Branch offices had no more than a dozen officers, at least half of whom were expected to provide security for meetings between sources and handlers, as well as writing up intelligence reports, updating the registry and researching future locations for meets.[21] Once a source provided information to his or her handler, the officer was debriefed by an RUC Source Unit, which made notes in a Daily Intelligence Book and passed important intelligence upwards in the form of an SB50, a slightly sanitised version of the source's information.[22] This intelligence was passed up the chain of command to the Head of the Source Unit, usually a Detective Chief Inspector, who, in turn, gave it to the Regional Head of Special Branch.[23] In Belfast, the Head of Special Branch typically called in the commander of the TCG and the officer in charge of the Source Unit to cross-check the veracity of the intelligence. Decisions on actionable intelligence were then made and filtered back down via Liaison Officers.[24] Sometimes, in areas like South Region, this information was not widely disseminated. In other areas, however, it was disseminated, which frequently led to inter-agency rivalry, including competition in recruiting sources and a reluctance to fully disclose every snippet of intelligence, a process that, on occasion, threatened ongoing agent-running and proactive intelligence operations. The sharing of intelligence was a balancing act and much of it came down to personal relationships between individual Intelligence Officers.

'It's very hard to describe the way people like myself and FT [Murray] thought,' said Murray's close friend, Ulster Unionist Party MP for Fermanagh Ken Maginnis. 'He wasn't somebody who took things at face value. He had the ability to put things into a bigger picture. "So, there's an attack going to happen? Who would do that? What does that mean?"' Murray had a penchant for making links:

> If he had enough information, he had enough background knowledge to put it into context. FT was the most honest person I ever, ever worked with. There wasn't a dishonest bone in his body. He knew his mission statement. He knew his responsibility, not only in fighting the IRA, but also to his own people. He was honest in the moral sense of the word. His aim was not to get out and kill a lot of IRA men. His attitude was to do his duty.[25]

★ ★ ★

Mullaghglass, near Rosslea, County Fermanagh, just before Dawn, 26 April 1986

Twenty-five-year-old Seamus McElwain and his close friend and comrade, 31-year-old Seán Lynch, were digging a shallow ditch on the side of the Dernawilt Road, the main road connecting the small towns of Lisnaskea and Rosslea near the border with the Irish Republic. They intended to bury an Improvised Explosive Device (IED) and take up position on higher ground, where they could detonate the device upon the approach of a Security Force patrol. The explosive charge inside the device was typically initiated in two ways – either by the victim stepping on it or by someone activating the firing mechanism at the end of the command wire, which sent an electrical current to the explosives and triggered the blast. It could take up to twelve hours for IRA members to dig in and conceal command wires to avoid discovery by Security Forces patrols.[26] On the outskirts of Rosslea that morning, McElwain chose to use a command-wire IED, which had an effective kill radius of about 20 metres. The likelihood of anyone in the vicinity of the explosion emerging alive was slim. If anyone did manage to survive the initial blast, McElwain planned to pick them off with rifle fire from a safe distance.

McElwain was originally from Knockatallon in Scotstown, County Monaghan, a few miles from Rosslea,[27] a part of Ireland steeped in the closely intertwined traditions of Catholicism and republicanism. Scotstown was principally bogland, punctuated here and there by narrow, straight roads. The first thing that visitors to the town saw was 'an open-air garage, surrounded by quietly rusting cars. The place was sleepy and unkept,' as Irish writer Colm Tóibín recalled. 'The whole place was desolate … depopulated, lonely.'[28] One of a family of seven, McElwain had a long republican lineage. His father was a Sinn Féin councillor in Fermanagh, having previously been a training officer for the IRA.[29] The younger McElwain followed in his father's footsteps, becoming a key leadership figure within the borderlands IRA. A dedicated volunteer, he had joined the organisation a decade earlier and soon gained a reputation for being 'highly motivated, courageous and inspiring'. Amongst border IRA men, McElwain was said to have 'placed himself continually at the tip of the spear, at the cutting edge of resistance, leading from the front, leading by example'.[30]

A six-year veteran of IRA operations along the border, McElwain combined youthful vigour with republican zealotry. While other IRA volunteers enjoyed vibrant social lives, McElwain put the armed struggle first. According to those who followed him on operations, he could be a little too rigid at times. They cited his calling of IRA meetings on Sunday nights – when most other young men preferred to go to discos – as evidence of his fanaticism. Day and night, he 'tortured areas', they said, eager for the men below him to increase their kill rate. So committed to hunting down the IRA's enemies was he that he tended to alienate IRA volunteers whom he saw as wavering in their commitment to the struggle, which was one group McElwain hated more than Protestant members of the British Security Forces.[31] He believed passionately that you could not be a proper IRA man

The IRA ambush of a British Army convoy at Warrenpoint, close to the Irish border on 27 August 1979, in which eighteen troops were killed. Warrenpoint was the military's heaviest loss of life in an operational theatre since the Aden Emergency in the 1960s. The incident was blamed on poor intelligence sharing and prompted the British Government to appoint a Security Coordinator in Belfast. Image Courtesy of Pacemaker Press.

Sir Maurice Oldfield had been Chief of MI6 in 1973–78. In 1979 he was recalled from retirement by Margaret Thatcher and appointed as Security Coordinator. Oldfield was the key architect of a new strategy designed to obtain secret intelligence from the Provisional IRA. Photo courtesy of Alamy.

Captain Herbert Richard Westmacott, a young Troop Leader with A Squadron, 22 SAS, was fatally shot in a raid on the IRA's M60 gang in Belfast in May 1980. Image courtesy of the Sandhurst Collection.

The body of Captain Westmacott lies on the pavement outside the house where the IRA's infamous M60 gang had holed up to ambush a passing Security Forces patrol. The SAS raid, codenamed Operation ARTICHOKE, was one of the first major intelligence-led operations mounted by the RUC, British Army and MI5 in the wake of the Warrenpoint ambush.

Twenty-nine-year-old Joanne Mathers, a married mother of one, was working as a census collector when she was shot dead by the Derry IRA on 7 April 1981. Her killing drove Willie Carlin to renew his contact with British Intelligence. Photo courtesy of Pacemaker Press.

Willie Carlin alongside Martin McGuinness at the offices of the NI Housing Executive in the 1980s. Carlin, a former soldier, had been recruited by MI5 in 1974 and sent back to Derry to report on republican activity. He was handled by Military Intelligence in the years 1981–85. Photo courtesy of Willie Carlin.

The funeral of an IRA volunteer killed by the SAS in 1985. British spy Willie Carlin, at the rear of coffin, can be seen looking directly at the camera. He is a few paces behind IRA Chief Martin McGuinness. Carlin was exfiltrated soon afterwards when his former MI5 handler blew his cover. Courtesy of the *Derry Journal*.

Martin McGuinness rose steadily through the Provisional IRA's ranks to hold positions as its Chief of Staff and Officer Commanding of Northern Command. As one of Britain's top intelligence targets, he was surrounded by informers and agents, like Freddie Scappaticci who is pictured here below McGuinness to the left. Photo courtesy of Pacemaker Press.

Graffiti in Derry referring to RUC Special Branch agent Raymond Gilmour. Gilmour had infiltrated the INLA and Provisional IRA in the city. In later life he suffered from psychological problems and alcoholism, dying in relative poverty in 2016. Photo courtesy of Alamy.

Secretary of State for Northern Ireland Tom King alongside RUC Chief Constable Sir John Hermon. By the end of his decade-long tenure, Hermon was regarded by some senior NIO officials as a 'powerful warlord'. However, he was widely respected by his officers and the architect behind the RUC developing its own in-house Counter Terrorism capability. Photo courtesy of Pacemaker Press.

The E4 Special Support Unit (later renamed E4 Headquarters Mobile Support Unit [E4 HMSU]) was formed in 1980 as a Quick Reaction Force for RUC Special Branch. Its members were trained in specialist tactics such as hostage rescue, sniping and Close Quarter Battle (CQB) drills. Photo courtesy of a Private Collection.

The Force Research Unit (FRU) ran the Army's human intelligence sources. The FRU's motto was 'Fishers of Men'. It handled several high-profile agents in the 1980s, including Willie Carlin.

Seamus McElwain was one of the IRA's most dedicated and ruthless volunteers. Originally from Scotstown in County Monaghan, he became a key leadership figure in the early to mid-1980s and a proponent of guerrilla warfare tactics. He was killed in an ambush by the SAS on 26 April 1986, the result of an intelligence-led operation coordinated by RUC Special Branch in South Region. Photo courtesy of Pacemaker Press.

The aftermath of the Enniskillen bomb attack on Remembrance Day 1987 in which eleven people were killed. A twelfth person later died from his injuries. The IRA tried to distance itself from the attack by blaming the Security Forces. However, some sources believe the operation was authorised by Northern Command OC Martin McGuinness. Photo courtesy of Pacemaker Press.

The Provisional IRA squad who launched an attack on the Loughgall RUC station. Clockwise from top left: Patrick McKearney, Tony Gormley, Jim Lynagh, Paddy Kelly, Eugene Kelly, Seamus Donnelly, Gerard O'Callaghan and Declan Arthurs. Photo courtesy of Pacemaker Press.

Today it is widely believed by former IRA members that an informer gave away valuable intelligence to the British in advance of the Loughgall attack. Although it has never been conclusively proven who leaked the information, security sources suggest Operation JUDY, the codename for the ambush, was the product of all-source intelligence. Photo courtesy of Pacemaker Press.

In many respects Operation JUDY was the culmination of a renewed close working relationship between the RUC, British Army and MI5, which began in 1980. Photo courtesy of Pacemaker Press.

The senior RUC officer behind Operation JUDY was Detective Chief Superintendent Frank Murray, who was head of RUC Special Branch in South Region. It was said of Murray that 'he used the SAS as his own private army'. Photo courtesy of Pacemaker Press.

Chief Superintendent Harry Breen pictured with an assortment of weapons taken from the bodies of the IRA volunteers at Loughgall. He was later assassinated by the South Armagh PIRA in a classic guerrilla ambush near Jonesborough on 20 March 1989. Frank Murray and his team had intercepted 'traffic' indicating that the IRA was on the move but were too slow to identify their target. Photo courtesy of Pacemaker Press.

Tom King with Lieutenant Colonel Andrew Freemantle (pointing). Freemantle was the only British Army officer to have served with the Australian SAS during the Vietnam War. An expert on guerrilla warfare, like his superior Tony Jeapes, Freemantle argued that combating terrorism required brains as well as brawn. Photo courtesy of the Royal Hampshire Regiment Museum.

The Gibraltar Three, Sean Savage, Mairead Farrell and Daniel McCann, were highly experienced IRA volunteers intercepted by the SAS as they plotted a bomb attack near the Governor's Residence in the territory in March 1988. Republicans believed the episode was the culmination of the 'shoot to kill' policy. Photo courtesy of Alamy.

Margaret Thatcher was a tough-talking Prime Minister with a deep interest in intelligence matters. Here she is on one of her last visits to frontline troops along the Irish border. She is accompanied by Secretary of State for Northern Ireland, Peter Brooke (far left). At that time, Brooke's officials were initiating secret talks with the IRA. Photo courtesy of Pacemaker Press.

Colonel David Benest OBE, the CO of 2 Para in 1994–97, meeting with the then Labour Leader Tony Blair. Benest was the commander of military operations in South Armagh in 1996–97. He believed that covert action was a necessary complement to Green Army tactics on the ground. Photo courtesy of Genevieve Clarke.

unless you were thinking, acting or dreaming about the republican cause twenty-four hours a day. He became deeply depressed whenever meetings resulted in decisions being taken to only attack property, rather than Security Forces personnel.

What he lacked in experience and knowledge, McElwain made up for in enthusiasm. 'A guerrilla is a fish that swims in the sea,' one of his friends recalled. North Monaghan was the sea in which McElwain swam. 'Seamie was special,' his friend said, 'he is not a person whom words could describe.'[32] McElwain did indeed see himself as a student of guerrilla warfare and liked nothing more than to read articles on the topic in *An Phoblacht*. *An Phoblacht* explained the IRA's style of warfare as follows:

> In the North all attacks are aimed at weakening the confidence of the British government. Through relentless struggles the IRA aims to break the will of the British to remain. So the IRA, with popular bases and material support secured, are organised and trained for a long, revolutionary war. Their strongest weapon, however, apart from popular support, is not the M60 or RPG-7, but is a simple condition of mind – the will to win and the determination to continue despite all set-backs. With such a mentality, lack of weaponry and explosives, loss of comrades to jail or death can be overcome.[33]

McIlwain was full of boundless energy in his commitment to the IRA and naturally he saw himself as part of a long, unbroken lineage of republican martyrdom. As one of his comrades later said of him, 'all of us knew what we were fighting for and let nobody tell you different'. These IRA volunteers were, he said, 'on precisely the same mission as the men and women of 1916 – to put an end to British Crown sovereignty in Ireland and to establish a 32-county republican government of national unity based upon democracy and social justice'.[34]

The editor of *An Phoblacht* at the time was Danny Morrison. He observed how ideas about guerrilla warfare and bloody republican sacrifice tended to resonate within a certain section of the IRA's support base:

> In as much as anything can be unified in a struggle. You've always got rural–urban divides, you've got generational divides, you've got political polarisation where some people who were supporting the republican movement, were supporting the IRA, would be against

contraception, would be against divorce, would be homophobic, would be anti-internationalist, would be violently nationalist. And then at the other extreme, you had people who saw themselves fighting a revolutionary struggle who would have read in jail Mao, or General Giap, or Frantz Fanon or Albert Memmi, taking all these into consideration, throwing them all up into the air, seeing where they could be applied. Were there any ideas to be borrowed? What thinking succeeded? But it was very improvised. And in that way unique because it was taking place in a Western consumer society with social democratic dimensions to it.[35]

In the wake of the hunger strikes, the IRA's hierarchy began to introduce formal lectures on protective security, interrogation techniques and Irish history and politics.[36] McElwain and others had benefited from this kind of education during their time in prison and would continue to do so even during their time on the run.

McElwain's zealotry gained him an unrivalled reputation amongst his peers, but it also led to him cutting a lonely figure. Born and raised in what many urban republicans regarded as a backwater in the IRA's struggle, he felt safer on his own two feet, trudging over long distances across the dark and foreboding landscape of the borderlands. It was said that he loved nothing more than to venture out on a long walk over many miles before closing in on his victims like a bird of prey. McElwain typified the commitment of rural IRA volunteers, who now saw themselves as guerrillas fighting a war against 'British occupation forces'. As one former IRA member recalled:

It was the development of the guerrilla tactic rather than what would have been a citizen's defence … A lot of stuff we would have learnt from the Brits themselves. A lot of stuff would have been learnt from other conflicts in the international context. Take a situation like Vietnam. It was shoot and disappear. As long as you had the support of the community behind ye, it was possible to do that in a protracted way for as long as you intended to do it. And that's what happened. It would have been impossible to do that without support on the ground. And there was very, very little the Brits could do to dilute that support. They hadn't got the capacity to be able to deal with people, to actually ween people away from support of the community. Plus the fact that even if people weren't totally 100% committed to backing the IRA, they weren't prepared to sell them out.[37]

As long as McElwain and his IRA squad had the backing of the people of Scotstown and other republican heartlands, they could continue swimming with the current in the waters of a supportive sea.

As one of the border IRA's most enthusiastic planners, McElwain liked nothing more than to pore over maps of an area before insisting on walking the area so he could memorise every hedgerow, river and farm on his way to the kill. It was said that his memory for places was so good that he only had to visit a place once in order to remember it. McElwain's arrest on 14 March 1980 brought his murder campaign to a temporary halt, though it did not lessen his commitment to the IRA cause. He spent much of his time in prison planning future campaigns of terror, as well as interacting with IRA men from across the Six Counties. Unsurprisingly, amongst these men he coveted his own reputation as a keen, young IRA volunteer from the borderlands who had inflicted serious damage on the Brits. Before his escape from the Maze, he was regarded by prison officers as being someone 'always anxious to be seen to toe the "party" line'.[38] In his knowledge of the ground, his dedication and commitment to the IRA, McElwain nevertheless became 'instrumental in leading the group of escapees across difficult terrain'.[39]

McElwain plotted and executed many operations against his enemies throughout 1984 and 1985. By 1986, he had the blood of several men on his hands and was considered one of the IRA's most active and dangerous gunmen. That morning in the spring of 1986, McElwain set out into the townland of Mullaghglass in County Fermanagh on yet another murder mission for the Provisionals. Accompanied by Lisnaskea man Lynch, McElwain took a meandering route to the objective. Both men were armed, with one carrying a Ruger rifle and the other an FNC assault rifle. As they walked across a field towards the IED, flares shot up and illuminated the sky, followed by a barrage of gunfire.[40] The reality soon dawned on them that they had walked into the middle of an ambush. They dropped to the ground, dodging hundreds of rounds fired by the SAS. It was a loud and aggressive show of force by the soldiers. Lynch crawled into a ditch, badly injured by bullet wounds to his abdomen, leg and hand. 'At one stage the SAS were searching just yards from where I lay seriously wounded,' he later told *An Phoblacht*. 'Despite their efforts, they failed to find me,' he said.[41]

The same could not be said of McElwain, who had died amidst a barrage of gunfire.

The soldiers who mounted the ambush had spent several hours carefully putting in place their plan. RUC Special Branch had briefed them on McElwain and his squad. They were told of how he had dispatched several of his victims in their homes or workplaces and that he did not distinguish between those who were on or off duty, those who were regular or part-time members of the Security Forces, those who were still in the ranks of the 'Crown Forces' or those who had retired from service. McElwain saw all of these men as representatives of the 'British war machine'.

As soon as news spread of McElwain's demise, locals in Scotstown began to grieve. The McElwain family farm became the centre of that grieving process. Soon, black flags adorned the windows and flag poles in the centre of the village. The Irish tricolour in the main square flew at half-mast. One of the village's own had been killed by the enemy.[42] At his funeral a few days later, Martin McGuinness, told mourners:

> We will all miss him. In prison yards all over Ireland and in Britain they remember him. He was a brave, intelligent soldier, a young man who willingly gave up his youth to fight for the freedom of his country. He was an exceptional soldier, who, after he escaped from Long Kesh, immediately returned to active service with the support of his family. In doing so he incurred the wrath of the British and Irish establishment, but the admiration of all others. He will be remembered in the towns and villages of Fermanagh and Monaghan; his name will live forever. What happened on Saturday morning was that an IRA Volunteer was murdered by British terrorists and it was terrorists who sent them. The sort of people who drop bombs on children in Libya – terrorists such as Thatcher and Reagan.[43]

By comparing the actions of the SAS to the American bombing of Tripoli, McGuinness was attempting to discredit the British government. To many IRA volunteers, these national liberation struggles were one and the same.

How had the British known that McElwain and Lynch would be in that place at that time? SAS ambushes were notoriously violent affairs. They were patiently organised and involved police requests for military support, orders issued in detailed briefings and secret soldiers deployed into the borderlands to kill or capture known IRA players. In fact, the intelligence-led operation to ambush McElwain was 'triggered by SB intelligence'.[44] But how was that secret information obtained? Some suspected an informer in their midst. As the great chronicler of militant republicanism J. Bowyer Bell once observed, there was only one thing worse than penetration from outside the IRA and that was penetration by way of the 'corruption of the faithful'. In such cases, family history and past service 'become cover to treason', he wrote.[45] The paranoia now spreading through the ranks of the IRA became highly corrosive. Perhaps this was exactly what Frank Murray had hoped would happen? The fact that McGuinness had secured permission from the Army Council to vet operations shortly before McElwain's death aroused suspicion in the broader climate of antagonism that was setting in between the IRA's squads in the borderlands and McGuinness' Northern Command.[46] However, according to journalist Mark Urban, although the operation was organised by Special Branch, the command wire had been discovered by an alert soldier on patrol, proving that the Green Army could be just as effective in providing secret intelligence that could be usefully exploited by their Special Forces colleagues.[47]

14

AGENTS WITHIN

'Intelligence work has one moral law – it is justified by results.'

– John Le Carré, *The Spy Who Came in from the Cold* (1963)

Major General Tony Jeapes' long career in Special Forces began in 1958 in the Malayan Scouts, with which he fought insurgents from the Malayan Communist Party. He later redeployed to the Jebel Akhdar in Oman, where he battled insurgents high above the city of Muscat in 1958–59. Jeapes would later return to Oman in 1970 as an SAS Squadron Commander to help raise several *firqats* (tribal militias) to fight communist insurgents in the south-western region of Dhofar. He had commanded the SAS in 1974–77, during which his troops helped Sultan Qaboos defeat the People's Front for the Liberation of Oman and the Arabian Gulf, as well as deploying to South Armagh at the request of Prime Minister Harold Wilson. Later, Jeapes found himself in charge of 5 Airportable Brigade in the Falklands War. He returned to senior operational command when he was appointed CLF in Northern Ireland in March 1985. By the mid-1980s, Jeapes was one of the British Army's most experienced leaders.

In Jeapes, the IRA had another formidable opponent. He understood the challenge posed by the IRA in all its complexity. In a book he wrote about SAS operations in Oman in 1980 while a serving colonel, Jeapes gave some insight into his thinking on military operations: 'Winning a counter-revolutionary war is like clearing a garden of weeds. It is what you plant afterwards that matters.'[1] Acutely aware of the aggressive potential of the SAS, he nevertheless remained a great believer in working with other branches of the security and intelligence apparatus to defeat Britain's irregular adversaries:

> Counter-revolutionary wars are first and last about people and throughout the campaign the need to gain the support of the people was continually stressed to the soldiers. The seizure of ground was

important only if it allowed Government forces to make contact with the people. Without their support guerrillas cannot exist, and it was their belief that they had lost this support and the consequent fear of betrayal, rather than the pressure of Government military operations, that caused the adoo to move their heavy weapons out of the Eastern Area as soon as they did.[2]

Jeapes was only in his role as CLF a matter of weeks when he decided to revise the Army's agent-handling guidelines. First laid down by Jimmy Glover in 1979–80, these were reissued by Jeapes as the 'Directive for the Force Research Unit (Northern Ireland)' on 26 July 1986. In setting out the parameters according to which the FRU was now to operate, he confirmed 'the command and control arrangements for the FRU', while also updating 'certain procedures for the handling of sources':

> The responsibility for Army source handling operations in the Province is vested in the Force Research Unit (FRU). The FRU is to continue to complement existing intelligence gathering agencies by acquiring from human sources within Northern Ireland intelligence related to terrorist activities. Army source handling operations are to be carefully coordinated with the RUC SB. The primary aim of such operations is to be the penetration of terrorist groups.[3]

Importantly, Major General Jeapes emphasised that '[a]ll operations are to be conducted within the Law and members of the FRU remain subject to Military and Civilian Law at all times.'[4]

The biggest challenge faced by the various agencies charged with penetrating the IRA was the competition that persisted behind the scenes, particularly between the FRU and MI5. This 'tussle' reverberated up and down their respective chains of command and put a strain on everyday working relationships. It was reflected in internal correspondence by MI5's Director of Counter-Terrorism, Sir Patrick Walker, who stated he was 'very angry about the FRU's actions' in relation to the recruitment of one source in particular.[5] As one high-ranking Special Branch officer later observed, all three intelligence agencies were now 'fishing in a very small pond' and despite 'all these problems being recognised in the 1970s', little was done to address them directly.[6] Although clear distinctions were made between political and operational intelligence, the competitiveness between agencies sometimes led to a lack of coordination. Resolving the territorial disputes between the various agencies became a difficult task, especially since many Special Branch officers believed that only Irishmen could handle other Irishmen. They frowned upon the FRU, which they regarded as 'Englishmen driving around the countryside with car boots full of money'.[7] The greatest disdain, however, was saved for MI5, which RUC detectives referred to as 'the rich cousins'. The territoriality of the three agencies hinged on two overlapping and complementary variables: institutional tribalism and clashing personalities. The 'need-to-know' principle only reinforced such divisions.

★ ★ ★

Falls Road, West Belfast, 15 August 1986

Thirty-year-old Patrick Murray was a builder from the Beechmount area of West Belfast. On 14 August, he was abducted in the Short Strand area of east Belfast and taken away for interrogation by the Nutting Squad. During his ordeal, he had his hands tied behind his back and his eyes taped over. He was tortured before being shot at point-blank range in the head.[8] In a lengthy statement issued to the press, the IRA outlined its case against Murray, who, the group claimed, had freely admitted his deception. The IRA alleged that there was considerable corroborative evidence against him. He was thought to have received £10,000 in payments over an eight-year period in return for information.[9] The IRA said Murray had not been directly involved in operations, though he had been privy to 'loose talk'.[10]

In reality, the charge against Murray was more complicated than the IRA's public rebuttal of its former member suggested. It seems that in the weeks prior to his death, he had been given £30 by the Short Strand IRA to buy fuel for a getaway car. However, Murray spent the money on alcohol. A few days later, he was spotted by another IRA volunteer as he climbed into an unmarked van on May Street, near the City Hall.[11] This was enough circumstantial evidence for the Nutting Squad to arrest him, torture him and shoot him in the head. Ever since the IRA's double murder of husband and wife Gerard and Catherine McMahon in September 1985, the organisation reserved the death sentence for those members who had been officially Green-Booked into its ranks.[12] Green-Booking was the formal recruitment of potential IRA volunteers into the organisation and came with greater responsibilities, including being given privileged access to the IRA's innermost secrets. Murray was a bricklayer by trade and one of the few the IRA relied on to construct what senior IRA commander Gerry Bradley observed were 'brilliant dumps'.[13] Bradley believed that Murray was 'sacrificed to protect somebody else: Scap, Magee? Who knows?'[14]

Not long after Murray's execution, the Nutting Squad were at work again. Operating out of a safe house in Omeath, a few miles across the Irish border, they interrogated suspected informer David McVeigh from Lurgan. On Wednesday, 10 September, the RUC in Newry received reports of a body on Flagstaff Road, the main arterial route between Newry and Omeath. The IRA released a statement that the organisation had been aware for some time that its operations in Lurgan had been jeopardised. During McVeigh's interrogation, he told the Nutting Squad that his spying career had begun when he was arrested in the wake of an attack on Lurgan Golf Club in January 1983. He was said to have met his handlers every three weeks and was paid £20 for each meeting, an indication, perhaps, of his status as a 'low-grade informant'.[15] The IRA claimed that the information McVeigh had passed on to the RUC led to the arrest of five of its members and the seizure of explosives, weapons and ammunition.[16] McVeigh's murder was the seventh IRA execution of a suspected informer over a twelve-month period and was promptly condemned by SDLP deputy leader Seamus Mallon, who said that the IRA had revealed their 'hypocrisy about injustices caused by Diplock courts and supergrasses when they decided to terminate a life in front of a kangaroo court on the evidence of gossip'.[17] The IRA was extremely paranoid about informers and turned to the Nutting Squad to plug the leakages of secret information.

One of Special Branch's most senior spymasters at the time recalled that, within the PIRA:

> You had three layers. You had ordinary people on the bottom layer who could tell you if something was up in an area. Then you had those in the next layer up – your eyes and ears – who were sat in public houses, around the table with the players, picking up on loose talk. Then you had the top layer – members of the organisation itself.[18]

It is impossible to know where the likes of Murray and McVeigh sat within these three layers, though the fact that they were Green-Booked members of the IRA would have – directly and indirectly – involved them in operational details. Regardless of their roles, however, they were both in a position to pass on information gleaned from 'loose talk', especially in public houses in which IRA volunteers socialised in their free time. Special Branch preferred to target individuals whom they could subsequently manipulate into key positions in the IRA's different departments. 'There were nine different areas the IRA needed to operate their organisation,' 'Peter' recalled. 'Everything from recruitment and training through to financing and ASUs. We opted for intelligence, ASUs and quartermasters. They were the three areas you needed to run a successful op.' Peter and other Special Branch officers often asked themselves the same question: 'Who do you recruit? You don't recruit the milkman nor is it Volunteer Third Class, the gofer.' In Peter's opinion, the best option was to place someone 'in each of the nine areas', with a preference for 'middle management who could explain away anomalies'.[19] According to Peter, time pressure often meant that they didn't have the luxury of spending a lengthy period recruiting agents: 'In the Cold War, you could spend six months recruiting an agent or a year boring a hole in the wall of the Czech embassy and nobody was going to get killed. Here it was a different matter.'[20]

As the infiltration of the IRA grew, the Nutting Squad began to take more drastic measures. One former IRA volunteer, 'Sean', recalled:

That was the difficulty at some point that had to be overcome, certainly within the movement and within … say by … the latter part of the 1970s, they realised what had gone wrong. That this open network structure that had existed was impossible to prevent from either infiltration or from sort of intelligence leaks. So, the development of the cell structure – where the only people who obviously knew who were [sic] doing what and when were the people in a very, very small group and they didn't find out until the very last minute what was going on, so the operation wouldn't be compromised. I think that did make a difference. That is what sustained [the armed struggle] and I think allowed the IRA to carry on for as long as they did. But even in that, you know, there were still people … who were informers, they were agents within. And there were probably agents at a rather high level within the IRA and had been working with the Brits for a long time. And one of my fears is – you know, in view of people I know who were found up back lanes with their heads blown off and were actually shot to make space for other people – it was to save somebody's else's life.[21]

After its year-long killing spree, the IRA believed that it had finally plugged the leaks that had been so damaging to the organisation over the previous five years. Outwardly, at any rate, the organisation believed that it was in better shape than it had been at any time since the 1975 ceasefire and had even appointed a new Belfast commander.[22] The IRA did not know that its squads in Ardoyne, Unity Flats, Short Strand and the Markets all remained deeply penetrated. Additionally, its commander in Unity Flats, Joe Haughey, was colluding with loyalists in plotting the assassination of their own high-ranking paramilitary leaders.[23]

Thirty-six-year-old John Bingham was the UVF's commander in the Ballysillan area of North Belfast. For much of the past decade, he had coordinated gun and bomb attacks on republicans and Catholic civilians across Belfast. On the evening of 14 September 1986, Bingham was lying in bed when four members of a special IRA assassination squad arrived at his home to kill him. Tasked by IRA GHQ, the gang was led by Gerry 'Whitey' Bradley and the gunmen were armed with a .38 revolver, an Armalite and a 9mm handgun. The death squad used an axe to gain entry to the house. Roused from his bed, Bingham attempted to close the steel-reinforced door at the top of his stairs, but was repelled by a burst of gunfire. Bradley and another man, Mr T, chased him into a bedroom and shot him dead. The gunmen then made off in a white Renault 18 'Deauville' car, which was later found abandoned in Jamaica Court in Ardoyne with the keys still in the ignition and a small radio transmitter on the back seat. When the car was inspected by police forensics, it was initially found that the ignition block was intact, though it would subsequently be damaged, allegedly, to make it look as if it had been tampered with.

The weapons used in the murder of Bingham were traced to three other murders, including that of Denis Taggart, a 33-year-old part-time member of the UDR who had been shot dead by two IRA gunmen outside his home on Battenberg Street in the Shankill on 4 August 1986. Another weapon used in the Taggart murder, a 9mm pistol, was subsequently used in the killing of another UDR man on 12 June 1987 and in the execution of another suspected informer, Eugene Wilson, by the Nutting Squad on 24 June 1987. Intriguingly, the .38 pistol used in Bingham's murder was traced to the execution of IRA man Paddy Murray in August 1986.[24] Whoever had been involved in Bingham's murder was also a member of the Nutting Squad or at least used weapons from the same IRA hide.

★ ★ ★

The IRA was under increasing pressure from their rank and file to escalate the armed struggle in the autumn of 1986. 'I don't like to see anyone killed,' Martin McGuinness told *Irish Independent* journalist Justine McCarthy, 'but if Margaret Thatcher had died at Brighton, it would have made the British less intransigent because it would have brought home to them that the IRA is not going to go away.' McGuinness was adamant that the IRA had taken their struggle to 'the heart of the problem', which was 'old granite face' herself, as he called the Prime Minister. The IRA's Northern Commander contradicted himself as he spoke: 'Republicans like myself have long since accepted that there can be no change without the democratic wish of the people', with reunification unlikely to be 'done by force of arms', he argued.[25] Two weeks later, Sinn Féin held their *Ard Fheis*, which saw the party vote narrowly in favour of abandoning abstentionism in Dáil Éireann. McGuinness, long regarded as a hard-line militant, gave a defiant speech in which he sought to reassure the rank and file of the efficacy of violence. 'The IRA freedom fighters and the Sinn Féin freedom fighters are one and the same thing,' he told delegates. The armed struggle would continue 'until the last soldier has left our soil'.[26] In reality, the IRA was a hierarchical organisation, so if the PAC and GHQ decided to replace people in its leadership with individuals who were compliant with the new stance on abstentionism, it would do so. 'There was no open discussion about alternative options,' recalled former IRA commander Tommy McKearney. 'Most volunteers were prepared to accept recommendation made by the leadership and endorsed their decision to enter parliament.'[27]

Although the IRA murdered an RUC Reservist in the run-up to Christmas, the organisation remained ostensibly in a state of ceasefire until the new year. In early 1987, the IRA killed an RUC officer in Enniskillen and an off-duty UDR member in Dungannon. On 10 March, they killed another RUC officer and, a few days later, a civilian whom the IRA squad mistook for an off-duty UDR member. Against this backdrop, Tony Jeapes hosted a visit from the Assistant Chief of the General Staff, Major General John MacMillan, on 13 March. MacMillan later wrote to him, expressing his thanks for 'a really excellent visit' during which he found the 'sense of purpose of everyone involved' a 'tonic to a Whitehall warrior'. For MacMillan, 'the edge was sharper than I had expected because of the real consciousness that everyone has of the effect of the collapse of the Supergrass trials and the number of old hands released'. On the intelligence front, he found:

> an even wider gap than I had previously recognised between the elements who are privy to intelligence and those who are operating in the field of protective duties and mundane support to the RUC. I know this is partly a product of the developing security consciousness of the terrorists, who leave so much less to chance than their unskilled predecessors used to, and partly to RUC primacy. I believe the motivation and effectiveness of the soldiers, and in consequence the effectiveness of the RUC, will only be fully achieved if we can make progress towards involving the long term units at least in 'thinking' as opposed to just the mechanical aspects of counter terrorism. I know the difficulties but it is something we used to be so much better at when it was in our own hands, and we cannot afford to miss any possible trick when success or failure in the campaign is so evenly balanced. The contrast with Tony Ling's boys was dramatic, and I was thrilled to hear their activity, though as ever there is a terrible similarity between their stories and the fisherman's tale.[28]

Jeapes remained acutely aware of the challenges of creating unity of purpose between uniformed soldiers, policemen and those operating in the shadowy world of covert action. As he reflected on his achievements during his tenure as CLF, Jeapes was also mindful that he would soon be moving on to a new posting within the Army.

In one of his final engagements as CLF, Jeapes flew to Bessbrook Mill on 2 April 1987 for a visit with Lieutenant Colonel Andrew Freemantle and the men of the Royal Hampshire Regiment. He was keen to see for himself how the regiment was interpreting his direction to support the RUC and defeat terrorism while upholding the law. Jeapes was impressed by what he heard in Bessbrook. A former SAS officer, like Jeapes, Freemantle was one of the Army's rising stars. He was perhaps the only officer in the British Army who had fought in the Vietnam War as a member of the Australian Army. Freemantle had a deep appreciation of the problem of guerrilla warfare and was often the first to correct those who saw killing terrorists as the only way to deal with terrorism: 'Whilst the impact of attrition should not be underestimated,' he wrote at the time, 'those with a wiser view appreciate that deterrence and reassurance are as, if not more, important.'[29] Jeapes returned to Lisburn content that Freemantle understood what his higher commanders were trying to achieve.

The area around Bessbrook remained calm until 7 April, when a series of bomb scares, an explosion and minor public order problems led to several attempted hijackings, a proxy bomb hoax and explosions for four solid days. Despite the high tempo of covert operations now being mounted against them, Martin McGuinness was driving some areas hard. Under the cover of civil unrest, the IRA's Nutting Squad continued to plug further leaks. On 12 April, they abducted Charlie McIlmurray, whom they accused of being an informer. He was taken to the safe house in Omeath, where he was interrogated, tortured and shot. It was almost midnight when the RUC in Newry received a report from the owner of McKevitts Garage on the Dublin Road, a 15-minute drive from Omeath, that a body had been found in the front passenger side of a small van. The vehicle had been hijacked on Concession Road earlier that day and the IRA had called the Daisy Hill Hospital switchboard claiming the murder.[30]

Four days after the discovery of McIlmurray's body, the South Armagh IRA parked a light blue Ford flatbed lorry, recently stolen from Camlough, resprayed and given new number plates, in a cul-de-sac 100 yards south of Bessbrook Mill. On-board were two banks of sixteen Mk 10 and Mk 10A mortars, which were fired directly into the base. Three mortars landed in the car park, destroying around twenty vehicles and damaging the headquarters building. Luckily, only three soldiers were injured in the attack, which lasted approximately sixty seconds. 'This mortar attack came as no real surprise,' wrote Andrew Freemantle. 'What is surprising, is that it has taken PIRA 10 years (almost to the day) to mount such an attack on Bessbrook Mill.'[31] In an in-house report on the incident, the Army confided that the irregular foot patrols around the base 'failed to deter a mortar attack'.[32] In an article in the battalion's newsletter, Freemantle thanked his men for applying 'relentless pressure on the terrorist' and reminded them that 'the events of 16 April should serve as a warning that we cannot relax our vigilance for one moment; don't let this happen to you. Go carefully.'[33]

On 18 April, the RUC stopped a vehicle at a VCP and promptly arrested four republicans, two Drumintee men aged 25 and 26, and two other men from Ardoyne in North Belfast aged 32 and 29. A search of the vehicle produced a sketch map of the RUC station in Lurgan and the surrounding streets.[34] A week later, an IRA squad placed an RCIED inside a blue Ford Cortina saloon, which had been stolen in Jonesborough six weeks earlier, and parked it on the hard shoulder of the northbound A1 dual carriageway. As 74-year-old Lord Justice Maurice Gibson and his 67-year-old wife Cecily drove the 3km stretch north from the Gardaí checkpoint at BCP5 to the British Army's Fathom PVCP 1 mile north at Killeen, the IRA exploded the device. The Gibsons were killed immediately. Like other members of the judiciary, Justice Gibson had been identified by the IRA as a target as early as 1974. 'This was a well planned, prepared and executed attack, which must have been based on good intelligence,' the Army concluded in its initial report on the incident. 'How the terrorist managed to target Lord Justice Gibson is still under investigation but it was, presumably, because he made all his travel arrangements in his own name.'[35] On the day of the attack, Secretary of State for Northern Ireland Tom King assured the House of Commons that the Security Forces would rise to 'meet the challenge of these new tactics by the IRA with the resolution and courage that have served them so well in the past'. He did not hesitate in offering them 'all possible support in their vital task'.[36] The next day, King travelled to Bessbrook to see for himself the progress that had been made by the Army. He was left in little doubt of the challenges that still remained on the ground.[37] However, King was convinced that more intelligence-led operations would be needed in what he had called 'this vital fight to defeat the terrorists'.[38]

15

THE MAN IN THE ARENA

'It is not the critic who counts; not the man who points out how the strong man stumbles or where the doer of deeds could have done them better. The credit belongs to the man who is actually in the arena, whose face is marred by dust and sweat and blood; who strives valiantly; who errs, who comes short again and again, because there is no effort without error and shortcoming; but who does actually strive to do the deeds; who knows the great enthusiasms, the great devotions; who spends himself in a worthy cause; who at the best knows in the end the triumph of high achievement, and who at the worst, if he fails, at least fails while daring greatly, so that his place shall never be with those cold and timid souls who neither know victory nor defeat.'

– Theodore Roosevelt, *The Man in the Area*,
23 April 1910[1]

Loughgall, County Armagh, 7.30 p.m., 8 May 1987

By the summer of 1986, Martin McGuinness had turned his attention to a new strategy designed to remove the Security Forces' footprint from rural areas and thereby create the impression that the IRA had established 'liberated zones'. The IRA had first unveiled this strategy on 28 July 1986 in a statement in which it threatened the lives of those it regarded as 'collaborators'. Two days after issuing the warning, the group shot dead 40-year-old Protestant contractor John Kyle in Greencastle, County Tyrone, with further assassinations carried out in August and October of that year and again in April 1987. In implementing his rural strategy, McGuinness had devolved much of the day-to-day targeting to the 31-year-old commander of the East Tyrone IRA squad, Paddy Kelly, and his second in command, 31-year-old Jim Lynagh.[2] Nicknamed 'The Executioner', Lynagh was born in Tully estate in Monaghan and attended the Christian Brothers school in the town. He hailed from a well-read and well-educated family and was described by his comrades in the IRA as 'impish' with a 'good sense of humour'. Lynagh joined the IRA after witnessing the displacement of Catholic civilians south of the border in 1969. Shortly after joining the IRA, Lynagh was involved in a number of bomb attacks and narrowly escaped injury when a device he was carrying prematurely exploded in December 1973. After a brief spell in prison, he found himself helping Seamus McElwain rebuild his IRA brigade, which subsequently murdered over a dozen members of the Security Forces, as well as 86-year-old Sir Norman Stronge, a former unionist politician, and his son James at Tynan Abbey in County Armagh in January 1981. Throughout all of these activities, Lynagh and his comrades believed that they were fighting a classic guerrilla war. In emulating their heroes from other parts of the world, they sought to overrun rural Security Force bases. The two men had led an attack on Ballygawley RUC station on 7 December 1985, killing two officers: 52-year-old Reserve Constable William Clements and 34-year-old Constable George Gilliland. They launched a further attack involving up to three dozen terrorists on 11 August 1986 at the Birches RUC station near Portadown. The IRA team hijacked a JCB digger, rigged it with an explosive device, drove it into the station and detonated the bomb. Kelly and Lynagh made rural RUC stations their prime targets in the execution of this military strategy. One of the stations on Lynagh's radar was the isolated, part-time police station in the tiny village of Loughgall.

Situated in a valley notable for its richly cultivated farmland and orchards, Loughgall takes its name from the local Lough Gall, which is overlooked by the estate of Sir Anthony Cope, one of the first planters in Ulster, who arrived in Ireland in the early seventeenth century. The Cope estate was inherited by the family of British general Sir Gerald Templer, who would achieve fame as the 'Tiger of Malaya'. Loughgall was also the site of the founding of the highly secretive Orange Order, which initially met in Dan Winter's cottage near the Diamond in 1795. The church in Loughgall had been built shortly after the formation of the order, in the same year that the United Irishmen launched a rebellion against English rule. As Kelly and Lynagh prepped their weapons and explosives for an attack on the RUC station in the village, the significance of Loughgall could not have been far from their minds. The plan, like the earlier Birches attack, was that two volunteers would drive a JCB digger into the outer wall of the station and explode a 300–400lb bomb carried in its bucket. Six other volunteers would follow in a Hiace van, dismount from the vehicle and open fire on any RUC officers they found alive inside the station. It was a particularly ruthless form of attack, the intention of which was to ensure that no officers survived.

However, the two IRA squads did not know that a team of undercover soldiers and police officers were lying in wait for them at Loughgall. According to Detective Inspector Ian Phoenix, a local RUC commander in the regional TCG, information 'gathered from a variety of surveillance sources disclosed that the Provisionals were planning another "spectacular" along the lines of the Ballygawley and Birches attacks'.[3] Twenty-four hours before the attack, all-source reporting confirmed to Phoenix and his colleagues that the target was likely to be Loughgall station. Following consultation with Secretary of State for Northern Ireland Tom King,, the Security Forces set in motion Operation Judy to protect the station from attack. They were well used to this kind of warfare. Establishing the movements of guerrillas was an essential part of the broader British counter-insurgency strategy. This precept had been laid down by Britain's celebrated counter-insurgency expert Sir Robert Thompson in his book on guerrilla warfare:

> The insurgent is just as vulnerable, particularly to small-scale ambushes. There is constant insurgent movement by forces, supplies, couriers, agents and the like. The pattern of this movement on the ground is like a spider's web, and if the intelligence effort is directed on it, many possible targets can be selected which will disrupt the insurgent supply organisation and deny continued freedom of movement ... When good intelligence is limited, sweep-and-clear operations in insurgent-controlled territory may be necessary to keep the insurgent forces stirred up and off balance ... When intelligence improves (or as a result of another operation or insurgent attack) and an insurgent unit can be definitely located, then 'fix-and-destroy' operations are required.[4]

As a former paratrooper who had seen action in Borneo and South Yemen, Ian Phoenix was well aware of the need to keep the IRA off-balance, whether through increasing the number of Green Army patrols or by creating intelligence-led opportunities to neutralise IRA squads in the act. Having soldiered alongside the SAS in various operational theatres in the 1960s, Phoenix knew the value of strike operations.

As Kelly and Lynagh led their men into the village, a back-up team of three other IRA men waited in a vehicle not far away. Within minutes, the men heard the 'rip of the bomb' as it exploded. 'There was a rattle of stuff (gunshots) and then there was a rattle of heavy stuff (British Army GPMGs),' the getaway driver later recalled. 'I turned to (Scout 2) and said: "They are giving her some rattle here."' After three or four minutes, the gunfire dissipated. When the IRA volunteers failed to materialise, the getaway driver drove into the village and encountered two SAS men on the road, who trained their Armalites on the vehicle. 'They knew we were involved. They had observed us for 20 minutes before it,' he said. The IRA back-up team could see the dead bodies of their comrades strewn around the Hiace van ahead of them. 'I knew they were wiped out at the time. I could see the carnage down at the van,' recalled the driver. After a short time, more British soldiers appeared and ordered him and other drivers to turn around and leave the immediate vicinity. 'I turned the vehicle thinking we were going to get emptied,' added the IRA volunteer. The group did not get far before they were stopped at an RUC outer cordon, though they promptly waved on by a police officer, enabling them to leave the scene.[5]

One of Phoenix's most experienced officers, 'Jack', a member of E4 HMSU, was based in the Operations Room of Castle Hill Barracks in Dungannon for the duration of the mission. The third largest town in County Tyrone, with a population of 15,000 people, Dungannon is situated some 40 miles from Belfast but just 12 miles from the Irish border. The seat of the ancient O'Neill dynasty, by the late 1960s it had become a hive of civil rights activism. The town grew up around elevated terrain known locally as Castle Hill. It was home to nationalist politicians Bernadette Devlin and Austin Currie, as well as the birthplace of IRA volunteer Gerry McGeough, a close friend of the IRA men shot at Loughgall. As the HMSU's Liaison Officer, Jack explained his role in the incident:

The senior district police commander went home after an hour. He wasn't too interested. Told us to give him a call if anything happened. The Army Colonel present said he didn't want to leave for a swim in case it kicked off. We had two officers inside who had volunteered to remain in place to man the station. It came over the net that an attack was in progress. The Army had two helicopters ready to provide air cover. As soon as we got the word, I opened an envelope and briefed the Colonel that it was Loughgall station under attack. I said I needed to get up in the chopper. The Colonel was brilliant. We went out and boarded the helicopter as the ARF.[6]

The flight time to Loughgall was a matter of minutes. Hovering 3,000 feet above the police station, Jack saw the bodies of eight IRA men on the ground below. Checkpoints had been erected by his HMSU colleagues up to 20 miles from the station in a bid to catch their accomplices.[7]

Loughgall was a watershed in the violent competition between the IRA and Security Forces in more ways than one. It was the IRA's biggest loss of life since the Anglo–Irish War of Independence in 1919–21.[8] Black flags were flown in Catholic areas as republicans mourned their dead, Gerry Adams addressed a crowd of 2,000 people and Danny Morrison hinted at revenge.[9] Broader sympathy for the dead IRA men from the nationalist community soon diminished when senior RUC officer for the region, Harry Breen, put the terrorist weapons recovered at Loughgall on display for the world press. The weapons had been used in over seven murders and ten attempted murders in the previous sixteen months, including the killings of contractors Harry Henry and John Kyle and part-time UDR man William Graham.[10]

In the months after the Loughgall ambush, Army units based in the borderlands recorded 'a marked decrease in the number of almost all types of terrorist attacks', a significant step change 'because this situation has occurred in a historically very active TAOR'.[11] In his end-of-tour report, the CO of the 1st Battalion, Royal Hampshires, 42-year-old Lieutenant Colonel Andrew Freemantle, recorded how this was doubly significant when placed in the wider context of 'the overall level of terrorist violence in the Province [which] has increased sharply'.[12] Freemantle put this down to four key factors. Firstly, the high level of professional overt 'Framework'-type operations launched in their area of operations, making the circumstances 'less attractive to the terrorist' and forcing the IRA to go elsewhere or to 'wait until the "coast is clearer"'. Secondly, and perhaps most importantly, he observed that 'Intelligence and the covert/overt interface has improved in a climate of growing appreciation by all parties of the part overt troops have to play, especially in the maintenance of normality'. Thirdly, he highlighted the use of electronic countermeasures to prevent bomb attacks on troops. The fourth and final factor was that they had 'been lucky'.[13] Overall, Loughgall offered immediate respite to members of the Security Forces under constant attack from the IRA. For Regional Head of Special

Branch Frank Murray there was much to celebrate. On the evening of the ambush, as Murray's officers and Special Forces soldiers returned to their barracks, Murray opened a special bottle of brandy he had been reserving for such an occasion with a friend.

★ ★ ★

The ambush at Loughgall conveniently removed key players who might have opposed Gerry Adams' political strategy.[14] There was now an urgent need to protect the Sinn Féin president, who was at the top of the hit lists of the two main loyalist paramilitary organisations. On 11 March 1984, the UFF attempted a drive-by gun attack on Adams, which was thwarted by an off-duty RUC officer and two plain-clothes military police officers who had been in the vicinity. A UFF statement named Adams as 'the Chief of Staff of the IRA, responsible for the campaign of murder and therefore a legitimate target of war' and warned that the organisation would 'get him again'.[15] The UVF's former Director of Operations has since confirmed that the UVF had a team with 'heavier artillery' ready to hit Adams on the same day.[16] A few years later, the UFF made good on their promise of another attempt on Adams' life'. On 20 May 1987, Brian Nelson, the UFF's Intelligence Officer and FRU agent, informed his handlers that an attack was imminent.[17] The E4 HMSU was tasked with protecting Adams. 'Jack', a member of the unit who had been on Operation Judy, recalled:

> We saved Gerry Adams' life more than once. At least twice, if not three times. The loyalists had a simple plan. It was to be simple and effective. There was a cinema down there – it's now a hotel – and behind there Adams held court in a wee clinic where people would have been able to bring their problems. He used an armoured car – bulletproof except for the roof – and loyalists planned to drive by on a motorbike and plant a limpet mine on the roof. We stopped that. We saved Adams' life.[18]

Other E4 HMSU members stressed that they did not discriminate against people and were only too happy to protect the life of the leader of the Republican Movement. They were at pains to emphasise that this proved that they were not involved in systematic collusion with loyalist paramilitaries. 'Ronnie' echoed Jack's sentiment: 'Collusion? If there had been collusion, we'd have cut off the head of the snake. As it was, we tore a few strips off its body and took away its rattle.'[19] Interestingly, some statistics, particularly of people killed and injured, tend to support the suggestion that loyalist paramilitaries were not being given a helping hand in their targeting of republicans. Between 1979 and 1986, loyalist paramilitaries killed seventy-seven Catholics, only three of whom were Sinn Féin members.[20] The vast majority of their victims were selected on the basis of their perceived community affiliation.[21]

As well as saving the lives of Gerry Adams and other leading republicans from loyalist paramilitaries, the Security Forces were also having some success disrupting the IRA's arms shipments. On 31 October 1987, the *Eskund*, a Panamanian-flagged vessel, was intercepted by the French coastguard off the coast of Brittany. It had set sail from Tripoli, where it had been pre-loaded by Libyan Intelligence Officers with 150 tonnes of arms and explosives.[22] The cargo was valued at somewhere in the region of £15 million to £20 million and included 1,000 Romanian-made AK47 rifles, 600 Soviet F1 grenades, 10 Soviet 12.77mm DShK ('Dushka') heavy machine guns with anti-aircraft gun mounts, a large quantity of anti-tank recoilless rifles and ammunition, Beretta M12 9mm Belgian machine guns, two tonnes of Semtex explosives with detonators and fuses, and a vast array of RPG-7 tubes and ammunition, a quantity of mortars and 50 tons of ammunition.[23] There was enough war materiel to equip the IRA four times over and there was strong speculation that this was the largest of four similar shipments that had landed in Ireland.[24] With the IRA 'better armed than at any other time in its history',[25] the organisation was planning to escalate its attacks in a 'Tet Offensive', which was named after the massive wave of coordinated attacks on United States and South Vietnamese military bases across the Republic of Vietnam in 1968. Despite the logistical setback, Martin McGuinness and the rest of his Northern Command team authorised their border squads to up the ante, regardless of the risks of collateral damage.

★ ★ ★

War Memorial, Belmore Street, Enniskillen, 10.47 a.m., 8 November 1987

A crowd of men, women and children started to gather outside the community centre on the corner of Belmore Road. It was Remembrance

Sunday and people were quiet and solemn, assembling to remember their dead from two world wars and many subsequent campaigns in far-flung colonial outposts of a now-decayed British empire. Some people had memories of family members who had served. The vast majority were keenly aware of the damage inflicted on their community by the IRA over the previous two decades. Meanwhile, inside the community centre next to the cenotaph, a time bomb was ticking. The device consisted of 30lb of home-made explosives, with a small commercial or military explosive booster, rigged to detonate at 10.45 a.m., when members of the local community had arranged to assemble to pay their respects to their dead.[26] One former bomb-maker has since explained how IRA Explosives Officers constructed these devices:

> Powdered fertiliser was a key component in IRA bombs, so I got grinding. The fertiliser could only be bought in the Republic – in the North, it was coated in plastic to ensure it couldn't be ground down. One bag, costing about a fiver, was enough to take down a medium size building.[27]

The service had only just begun when the bomb exploded, resulting in the deaths of William and Agnes Mullan, both aged 73, who ran the pharmacy in the town; 73-year-old Kit Johnston, a retired ambulance driver, who was killed along with his wife, Jessica; 52-year-old Ted Armstrong, an off-duty RUC officer; 49-year-old Samuel Gault; 68-year-old John Megaw, a local pastor; Georgina Quinton, a retired RAF servicewoman; 62-year-old Wesley Armstrong, who was killed along with his wife, 53-year-old Bertha Armstrong; and 20-year-old nurse Marie Wilson.[28] Of those caught up in the blast, six belonged to the same Presbyterian church. In the aftermath of the explosion, an *Irish Times* journalist observed that the two communities managed to 'live their lives on two levels: privately, people can be viciously sectarian but publicly they can be the best of neighbours, and genuinely so'.[29]

The massacre at Enniskillen was regarded as one of the worst atrocities of the Troubles. At the time, IRA spokesmen denied that the group had deliberately targeted civilians and blamed the bomb on poor discipline within the ranks of a locally based squad. However, other IRA sources maintain that the group's Northern Command, the clearing house for all IRA operations, had approved the attack.[30] The organisation's statement read: 'The IRA admits responsibility for planting the bomb in Enniskillen yesterday which exploded with such catastrophic consequences. We deeply regret what occurred.'[31] Callously, the IRA even attempted to shift the blame to the Security Forces. 'The bomb', they claimed, might have been 'triggered by the British Army scanning high frequencies', reflecting 'an ongoing battle for supremacy between IRA and British Army electronic engineers over the use of remote control bombs'.[32] *Irish Times* journalists were not convinced: 'The graveyards of Northern Ireland bear silent testimony to the Provisionals' mistakes', the newspaper's editorial read.[33] For Adams and the political wing of the Republican Movement, a question mark hung over their 'direct influence over PIRA's operational planning'.[34] Attention now turned to the Security Forces, who came under pressure to stop further atrocities.

★ ★ ★

Sprucefield Roundabout, near Lisburn, 2.20 p.m., 3 February 1988

A large refrigerated lorry was making its way towards Lisburn when it was stopped at a joint E4 HMSU–Army checkpoint at the Sprucefield roundabout near Lisburn. In a search of the vehicle, police officers discovered 12,000 rounds of ammunition for pistols and rifles, two RPG rocket launchers and thirteen warheads, twenty RGD hand grenades, twenty limpet mines, fifteen AK-47 assault rifles, twelve handguns and one heavy machine gun with 2,500 rounds of 7.62mm rounds.[35] The seizure followed an announcement by Sir John Hermon some weeks earlier that the IRA was preparing to escalate its activities. Hermon accused the IRA of 'grasping at straws' after Enniskillen. 'Even among their own supporters the initial reaction was one of shame and disgust', observed journalists Patrick Bishop and Eamonn Mallie.[36] A senior IRA spokesman even admitted to both journalists that Enniskillen signalled the emergence of a new breed of IRA volunteer who was unfazed by the risks posed to civilians by such an attack. Despite assuring Bishop and Mallie that there would be 'no more Enniskillens', the seizure of weapons told a different story.[37] It was around this time that the Irish government passed its Extradition Act as a deterrent to IRA activities south of the border. In a coordinated effort, Irish Foreign Affairs minister Brian Lenihan dispatched his diplomats to take soundings from key members of the nationalist community on IRA thinking.

One Irish diplomat based in the Maryfield Secretariat, Brendan McMahon, paid a visit to the Maze Prison to meet head chaplain Father John Murphy. McMahon heard that IRA prisoners were actively monitoring Gerry Adams' talks with John Hume.[38] Father Murphy said the talks were happening 'against a background of a certain unspoken feeling among some Republicans that the "war" is probably not winnable in the short to medium term'. Interestingly, he also noted how older IRA prisoners were more inclined to support political initiatives while their younger comrades wanted the group to go ahead with 'one last push'. The effects of the Life Sentence Review Committee (which oversaw the extension of life sentences from ten or eleven years to thirteen or fourteen years) meant that those who had served lengthy prison terms were unlikely to return to active service. Father Murphy observed that there was now a 'significant difference between the generations, with the younger generation being less pure in its idealism and less disciplined with the result that there are differing perceptions and priorities between the generations'.[39]

Against this backdrop, Tom King issued a statement in the House of Commons on the Stalker and Sampson reports into the RUC 'shoot-to-kill' allegations that had arisen in the wake of the shootings in Lurgan in 1982. Both inquiries had formerly concluded, finding no evidence to suggest a cover-up. However, they did find proof of a breakdown in internal disciplinary processes and decision-making. As King told the House:

> Those questions go to the heart of the problems faced by a police force using the normal processes of the law while fighting a vicious and ruthless terrorist enemy. Intelligence is the lifeblood of that fight. Without it, the Security Forces are seriously handicapped. It is vital that it is protected. Moreover, knowledge of even the procedures used by special branch and other RUC officers will not only make their task still more difficult, but it will put lives at even greater risk. That is why the Security Forces are understandably and rightly so committed to protecting intelligence. But the lessons of those incidents show clearly that that desire must not operate outside effective accountability and control.[40]

King urged police officers to keep a sense of proportion at the forefront of their minds when dealing with terrorism. It was an unenviable task, according to recently retired Army commander, General Sir James Glover.

'The IRA can never be defeated,' he said on an episode of the BBC's flagship current affairs programme *Panorama* on 1 March 1988:

> The Army's role has been for some time to help to create the conditions where a full democratic peaceful political solution can be achieved. The IRA was much more professional. They are not just a bunch of mindless hoodlums and hooligans. They do have in their midst some astute, highly intelligent and very professional terrorists.[41]

The IRA's 'Long War' would continue, particularly as the group had the stamina and political motivation to do so. Glover alleged that Gerry Adams had restructured the IRA into 'less informer-susceptible four-man cells', claiming that 'no substantial military operation in Belfast could be mounted without his personal approval'.[42] Despite Glover's allegations, it was actually Northern Commander Martin McGuinness who was making many of the IRA's day-to-day operational decisions, in conjunction with the group's Chief of Staff, Kevin McKenna.

The E4 HMSU unit that had intercepted the Sprucefield arms cache was re-tasked to South Belfast to provide close protection to a building contractor earmarked for assassination by the IRA. 'Jack' recalled the routine he and his men followed while on protective duties:

> He got up at 6 a.m. every morning and was downstairs at ten past dressed in his shirt and clip-on tie … He worked around the clock. The intel suggested that he would be whacked by an IRA team as he sat in traffic. He always had an escort with him who travelled in an unmarked car. The plan was reactive. If the IRA attacked him, the Troop [SAS] would respond. One morning we were performing a CTR [Close Target Reconnaissance] on his house and I spotted Sean Savage riding past on a bicycle. He was a dedicated IRA volunteer. Next thing we know he didn't show up on the morning we thought he might attack the businessman. Then we were pulled from the op. It happened a lot. We didn't know why.[43]

Twenty-three-year-old Seán Savage had been an IRA member for only six years when he conducted his recce on the building contractor. He was a bright young man who had left school with eight O Levels and was said to be a keen cyclist, GAA player and photographer.[44] A dedicated volunteer,

Savage was regarded as a talented bomb-maker. GHQ plucked him from the contractor job and sent him overseas on a special mission.[45] Savage found himself playing a key role in Kevin McKenna's ambitious, multi-pronged strategy of attacking British national security targets in Northern Ireland, the UK and on the European mainland. Directly overseen by McKenna, the IRA embarked on a renewed offensive, which began with the bombing of the Officers' Mess at Rheindahlen Military Barracks, close to the border with Holland, in March 1987.[46] This was the first bombing in Germany in the six years since its ASU had attacked Herford Barracks. Then, almost a year to the day after the IRA bombed Rheindahlen, IRA volunteers were back on the Continent poised to carry out another, more deadly operation against a prestige military target.

16

THE BUTTON JOB

'I could never be satisfied with intelligence gathering until it was virtually perfectly able to tell us what is likely to happen.'

– George Younger, Secretary of State for Defence,
3 May 1988[1]

Rock of Gibraltar, Afternoon, 6 March 1988

The Joint Operations Room was alive with chatter. SAS soldiers intermingled with policemen and MI5 officers. There was a unity of purpose in the tasks they were carrying out professionally and collegiately. Everyone was aware of the gravity of their mission. Four weeks earlier, Spanish authorities had alerted the UK to the presence of three known IRA terrorists in Malaga, some 80 miles north-east of the Rock. This sighting was confirmed on 4 March, when the squad was spotted in the Spanish Riviera. MI5 cross-checked its intelligence with RUC Special Branch sources reporting almost certainly from inside the IRA's GHQ.[2] Once the intelligence was confirmed by surveillance undertaken in Gibraltar, it seemed that the likely target would be the Royal Anglian Regiment Band, which assembled for the Changing of the Guard ceremony outside the Governor's Residence every Tuesday morning at 11 a.m. The intelligence-led operation had been in place for many months. MI5 officers had even watched IRA member Siobhán O'Hanlon conduct a reconnaissance of the intended target on 20 February. After checking a poster advertising the Changing of the Guard event, she entered a Catholic church and lit a candle before kneeling in prayer. The next morning, she phoned IRA member Danny McCann and told him she would be staying on for a few days to observe the ceremony. After crossing back into Spain, O'Hanlon spotted a tail, which prompted her immediate return to Belfast.[3]

Despite O'Hanlon having been compromised, the operation was given the go-ahead by the IRA's GHQ, which had handpicked a special team consisting of 31-year-old Mairéad Farrell, 30-year-old Danny McCann and Seán Savage. Farrell was one of the organisation's most recognisable volunteers, having been the leader of IRA prisoners inside the women's prison in Armagh throughout the 1980s. A poster girl for the 'dirty protest' and the hunger strike, she was something of a radical in the more conservative ranks of the IRA. After her release from prison, she became an advisor to the PAC.[4] Farrell believed that women should be treated equally to men, particularly on IRA operations. Prior to the Gibraltar mission, she had been working on an operation to infiltrate the Police College at Garnerville in East Belfast, where she reportedly gave a lecture on human rights.[5] McCann was one of the IRA's 'most bloodthirsty gunmen' and had previously served a two-year sentence for possession of explosives. Along with Ivor Bell, he had been expelled from the organisation in 1985 for his dissenting views and had only recently been reinstated.[6] RUC Special Branch believed McCann to be 'responsible for a number of botched rocket-propelled grenade attacks' and linked him to twenty-six murders, including the deaths of two Special Branch officers in Belfast docks in 1987.[7] Savage was the nephew of IRA Army Council member Billy McKee[8] and an expert Explosives Officer who was part of the IRA's Engineering Department in Dundalk. The fact that the IRA had sent a recently released prisoner, a volunteer who had been court-martialled for being too hard line and a young master bomb-maker to Gibraltar highlighted the importance of the operation for the IRA.

MI5 officers from A Branch mounted surveillance of the three terrorist suspects.[9] Based at Euston Tower, near King's Cross in London, A Branch was a small group of technical surveillance specialists who watched terrorist suspects from 'vehicles, on foot and from fixed observation posts'. They were a 'curious mixture of people' from diverse walks of life: some were retired members of the military while others were supermarket managers.[10] The 'A Team', as they were known, provided technical solutions to security problems, often working in pairs to follow unsuspecting targets. One of their principal jobs in Gibraltar was to man static observation posts in buildings in the vicinity of the likely target.[11] This would be the A Team's 'biggest deployment so far, either at home or abroad'.[12]

As the A Team was setting up its equipment on the evening of 5 March, Gibraltar's Police Commissioner Joseph Canepa began his briefing in the Joint Ops Room. In attendance were seven members of the A Team, seven SAS soldiers and five police officers, including Chief Inspector Joseph Ullger, the Head of Special Branch in the colony.[13] Canepa dealt with the police aspect of the operation, while a senior member of the A Team explained the nature of the intelligence reporting and a senior SAS NCO covered the role of the military. MI5 were confident of the quality of their intelligence. The senior MI5 officer used a slide projector to show photographs of all three IRA suspects to those gathered. He briefed them, stating that all three suspects were 'dangerous terrorists who would almost certainly be armed and who, if confronted by security forces, would be likely to use their weapons'. In terms of the operation, he said that the terrorists would most likely use a car bomb. He was confident that the bomb would have been prepared in Spain and primed in Gibraltar. The MI5 officer discounted the likelihood of the IRA squad using a 'blocking' car to keep the space open into which the bomb vehicle would be driven open prior to the attack. He thought the IRA would not jeopardise its operational security by making two trips. As the briefing continued, the Army's Explosive Ordnance Disposal (EOD) expert described the device that would likely be used in the attack, making mention of a timer such as the one the IRA had used a few months earlier in Enniskillen. However, as the IRA's slaughter of civilians had caused an international outcry, it was deemed unlikely that they would repeat their mistake. The EOD expert informed the police officers, soldiers and Security Service officers that the device would most likely be remote-controlled, known colloquially as a 'button job', which meant it could be activated by the press of a button. The SAS NCO stressed to his men that the terrorists were 'ruthless and if confronted would resort to whatever weapons or "button jobs" they carried'.[14]

At 2.50 p.m., the IRA trio was spotted deep in conversation as they looked at the white Renault car they had parked in the vicinity of the Governor's Residence. Five minutes later, MI5 officers told Special Branch officer Detective Constable Viagas that they were 80 per cent certain that the three suspects were indeed Farrell, McCann and Savage. Thirty minutes later, Commissioner Canepa asked for positive identification, which he promptly received. The EOD expert was then tasked with checking the vehicle. He returned to the Joint Ops Room to confirm that the vehicle was a 'suspect car bomb'. At 3.40 p.m., Commissioner Canepa signed a form ordering the SAS to intercept and arrest the suspects. Once the form was signed, an SAS officer issued instructions to his men on the ground via the radio network. Within a few minutes, the soldiers confirmed their sightings of Farrell and McCann and, after a moment, Savage, who had just broken away from the other two and was walking in the opposite direction, along Winston Churchill Avenue. The soldiers were told that they could make an arrest.

As they closed in on Farrell and McCann, McCann looked back over his left shoulder. One of the soldiers drew his pistol, 'intending to shout a warning to stop at the same time, though he was uncertain if the words actually came out'. He claimed that McCann moved his hand as if he was going for a detonator. The soldier shot McCann in the back. Farrell also moved, 'grabbing her handbag under her left arm'. In the belief that she was 'going for a button', he shot her in the back.[15] Both IRA volunteers were shot at point-blank range. After they fell to the ground, a soldier fired another shot into McCann's body and two rounds into his head. Over twelve rounds of ammunition were fired at both suspects. Eyewitnesses later disputed the soldiers' recollection of events, with two civilians living in the apartment block across the road maintaining that they saw a woman and a man holding their hands above their heads as if surrendering before a 'fusillade of shots' rang out.[16] Four eyewitnesses, including three police officers, recalled hearing a warning of 'Police! Stop!' being shouted before the shooting began. Simultaneously, soldiers attempted to intercept Savage, who 'moved his right arm down to the area of his jacket pocket and adopted a threatening and aggressive stance'. A soldier shot him nine times in rapid succession. Given that the soldiers involved in the shootings had been dressed in civilian clothes, they immediately took out berets, pulling them onto their heads to distinguish them from terrorists as the police arrived. In total, the three IRA volunteers were hit twenty-seven times at close range, including several bullets fired into their heads as they lay on the ground.[17]

At 3.47 p.m., a message was received by the Joint Ops Room that the suspects had been apprehended. It did not become apparent that they had been shot dead until fifteen minutes later. Once the military handed back control of the situation to the police, a search of the three suspects' clothing and belongings yielded no weapons or detonating devices. The bomb disposal team found the boot of the suspect car empty. A hire car key ring found in Farrell's handbag led Spanish police to a Ford Fiesta parked in a basement car park in Marbella. When they searched the second vehicle, officers from the Malaga bomb disposal team discovered an explosive device concealed in the spare-wheel compartment of the boot. It consisted of five packets of Semtex explosive (weighing 64kg or 141lb), with four detonators and 200 rounds of ammunition. Attached to the bomb were two timers, marked ten hours forty-five minutes and eleven hours fifteen minutes respectively.

The device had not been primed, but if it had been, it would have caused considerable carnage. Explosions release a rapid burst of energy that forces light and heat outwards along with a shockwave. The average car bomb can carry up to several hundred pounds of explosives. The bigger the bomb, the bigger the blast radius. To ensure that they caused maximum damage, the IRA trio packed the rounds of ammunition around the explosive device, which meant that anyone within the blast radius of 500 feet would have been killed or seriously injured, with buildings damaged beyond repair.[18] Intercepting the IRA bomb team in Gibraltar, therefore, saved lives,[19] as well as strategically impacting on the organisation's ability to wage war.[20]

An IRA statement released a few days later was defiant. The group claimed that the 'only rules that the British have ever operated against our nation were "shoot-to-kill"' and said that the IRA remained 'undeterred'.[21] The final, haunting words on the matter were spoken by Mairéad Farrell, who had been interviewed for a television documentary shortly before her death: 'They can't control our minds, they can't get inside them: that's their failure.'[22] In another interview with *An Phoblacht*, Farrell highlighted the risks involved in IRA operations: 'You have to be realistic,' she said, 'you realise ultimately you're either going to be dead or end up in jail. It's either one or the other. You're not going to run forever.'[23]

However defiant the IRA may have been, Gibraltar was a major setback for Kevin McKenna and Martin McGuinness, who were overseeing the IRA's multi-pronged campaign. It seemed that Britain was moving at a brisk clip to contain the group within Northern Ireland. Good teamwork between the intelligence agencies was essential to the success of this strategy.

★ ★ ★

In the Shadow of Slieve Gullion, South Armagh, Summer 1988

At 1,893ft, Slieve Gullion is County Armagh's highest peak. Its summit affords a commanding view of the surrounding undulating landscape: hundreds of small fields bordered by dry-stone walls topped with blackthorn hedges and interspersed by farms and lakes. To the south of the peak is Dundalk Bay, with Bessbrook to the north, Cullyhanna to the west and the large town of Newry to the east. At the bottom of Gullion's eastern slopes lies the village of Killeen and the A1, one of the major routes from north to south. On the southern slopes lies the Ring of Gullion, which is thought to date back 6,000 years. These are remote and hilly parts of the Irish frontier and, like South Armagh generally, have long resisted external attempts to conquer and pacify them.[24] In this area, the British faced hostility unlike anything they had witnessed in any other part of their expansive empire. For much of the 1970s, South Armagh IRA squads were the tip of the militant republican spear. These close-knit groups were suspicious of outsiders and held republican convictions inspired by the geography, history, culture and traditions of the region.[25] Lieutenant Colonel Andrew Freemantle, the Hampshire Regiment CO who had previously served in the Australian Army during the Vietnam War, characterised South Armagh as 'a sort of Dallas/Hillbilly society that has, for many hundreds of years, operated on the fringe of the law', with many people in the area having done 'very well out of the current situation and profited handsomely from the proximity of the border'.[26] With considerable experience of counter-revolutionary warfare under his belt, Freemantle, like most commanders who soldiered in the area, judged the greatest threat to be 'the Provisional IRA and, in particular, the Crossmaglen PIRA who are possibly the most dedicated and professional terrorists in Northern Ireland'.[27] The bonds of loyalty shared between these volunteers was stronger than their loyalty to the broader Provisional movement. 'They were referred to as "the munchies" from the Irish *Muintir na hAite* for "locals"', recalled 'Síomón', one of the very few British agents ever to infiltrate the borderlands IRA.[28]

Thanks to the work of agents like Síomón, both Military Intelligence and Special Branch knew a considerable amount about the six men who sat on the South Armagh Brigade Staff.[29] They knew, for example, that the oldest man was 44 years of age and the youngest 32. They also knew that the Crossmaglen IRA, drawing its membership from Crossmaglen/ Cullaville and Silverbridge, consisted of some twenty-two members, the average age of whom was 31. Two of their more notable members were Brendan Burns and Brendan Moley, who died when a bomb they were transporting exploded prematurely on 29 February 1988. The unit was headed by Mr K, who was a specialist in home-made mortars and directing heavy gunfire at helicopters. He was also responsible for coordinating many of the hijackings and robberies in the area. The 'Cross Boys', as the squad were known locally, were the nerve centre of IRA operations in South Armagh, though IRA squads were spread right across the county, with an estimated sixteen members in the Camlough/North Lough IRA, eight in Castleblaney/Keady IRA, ten in Newry, nineteen in Dundalk, thirteen in Armagh City, thirteen in Monaghan, nine in Downpatrick, thirteen in Castlewellan/Newcastle and six in Kilcoo. A further fourteen men were to be found in South Mourne and seventeen in North Armagh. In total, the South Armagh Brigade numbered somewhere in the region of 166 members in 1988 and was heavily armed with 0.5 Browning heavy machine guns, Second World War-era MG-3s and M-60 general purpose machine guns, Armalite rifles (AR-15 and M16), M1 Garand 30.06 calibre rifles, Ruger Mini 14s and an assortment of 7.62mm calibre weapons. Additionally, the brigade was well equipped with the latest shipment of arms and explosives from Libya, including Semtex, SAM-7 missile launchers and RPG-7s.

The South Armagh Brigade was the biggest IRA unit outside Belfast and presented the single greatest security challenge to British Intelligence.[30] Síomón recalled: 'These guys were tight and ruthless; two ingredients which made it nearly impossible to compromise them.'[31] Opportunities, however, did present themselves, particularly as individual members were arrested or killed on 'active service'. After the killing of Seán Savage in Gibraltar, one such opening occurred in the IRA's Dundalk bomb factory. Síomón was one of those who got the call. 'Boy's a dear, I loved it. Where else would you get the chance to play with guns and blow things up?'[32] After several years of building up his cover, he found himself being 'Green-Booked' into the IRA only a few months prior to Savage's death. For the Security Forces, agents like Síomón were invaluable for they alone offered a glimpse inside the South Armagh IRA.

Forty-three-year-old Brigadier Charles G.C. Vyvyan had only been in charge of the newly reformed 3rd Infantry Brigade for a matter of months when he found himself overseeing one of the most dangerous regions in Northern Ireland. He was a great believer in creating uncertainty in the minds of terrorists by using intelligence to pre-empt attacks before they could be launched. He believed that every single soldier under his command needed to collect low-level intelligence, much of which could be gathered using a technique known as 'chatting up the farmer's daughters'.[33] Beyond this, Vyvyan said, it was up to individual COs to form good working relationships with Special Branch, which he saw as vital. There was considerable work to do here, including persuading the RUC that the Army was 'a precise and delicate instrument and that, given proper direction, it can work for them and produce results for them without jeopardising source security or other operations'.[34] Jeopardising long-term operations for short-term gains was discouraged by Vyvyan. Crucially, he was also convinced that the responsibility for recruiting sources was not limited to the FRU. He wrote:

> This perception must change; the recruiting of some of the best sources available over the last 19 years has frequently been started at the very lowest level with the right approach from a junior soldier on a routine task. All ranks must be made aware of the importance of being alert to the individual who shows any sign of being prepared to chat.[35]

Much would depend on how battalion intelligence sections briefed the men out on patrols on the ground.

By the late 1980s, Project 3702 had been replaced by 'two systems: "Vengeful", dedicated to vehicles, and "Crucible", for people', which drew on vast amounts of surveillance data on the population.[36] Green Army 'framework patrolling' was designed to assist in the profiling of the patterns of life of the main players, which were then fed into the system so they could be exploited by specialists in the FRU and Special Branch.[37] Beyond the deployment of soldiers to man checkpoints and conduct long-range COP duties, the British had developed a sophisticated network of surveillance towers along the border. This was labour-intensive. During their deployment in South Armagh, for instance, 40 Commando averaged some forty-five patrols every day, moving 1,000 men and 25,000lb of stores by helicopter, running 200 vehicle checkpoints and checking over 1,200 cars. One hundred and fifty men constantly manned sangars and OPs in watchtowers along the border.[38] In total, there were thirteen watchtowers located at Camlough and Camlough Mountain, Jonesborough Hill, Croslieve Hill, Sturgan Mountain, Glassdrumman, Cloghoge, Tievecrom, Sugarloaf Hill, Creevekeeran and Drummuckavall.[39] The most important of these was located at Glassdrumman. Its function was to provide 'surveillance of the surrounding countryside, enabling us to observe activity in the local area, including across the border, and to guide and support both military and RUC patrols. With constant surveillance we are able to build up a pattern of local life and hence unusual or suspicious activity is quickly spotted.'[40]

This surveillance offered the military a competitive advantage over the IRA, but it was arduous work. One troop of about thirty men would man the OP while the others patrolled the Crossmaglen and Forkhill areas. Most Marines spent up to three weeks in the towers, which were typically nothing more than a 70-foot-tall 8-foot square box atop 'submarine'-style accommodation in an underground bunker. 'The opposition', as the Marines termed the IRA, was 'well aware of the obstacle which the towers provide to their operations', and had 'been persistent in trying to rid themselves of the problem with marches and demonstrations, car bombs and mortar attacks'. Since July 1986, the watchtower at Glassdrumman had been targeted by the IRA in three mortar attacks and a proxy bomb attack. 'We spend much time in careful observation and logging to build up information, but the adrenalin spurts when occasional bangs and flashes occur around us,' one Marine recorded in his regimental magazine. 'Old border hands will be pleased to know that "Slab" [a prominent republican] is alive and well, only 2k from GDN.'[41] 40 Commando were eventually replaced by 1 PARA in July 1988.

The IRA was not a static organisation. The group was constantly under pressure from the Security Forces and had little room for manoeuvre. Despite the enormous human and signals intelligence and surveillance directed at them, they had developed their own sophisticated intelligence-gathering capability. With members and supporters in key roles at British Telecom, the Driver Licensing Authority, customs offices and post offices, they were able to acquire the ex-directory telephone numbers, addresses and vehicle registrations of many members of the RUC and the Army.[42] As one Special Branch officer observed, 'I would have presumed, and still presume, that they knew all our identities and to the best of their ability they would have known the vehicles we used as well. That was part of their – they had quite an effective intelligence capability.'[43] Some IRA volunteers openly admit that they were dispatched to Belfast to obtain maps of the local Newry and South Down area from the Ordnance Survey office on the pretext that they were pigeon fanciers.[44] The IRA used the maps to plot the trajectory of the mortar rockets they would use against British barracks. Flat-bed lorries would be used to transport the rocket systems, with black tape stuck onto the driver's window so that IRA volunteers could properly sight a vehicle in a firing position, thereby ensuring their deadly cargo was delivered onto a target such as a Security Forces base.[45] On 23 June 1988, the IRA managed to shoot down a Lynx helicopter in a multi-weapon attack, with a 12.7 DShK heavy machine gun used for the first time in Northern Ireland.[46]

By the late 1980s, the Security Forces determined that the South Armagh IRA was increasingly liaising with other units for assistance, with up to fifteen to twenty men involved in most attacks. As well as the terrorists pulling triggers or pressing switches on explosive devices, the IRA employed drivers, dickers (lookouts or scouts), explosives officers, escorts, engineers, financiers and quartermasters. Large-scale operations required more men and facilities. In the wake of an increase in IRA activity across the region in the summer months, South Armagh became more centralised, with two large squads concentrated in the north and another around the Newry/Dundalk border. This reorganisation was undertaken to preserve operational security. It was reported that one man, Mr Z, was so eager to take the IRA's war to the Army's bomb disposal experts that he began to appear at the scene of hoaxes to observe the Army's Tactics, Techniques and Procedures.[47]

On the morning of 23 July 1988, Mr Z and other members of his squad lay in wait for a passing vehicle on the Dublin Road, close to a Texaco garage, where they planned to explode a landmine and kill a member of the judiciary, Lord Justice Higgins. Instead, they murdered three members of the Hanna family, who were travelling home in their Mitsubishi Shogun from Dublin after a holiday in Disneyland in the United States. The force of the explosion blew the vehicle into a neighbouring field, completely destroying a nearby house and damaging a red Fiat and a cream Lada also travelling on the road. Soldiers from the Royal Regiment of Fusiliers were on a routine foot patrol about 2 kilometres away when they heard the explosion. An ambulance arrived within ten minutes to take the injured to hospital, while two other ambulances removed the bodies of the Hanna family. By the evening, Army bomb disposal and Scenes of Crime Officers were on the scene. One Army intelligence report read:

The murder of the HANNA family, although a grave mistake by the terrorist must have been a carefully planned operation with certainly few indicators that such an attack might take place. Serious questions must be asked about VIP's using the A1 Dublin route to the South, and how the terrorist can plan this kind of operation to such potential accuracy.[48]

As news reports of the attack started to filter through, one IRA man in the region who went by the nickname the 'Sick Psychopath' was in his local bar in Newry. It was said that he started to laugh and suggested to one of his comrades that they 'should go down and get the presents for the kids', referring to the family's gifts, which were strewn across the road after the explosion.[49] The CO of 1 PARA at the time, 39-year-old Lieutenant Colonel John Reith, observed in a report:

> It is difficult to believe that PIRA could have mistaken the Hannah [sic] family for that of Justice Higgins. In PR terms it would suit them far better to admit this than that a 'volunteer' had panicked at the approach of the patrol. In my view the latter is a more probable reason for the explosion occurring when it did.[50]

A few days later, the IRA struck again, detonating a bomb as a joint RUC–Army foot patrol passed along the Skerriff Road in Cullyhanna. One soldier was killed and several others were wounded.

As autumn approached, the RUC admitted that they were finding it almost impossible to neutralise all of the new explosives now in the IRA's inventory.[51] Semtex, the military-grade explosive manufactured by the Bohemian Chemical Company in Czechoslovakia, enabled the IRA's Engineering Department to develop innovative weapons. With the assistance of the NIO, the RUC commissioned a media campaign, appealing to the public to come forward with information on the IRA by calling the Confidential Telephone. Behind the scenes, the NIO increased the amount of money being transferred into the Chief Constable's 'B Account'. *The Times* newspaper reported an increase from an average payment of £5,000 to informers to a staggering £100,000 for information leading to the arrest of IRA leaders. Crucially, the paper also reported the formulation of new Standard Operating Procedures (SOPs) for a Joint Committee, involving the Army, the RUC and MI5.[52]

★ ★ ★

Heinsburg, German–Dutch Border, 11.33 p.m., 30 August 1988

Thirty-year-old Gerry McGeough had dreamt of being an IRA volunteer ever since he was a child. Fifty years after the Easter Rising, McGeough was enacting scenes of derring-do from RTÉ's drama series *Insurrection*, which he watched with his grandmother at her farm in Tyrone. As soon as he was old enough, the young McGeough joined the PIRA and established himself as one of its most active members.[53] On 13 June 1981, he had been involved in the attempted murder of UDR member Samuel Brush. With the Security Forces hot on his tail, he went on the run and became involved in acquiring arms for the IRA from the United States.[54] On 30 August 1988, McGeough and his close comrade, 29-year-old Gerry Hanratty, were in Europe attempting to cross the German–Dutch border, when they were apprehended by a border guard. A search of their vehicle yielded three .38 Webley Mk IV revolvers, with live and spent ammunition, two AK47 assault rifles, seven full magazines and one empty magazine, two fake Dutch number plates, two radio transceivers, 420 Deutschmarks, 2,800 Belgian francs and an assortment of Irish and Egyptian banknotes.[55] The two men had been in the lead vehicle in a two-car IRA move across the border into West Germany; however, the other car, a white Volkswagen Golf, anticipating trouble at the checkpoint, made a quick escape. An MI5 report on the incident confirmed:

> Ballistic tests have established that the two AK47s are the same weapons that were used to fire upon a German police car following the bombing of Glamorgan Barracks, Duisburg on 13 July (Box 500 132/88 refers). One of these weapons was also used in the murder of SAC Ian Shinner at Roermond, the Netherlands on 1 May. Ballistic comparisons of the rounds which killed Warrant Officer Heakin on 12 August at Ostend with the .38 Webley Mark IVs will be made on 6 September when a Belgian ballistics expert will visit the BKA. Of the two AK47s recovered only one still has its serial number. This is 1983 NK 1406, which reveals the weapon to be Romanian made fixed butt AKM of the type provided to PIRA by the Libyans. Over 250 of these weapons have been recovered in Northern Ireland and the Republic since early 1986.[56]

In light of the Gibraltar killings, the capture of McGeough and Hanratty by German authorities administered a *coup de grâce* to Kevin McKenna's multi-pronged strategy. Thereafter, the IRA would switch its focus back to Great Britain and Northern Ireland. The British were now in a much better position to defeat the Provisionals.

17

GRIPPING THE IRA

'The standard of intelligence and surveillance has reached a point where carrying out acts of terrorism has become highly risky.'

– Mark Urban, 'The secret war of Ulster's SB spooks and IRA touts', *The Independent*, 5 August 1989

38 Kildrum Gardens, Derry, 31 August 1988

Derry suffered irreparable economic damage as a result of the IRA's bombing campaign throughout the 1970s. Martin McGuinness had sent cars laden with explosives into the city centre, levelling some of the old, established businesses and deterring new investment. The violence had a direct effect on the city's prosperity, which ultimately deprived the people who lived there of jobs. Another consequence of McGuinness' campaign of terror was the forcible displacement of people from their homes, particularly in Protestant enclaves. High unemployment and sectarianism were a deadly mix. In Catholic, working-class areas, many young men eked out a meagre existence on the dole. The morale of both communities was low. The Inner City Trust, a not-for-profit organisation dedicated to improving socio-economic conditions in Derry, was 'transforming many derelict city centre sites', while the Northern Ireland Housing Executive demolished old terraced housing and flats to make way for more modern housing and new greenfield sites. Some community leaders, such as Protestant trade unionist Glen Barr, were calling for the appointment of a business tsar to help breathe new life back into the city and create new jobs.[1] The Brandywell, Martin McGuinness' own estate, had been badly affected. With the aid of community activists like Willie Carlin, the situation began to improve, but after Carlin's exfiltration, Sinn Féin seemed to lose direction at the local level, in large part thanks to the inability of activists to liaise with statutory bodies. Sinn Féin's mortal political enemies in the SDLP joined forces with unionist representatives to lobby the British government to meet the needs of ambitious regeneration projects.

Despite these attempts at economic modernisation, the two communities in Derry had moved poles apart. The drop in the number of Protestants living on the west bank of the River Foyle was stark. In 1971, 8,459 Protestants lived there, but by 1981 their numbers had declined to 2,874 and by the end of the decade only 1,407 Protestants lived on the west bank, with the number of Catholics growing from 33,951 to 48,233.[2] Fifty-four Protestants had been murdered in the city, in comparison to 109 Catholics and sixty-four members of the British Army.[3] Irish Congress of Trade Unions Northern Chairman Thomas Douglas told trade union delegates at a conference in the city that unemployment was helping paramilitary organisations to win more recruits: 'It is these ... conditions which lead to anger and frustration and provide an excellent recruitment opportunity for the men of violence.'[4] In spite of the early successes of the Fair Employment Agency, Catholics were more likely than Protestants to be unemployed. 'To a young Catholic who was unemployed in west Belfast or Derry,' *The Irish Times* reported, 'the fact that Catholics in the civil service or the public boards, or with jobs such as scientists, statisticians and professional engineers, may have increased, was irrelevant.' For a young Catholic at the bottom of the social strata, the 'harsh reality that he faced was that over the last decade it had become much more difficult for him to find a job and he suspected that his Protestant counterpart did not have the same difficulty, and he was right'.[5] Despite attempts to rejuvenate Derry's ailing economy, young unemployed men continued to swell the IRA's ranks.

This disaffection manifested itself chiefly in attacks on Army and police patrols, with the RUC sounding repeated warnings about the IRA's acquisition of Semtex. The Provisionals were increasingly using improvised grenades in these attacks.[6] The IRA had also developed a new technique that made defusing bombs even more challenging for the Army. In one public statement, the organisation said:

> When car bombs are planted, a small smoke grenade will explode shortly afterwards allowing members of the public to immediately identify the car and the area in question. Simultaneous with the smoke grenade going off, a microswitch will be activated which will sensitise the car to the extent that efforts to defuse it, using controlled explosions will immediately set off the main charge before its timing device has expired. British Army bomb disposal squads who attempt

to defuse car bombs early and before areas are properly evacuated will be responsible for endangering civilian lives.[7]

One of the bomb-makers pioneering this new technique in Derry was 28-year-old Paddy Flood. For much of the previous year, Flood had been one of the tiny number of volunteers with privileged access to the IRA's deadly new batch of Semtex explosives smuggled into Ireland from Libya.[8] MI5 had briefed Tom King regarding these explosives, prompting him to issue a statement to the press: 'At the moment, we do undoubtedly face a serious threat of terrorist violence which has been made worse, of course, by the support of Colonel Gadafy [*sic*], and the substantial weapons and explosives that he has made available.'[9]

Paddy Flood was eager to test out the Semtex with new IEDs in combination with a deadly new tactic.[10] The 'come on' (also known as 'the lure') had been used by the group in the murder of a civilian prison worker and two RUC officers at Magee College, and by 1988 they were employing it frequently. RUC Special Branch were keenly aware of this particular *modus operandi* and had issued a general warning to uniformed police officers and soldiers to avoid unverified call-outs. On 5 August 1988, the IRA hatched a plan to lure Security Forces to a house in Derry in order to kill them. This information was passed on to all police stations in the city so that their officers could be made aware of the threat. No address was given. Although the decision had been made to raise awareness, the Branch had 'no specific intelligence' with regard to any active terrorist plans.

Three weeks later, at 10 p.m. on 31 August, the IRA launched an audacious gun and bomb attack on Rosemount police station at the top of Creggan Hill. Two devices were thrown at the barracks and several shots were fired by a lone gunman. When the police and the Army deployed to secure the perimeter of the base, they discovered two unexploded devices, as well as both live and spent ammunition. Twenty minutes later, Special Branch recommended a halt to any further search of the area. Although no explanation was given, it is reasonable to assume that the attack was interpreted as part of an elaborate 'come on'.

At 10.35 p.m., the IRA abandoned a car in Kildrum Gardens, less than 2 miles west. Two calls were made to RUC Strand Road at 2.10 a.m., reporting an abandoned car in Kildrum Gardens. Eyewitnesses reported two men running away from the car shouting that there was a bomb inside. The bomb exploded twenty minutes later. The Security Forces refused to attend the scene as they suspected that a secondary device might be present. The information received by police switchboard operators was selective, suggesting that some of those who placed calls were complicit in the 'come on', either out of fear of or sympathy with the IRA. Special Branch recommended a moratorium on follow-up operations until the credibility of the threat posed to their colleagues could be checked with their network of sources in the city.

The next day, the Security Forces deployed to the area only to abandon their search efforts a few hours later, at 4.30 p.m., as a result of serious rioting. Initial inquiries by CID officers revealed some evidence that the bomb may have been an elaborate plan to kill Security Forces. At 4.56 p.m., the area was finally placed out of bounds by Special Branch. The information on which they were acting came directly from an agent who was graded as 'reliable', but who had 'limited access to local PIRA'.[11] At this stage, senior RUC commanders decided to 'let matters remain as they were until further intelligence could be obtained or a clear indication was received from the PIRA, which would pinpoint the device'. This decision was made in order to protect the source who had provided the intelligence, as well as the Security Forces in the vicinity of Creggan. For the Branch to have disclosed the nature of this secret information 'could have had fatal repercussions for the agent providing the intelligence on the booby trap device and that agent's active attempts to pin down its location'.[12] Those in receipt of the intelligence said that they had opted to allow their agent to locate the device and its technical specifications, which, they maintained, was the most 'rational and proportionate tactical decision'.[13]

The Derry IRA remained undeterred in their bid to lure Security Forces into the area of Kildrum Gardens. At 12.50 a.m. on 28 August, two armed men robbed a shop on Beechmount Avenue, conveniently dropping a piece of paper with a Kildrum Gardens address on it. The detectives investigating the robbery surmised that it may have been part of a 'come on'. However, they had limited access to the full intelligence picture because of the need-to-know principle. Additionally, they had not been made aware of the IRA's kidnapping of the man who lived at the property at 38 Kildrum Gardens. On 31 August, the man's neighbours, 54-year-old Sean Dalton, 68-year-old Sheila Lewis and 57-year-old Gerard Curran, were so anxious to establish their neighbour's whereabouts that they attempted to gain access to the flat themselves. Before they could do so, an explosion ripped through the building, killing Sean Dalton and

Sheila Lewis instantly and severely injuring Gerard Curran who died seven months later. Shortly after the explosion, the IRA issued a statement: 'This operation was designed to inflict casualties on members of the British Army search squad who were in the area. At no stage was it anticipated that a member of the public would enter the flat and open the booby-trapped door.'[14] The IRA's elaborate 'come on' had placed civilians in harm's way. Nevertheless, the delay in cross-checking the initial reports of an abandoned car in the area with two-legged sources, combined with a reluctance to share information, made a bad situation worse. The net result was an intelligence failure and the deaths of civilians.

This sluggishness in the sharing of intelligence was not limited to the RUC. There were still severe limitations on the central coordination of intelligence within the highest departments of the British state. Civil servant Peter N. Bell headed up the NIO's Security and International Liaison Division (known as 'SIL') in Whitehall, which had responsibility for harmonising relationships between the NIO, the Army, police and MI5. In a letter to his opposite number in the FCO, Ivor Roberts, Bell complained that there 'still remains too much "ad hoccery" in the way Whitehall grips, at the political levels especially, the kind of problem which IRA terrorism is likely to present us with over the coming months'. Citing the Gibraltar episode, he added:

At the beginning, the official arrangements for handling the operation were distinctly shaky – and led to a great deal of criticism of officials by Ministers. That has all ended now happily and new machinery is now in existence for dealing with any future counter-terrorist incidents of that nature. But I still remain concerned that in a less clear-cut situation, for example the flurry arising from alleged IRA activities in Sweden … we may be missing tricks owing to a lack of central direction and, possibly, deficiencies in co-ordination between the overt and the covert channels.[15]

Roberts replied to Bell a week later, empathising with the problem of bureaucratic inertia, though:

I think you are scratching the surface of a very deep pool. The arrangements for gripping PIRA are very political, as you know. MPSB, Box 500, and the RUC each have their role on the intelligence side.

Any one of the three will tell you privately about the shortcomings and lack of cooperativeness of the other two. I make no judgement on this – but the fact is that for all our natural advantages we do not have much really hard intelligence of attacks on the mainland or overseas. 'Flavius' was the exception rather than the rule, as shown by the string of shootings and bombings that preceded and followed it. But the entrenched interests and expertise involved are, I suspect, too great for this division of responsibility to be improved at anywhere below Ministerial level.[16]

Whitehall had clear difficulties in unifying its various security and intelligence tribes in Northern Ireland, divisions which, ironically, were reflected inside the IRA. The killings in Gibraltar sparked an internal inquiry within the IRA about how the British could have known about the operation. Its findings pointed to 'loose talk' amongst those involved, as well as leaks in West Belfast and County Louth.[17]

After Gibraltar, the IRA began to switch its focus back to England. Its recruitment of 'clean skins' and the establishment of a working alliance with criminal elements in gangland Britain increased. On 20 December 1988, a nervous IRA gunman opened fire on a man who approached him as he sat in a car outside a flat in Staplehurst Court in Clapham, South London. In a follow-up search of the area, armed police officers found guns, ammunition and 48kg of Semtex. Four weeks later, they discovered a target list of 100 prominent people the squad was planning to assassinate.[18] Home Secretary Douglas Hurd was livid. He told BBC Radio 4 listeners: 'With the Provisional IRA and some of these Middle East groups, it is really nothing to do with a political cause any more. They are professional killers. That is their occupation and their pleasure, and they will go on doing it. No political solution will cope with that. They just have to be extirpated.'[19] Hurd's tough talk reflected a view now prevalent in Thatcher's Cabinet after Gibraltar that the only way to deal with the IRA was by responding with force as and when the opportunity arose.

★ ★ ★

Around noon on 20 March 1989, Detective Chief Superintendent Frank Murray noticed an increase in signals traffic in South Armagh. Something big was happening and it had roused the entire network of IRA members in the region. Murray could not be certain what was causing the spike and rudimentary traffic analysis could only tell him that a large group of people was on the move, not why.[20] He spent the rest of the afternoon checking with his source handlers and Army COP teams to determine which key players were moving around. South Armagh PIRA was something of a sleeping giant at times like these, shaking the ground as it awakened from its slumber. If the group was roused, something serious was afoot. Murray had to find out what, but by the time he had roused his own team, the IRA operation was nearing its culmination.

At 3.35 p.m., two of the RUC's most senior officers for the region, Chief Superintendent Harry Breen and Superintendent Bob Buchanan, were leaving a meeting with the Gardaí at which they had been discussing a major cross-border operation against prominent republican Thomas 'Slab' Murray.[21] The operation had been personally ordered by Tom King at a function in Stormont Castle a week earlier and, despite some apprehension amongst the police officers, was scheduled to take place within the coming weeks.[22] After the meeting, Breen and Buchanan made their way along the Edenappa Road in Buchanan's unmarked vehicle. As they neared Jonesborough, Buchanan spotted men in combat gear up ahead. Slowing down in anticipation of an Army patrol, the RUC men realised that they had driven into an IRA ambush. The rear doors of the van up ahead of them were flung open to reveal several men armed with AK47 rifles. Buchanan quickly put the car into reverse, but it was too late. A round passed into his skull, killing him instantly and causing the car to crash into a dry-stone wall. In a panic, Breen attempted to radio for support before climbing out of the car holding up a white handkerchief as if to surrender. An IRA gunman walked up to him and shot him in the head.[23]

The double murder of such high-ranking police officers was a body blow to Thatcher's policy of increasing cross-border cooperation under the Anglo–Irish Agreement. In the aftermath of the attack, Frank Murray was furious that he hadn't been able to crack the code to the traffic analysis in time. The Army's Intelligence Officer attached to TCG South at the time was Major Ian Liles. He later remembered that, 'after considerable analysis' of the traffic, it was determined that an IRA operation was underway, involving 'up to 70 personnel, not all of them would have known what was happening, there is no doubt about that, and this would have included what were referred to as dickers, lookouts, people checking for helicopters, checking roads for army and police patrols'.[24] If this is true, this operation involved just under half of the South Armagh Brigade and would have required considerable discipline to limit the flow of information regarding the intended target.

The murders of Breen and Buchanan did not terminate the RUC's investigation into IRA criminality; if anything, it re-energised those involved in the investigation. So, in a bid to obliterate any prospect of a coordinated Gardaí–RUC move on smuggling, the six men on the South Armagh Brigade Staff decided that it was time to send out a warning to anyone thinking of supplying information to the police.

Forty-eight-year-old John McAnulty was regarded as something of a loveable rogue in the town of Warrenpoint. Nicknamed 'Big Note', McAnulty had, for many years, been involved in cross-border grain smuggling, which brought him to the attention of the IRA.[25] One summer's evening in July 1989, McAnulty was abducted by six armed and masked men as he left the Rosewood Country Club near Dundalk, where he had been enjoying a meal with his ex-wife.[26] The IRA squad that abducted him cut the telephone wires, making it impossible for his wife to call the police. When she returned to the scene, she found her ex-husband's blood-stained wedding ring lying in the car park.[27] Like so many others before him, McAnulty had been spirited away to the Omeath safe house, where he was interrogated and tortured. His body was later found face down in a ditch on a road near Cullaville. His head, marked only by a single gunshot wound, was covered with an orange shopping bag. In a press statement, the IRA claimed that McAnulty was an informer and had met his RUC handler in a car park in Banbridge and that the officer was based in Bessbrook. The organisation stated that, 'He admitted under questioning that he had supplied specific information concerning IRA activities in the area.'[28] There is still considerable controversy regarding the IRA's motive for killing McAnulty. If he was a criminal, it is plausible that rubbing up against the IRA and his refusal to pay protection money was the reason for his demise. Whatever the real reason, *The Irish Times* concluded that a 'chill atmosphere' had descended on South Armagh:

> The people of South Armagh are depressingly familiar with the deadly undertow of violence in the murky waters of what has come to be accepted, in some areas, as everyday commerce; where the barely legal rubs shoulders with the blatantly illegal and invasions of both by paramilitary gangsterism are commonplace.[29]

Crime reporter Jim Cusack went further, speculating on the IRA's *modus operandi* in terms of its abductions of suspected informers:

> His killing fits a well established pattern established in the area in the past decade. Both the IRA and INLA have operated this system of killings, whereby they abduct and shoot their victims in the Republic and then dump the bodies inside the North. This means the Gardaí are left investigating one part of the crime, in this case the abduction, while the RUC investigate the actual murder, as the murder investigation takes place in the jurisdiction where the body is found.[30]

McAnulty was the twelfth person accused of being an informer to have been shot and dumped on a lonely border road.

Fifty-five-year-old Peter Brooke had not been in his job as Secretary of State long when his advisors suggested that he convene a press conference to mark his first 100 days at Stormont. Brooke was a shrewd political operator, adept at fielding difficult questions, but even he could not dodge the question preoccupying the minds of many people at the time: could the IRA be defeated? Brooke stated:

> In terms of the late 20th Century terrorist, organised as well as the Provisional IRA have become, that it is difficult to envisage a military defeat of such a force because of the circumstances under which they operate though the Security Forces can exercise a policy of containment to enable, broadly speaking, normal life to go on within the province.[31]

He continued:

> It would require a decision on the part of the terrorists that the game had ceased to be worth the candle, that considering the lifestyle they have to adopt, that the return which they were securing from their activities did not justify the costs that it was imposing in personal terms on those who were engaged in their activities.[32]

Brooke concluded by telling the reporters gathered, 'I'm not going to be inflexible in my language now and in any way hem in what position we might adopt at some stage in totally different circumstances,' he said.[33]

Brooke's comments were immediately seized upon by Gerry Adams, who said he was 'prepared to talk at any time to bring about the conditions for a lasting peace in Ireland'. Amongst unionists, however, the comments caused uproar. However, Brooke's remarks came in the wake of similar views expressed publicly over the preceding twelve months by retired generals Harry Tuzo and Jimmy Glover, both of whom had been at the forefront of operations in Northern Ireland in the 1970s and 1980s. Interestingly, Brooke drew a comparison with Cyprus, where British Security Forces had fought George Grivas' EOKA terrorist group in the late 1950s, a situation that had set a precedent for talking to terrorists. Nevertheless, Brooke's comparison rang hollow with many unionists and he was rebuked by Democratic Unionist Party (DUP) leader Ian Paisley. The only person to voice support for Brooke's position was Liberal Democrat leader Paddy Ashdown, who also had first-hand experience of soldiering in Northern Ireland. In an incredibly far-sighted observation, Ashdown explained that 'oppressive military action' offered only a short-term solution to what was, at its heart, a political problem.[34] Brooke subsequently qualified his remarks by suggesting that the terrorists could not hope to win. Behind the scenes, the DCI, John Deverell, had just learned of an operation by his counterpart in MI6, Michael Oatley, to establish a secret 'bamboo pipe' to channel messages between Intelligence Officers in London and the PIRA. Oliver Miles, who served as the political adviser to Peter Brooke, said that he was unaware of this clandestine rapprochement with the IRA, which suggests that Brooke may have, initially at least, been kept in the dark regarding these developments.

★ ★ ★

On 13 December, members of the Newry IRA launched a flying column-style attack on the PVCP at Derryard in Rosslea, County Fermanagh. Manned by troops from the King's Own Scottish Borderers, the attack killed two soldiers and wounded several others. The weapons used in the attack had been part of the earlier Libya shipments. 'Síomón' was close to those who carried out the attack. He recalled that those involved later boasted about what they had done:

Mr V and Mr Y were on the Derryard job. That came from Dundalk. They'd a jimpy [GPMG] on the side of the lorry. They took over a house the night before. Those boys had body armour on. They attacked the PVCP and shot the soldiers. Mr Y killed two of the soldiers. Shot them close, then Mr V went up and finished them off. He took a brand new Browning Hi-Power pistol from the body of one of the soldiers. The IRA had AKMs with them. One of the boys had sawn off the front grip on his rifle. They used pipe bombs, stuffed with Semtex and copper as directional charges. They wrecked the place. Bean tins with copper inside – a copper cone – if you look at a lot of stuff from the Second World War, it's all there.[35]

Through agents of influence like Síomón, the Security Forces were able to compile *post hoc* information on attacks like Derryard, even if they could not necessarily prevent them. It was also necessary to turn intelligence into evidence for the courts, a challenge that forced the Security Forces to practise the art of strategic patience. Journalist Mark Urban observed at the time:

Sometimes security chiefs are presented with the dilemma of knowing that an operation is about to be carried out but fearing that arresting the would-be perpetrators would alert the IRA to the presence of an informant, so placing his or her life in jeopardy. Under such circumstances, patrols or checkpoints by uniformed soldiers may be stepped up and these often deter the terrorists. The IRA cannot be certain why the patrols were increased, so the identity of the mole is protected.[36]

The human factor made it difficult to fully manipulate events on the ground, as an incident in West Belfast in the new year would illustrate perfectly.

18

FOOLS HANDLING FOOLS

'No matter what's down on paper about the number of spies, you always have to factor in fools handling fools. That it can happen. That you give some fool the job of handling another fool. And what really comes out of it?'

> – Anthony McIntyre, former member of the PIRA (2019)[1]

'We're from the IRA security unit – don't move or we'll fucking shoot ye,' recalled one man who claimed to have insights into the IRA's Internal Security Department's *modus operandi*:

> Once the fella was arrested, he'd be stripped, his clothes swept for bugs and he'd be told to put on a boiler suit. His hands would be plastic-cuffed and he'd be ordered to get down. A van would have been hired a few days before and a curtain put up behind the driver so they couldn't see out. Those arrested would be told [prior to their abduction] that they'd be going on a training camp for a week so they could tell their families they'd be away. After the gun was produced [if he resisted], it'd have been got rid of on the off chance the Guards stopped the van at a checkpoint. If that happened, the cuffs would be snipped and the fella would be told to say 'we were out for a spin'. So, they couldn't say they were tortured [if they were released], cotton wool pads would be placed over their eyes and their head wrapped in crepe ties [like medical staff would have done to the victim of a head injury]. No violence was inflicted [unless they struggled]. Everyone was told shhh! Silence. Deadly quiet. Then, when we got to the cottage, they'd be marched up into the house. When the interrogation was ready to start, they'd be brought into the kitchen or the living room.[2]

It was a lonely experience for abductees, who were frequently subjected to psychological torment during their captivity. The 'shock of capture' and the need to keep the abducted person off-balance was greatly accentuated by the Nutting Squad, which 'routinely used violence and sensory deprivation against suspects and employed the IRA equivalent of water-boarding against some'.[3]

The success of the IRA's very own gestapo in extracting the information they needed from people owed much to the presence of former soldiers in the ranks of the Nutting Squad. The leader of the squad for over a decade was John Joe Magee.[4] Born in 1929, Magee had served in the Royal Marines and Special Boat Service in the 1950s and 1960s before returning home to his native Belfast, where he promptly joined the Provisionals. 'J.J. Magee had apparently been caught with ammunition in a house in Drew Street in 1970,' former IRA volunteer Anthony McIntyre recalled. 'He was on the battalion staff and the camp staff. I knew him in Magilligan in the early 1970s and mid-1970s until his release.'[5] Although originally from Belfast, Magee later relocated with his wife and family to a modest three-bed terraced house not far from the GAA stadium in central Dundalk.[6] The majority of the interrogations of suspected informers took place within a 15-mile radius of his home near the Cooley Peninsula.

Magee's squad liked to abduct suspected informers in Northern Ireland and take them over the border to Omeath in County Louth, which had long been a safe haven for the IRA and the launch pad for its massacre at Narrow Water on 27 August 1979. 'It was one of the most picturesque parts of Ireland,' recalled 'Síomón', a former IRA associate, who said 'the smell of sea air was the first thing to hit the back of your throat. It was beautiful.'[7] Surrounded by quaint emerald fields and hedgerows was an IRA safe house belonging to the brother of a member of the organisation who was frequently away on business. Magee and the Nutting Squad brought their captives to this house on several occasions during its most active years. Síomón recalled: 'If it was decided they'd be killed, they were shot there and then. Sometimes brains went everywhere; at other times, the head just swole up and they looked stunned before they dropped.'[8]

Síomón continued:

> The arrested man would have to sit a test set by John Joe Magee. It was like the Eleven Plus. He'd be quizzed for days. His answers pored over and interrogated. It was impressive to watch. J.J. would have gone over and over the small details. Then the cassettes would've been taken from J.J. to 'Mr W.' [an IRA commander in South Armagh, who

was the 'link man' to the Army Council]. He'd run the tape through a stress analysis machine the IRA had brought in from the US. The whole interrogation process was planned for days. Toilet roll and food would've been collected and plastic sheeting put down. Once the guys went in, they wouldn't want to come out for a week. John Joe was an ignorant big shite but he was very methodical. He was a details man. I'd never seen anything like it.[9]

Magee was a stickler for IRA rules and regulations. Given that the IRA was a hierarchical organisation with a chain of command, its actions were rigorously policed by enforcers like Magee, who swore by its *Green Book*, which explicitly dictated that '[n]o members should succumb to approaches or overtures, blackmail or bribery attempts, made by the enemy and should report such approaches as soon as possible'. The penalty for those found guilty of treason was death. Additionally, it maintained that any volunteer who 'seizes or is party to the seizure of arms, ammunition or explosives which are being held under Army control, shall be deemed guilty of treachery. A duly constituted Court-martial shall try all cases'. The *Green Book* made it clear that the death penalty and other sanctions 'must be ratified by the Army Council'.[10]

Although he was considered one of the originals, some of Magee's IRA comrades regarded him with suspicion. As Anthony McIntyre explains:

> In 1977 a member of the Army Council [believed to be Billy McKee], after John Joe Magee came out of prison, directed that John Joe Magee be shot dead – along with two loyalists – for running a brothel on the Falls Road and that each of the women, sex workers, were to be shot in the leg, not killed. J.J. Magee was seriously, seriously mistrusted back in the '70s. How he emerged to come to the position he did later on ... I don't know. And I don't have any evidence. But there were serious suspicions that J.J. Magee was an informer.[11]

McIntyre recounts a conversation he had about Magee with Brendan Hughes, one of the IRA's most respected senior commanders, in his cell in 1986:

> In 1986, in the jail, Brendan Hughes came to me and we were talking about IRA strategy – where the Army should go [etc.]. And I'd said

to Brendan, 'We will be penetrated.' And I said, 'I'm convinced we are being currently penetrated.' [And Brendan asked] 'Where?' And I said, 'By the Security Department.' And he asked me, 'Why?' And I said, 'Because the Security Department are in position for a long time. They don't go to jail and they would be a great asset to have for the British. You know your man's guaranteed to be there.' And as myself and Brendan sat down, he came to a conclusion – he ended up agreeing with me – because he had his own suspicions about two people. And he thought one of them, definitely, had to be an agent. He didn't know which one, but he thought one of them would be. And it was because they were so centrally placed. They were like the electrical junction box that every wire went through. They called them the 'Clapham Junction'. They knew who were coming into the IRA because they had to give them security clearance. They had to go in and investigate IRA operations that went wrong and, of course, in investigating IRA operations that went wrong, they would have known who were doing the operations. And if you are in the Northern Command or GHQ Security Department and you are going into every other area, you very quickly get a map of the IRA. But, because it's not your job to know about an operation in advance, you'll not be part of an inquiry into an operation that goes wrong but you've already told your handlers who the key players are. So, they just have to watch the key players. They just have to watch the patterns. And then they catch them. And then when the IRA go in to do its investigation, even if the agent himself is not managing the investigation, nobody can trace this back to the agent 'cause the agent had no knowledge in advance of the operation. But he had enough information for the British to know who the key players were and from there on to focus on them. And, slowly, slowly, softly, softly, catch the monkey.[12]

Not long after his conversation with McIntyre, Hughes was released from prison. His first action was to report back to the IRA. He was soon appointed to Northern Command and placed in overall charge of IRA Internal Security.

'There was a major problem with informants,' Hughes recalled. 'And one of the jobs that I had taken on was to try and find informers. The Army, the IRA, always had a problem with informers; there were always informers around – low-level informants, high-level informants – but by that stage, by the late 1980s, there was an awful sense of mistrust.'[13] Penetration of the IRA had reached a peak by the late 1980s. Many operations had to be cancelled or aborted, even while in motion, because of extensive intelligence coverage. McIntyre recalled that Hughes began to harbour serious reservations about John Joe Magee:

> There is suspicion. Brendan Hughes said J.J. Magee was an informer and working for them [British Intelligence]. Brendan Hughes told me that J.J. Magee's flat in Distillery Street, where he lived, was bugged. J.J. Magee was responsible for serious investigations by the IRA Internal Security Department in … Armagh … And Brendan said there were serious issues with J.J. Magee, John Joe, and he thought he was an informer.[14]

McIntyre said Magee was not considered 'beyond reproach' within IRA circles. 'I spoke to the person who was on the Army Council at the time,' said McIntyre:

> At one time he was the President of the Army Council – and he told me very, very emphatically about J.J. Magee. So, he was not regarded as somebody who was beyond reproach in the way you have senior figures like Seamus Twomey and those people, [including] Billy McKee, were all regarded as being beyond reproach because they had been there from the '40s.[15]

As Hughes closed in on suspected informers, he found himself promoted again, this time to a position on the Army Council. In his new position, he was preoccupied with more strategic matters and never did find conclusive proof that Magee was an agent.[16] However, events in the new year further fuelled suspicions about informers inside the IRA.

★ ★ ★

Carrigart Avenue, Lenadoon, West Belfast, Evening, 5 January 1990

It was a bitterly cold winter's evening. Thirty-seven-year-old Danny Morrison, Sinn Féin's Director of Publicity, and his party colleague, 39-year-old

John 'Anto' Murray, were on their way to meet a man who had just admitted to being a police informer.[17] Thirty-four-year-old Sandy Lynch was part of 'an IRA intelligence unit responsible for selecting targets' when he was arrested by IRA Internal Security and taken to a house in a quiet cul-de-sac in the Lenadoon Estate in West Belfast for interrogation.[18] The IRA believed that Lynch had been passing information to the RUC Special Branch for a regular payment. During his interrogation, he was allegedly told by one man, Freddie Scappaticci, that he was a 'touting bastard' and faced the prospect of being taken to remote parts of South Armagh 'where he would be "hung upside down until he confessed"'.[19] It dawned on Lynch that he was in the same place another suspected informer, Joe Fenton, had been taken to almost a year earlier.[20] Fenton, a 35-year-old father of four, was an estate agent who had allowed the IRA to use several of his properties across Belfast. The IRA said he had worked for Special Branch for almost a decade as a result of a mixture of 'threats and blandishments'.[21] Fenton's suspected betrayal of IRA volunteers was discovered by Brendan Hughes, who told journalist Martin Dillon that he believed Fenton was sacrificed by British Intelligence to keep a more important agent in place. 'Fenton was not the first and will not be the last,' Hughes warned.[22]

As Danny Morrison approached the house in Carrigart Avenue, he heard the distinctive roar of RUC Land Rovers. He attempted to escape by making his way to the back garden, where he narrowly avoided being shot by a soldier who was lying in wait. Although he was ordered to halt, Morrison jumped over a fence and entered an adjacent property, the startled occupants of which had been relaxing in front of the television. He was promptly arrested by police officers, along with the occupants of the house where the interrogation of Sandy Lynch was taking place.[23]

Lynch's rescue and Morrison's arrest were a coup for the authorities. They had netted one of the highest-profile republicans in the city, though the subsequent trial threatened to unravel when Lynch admitted to lying. Lynch also made a startling revelation that he had taken part in a bomb attack on the Shorts aircraft-manufacturing plant in East Belfast. As he told the court, 'I had no option but to take part. I was told to get involved. I defused one bomb and made sure two others would not go off.' Lynch claimed that he became an RUC informer in order to 'save lives'.[24] Lynch was one of the lucky ones. Up until that point, the IRA had executed several people whom it had accused of passing information to the authorities. IRA volunteers like Tommy Gorman had little sympathy for those who betrayed the organisation. As he recalled, 'It was a minority of people who were active on IRA operations. The other people were a lot of dead wood.' He argued that it was in this latter group that 'the touts can thrive. I mean hidden away in the undergrowth, you know. You wouldn't know they were there.'[25]

The ability of agents to hide in plain sight had concerned Brendan Hughes ever since the UVF murder of 33-year-old Brendan 'Ruby' Davison on 25 July 1988. Davison had joined the IRA at the outset of the Troubles and was later imprisoned for his role in a bomb attack on Security Forces in 1971. After his release in 1980, he steadily rose up through the ranks of the IRA to become the OC of the Markets area. Much of Davison's reputation was based on his experience as an interrogator in the Nutting Squad and as the man who 'played a big part in holding things together' for the Belfast IRA in the mid-1980s.[26] According to some reports, Davison was killed in retaliation for the IRA assassination of prominent UVF member Robert 'Squeak' Seymour on 15 June 1988. One loyalist said that the information given to the UVF at the time came 'from Davison's own people', who wanted him dead because of his involvement in child abuse.[27] It was not the first time Davison had been targeted by the UVF. He was shot four times by the group as he stood in a bookmakers on 30 May 1987.[28] Davison was such an important IRA figure that Gerry Adams carried his coffin. Davison's uncle by marriage was Freddie Scappaticci, who marshalled the cortège at his funeral. It has since been alleged that Scappaticci knew that Davison was an informer and had even 'tried in vain' to deflect the cloud of suspicion.[29] In any case, the UVF saved the IRA the trouble of having to abduct, torture and execute a man who many believed had betrayed his comrades when they shot him dead.

★ ★ ★

Stormont Castle, Belfast, 23 January 1990

Fifty-nine-year-old Sir John Blelloch was the only Permanent Under Secretary of State to have returned to serve a second senior appointment in the NIO. He had developed a great affection for Northern Ireland and 'enjoyed the professional bonus of knowing the background to almost all issues that arose'.[30] He had considerable insight into security matters, having served as a Deputy Secretary in the MoD Main Building before returning to Belfast. Blelloch had joined the civil service after graduating from Cambridge and was appointed Private Secretary to successive Parliamentary Under Secretaries of State for War, Fitzroy Maclean and Julian Amery, in 1956–58.[31] A 'neat, slightly stooped man, with a twinkle and a wry sense of humour', Blelloch 'looked, spoke and behaved like a quintessential civil servant'. He was considered 'able, patriotic and sympathetic' and it was felt that the NIO was in safe hands as he moved into his final year at the helm.[32]

It was late January 1990 when Blelloch sat down to draft a comprehensive strategic analysis of the security situation. Known as the 'Defeating Terrorism Papers', Blelloch wrote of tackling terrorism 'vigorously', emphasising that the 'ultimate objective of security policy is, therefore, to force PIRA to end its campaign of violence' and, pending the achievement of this objective, the aim is to 'secure a quantifiable reduction, and a continuing downward trend, in levels of violence'.[33] Intriguingly, the government sought to measure success through increasing prosecutions, arms finds, the interdiction of operations and the disruption of sources of weapons and explosives supplies. Blelloch was eager to provide the basis for a whole-of-government approach to combatting the PIRA. The Defeating Terrorism Papers covered three principal themes: strategy, threat and context. Blelloch classified the IRA's objectives as 'long-term' and 'intermediate'. The IRA's long-term objective was British withdrawal, which seemed oblivious to the reality that there were one million unionists living in Northern Ireland. Blelloch believed that this long-term objective was unlikely to be achieved and so the IRA would, instead, seek to secure their intermediate goals of making Northern Ireland unworkable, provoking the Security Forces into overreacting, thereby compromising the British state's legitimacy, and, lastly, destabilising everyday life in Northern Ireland.

Blelloch identified three categories of resources that the IRA needed to sustain their campaign. The first was people, as the group needed to be able to draw on a significant pool of volunteers. 'PIRA's terrorist operations are now carried out chiefly by small self-contained cells or units,' wrote Blelloch. These were 'increasingly independent of wider nationalist community support and correspondingly harder for the Security Forces to penetrate'. Second, motivation – the IRA could draw on a well-motivated cadre of individuals who believed that Britain would eventually withdraw from Northern Ireland if republicans continued with their 'armed struggle'. Thirdly, Blelloch believed that the IRA had the materiel, in terms of weapons, explosives and money, to 'sustain their campaign into the foreseeable future'. In Blelloch's view:

> The PIRA campaign of violence will end when PIRA and/or its supporters are brought to the point when even they recognise its futility. They must be 'motivated' to end it. Continuing pressure by the security forces, equipped with the necessary resources, will be a necessary condition for achieving that objective; but it will not itself be a sufficient one. It must therefore be reinforced by effective Government action in the political, social and economic fields. All the Government's policies seek to take account of the wider geographical, social and political contexts.[34]

In a note circulated to his Permanent Secretaries in the Northern Ireland Civil Service departments, Blelloch outlined that 'there are *no* short cuts, and that we will only win in the end if we continue on our present course as long as it takes, giving the opposition no grounds whatsoever to believe that, under any political dispensation in the United Kingdom, they can hope to achieve their fundamental political goals by violence'.[35] Drawing on intelligence reporting, Blelloch observed: 'Happily, there are growing signs of self-doubt within the Provisional movement. All the more reason, therefore, to keep up unremitting pressure on all fronts.'[36]

Blelloch was an ardent proponent of dealing with terrorism within the parameters of the law, which meant 'not only that terrorists are treated as criminals amenable to the law but also that the actions of Security Forces are themselves subject to the law'. As he explained:

> The prime objectives are to pre-empt terrorist operations and in particular to remove known terrorists from the scene while acting within the law; also of key importance are finds and interception of weapons, cutting off the terrorists' supplies of money, etc. For these purposes, good operational or tactical intelligence is essential; and every effort is being made to provide it. But not all operations need be, or are, pro-active: there is an important role for a deterrent security force presence, especially at particular times and places.[37]

After receiving comments from his top civil servants, Blelloch believed that the next logical step would be to see 'how the work of Government *as a whole* can be further mobilised in support of our strategic goal [to defeat terrorism]'.[38]

In implementing this whole-of-government approach, Blelloch found a ready ally in long-serving Parliamentary Under Secretary of State, Richard Needham. At the time, Needham was beginning to think about ways in which he could better accomplish the government's goal by using the economic instrument of state power to drain the bottomless pit of disaffection in republican areas by creating jobs and other opportunities under the newly created Fair Employment Agency. He had always believed that the best way of sapping energy from the IRA's campaign was to lay firm economic foundations by rebuilding those cities, like Belfast and Derry, devastated by IRA bombs, while the Security Forces went 'on the offensive against Sinn Féin and the IRA'. Under the leadership of Blelloch and Needham, the NIO authorised the activation of the 'bamboo pipe' to facilitate exploratory talks with republicans, though they 'never told the Secretary of State'.[39]

19

NOT AN ABSOLUTE SCIENCE

'There wasn't the real ... liaison that there should have been. There were too many people in Special Branch – and this is the whole culture of counter-intelligence, I mean, it doesn't matter where you go in the world, it's always the bloody same. People with good intelligence sources are very reluctant to let anybody else share it [*sic*]. And, I mean, it was endemic ... If you were clever enough you could catch it on. But it wasn't an absolute science by any means.'

– 'Jimmy B', former E4 HMSU Commander (2011)[1]

Fifty-four-year-old Michael Oatley was growing tired of the spy game. Much of his disgruntlement resulted from the realisation that he had been passed over for promotion to the top job of Chief of the Secret Intelligence Service in favour of Colin McColl. He blamed this on the attitude of the Thatcher government. As he told Brendan Duddy at the time, 'She was still in power, wanted *nothing* whatsoever to do with Republicans and therefore the line of communication was being kept in cold storage ... Thatcher had practically put an embargo on all operations.'[2] Oatley took the opportunity to catch up on some leave. He travelled to Ireland to stay with Duddy for three days over the Easter holidays. Duddy recalled that Oatley 'was disappointed that he had not been made No.1' and that he had 'turned real sour about his job'. According to Duddy, Oatley only wished to talk about three things during his stay: 'his retirement, Thatcher's attitude and money'.[3] Duddy and his friend, who was in fairly low spirits, talked through a means by which Oatley might become 'an independent, highly paid consultant for the Brit. Gov. after his retirement'.[4] Subsequently, Duddy recalled, Oatley had a 'major row with his people + was angling for a job as a consultant for MI5 working with B.D. [Brendan Duddy]'. Duddy observed that '[h]is proposal of £1,000/day + expenses was refused by MI5. MO [Michael Oatley] was threatened with having his pension withdrawn, etc.'[5]

By this point, McGuinness had stepped back from his operational role as OC Northern Command, passing the torch to his Director of Operations, Mr X. This freed him up to invest more of his time in developing the IRA's capacity for engaging in a process few would have thought possible only a few months earlier. On 22 February 1990, McGuinness gave an interview to *An Phoblacht* in which he indicated that he was open to dialogue with the British. McGuinness and Adams were conscious of the difficulties that would be involved in getting the British to agree to face-to-face talks. This was part of the reason why Adams engaged Hume in dialogue in 1988. At first, Secretary of State for Northern Ireland Peter Brooke did not welcome Adams' overtures. 'Sinn Féin cannot expect to be treated as any other political party,' he said at the time, a position that was criticised by *An Phoblacht*. The republican newspaper claimed that Britain 'had no plans of peace – only ones of war' and stated that Brooke's comments demonstrated 'all the arrogance and inflexibility of the colonist. For him "peace" is another word for crushing your opponent.' Adams condemned Brooke's stance: 'A whole new and flexible approach is necessary if this war is to be ended. Republicans are genuine in their commitment to the search for a lasting peace. Peter Brooke's comments suggest he is not.' *An Phoblacht* dismissed as 'spurious' rumours that the IRA was contemplating a ceasefire. McGuinness stated that instead of 'people talking about ending the armed struggle they should be talking about continuing the struggle for the rights of the Irish people to be free and united'.[6] The onus was now on Britain to create the conditions necessary for dialogue.

It fell to Oatley to create the conditions for this dialogue by making contact with Duddy and returning to Derry in October 1990.[7] Oatley 'intimated' to Duddy that 'if he had to be in a room with MG [Martin McGuinness], he wouldn't run away'. McGuinness duly arrived and engaged in a 'lively' two-hour discussion with Oatley, who, Duddy noted, held a 'tight, straight Brit line'; McGuinness held a similarly controlled republican one.[8] The single item on the agenda was how to move forward with peace talks. Oatley intimated 'that there would be an effort made to reactivate a long-standing line of communication'. But first there had to be a cessation of violence. McGuinness said the British would 'need to have a clear agenda of what their position would be in the event of a cessation'.[9] The last half hour of the meeting between the two men was spent talking about McGuinness' passion for fishing. Apparently McGuinness 'fantasised about what it must be like to be free to travel around Scottish trout and salmon areas, stay in BnBs etc and not have to worry about Security Forces constantly on your back.[10] Oatley was 'fascinated by this', Duddy recorded, and after the encounter, Oatley told Duddy that he had found McGuinness 'so very articulate and would have made a very good Guards officer. He mused about McGuinness being one.' Duddy was quick to respond: 'It was typical of the British not to realise that there were other armies besides their own, and that MG [Martin McGuinness] could well be holding a position in one such army which was a lot higher than that which MO [Michael Oatley] was just now imagining him in.'[11] After the meeting, Oatley reported to the NIO at Stormont, where he met the new Permanent Under Secretary, Sir John Chilcot, and the DCI, John Deverell.[12] After a further meeting with Peter Brooke, Oatley returned to Duddy's home, where the two men 'worked at great length to produce the "no selfish or strategic interest" speech + the other speech by Brooke ... SF "setting the record straight" (pp 16) acknowledges an advance copy being sent to them'.[13]

The 'big change' came, however, in November 1990, when Thatcher was on her way out. Duddy believed that the speech given by Peter Brooke in early November was 'obviously connected somehow to the October meeting between MO and MG'. Once he started to talk about retirement, Duddy became unhappy. Everyone he had ever worked with, including James Allen on the 1974/75 ceasefires and Robert F. Browning, had been promoted and gone home. Allen became Governor of Mauritius and Browning became a Director General in the Ministry of Defence in Oman. It soon dawned on Duddy that Oatley wanted him to step down as the link essentially in order to privatise the process. Duddy recalled having several meetings with Oatley to discuss whether he, Duddy, should be 'in' or 'out'. If he stayed in, the British would likely send a low-ranking official to liaise with him. Duddy dreaded this, for he found it painful when 'the Brits would change their man and send in someone who simply did not have a grasp of the situation'.[14] After twenty years of acting as the link, Duddy was getting fed up. For the remainder of Oatley's visit in the autumn, he and Duddy strategised on the best way to bed down the secret dialogue they had been responsibile for instigating.

Behind the scenes, such rhetoric remained just that – rhetoric. Senior republicans, including Danny Morrison, knew that the context was beginning to shift as the IRA turned to the link provided by Brendan Duddy:

Read the IRA statements of Easter '87, '88, '89. All of them are
stating ... 'There'll never be a ceasefire. There'll never be a ceasefire.'
Now, I was arrested in January '90. I'm in the Crum on remand on a
conspiracy to murder and kidnap charge and on the news comes that
there's a Christmas ceasefire in December 1990, four years before the
main ceasefire. Because of the perceived senior position that I held,
you know, I had a view that that would not have taken place had there
not been something tentative or exploratory between ourselves and
the British. That would not have appeared out of the blue. You do not
concede ground like that unless something is happening.[15]

Despite the IRA calling a three-day ceasefire in December 1990, the Security
Forces continued to pursue IRA squads and the IRA, in turn, prepared for
a return to violence by planning a fire-bomb campaign of retail businesses
in Belfast.

★ ★ ★

If the IRA was looking for a way out of the conflict, this was not reflected
in its words and deeds. In its New Year message in January 1991, the IRA
appeared to be uncompromising. It looked forward to marking the tenth
anniversary of the hunger strikes and the seventy-fifth anniversary of the
Easter Rising. Along with the usual rhetoric of stoic republicanism, it
informed supporters: 'Momentous changes are occurring across the world,
yet little has changed in this British-created sectarian statelet since the violent
imposition of partition.' Saluting its comrades, it stated that the 'challenge of
1991' was 'the achievement of a just and lasting peace in a free Ireland. The
challenge to the NIO and Downing Street is to face up to the inevitability of
Irish unity rather than trying to revitalise a dying colonial rule.'[16]

On 7 February 1991, Duddy travelled to London, where Oatley had
arranged for him to meet 'some very senior people'. Duddy had been in
Israel and flew back to London for the meeting. It was the same day that the
IRA bombed Downing Street. Duddy recalled that it was a 'crazy situation'.
He, Oatley and his people were in phone boxes in central London, where
'wisdom eventually prevailed, and the meeting was called off'. Duddy
returned to Derry and Oatley later telephoned him to say he was 'having
difficulty with the government'. According to Duddy, Oatley was 'threatened
with pension withdrawal and worse' if he did not 'concede his position' as

the liaison with the Provisionals. In his last meeting with Duddy, in May 1991, Oatley said he had agreed to brief 'Fred', whom he described in 'very uncomplimentary terms'. Oatley knew that his personal connection with Duddy might also be severed as a result of his impending retirement from MI6. He was also concerned that the link would come under the control of the UK's domestic intelligence agency, MI5, essentially freezing out Oatley's own agency.

By the summer of 1991, Brendan Duddy began to receive strange telephone calls from a man purporting to represent an English commercial company. The man gave no name, but asked to meet the Duddy to discuss inward investment in Derry. Duddy was suspicious and immediately directed the caller to the Chamber of Commerce. The caller rang back, said that he was in the Waterfoot Hotel and asked if he could speak to Duddy for ten minutes. Surprised and intrigued, Duddy agreed. When he met him in the Waterfoot Hotel, the man introduced himself as 'Fred' and said that he had taken over from Oatley. Fred then handed Duddy a typed letter on official government-headed notepaper. It was personally signed by Peter Brooke and acknowledged that Duddy had been involved in the important 'work for peace over many years'. The letter pleaded with Duddy to 'stay in the job and see it through'. Duddy thought it was 'actually begging in tone'. After reading the letter, Duddy folded it and handed it back. He then asked Fred, 'What do you want me to do?' Fred smiled and asked, 'Will you work with me?' Duddy agreed and the two men took their seats in the restaurant for what amounted to a three-hour discussion, in which Duddy told the Intelligence Officer that he had begun to feel 'that the Brit Gov were not serious about peace' and that he was 'out'. According to Duddy, Fred replied, 'The British Government is very serious about peace and that it would be soon made clear.' The two men parted, after which Duddy quickly contacted Martin McGuinness to brief him about the meeting. McGuinness asked Duddy for a few days to 'discuss the Republican movement's attitude' towards the approach. A week later, McGuinness telephoned Duddy and asked him to 'carry on'.[17]

★ ★ ★

The central figure controlling the secret dialogue facilitated by Brendan Duddy and involving Fred and Martin McGuinness was the DCI at Stormont, John Deverell. Born in Nairobi, Kenya, on 15 July 1936, Deverell was the son of a distinguished colonial mandarin, Sir Colville Deverell, a Dublin-born former Governor of the Windward Islands and Mauritius.[18] Deverell had joined MI5 in 1971 and rose quickly through its ranks to become a Section Chief. His most notable success was leading a counter-espionage operation against Soviet spies, which led to the arrest and conviction of Michael Bettaney in 1984 and the East German spies Reinhard and Sonja Schulze in 1985.[19]

Deverell had assumed his new role at a time when inter-agency competition was at its peak. As a result of the huge media and political storm caused by the arrest of FRU agent Brian Nelson, Deverell personally visited the MoD to discuss the matter with Secretary of State for Defence Tom King on 26 September 1990. Deverell argued that Nelson's pending prosecution risked exposing the secret techniques used by the FRU, Special Branch and MI5, which, he argued, were 'really one and the same thing'. Deverell believed that '[i]f one service's techniques were exposed it exposed the others because they were very similar'. Deverell then proceeded to give a masterclass in agent-running, informing those present:

> how agents are run, directed, briefed, steared [sic] to particular areas of activity, and specifically tasked to gather information or intelligence in particular areas. He also pointed out that in order for the best of them to be effective they may well have to be part of a terrorist gang and that they may have to commit low level crime in order to maintain their cover within that gang. He mentioned perhaps that [they] may have to steal a car, refusal to do so would merely cast suspicion upon them. Secretary of State understood the point being made and commented that really the law didn't seem to adequately cater properly for the running of agents.[20]

At the same meeting, it was revealed that Army agents were 'regularly reminded not to become involved in criminal acts'.[21] In a follow-up report that he prepared for GOC John Wilsey, the Army's Chief of G2 at HQNI assured the general that the FRU kept 'extensive and detailed records' on the threat posed by loyalist and republican terrorists. The work of the Army's agent-running unit remained vital:

> The continuing existence of FRU, an Army intelligence gathering unit whose personnel cannot be suborned by the RUC pressure, and which

works to national and not regional masters, will always be a contentious issue. The Chief Constable has publically [*sic*] accepted before the GOC, that FRU is a valuable unit in the fight against terrorism, yet he now wishes to see it removed, or put under the direct control of the RUC SB. This is perhaps not surprising in the circumstances but is it wise and in the overall interests of HMGs fight against terrorism? Are we prepared to allow soldiers to be commanded by policemen in this extremely sensitive and difficult area? In short is this not an example where divided responsibilities is [*sic*] in the national interest?[22]

The Chief of G2, however, admitted that the relationship between the FRU and MI5 'has never been particularly easy'. He believed that the Service was a 'small organisation with its fair share of officers of dubious quality' and that MI5 was being protective of its charter, 'particularly in the area of agent running operations', noting, interestingly, that the Army could only run 'sources', not 'agents', 'except under the supervision of … the Security Service'. The Army's Intelligence Chief said that Jack Deverell was 'well versed in these rivalries' and 'would lose no sleep at the removal of the Army's most effective source running unit'.[23]

These arguments were well understood by Tom King. 'Intelligence from agents and informers is the most important source of information we have about the policy, plans and psychology of the terrorist groups we are fighting', the Defence Secretary told Attorney General Sir Patrick Mayhew on 3 October 1990.[24] The key importance of human intelligence in the intelligence war against the IRA and loyalist paramilitaries was accepted by all of those attending high-level meetings at the time. Sir Michael Quinlan, the Permanent Under Secretary at the MoD between 1988 and 1992, later observed how intelligence tradecraft 'involves doing things which would normally be reprehensible – concealment, untruth, subterfuge, intrusion, illegality at least abroad, co-operating with or employing disreputable people, suborning individuals from their formal responsibilities'.[25] Quinlan was comfortable with this. He wrote: 'Secret intelligence cannot be conducted without all or anyway most of these actions, and I am not minded to condemn them accordingly.' A deeply religious man with strong Christian beliefs, Quinlan pioneered ethical thinking on the use of nuclear weapons during his time at the MoD. On the use of HUMINT, he concluded that 'it would seem to me manifestly contrary to moral common sense to hold that, for example, we were not entitled to do certain of these things in order to penetrate and weaken murderous clandestine organisations in Northern Ireland'.[26] Nevertheless, while all concerned accepted the need to obtain secret intelligence through these means, they were far from united on how this intelligence should be obtained in practice.

NIO official Peter Bell noted that these inter-agency tensions had become more noticeable since his move from SIL to the Security Policy and Operations Division in the NIO. Against the backdrop of an 'intense' security threat, he believed it 'particularly important that all Security Forces resources are used as efficiently as possible, and that the police and Army work harmoniously together', though he now detected 'accumulating evidence that this is not everywhere the case'. With Wilsey now 'a clear advocate for a Province Executive Council', something of a 'controversial idea', Bell noted, relations might only worsen.[27] Higher up in the NIO, some ministers even believed that the RUC had been a little too 'proactive' in its pursuit of the IRA. Richard Needham regarded the recently retired Chief Constable, Sir John Hermon, as a 'powerful warlord' who 'did what he liked'.[28] In Needham's view:

> What really concerned me about the police was – the Special Branch were a law unto themselves anyway – that there was no political control from the Northern Ireland Office or the Police Authority, and therefore there was no intelligent strategic direction. There was no proper managerial oversight; things that had to be done never got done. But that was not the problem of shoot-to-kill. Whatever control you had over the police at the top, you would still have policemen shooting to kill because there was no political way of dealing with them.[29]

Hermon's replacement by Hugh Annesley offered the NIO a perfect opportunity to steer the state towards challenging the IRA on socio-economic grounds.

Although such disagreements over strategy were healthy, they could not disguise the fact that, a decade on from the establishment of the Oldfield System, intra-government disagreements threatened to derail Blelloch's whole-of-government approach to achieving the strategic objective of defeating the IRA.

While the Army, the police and the NIO remained locked in inter-agency rivalry in Northern Ireland, MI5 continued to lobby the Cabinet

Office in its bid to take over responsibility for combatting the IRA in Great Britain from the Metropolitan Police Special Branch. They were successful. On 8 May 1992, Home Secretary Kenneth Clarke announced the change to the House of Commons.[30] By gaining control of UK counter-terrorism, MI5's new Director General Stella Rimington scored her first success. Rimington had been appointed partly because of her expertise on counter-terrorism and partly because she was the protégée of outgoing Director General Sir Patrick Walker. Twelve years after accompanying Alan Rees-Morgan to his final debrief of Willie Carlin in December 1980, Rimington was now in a position to use MI5's 'superior financial backing to penetrate the Provisionals at a high level'.[31]

★ ★ ★

For those in the upper echelons of the Republican Movement, it was imperative to keep the channel of communication open. Danny Morrison was keeping up to date with developments from behind bars. He was asked by Gerry Adams to sound out prisoners on the prospect of entering into talks with the British:

> I think that the IRA *on its own*, relying on its own thinking and relying on its own analysis, was of the opinion that its military campaign – despite the fact that they were heavily re-armed – had reached deadlock. And, as I pointed out to you, they had a variety of choices. They could go at it *madly* for a short space of time to try and break the British. They could go down the road of terrorism, which could never have been contemplated, which would have been unconscionable as far as I was concerned. Totally unjustifiable and complete madness anyway. So, they opted for exploratory peace talks. And it was very difficult for them. Did everyone in the IRA go along with it? Clearly not ...[32]

Brendan Duddy remained abreast of developments in his role as intermediary. In a communique from the British, the Intelligence Officer known as 'Fred' wrote: 'Neither your side nor ours seems to have the ideas to bring peace closer – I know you need an honourable peace (with all that implies) and you know our basic condition before we can talk. Somehow we must find a way – for all our sakes – and I will keep at it till we do.'[33] On 18 February 1992, Adams started to press for direct dialogue, but the British refused. 'We have no wish to appear discourteous, nor to question the good faith of those seeking a constructive exchange,' Fred's message to Duddy read. In rebuffing Adams' advances, the British made it clear that the 'circumstances do not exist at present, nor (despite certain statements) do we detect in action on the ground any signs that they are yet evolving'. The British believed that it was up to the leadership to 'pass on to others their impressions of our views' and that a 'good test' would be the consistency between the impressions behind the scenes and the 'publicly stated positions'.[34] On 22 June 1992, the IRA sent another message to the British via Duddy, which was never disclosed by Sinn Féin. It read:

> The Republican Movement recognises a strong desire among the people of Ireland and Britain for a lasting settlement of the conflict to be arrived at.
>
> The Republican Movement can and will contribute to this process.
>
> We recognise that a sustained period of peace is necessary, and we ask: Is the British Government willing to explore the conditions and timings needed for this dialogue to begin?[35]

Thus began a more sustained period of clandestine engagement between the IRA and the British.

★ ★ ★

The ramping-up of loyalist attacks forced MI5 to turn its attentions to those Young Turks who had replaced the old guard in the UVF and UFF. For UFF commanders like Johnny Adair, the 'auld lads' in charge of their organisation were nothing but 'touts' working at the behest of RUC Special Branch. Adair has since claimed that he himself became a target not only of the IRA, but also of agents and informers within his own organisation. He recalled:

> These people were at their work. I was doing a brilliant job in the early '90s. Brilliant. The organisation was armed to the teeth, the recruits were flooding in. The boys came up to see me in jail. Spencer, Big Winkie, Donald. 'We've got bad news for ye [they said]. They were going to kill ye in 1990. It wasn't the 'RA.' And I said, 'Tell me more.'

The bastards devised a plan to kill me for no other reason ... [than] I was a thorn in their side ... Those cunts were gonna kill me.[36]

Adair says he was well aware of attempts to turn the men under his command, though the authorities could 'never buy my soul':

My war was with the republicans but first and foremost the war was within. When you were getting up in the morning you didn't know, 'Is he working [for the Branch]. Has he been recruited?' Because the Special Branch, we know how they work. We know what their job is. Their job is not to police the area with RUC uniforms on. Their job is plain clothes – to go out and try and recruit people. And that was their job. They tried it with me. And so many people would come forward to me and say, 'Johnny – they offered me this and they offered me that.' But how many people did not come forward till [sic] me and accepted their offers? And that was my biggest threat – the 'enemy within' I used to call it. I was always trying to lay wee traps to try and smoke them out. And I would set wee traps. And sometimes it worked because, I mean, you're trying to kill republicans who's [sic] killing your people and blowing your country to smithereens. But at the end of the day you've fuckin rotten bastards who – for reasons either to stay out of jail or just for money and greed – were putting their own people in jail. Oh. I hated that and that was my biggest challenge was to deal with the 'enemy within' ... Sadly the loyalist paramilitaries were awash with fuckin' informants. You go back to that report where John Stevens stated that 103 [sic; 207 out of 210] were working for [the Security Forces]... I would believe that right. We were successful. And I've all the time in the world to think. Times when I couldn't think ... But now when the dust settles things become clear ... In modern-day loyalism, it seems who is not a tout? They're all fucking touts.[37]

Under Adair, C Company became an efficient killing machine. In the period between 1990 and 1994, loyalist paramilitaries killed 175 Catholics, twenty-two of whom were republican paramilitaries or ex-paramilitaries and thirteen of whom were Sinn Féin activists. Thus, only 20 per cent of these victims were linked to the Republican Movement, which indicates that loyalists found it much easier to target Catholic civilians, especially given the severity of residential segregation.[38]

Despite the UVF and UFF ramping up their armed campaigns in the early 1990s, Special Branch officers were having some success in preventing attacks. A former member of the UVF, 'Matthew', recalled that a team was sent to kill Martin McGuinness and his close associate Sean 'Spike' Murray in Belfast, but that their intended targets had been tipped off and the police were waiting for them.[39] They were promptly arrested and imprisoned. There is evidence to suggest that this was part of a wider pattern. One estimate for 1986–93 puts the number of loyalists arrested vis-à-vis republicans at a 2:1 basis, which highlights the ramping up of Security Forces operations against loyalist paramilitaries.[40] The prevention of attacks also took other forms, including the cultivation of agents inside loyalist paramilitary groups. One such agent reached a leadership position in the UVF and began to report extensively in the 1990s, assisting British Intelligence in intercepting one of the group's largest ever shipments of illegal weapons and explosives in November 1993. Had loyalist violence gone unchecked, loyalists would have succeeded in killing high-ranking republicans and thus jeopardised the secret dialogue that was underway. As one republican observed:

Once loyalism went on the rampage, directed against the Catholic community and – at points – against the republican community, certainly that was the opportunity for the Brits. You know, these were guys that they could use. And that's where the whole thing about 'collusion' comes up. And that's one of the other difficulties, you know. When the agents of the state who are supposed to be the people responsible for upholding the law and order actually bend and break and rewrite and redraft legislation to suit themselves, and, you know, to give them, practically, immunity because they are so far detached from deaths or killings or assassinations ... At what point can you actually decide these are people we need to negotiate with? That was one of the long phases, I think, in the creation of the peace process. How – and who – do we get to trust? You know, even after the army left the streets there was still an intelligence element left here guiding the hands of the loyalists. So yeah, collusion would be one of the big issues you know what I mean. There was probably as much damage done – certainly targeting wise to the Republican Movement – through collusion than there was through 'in the field' action ...[41]

20

'THE MADNESS WAS SO REAL
YOU COULD TOUCH IT'

'The British System is perfectly capable of going in many different directions at the same time, each section pushing to develop its own particular agenda.'

> – Brendan Duddy, the secret link between the
> IRA and British Intelligence (1993)[1]

GOC's Office, HQNI, Early 1993

Fifty-one-year-old Roger Wheeler had been Assistant Chief of the General Staff (ACGS) for two years prior to assuming command as GOC Northern Ireland in late January 1993. He recalled the thinking that had percolated in the MoD in the 1970s and 1980s, which resulted in an entire generation of middle- to senior-ranking Army officers asking themselves the same question: 'Why haven't we remembered the lessons from Malaya?' Wheeler was a student of insurgency, having lived in Cyprus during the revolt when his father was CO of the Royal Ulster Rifles in the late 1950s and having spoken to his father about his experiences as brigade commander during the last stages of the IRA border campaign. He had also studied Templer's methods in his early years as a commissioned officer:

> Templer was the one who pioneered having the politics, the social policy, the economic policy, the security policy in the place of the military all run together. And, there was quite a strong feeling, I think, amongst the sort of middle to senior people that it took us quite a long while to organise ourselves in dealing with the problem in Northern Ireland in such a way that all those strands were drawing together.[2]

Wheeler had not served in Northern Ireland, though part of his job as ACGS was to liaise with senior commanders in Northern Ireland every six weeks. To his astonishment, as he had no operational experience, he was appointed GOC in late January 1993. He now found himself in command of troops fighting an intelligence-led war, which came down to two key factors: organisational and the personal relationships.

'By then we really had sorted out the proper coordination,' he recalled.[3] The formation of the Province Executive Committee (PEC) on 16 December 1992 had linked the SPM with the TCGs who were carrying out the tactical battle against terrorism.[4] Below the TCGs were the newly formed co-terminous RUC and Army boundaries, which enabled closer working relationships between the Security Forces. As Wheeler recounted:

> There wasn't a cigarette paper between the RUC and the military. There were undoubtedly personal difficulties sometimes when you had a strong personality coming in. I can remember saying to the incoming Commanding Officers: "The RUC, like any UK police force, operates on the basis that even a Constable can make a decision and do something as an individual. We provide that individual – of course, in a coordinated way, having discussed the patrol guidelines and all of that – with a concentration of force because that's what we do. We needed to remember that.' And, indeed, I think I said rather irreverently, 'If necessarily, if you come up with a bright idea, then for God's sake make sure the RUC man at your level that you're dealing with thinks that he had the idea in the first place and then it'll work.' With such close working relationships in place at all levels, there really was a joint effort to pool intelligence and exploit it.[5]

In order to ensure that the military subordinated itself to these structures, Wheeler turned to Lieutenant Colonel David Richards to 'research and then write the Army's first formal campaign plan for Northern Ireland, a mere twenty-three years after British troops first arrived on the streets of Belfast.'[6] Fresh from a tour in charge of soldiers at Drumadd Barracks, Richards at first struggled with the enormity of the task. 'It was hell,' he later wrote in his memoirs.[7] Although he visited all three brigade commanders at the time – Anthony Palmer, Douglas Erskine-Crum and Alistair Irwin – and all were 'generous with their time and had many excellent ideas', Richards' major finding was that, ultimately, 'this was a political problem that would require a political solution. The role of the military was to facilitate that.'[8] However, Richards gained his greatest insight into the nature of the security problem when he attended a seminar held in TCG South in Portadown. There, Richards 'met an amazing character, who was reputedly held together with wire. A tough Northern Ireland policeman, he was a long-serving Special Branch officer, someone who had devoted his life to what he believed in. He'd been blown up at least twice and we lesser mortals were all in awe of him.'[9] Following Richards' encounter with Frank Murray, he believed that the Army needed to take a more flexible approach towards the IRA, which meant doing things that 'didn't appear to make much sense', ranging from being 'very hard on certain IRA terrorists in order to reinforce the fact that you meant business until they came to the table', while perhaps refraining from doing things that 'militarily made sense in order to induce constructive behaviour'.[10] Richards had learned much from writing the campaign plan. 'The question was how could we, a conventional Army, outwit and outmanoeuvre them at the tactical level, playing our part intelligently within a wider strategy?'[11] This was the central question facing the Security Forces. Part of the answer would soon emerge from the most unlikely quarter: within the IRA itself.

★ ★ ★

Brendan Duddy's House, Derry, Mid-1993

Brendan Duddy was a proud but conflicted man. Since the 1970s, he had enjoyed the confidence of both high-ranking members of the IRA and the British government. He had worked with representatives of both sides in order to secure a ceasefire in the mid-1970s. Although it didn't last, it led Duddy to place a premium on dialogue between warring factions. He had arrived at this conclusion with a little help from a close friend and fellow peace activist, Gordon Lawrence. In his correspondence with Lawrence, Duddy appeared to rededicate himself to his work as 'the link'. Although the dialogue floundered on the day the IRA sent three mortar rounds into the back garden of 10 Downing Street, Duddy still managed to persuade Martin McGuinness and the PAC to return to dialogue in 1992. Throughout 1992, 'Fred' kept the Republican Movement apprised of inter-party talks, though he overstretched by revising a message from his political masters in London to the IRA in which he used the phrase 'the conflict is over', apparently 'in the hope that it would encourage the British Government into commencing intensive dialogue with republicans'.[12] A significant breakthrough was eventually made on 10 May 1993, when Duddy, the primary contact, called a meeting with 'Tax' (apparently Noel Gallagher) and 'Star' (apparently Denis Bradley) at his home. They were visited by 'Walter' (Martin McGuinness), who handed them what Duddy called 'a speaking note' to read out to the British, which included the phrase, 'it is clear that we are prepared to make the crucial move if a genuine peace process is set in place'.[13] The message included recognition that the British required 'a private assurance' in order to publicly defend entering into a dialogue with republicans – 'we have proceeded to this stage without assurance'. Duddy realised that he was being asked to go to the British with 'an offer of a ceasefire on behalf of the IRA to enable talks to take place'.[14] Duddy immediately made arrangements to travel to London and deliver the message directly to Fred and someone he called 'David'. In his recollection of the meeting, Duddy recalled 'a lady being present also – could have been Catherine, Joanne or the girl who died in the plane crash'.[15] Although Permanent Under Secretary Sir John Chilcot was upbeat about the proposal, Patrick Mayhew expressed reservations. The IRA responded to such prevarication by exploding a bomb in Oxford, thereby demonstrating its willingness to continue with its armed campaign. Despite the oscillation from dialogue to violence, communications remained open.

'Chiffon' was the codename given to this secret dialogue between the British government and the IRA. This dialogue was so secret that many middle-ranking officials in the NIO were unaware that it was taking place. Chris McCabe, an Ulster-born official in the Political Affairs Bureau, recalled two clergymen close to republicans on the ground with whom he kept in regular contact coming to him after being told by a man in a long white trench coat in London to 'back off'. McCabe recalls relaying the message to Chilcot, who told McCabe:

> I'm afraid I can't tell you much but you do need to know that there's a credible process of engagement involved. It's being driven by London and it's starting to produce results. Your contacts have been useful in providing some corroboration for what we're hearing, but we're moving into a very sensitive phase where the risk of sending mixed messages is too high to let you continue.[16]

Chilcot had good reason to bring up the need-to-know principle. He himself had been unaware of the link when he took over as Permanent Under Secretary in 1990. 'It was evident, even when I took over in Peter

Brooke's time,' he recalled, 'that Tom King had his means of indirect communication, serviced in my time essentially by the security service and by well-wishers on both sides.'[17] The British were always unsure whether they were hearing exactly what the speaker had said or 'interpreted words or words that another party in the chain wished had been spoken.'[18] By 1993, Chilcot was 'reasonably confident that what was coming through was what was being sent'. In order to be sure, the Permanent Under Secretary relied heavily on 'third-party observer-style intelligence assessment on the toings and froings of communication.'[19] The sorts of questions to which the NIO, as the primary consumer of intelligence, needed answers were, in Chilcot's words, 'How far are these guys in control of their situation? What is their understanding of our political position and our government, and what do they think and how is the Ard Fheis going to go? These were the key considerations and informed much of our approach.'[20]

For the British, this was the moment when they realised that they were dealing with an armed grouping that seemed serious about ending its violence. They had been here before with armed groups in their various colonial outposts, particularly in the last days of empire. As the sons of empire, Blelloch, Deverell, Oatley, Chilcot and other members of the British establishment now believed that the time had come to engage with their opponents in order to seek an honourable compromise that both sides could live with. The only way to really do this was to develop what one notable authority has called a 'cooperative relationship'.[21] This approach was characteristic of the public school-educated elite, as academic Paul Kingsley wrote at the time:

> It is an essential part of English political thinking that we should identify the 'moderates' and 'extremists' in any given situation in order that we can give concessions to the 'moderates' and isolate the 'extremists'. This is the policy which was tried in the colonies. We have seen that it met with mixed results and was only effective where the 'moderates' and 'extremists' had the same goal, and the intention was to concede this objective to the good guys rather than the bad guys. In effect, the plan is to punish the 'extremists' by giving something to their 'moderate' opponents.[22]

Kingsley understood better than anyone else what George Orwell meant when he observed that while 'the battle of Waterloo *was* won on the playing fields of Eton', the 'opening battles of all subsequent wars have been lost there'.[23] He knew what Whitehall was prepared to sacrifice in order to contain the Northern Ireland 'problem', but also that they were capable of finally accepting another truism. 'Someone once asked how you defeat an idea,' Kingsley concluded. 'The answer is that you deny it all hope. When hope has gone, action is pointless'.[24]

News of the dialogue between the British government representatives and the IRA leaked out at the end of November, before a secret deal could be struck, causing widespread public opprobrium. Duddy was blamed and subsequently interrogated by the IRA. The PAC believed Duddy had over-extended his remit as a mediator and was guilty of playing a double game between the two sides. Sinn Féin was angry and the British were embarrassed and feared a negative political and public reaction. Duddy was asked by Sinn Féin President Gerry Adams to resign from his position, which he did. A few weeks later, Duddy took his family on a holiday to the Canary Islands, where he spent much of his time in the sun worrying about the consequences of his high-risk negotiation strategy. He worried that his life was in jeopardy, particularly from the IRA. For a man who had dedicated a quarter of a century of his life to finding a solution to the Irish conflict, Duddy was now in a precarious position. In a letter to a friend, known only as 'Elizabeth', Duddy confided that '[t]he madness was so real you could touch it'.[25] What Duddy did not appreciate at the time was that the IRA leaked like a sieve. This has been denied, even by prominent members of the Republican Movement, including Danny Morrison, who observed that:

> The IRA were never infiltrated at leadership level because if you go down that road, you're saying the British government allowed the IRA to blow up Brighton Hotel and kill Mrs Thatcher. If the IRA was infiltrated, how did the escape take place out of the H Blocks in '83? If the IRA was infiltrated, then how did the mortar attack in Downing Street come off in '91?[26]

However, it would later transpire that senior members of GHQ, including its intelligence cell, were compromised. One of those responsible was Denis Donaldson, an IRA member from the Short Strand area of East Belfast. The extent of Donaldson's treachery has never been revealed, but we do know that he had come to be viewed with suspicion by other members of GHQ.[27]

Given the amount of technical and human intelligence penetration of the IRA leadership by the early 1990s, therefore, news of the secret dialogue could have originated from a range of sources.

★ ★ ★

By early 1994, John Deverell had established himself as the senior authority on all intelligence matters in Northern Ireland.[28] He had a steady stream of MI5, Army and RUC officers coming to visit him to brief him on ongoing operations. As 'Jimmy B.' recalled:

> The Regional Head of Special Branch in Belfast, say ... would have had ultimate control but he in the end of course ... the big master was the Director and Controller [*sic*] of Intelligence ... I remember the guy that was killed in the Chinook [crash] was John Deverell. And you would have been reporting to him. I remember reporting to him. And unbeknown to me – it came out later on, of course – the British Government were negotiating directly with the IRA. So here you were, you know, and that was typical, of course, of MI5. They played their cards [close to their chest]. And rightly so. They had a bigger perspective to work to but where the conflict came [was in working together] ... One question I asked right away – and I was just a naïve policeman at that stage – why did the Army need their own intelligence collation office in every police headquarters? And they did. I was told that the Army don't go anywhere without their intelligence system ... The police had their collators and the Army had their own intelligence office. But the real intelligence went across to Lisburn where you had the real movers and shakers. But there was that conflict.[29]

Shortly after Jimmy B. had made his office call to Deverell, his boss, 53-year-old Brian Fitzsimmons, the Head of RUC Special Branch since 1989, was also summoned to Stormont Castle to a meeting with Deverell. Before he left Special Branch headquarters, he called in to see one of his officers, 'Toby'. 'I have been asked why we are allowing the Army to run agents,' he told Toby. 'I was going to tell him that the Army had some advantages, including approaching people in a different way, and that we should allow them to get on with it,' Fitzsimmons added. Toby agreed with him. A former soldier himself, he, like Fitzsimmons, knew that the military could offer some advantages to the RUC. Fitzsimmons had been the Deputy Head of Special Branch for two years prior to his promotion to ACC and was 'generally acknowledged to be the key figure directing the RUC SB's operations during this period and was the essential liaison point for [the FRU CO] and senior Security Service officers such as the Director and Coordinator of Intelligence (DCI) and the Assistant Secretary Political (ASP)'.[30] Fitzsimmons was a firm believer in the use of agents, as illustrated in an internal RUC report he had written a few years earlier:

> Quite often, post-incident investigations fail to make seasoned terrorists amenable to the law and, for the sake of community well-being, it falls to intelligence-led operations to prevent attacks taking place and, where possible, to arrest those involved. In consequence, all sources of useful intelligence are sought out and, because of their scarcity, carefully protected. The protection afforded is not merely in the agent's interest but also the public's interest.[31]

Toby shared Fitzsimmons' view:[32] 'There was no warehouse full of evidence against senior PIRA. It doesn't exist.' In his conservative estimation, the Army handled around 1 per cent of all agents and that number increased if a clear distinction was made between a 'casual source' and a 'full-blown agent'.[33]

★ ★ ★

By 1994, the Security Forces were fighting a war on two fronts. As a result of the activities of Johnny Adair and Billy Wright, commander of the Mid Ulster UVF, loyalists were quickly overtaking republicans in killings. E4 HMSU's long-time commander Jimmy B. explained how things had shifted:

> If you were looking at things from a more strategic perspective … the war against the Provos was largely won in Belfast. It was won in Belfast. It wasn't won in South Armagh because of the border; because there never was the level of cooperation, until later on, in the end, with the Garda that there should have been. But you could structure the whole Provo organisation, to who was doing what because of the way they were structured, and right down to who was the operations

officer and who are the targets so if you were mounting a surveillance operation, you could go and say, 'Look, Mr X is the target.' And you would have had intelligence coming from two-legged sources. You would have had surveillance intelligence. And you would have had all sorts of [intelligence] that would have enabled you to do that.[34]

Other Special Branch officers active at the time concur with this analysis. In the view of William Matchett, the IRA ceasefire announced on 31 August 1994 meant the Branch 'had achieved its objective. It won the intelligence war. By design it was a secret victory,' adding, importantly, that the 'Whole of Government strategy had worked.'[35]

IRA volunteers on the ground, like Brendan Hughes and Tommy Gorman, felt a sense of bewilderment. Hughes saw the ceasefire as a defeat; his whole being 'screamed out in protest against it' and he saw it as 'the ultimate capitulation, the abandonment of republicanism.'[36] Gorman recalled that discussion about the idea of a ceasefire was closed down by those under the spell cast by Gerry Adams. The Bobby Sands Discussion Group, which consisted principally of IRA members, including Gorman, met regularly to discuss a range of topics, from the socialist aspect of the armed struggle to abortion and women's rights. The announcement of the ceasefire had caught the group by surprise. Indeed, several of those in the group had even attended the recent General Army Convention, which had voted against the idea. Nonetheless, the group believed that they had 'something substantial to get our teeth into', so they organised workshops and invited along senior members of Sinn Féin to address them on the political way forward.

Gorman recalled that a few days after the ceasefire, he organised a bus to take the members of the discussion group to Derry to speak to Mitchel McLaughlin, by now the national chairman of Sinn Féin. 'Mitchel got a pretty hard time,' Gorman recalled. The IRA men asked him bluntly, 'What are the leadership doing? Why didn't they discuss this development with anybody on the ground? Where are we going from here?' McLaughlin apparently 'lost the bap'. 'Who are *you people* to determine policy? You aren't within the circle!' he told Gorman. The members of the discussion group felt that they had been sidelined. The meeting ended in acrimony and the IRA volunteers returned to Belfast. A few days later, Gorman received a house call from two senior IRA men. They were there to see him about something 'ostensibly quite separate', but they asked pointedly whether he had been 'at the meeting in Derry the other night?' Gorman soon twigged why they had come to see him. 'Away to fuck. Are youse the thought police?' he told them. 'Are people not allowed to discuss things within the movement!' he exclaimed. He was angry. 'It's okay to go out and kill someone on behalf of the movement, but we're not allowed to discuss the way we're going?' Gorman realised at that moment that there could be no 'rocking the boat' – 'a gravy boat, in my opinion', he said – and that he would have to fall into line with the decision.

Disagreements within the IRA, however, did not diminish. Hughes and Gorman were soon joined by others. The dissent threatened to fragment the organisation. Danny Morrison was one of the key proponents of the Sinn Féin strategy and lost little time in defending the IRA's decision to call a cessation:

> I was in charge of Sinn Féin in the H Blocks in '94 and '95 and in charge of commissioning the debates and framing the debates and I was absolutely of the view that they were going to have to compromise. I was also of the view that there would be a devolved assembly. I was also of the view that Sinn Féin would have to take their seats in it. Now, had you said that openly to a lot of people they would have said, 'Hold on a minute, I'm not going down that road.' At each new stage they saw the logic. They saw the value. [The visit by Bill] Clinton. All of those little things. Then, of course, the prisoners getting very generous parole. The tension in the prison was getting relaxed. This created a sense of, 'If this is handled [well], we will receive a variety of rewards including an increased mandate.'[37]

This logic had its critics, including amongst public intellectuals who were closely observing the politicisation of the Provisional movement:

> Given the long-term security service penetration of the Provisional movement at all levels, British ministers were probably in a better position to know the real intentions of both its military and political leadership during the peace process than were ordinary Sinn Féin activists and IRA volunteers.[38]

Could this penetration of all aspects of the movement have given the British a strategic advantage? Disgruntled hard-line members of the IRA believed that it did, which led to the consolidation of a dissenting view within the movement in the immediate aftermath of the ceasefire.[39]

★ ★ ★

That the IRA had called a ceasefire did not lessen the demand of the consumer base of senior government officials for more intelligence product. Thus, MI5 officers continued to provide technical expertise to the RUC while running agents inside the IRA and Sinn Féin. The Head of Assessments Group (HAG) was responsible for analysing the majority of this secret information prior to its dissemination to consumers. HAG sought to monitor the thinking of the Republican Movement's senior leadership and, importantly, gauge their commitment to the emerging peace process. The vast majority of tactical and operational intelligence on the day-to-day activities of the IRA and other groups fell to the RUC, with the support of the military.[40] Intriguingly, the breakdown of the IRA ceasefire in February 1996 brought further pressure to bear on Special Branch, especially in relation to the timely dissemination of operational intelligence. The fall-out from the Canary Wharf bombing and subsequent IRA bombing in Manchester prompted the arrival in Northern Ireland of Whitehall's Intelligence Coordinator – and a contemporary of Sir Maurice Oldfield – Sir Gerry Warner. His terms of reference were to examine:

> The methods of operation; with particular emphasis on securing, analysing and acting on intelligence; the methods and effectiveness of liaison within the Force and with other bodies, e.g. the Security Service, HQNI [i.e. the Army], and NSY [New Scotland Yard]; use of information technology and the appropriateness and value of interchanges between RUC SB and the Security Service.[41]

It was the first time Special Branch's activities had been put under the microscope. As one MI5 officer told a public inquiry a decade after the second IRA ceasefire:

> The review carried out by Sir Gerry Warner followed the breakdown in the first IRA ceasefire. There was a feeling, both politically and amongst the intelligence agencies, that that had been an intelligence

failure. Although there were plenty of indications that there were stresses in the ceasefire, there was not a clear indication that it is going to rupture. I mean, I think an assessment we issued said that if nothing happens within the next month or two, there is likely to be a breakdown. In fact, it happened about a fortnight after that assessment was issued, but there wasn't pre-emptive intelligence that said, 'The ceasefire is going to break.' That was seen as an intelligence failure. For that and other reasons, Sir Gerry Warner was asked to come across and review the intelligence structures and arrangements. On the basis of the evidence that was given to him, he recommended that the RUC, as they then were, their arrangements for processing and dealing with intelligence needed to be enhanced and improved, and in particular their arrangements for extracting from the intelligence they received political and strategic intelligence need to be improved [sic]. So the specific recommendation he made was that the Security Service should put some of its staff into Special Branch to help them to up their game.[42]

Even though John Deverell had tragically perished in the Mull of Kintyre disaster, MI5's ambition to assume greater control over intelligence operations to support the nascent peace process survived. After Canary Wharf, MI5 'continued to achieve a mixed record in preventing Irish terrorism on the mainland', but even its 'most hostile critics would be hard-pressed to ignore its victories against the IRA'. A new generation of Security Service officers, like their predecessors, made a significant contribution through their 'diligent handling of agents and informants'.[43]

One of those recruited for a 'short term infiltration job' was 'Tony'. He was asked to get close to the family of a prominent member of the PIRA. As an agent of influence, he had one mission: 'To sow division amongst his nearest and dearest while gently persuading them to abandon their support for terrorism.'[44] The extended family was at the core of Irish republicanism. It gave sustenance, shelter and unqualified support to the sons, fathers, brothers, uncles and nephews who formed the nuclei of many IRA squads. From the early 1970s, the Prices, Hartes, McKearneys and Carlins constituted key nodes within the Republican Movement. It might be easy for individuals within a community – even one as tightly knit as the republican community – to betray their comrades, but families would never betray each other. Consequently, the intelligence agencies found it almost impossible to penetrate these squads. In order to extract information, it was sometimes necessary for someone to get close to them when they were outside Ireland. Intelligence agencies are nothing if not creative. It was in this context that Tony was sent to Spain to ingratiate himself with 'Persons of Interest'.

Tony operated alone on these missions, but MI5 occasionally provided him with technical support. It wasn't long before he was drinking in the same bars as his Persons of Interest. On one mission, he was tasked with getting close to a woman who was the sister of a prominent IRA member. He found it easy to engage her in conversation, though her entourage was less welcoming. 'I found the brother to be something of a village idiot. He'd a thick set of glasses and wonky eyes. He was a pathetic character, really,' Tony recalled. A former soldier, Tony had served in Northern Ireland at the height of the Troubles. He was resourceful and resilient, two attributes required for such undercover work. Tony recalled spending a considerable amount of time getting into character. He changed his appearance, dressing in a more bohemian way. He also hammed up his West London accent and developed a 'legend' (what undercover operatives call their backstory) as a petty criminal. He assumed the role so well that he developed some psychological problems when he returned to England due to the multiple personalities he had created. 'I was spending my time with some pretty nasty people and that transferred itself back home when I returned from a mission.' One day in London, Tony became extremely agitated, telling another man who made him angry to 'fuck off'. It was around this time that Tony's wife began to notice a change in his moods. He became irritable. He soon realised that his family life was suffering because of his role playing for the Service. On another mission, Tony was challenged about his backstory by IRA sympathisers. He managed to convince them that he was who he said he was. But the incident left its mark and Tony retired soon after his involvement in a major sting operation against arms traffickers. Tony said that lies work best when you stick as close to the truth as possible. When the truth became blurred by lies, for him, however, he knew that it was time to walk away. Even in the context of a fledgling peace, it was proving difficult to recruit and run agents of influence inside the IRA. Those who remained 'behind enemy lines' were extremely dedicated, cunning and resourceful. Yet, even they couldn't plug the intelligence gaps now emerging in Northern Ireland.

21

A 3D WAR

'Certainly I think from a Special Branch point of view that's something that terrorist groups were doing on a continual basis, and indeed their structure and their methods of operations were always sort of constructed in such a way that it would reduce the infiltration of their organisation and they were always very suspicious of individuals and, of course, if things went wrong, it is much easier to blame a source, an agent, a tout, than it is to look at your own shortcomings as an organisation.'

– Deputy Regional Head of Special Branch
in Belfast, 1996–98[1]

Bessbrook, South Armagh, Evening, 12 February 1997

Twenty-three-year-old Stephen Restorick lived life to the full. He worked hard and he played hard. Always smiling, laughing and joking with people, he had spent the Christmas leave period of 1996–97 at home with his family in Peterborough in the north of England. His mother, Rita, remembered that she and Stephen's dad had hardly seen him: 'He was always out and about in pubs, clubs and at the cinema.' He told his parents that his shifts at the PVCP in the South Armagh border town of Crossmaglen were long, but he never complained. One of his closest childhood friends, Lisa Fellows, recalled that they had got drunk together and sang Christmas carols. By early January, Stephen was back in Northern Ireland, 'stagging on' at the PVCP. On a particularly biting winter's evening, Lance Bombardier Restorick stopped a car belonging to Lorraine McElroy. Her husband, Tony, and their two children, 13-year-old Sean and 1-year-old David, were also in the car. As Mrs McElroy handed her licence to the soldier, he thanked her politely and smiled. 'Then there was a crash and a terrible flash of light,' she said. 'He dropped by the side of the car and was lying on the ground moaning.' Another soldier quickly ran to his aid, shouting, 'Steve, open your eyes, open your eyes – keep them open.' Mrs McElroy recalled that he had seemed 'very happy' and said that he was a 'smiling cheerful, young man. I'll never forget.'[2]

In the twelve months since the organisation had returned to war, this was only the second time that the IRA had killed a soldier. Michael Caraher and Bernard McGinn had been active Provisionals for two decades and so this wasn't their first outing with the group's prestige, high-velocity .50 Barrett rifle. Most of the South Armagh sniper team's other attacks had taken place between 26 March 1990 and 26 June 1993, after which it had stopped in advance of the ceasefire in 1994. According to *Irish Times* journalist Jim Cusack, South Armagh had simply 'been biding their time before launching any attacks', the first of which was the attack on the PVCP that killed Stephen Restorick.[3]

There were two reasons why South Armagh was unable to launch a concerted campaign in their own backyard. Firstly, Officer B, Frank Murray's successor as Head of Special Branch in South Region, had authorised a major surveillance operation against the IRA in the region as early as April 1996, which was designed to 'monitor paramilitary activity using rural locations close to the South Armagh border with Ireland'.[4] The operation cast a wide net, according to Officer B, and was 'not just of a local nature but involved the "crème de la crème," who were possibly acting on a national and international basis'.[5] The second reason – and, perhaps, the primary reason why South Armagh PIRA had failed to kill any soldiers in the previous twelve months – was the by-now well-honed TTPs of the Green Army.

Forty-three-year-old Lieutenant Colonel David Benest had been in command of 2 PARA since 1994, when the battalion was deployed on a residential tour of Northern Ireland. A veteran of several tours in the most dangerous parts of South Armagh and West Belfast, Benest had also been the Regimental Signals Officer when 2 PARA defeated the Argentine military in Darwin and Goose Green during the Falklands War of 1982. In September 1996, he found himself in command of the 2 PARA battle group in South Armagh, which included a company of soldiers from the Grenadier Guards and a battery of troops from the Royal Horse Artillery. He and his men were responsible for all military operations in the TAOR. He was one of the Army's most experienced commanders. He spent much of his time reflecting on ways of preventing the IRA from returning to war:

> What I did was to apply my thinking from being a Company Commander in West Belfast [in 1989–90] ... We knew they [the IRA] were there.

We knew what they were trying to do with the anti-armour grenades and so on, and the command wires, and the sniping. So … I took my own view – I got no instruction at all – that when we go on the ground, we are going to go in such strength that the PIRA will say, 'This is too risky.' And I learned that, funnily enough, from the Falklands … I saw … how the Royal Navy deployed to the South Atlantic. It deployed as a task force, which is extremely strong. Submarines, air, you know, it's a 3D war … So, I started in West Belfast, the idea of three-dimensional patrolling. Helicopter, where possible; observation posts; soldiers on the ground, certainly. And that backed up by armoured vehicles … This is no different to World War II tactics. Tank, infantry cooperation in an urban environment. Exactly the same … All I can say is that in eighteen months, not a single attack … Not a single soldier lost in eighteen months in West Belfast … I'm very proud of that … And I thought, right, 'If it can work in West Belfast, we can try it in South Armagh' … And we know from our Special Branch links that the PIRA were increasingly frustrated. They couldn't attack the PARAs because we were too clever. So, it wasn't to do with brute force, it was to do with intelligence and intelligent thinking … And, frankly, intelligence was almost non-existent. I didn't really need it. I just wanted to say, 'If we can stop the attacks in South Armagh for six months, not bad.' In the end we were defeated, sadly, with [the killing of] Stephen Restorick.[6]

Despite employing advanced TTPs on the ground, British soldiers remained vulnerable for two reasons. Firstly, covert action had failed, giving rise to tensions within TCG South, and, secondly, because of a natural blind spot. The Army's watchtower, Romeo 13, was high above the checkpoint on Camlough Mountain. There was millions of pounds worth of sophisticated electronic surveillance equipment inside the watchtower. However, the equipment did not have a direct line of sight to the PVCP. A single evergreen tree obstructed the line of sight. Guerrilla forces tended to know the ground better than their Security Forces enemies. The IRA exploited this by mounting a static gun position behind tree cover. On the day on which Lance Bombardier Restorick was shot, the sniper team parked their Mazda as close as they could to get a clear line of sight to the PVCP. It was a prime location and their strategy would prove effective.

A day or two after Stephen Restorick's murder, David Benest and his soldiers received a visit from the Secretary of State for Northern Ireland,

Patrick Mayhew, and the Assistant Chief Constable for the region at Bessbrook Mill. Benest remembered that the meeting had been scheduled well in advance of Restorick's murder, but went ahead despite the attack. Emotions were running high. Benest took the opportunity to highlight the failings of the local Security Forces in his briefing to Mayhew and his NIO advisors:

> And I said, 'Come on, that tree has got to go!' And they all went into a huddle about community relations. 'What? Can we really cut down a tree outside Bessbrook, you know, [asking themselves] what does this mean for the community?' And I said, 'For fuck sake, I've just lost a soldier because of that effing tree.' And, in the end, they said, 'No'. And the police said, 'Too bad'. And I then turned to the police and said, '*You, you people* should be on that checkpoint. It's not our job to protect the checkpoint and check people's licences. It's *your* job. Our job [is to provide cover on the hill], stopping snipers, whoever. Our job is to be out there, not to be sitting on effing checkpoints.' And – needless to say – that was not received well … And it's, 'You're the Army. Tough shit. You've lost a soldier.' And that's how it felt to me and I'm sorry to say I have a very low opinion of the uniformed branch of the RUC. Special Branch, in my view, were fantastic. Brilliant. Very, very bright people who really knew what they were doing …[7]

As the veteran of multiple tours in Northern Ireland, Colonel Benest knew the limits of what the Green Army could do better than anyone, particularly since the breakdown in the IRA ceasefire. He was also a pragmatist and knew that 'the people who are going to get these people are the Special Forces, the covert capability. The beauty of it was that because I had worked with them, they knew me very well.'[8]

Covert operators remained essential in the pursuit of those terrorists who had murdered Stephen Restorick. One former RUC officer alleged that one of the sniper team, likely Bernard McGinn, was tracked down to a hotel in central Belfast and offered a suitcase of money to stop shooting people. 'He told them to "fuck off"', said the former officer. A follow-up operation involving an even bigger suitcase was then mounted and was met with the same response. This particular member of the South Armagh PIRA could not be bought off.[9] Not long afterwards, the TCG mounted a more aggressive arrest operation against those involved. In a raid on a farm at Creggandan Road in Crossmaglen on 10 April 1997, the Security Forces arrested four men. They found a resprayed Mazda, inside of which there was an elaborate metal device that served as a firing platform and a CB radio used for communications. Gunshot residue in the vehicle indicated that a weapon had recently been fired from the platform. In a corrugated metal barn, soldiers found a small cattle trailer modified to serve as a portable arms cache. Inside the trailer, they found an AKM assault rifle, a .50 calibre Barrett sniper rifle and 50 rounds of ammunition. The four men were taken to Gough Barracks for interrogation.

RUC detectives cautioned Bernard McGinn on the charge of membership of the IRA and his alleged participation in a planned terrorist operation. 'Make me an offer I can't refuse,'[10] McGinn said during his eighth interview with the detectives. The CID officers thought that it was an odd thing for him to say. When asked what he meant, McGinn replied, 'You know what I mean.'

McGinn was born in Castleblayney in County Monaghan. His father was a Sinn Féin councillor and his brother-in-law was destined to become a TD. An accomplished terrorist by his early twenties, McGinn murdered Gilbert Johnston, a former member of the UDR, in 1978.

At his next interview, Detective Sergeant Burns asked McGinn what he had meant by his comment. McGinn replied that he didn't want any notes taken. He proceeded to tell Burns that he wanted freedom for the sake of his 7-year-old son. In exchange for a deal, he would tell the RUC 'what was going on in South Armagh'. If he was released after a drastically reduced sentence, he 'could work for them'. The detectives told him that they couldn't authorise that kind of a deal, but would speak to their superiors. 'Do you want to stop another Canary Wharf?' he asked them. McGinn was offering himself up as a source. He confessed that he had mixed the explosives for the London bombing and for another job planned for Birmingham city centre that had been cancelled at the last minute. He told the detectives that he 'rode shotgun' in the Barrett sniper rifle attacks, armed with the AKM. The day he was arrested, McGinn claimed that his squad was preparing to go and shoot another soldier in the area. In the end, McGinn's advances were rejected and on 19 March 1999 he was sentenced to twenty-five years' imprisonment.

★ ★ ★

As the Provisionals approached yet another Easter Sunday without having advanced towards their long-term objective, Gerry Adams made his way to Milltown Cemetery, where he addressed his supporters. 'In a few weeks there will be a new British government,' he told them confidently. 'Will it create a new opportunity for peace? Will it take responsibility and give leadership where John Major has chosen to form alliances with David Trimble? Will it accept the imperative of opening real and credible negotiations?' These were tough questions, but Adams believed that Sinn Féin stood 'ready to play our part'.[11] A view within the Republican Movement at the time held that the IRA was in a strategic position and could use the threat of force to gain re-entry into all-party talks, but much would hinge upon Adams' prophecy of a New Labour government. Danny Morrison had been released from prison in 1995 and would go on to contribute to Sinn Féin's submission to the Mitchell Commission on Decommissioning. As he observed:

> I mean, the IRA didn't go at it full hog. I mean, the IRA didn't throw everything into the mix. I mean, it was fairly restrained. A couple of bombs in London, [an] explosion at Thiepval Barracks, two RUC officers killed in Lurgan, but that wasn't a full-blown campaign. They were just treading water until the Labour Party came in but needed to assert themselves to show that they weren't going to roll over. Was there massive disagreement? I think a lot of people were unsure about where it was leading to.[12]

By the middle of July 1997, it was obvious where it was headed. The organisation said in a statement:

> After 17 months of cessation in which the British government and the unionists blocked any possibility of real or inclusive negotiations, we reluctantly abandoned the cessation. The IRA is committed to ending British rule in Ireland. It is the root cause of divisions and conflict in our country. We want a permanent peace and therefore we are prepared to enhance the search for a democratic peace settlement through real and inclusive negotiations.[13]

The IRA instructed its units to cease military operations from midday on Sunday, 20 July.

One of those who believed he knew where the IRA was headed was former volunteer Anthony McIntyre, who had spent eighteen years in prison, including four years 'on the blanket':

> The IRA was beaten. I have absolutely no doubt about that ... What was the British state's intention in this whole conflict? It wasn't for the British state to stay in Ireland for forever and a day. The British state were not opposed to Ireland being united. The British state were only opposed to Ireland being united under Provisional IRA terms, which was the coercion of the British state out of Ireland and the coercion of all the unionist community into the unitary state. The British state wanted a situation whereby its strategic objective was to defeat the Provisional IRA by removing the *raison d'être* for its campaign and, therefore, it brought the Provisional IRA to accept the consent principle. Once it did that, the Provisional IRA were defeated, whether it came as a result of intelligence or whether it came as a result of the agents of influence moving it in that direction. I think that, ultimately, the IRA were defeated. They failed to secure their strategic objectives and they settled for the objective that the British always had on offer anyway – unity by consent. So, how we can say it was an IRA victory, I do not know. Even if it was an IRA draw, a draw in that situation would have been Joint Authority. The IRA accepted partition and they accepted the term for getting rid of it, which was by consent of the majority in the North. Now, how did we reach that defeat? That's another matter.[14]

McIntyre is one of many former volunteers who suspect that the IRA defeat was brought about – to an extent – by intelligence operations.

The IRA's defeat is disputed, of course, by both proponents of the Provisional narrative and by some academics who believe that neither agents, 'nor other aspects of the intelligence war influenced republican armed or political strategy to any great extent during the conflict'.[15] Such conclusions are just as one-dimensional as those which argue that agents – as just one intelligence-gathering tool – were chiefly responsible for bringing about the end of the IRA's campaign. The utility of intelligence, like the use of force, can only truly be evaluated in the context of strategy. In other words, the methods of intelligence collection must be seen in light of the strategy adopted by those who use them for a stated political purpose. Underplaying the role of this strategic process in Britain's counter-terrorism efforts to end the IRA's armed struggle leads to counter-factual interpretations according to which the Provisionals' long-term objective of forcing a united Ireland was merely 'designed to motivate volunteers' and the British state only really used the intelligence war to reduce armed activity over time to an 'acceptable level'.[16] In fact, as Blelloch's Defeating Terrorism Papers and the subsequent formation of the Province Executive Committee (PEC) were to prove, the intelligence-led system, first mooted by Sir Maurice Oldfield in 1979–80, was explicitly designed to help the government defeat the IRA and return Northern Ireland to something resembling normality by Western liberal democratic standards.

Even former Military Intelligence Officers, like 'Bob', suggest that intelligence operations only really brought the IRA to a 'culminating point' and that the 'crucial dynamic' lay in how 'the political people faced down the military people. It was political people who went straight to the Army [and police]. They betrayed military operations. Not all of this was due to self-initiative. In fact, many of those had been agents of influence.'[17] This point of view is confirmed by former senior members of Special Branch, who make the point that it was the way in which the 'political people' faced down the 'hard men' of the IRA that helped move the IRA towards ending its armed struggle.[18] This perspective has been elucidated by Anthony McIntyre:

> People are constantly onto me trying to assert that [Martin] McGuinness was an informer. I'm not convinced that McGuinness was an informer. I'm not convinced [Gerry] Adams was an informer. I'm not convinced they were agents. But I do think they were assets. And I think you can be an asset, I mean, without knowing it. You might be an asset and you know you're an asset because your interests are dovetailed with the interests of the people who wish to have you as an asset. I think the British regarded McGuinness and Adams as assets because they felt that they were the people who would ultimately bring the IRA to the type of conclusion that the British wanted it brought to. However, there are now many people saying, 'They're all touts' ... There is a view that there were a lot of informers and agents of influence. And the problem with an agent of influence is that the agent of influence doesn't give the type of information that leads to arrests and, therefore, there's no trail that the IRA can follow in

terms of finding out what went wrong. The agent of influence nudges you in a certain direction. Denis Donaldson was certainly an agent of influence; he may also have been an informer. I think it's a very useful distinction ... Denis Donaldson was an agent of influence who would have pushed the ideas that the British and the leadership [of the Republican Movement] wanted. And he would have been responsible for protecting the leadership; ensuring that its critics were smeared.[19]

Unsurprisingly, Danny Morrison downplays Donaldson's influence on the Republican Movement: 'Denis Donaldson didn't have access to IRA secrets. Denis Donaldson was a political spy and what he was doing, in my opinion, was giving the British a paper on Friday which Sinn Féin would have been giving the British on Monday, you know ... Denis could not have had access to anything.'[20] Nevertheless, the scandal involving Donaldson and other agents, including 'Stakeknife', persisted. Estimates of the number of agents inside the IRA vary. One former Special Branch officer, William Matchett, suggests that '15 well-placed agents were active at any one time in the IRA.'[21] Journalists like the late Liam Clarke, long familiar with intelligence matters, gave credence to the estimate that 'half of all senior IRA men' were 'working for intelligence services'.[22] It is impossible to know for sure how many 'casual sources' and agents had an effect at any given point in time. There is no doubt, however, that they were just as effective in bringing to an end the IRA's campaign of violence as the Green Army tactics and covert action.

Epilogue

COLLECTING PEOPLE

'For the intelligence services' work to be effective their operations, sources and methods need to remain secret if they are to continue to perform their task and to protect British interests and often save British lives.'

– Baroness Park, former senior SIS officer, speaking on the Intelligence Services Bill (1993)[1]

Hotel Lobby, Belfast, Afternoon, early October 2018

The fire burns brightly in the lobby bar of a central Belfast hotel. It's a mild autumnal day and I'm patiently waiting for my contact to arrive. I'm here to meet 'Peter', a former Regional Head of RUC Special Branch. He's one of the most knowledgeable spymasters I've encountered in twenty years of researching the Northern Ireland conflict. I spot him as he enters and stand to greet him. I order him a sparkling water as he settles into his seat. 'I've just come from a meeting about the government's legacy consultation,' he says as he hands me a copy of the morning's *Belfast Telegraph*, which bears the headline 'Retired police officers body says Northern Ireland legacy plans "unfair and unworkable"'. 'It's not good,' he tells me. 'We will see what can be done.' I quickly scan the story before spotting a smaller column on a South East Fermanagh Foundation remembrance service held in Ballygawley, which I had attended the day before. The gathering was held in a small Presbyterian church and attended by First Minister Arlene Foster. During the service, a local woman spoke emotionally about the events surrounding the IRA's murder of her father, a serving RUC officer. I sensed sorrow amongst the congregation that day. These were the people who had borne the brunt of the IRA's campaign in the borderlands. They'd suffered unimaginable horrors, inflicted on their community by the likes of Seamus McElwain, Jim Lynagh and Paddy Kelly. Along with Detective Chief Superintendent Frank Murray, Peter had spent his entire career trying to keep these people safe. I had no doubt that those attending the service, including myself, owed our lives to the good police work of FT Murray, Peter and his colleagues.

'I think if you were to work out in an academic way what lessons are to be learned from what happened here, it would do justice to those who made the sacrifices,' Peter says. In my dealings with Peter over the years, I've come to empathise with the challenges faced by him and his colleagues. We've spoken before about how difficult it is to square the moral and ethical debate about the use of human sources and the resulting security benefits. It was Sir Desmond de Silva, the experienced QC appointed by David Cameron to review intelligence material relating to the loyalist paramilitary murder of solicitor Pat Finucane, who observed how 'the running of agents in terrorist organisations was one of the most effective methods by which the security forces could frustrate terrorist activity and save lives'. This is certainly something republicans have challenged both politically and legally. Yet, it brings us back around to the state's difficulty in seeking to defend its national security and its people amidst a concerted terrorist campaign. 'The work of the intelligence agencies in running agents played a significant role,' de Silva concluded, 'in containing terrorist activity to such an extent that all paramilitary groups began to realise that their aims were unachievable by violent means.'[2] My conversations with Peter have contained many of the same reference points, though it is unlikely that Peter agrees with de Silva's conclusions.

Like 'Toby', Peter believes that politicians did not always offer the appropriate guidance or pass the right laws to protect those who were charged with enforcing them. 'We inhabited a sort of "Middle Earth",' Peter tells me, 'where violent and unexplainable things happened.' I know from my conversations with Dr William Matchett, another former Special Branch officer, that he shares the same views. He believes that reviews such as de Silva's 'showed the shortcoming' of the intelligence war. 'It was not ideal,' he writes in his highly informative book, Secret Victory, 'but in an irregular war nothing is. There are no failsafe systems. But the system saved more lives than the alternatives.'[3]

One of those who observed the effective police work of Special Branch officers in the killing fields of Fermanagh was Ulster Unionist MP Ken Maginnis. He was a close friend of Frank Murray and he knew the intense pressure he worked under. 'I don't think we won a military victory,' he says, 'but we won a moral victory.'[4] Lord Maginnis has much admiration for the work of Special Branch and he has taken many opportunities in both Houses of Parliament to defend those who have come in for criticism.[5]

Notwithstanding the efforts of those who have defended the intelligence war against terrorism, I wanted to ask those agents of influence who penetrated the heart of the Provisional Republican Movement for their views. After all, it was they who put their lives in immediate danger to bring back secret information from the front lines in this intelligence war.

★ ★ ★

British Library, St Pancras, London, Afternoon, Early June 2019

It's a particularly balmy summer's day in London. Outside the British Library, I see Willie Carlin standing on a street corner, sporting a light summer jacket and a pair of dark glasses. We shake hands and exchange pleasantries as we walk into the building. In the library's busy café, I'm anxious to secure a table away from prying eyes. We have serious matters to discuss and you never know who might be within earshot.

I tell Willie that I'm interested in hearing more about his tradecraft. I ask if he received any training during his eleven years as a mole inside the Republican Movement. 'None whatsoever. Absolutely nothing, even when I became "important", he responds. 'Even when I was in London. You know, I've read about people who claimed that they were this or they were that and who were brought to London and were trained in picking locks and all sorts …'

I'm intrigued. 'What about taking photos?'

'Absolutely nothing,' he says dismissively.

'Making recordings?' I ask.

He responds more forcefully now:

> No. Look, back then there was no Internet. There was no WiFi. You couldn't have a wee tape recorder on you. If the RUC caught you, you were fucked. You couldn't write things down because you were fucked if you were caught. I had to develop how to remember things. And I got quite good at it. I still am. You name me a part of my life and I'll not only tell you when it happened, how it happened, but what the bus was like that drove past at the same time, and the birds in the trees,

and what the song was playing in the café beside me. I don't know where I got that from. I have no idea. But it has always been there, in my life. I can give you an example, which you probably know about anyway. I saw a car go past Tommy McGlinchey's house one day and I thought, 'Fuck, I must remember the registration number of that car,' and I repeated it over and over and over in my head. BYI 7613. Still remember it. A white Cortina. Undercover cop car. And, sometimes I forgot it … And I got to the point where I could remember ten pieces of information when I drove past the chapel. And I must have passed the Waterside chapel five times a day. And every time I passed it, I opened that part of my brain where I repeated the ten pieces of information. Somebody's name, somebody's registration number, the time I seen somebody at. And I could remember the ten pieces of information every time I pass the chapel. And I actually got to the point where I had to visualise, not even go there, passing the chapel, and I could remember the ten pieces of information. Now, nobody trained me to do that.[6]

Carlin's memory helped him perfect his deep cover personality. It was one of the reasons he was such a valuable asset. How does he explain it?

My point of view is, you know, I've probably always been an actor since a wee boy. And I learn my lines. Even today, when I get ready to come to meet somebody or go out into the world, the last thing I do after I get myself ready … I look in the mirror – I'm ready to go on stage. And when I walk out the front door, I'm not me anymore …

'So, you're in character?' I ask him.

He responds, 'It's scary but I can do this. I can sit in the middle of a debate and be the biggest, fucking staunchest republican, and I can win my argument … What I'm trying to tell you is I was never trained in anything …'[7]

In many ways, Carlin was pragmatic about his mission. He was prepared to take the risks, even though he operated alone and, at times, without precise instructions. I was eager to probe him further regarding his drive as an agent.

'How do you build up that cover personality that wins across people – who are pretty militant, extreme people – who could snuff you out in a second?' I ask. 'How do you develop that in the knowledge that you make one mistake and that could be it?'

'The answer is don't think about it,' he says, 'because if you start thinking about it, you have a doubt. And I tell people, "Never have a Plan B. Never have a Plan B." Because if you're not sure, walk away. Don't do it.' Willie knew this better than anyone. His cover had been blown and he was exfiltrated in March 1985 on-board Margaret Thatcher's ministerial jet, which brought him to RAF Northolt, after which he was taken from safe house to safe house until eventually, with a little help from John Deverell, he disappeared into anonymity.

★ ★ ★

Royal Festival Hall, South Bank, London, Lunchtime, Late August 2019

Tourists crowd the South Bank. It's still warm in the city. I'm here to meet 'Síomón', a former agent who penetrated the IRA for British Intelligence. We meet at the Nelson Mandela bust outside the Royal Festival Hall and take a short stroll before ordering a coffee in a restaurant by the riverside. 'It's good to see you,' I tell him. He's busy playing with his phone and smiles in response. He's interested to hear how I'm getting on with my research. 'I've found our conversations fascinating,' I tell him, 'though I've had to do some digging to find out more about some of the personalities you've mentioned.' On different occasions, the names of prominent republicans have come thick and fast: John Joe Magee, 'The Hawk', Mr Z, the 'Sick Psychopath', 'Diddley' and 'The Goat'.

'I'd like to clarify a few things about your story,' I tell him.

'You just didn't walk into the IRA,' he says. 'It takes years to be trusted. I was told to get in and get as far up the ladder as I could, preferably to save lives. It was long-term infiltration, not a quick informant job. You can't pretend to be one of them. It was Eric Anderson who said, "Altar boys are no good to me."'

We talk over operations, strategies and tactics. At one point, he takes a napkin and draws a firing mechanism on it. The last person to draw something like this for me was a PSNI detective I spoke to who was investigating a particularly nasty explosive projectile used by dissident republicans. I find it interesting that the same weapon system was developed by the borderlands PIRA almost thirty years ago. The same device was also subsequently employed with devastating effect by the Jaysh al-Mahdi militia in Iraq.

After coffee, Síomón and I walk along the banks of the Thames. 'Detectives collect evidence. Intelligence operators – MI5, Police and Military Intelligence – they collect people,' Síomón says. 'I'd a team behind me, my handlers. I knew that when I stepped forward the team was behind me. You had to be convincing … The hardest person you have to convince is yourself. If you can convince yourself, you can convince anybody.' I'm intrigued. I have no doubt that he was courageous, but I'm interested in the psychology behind this approach to deception.

'How do you cope with telling lies?' I ask.

'It's not lies,' he tells me emphatically. 'You're just not telling them the full truth. You just can't pretend to be a terrorist. When you're dealing with terrorism, you have to deal with some nasty people.'

Síomón's observations tally with my own views on terrorism. I've spent two decades interviewing people on all sides of this dirty little war and, as far as I'm concerned, terrorism is something of a minority sport. Moreover, not everyone who engages in it can live with what they have been party to, regardless of how they might dress it up with political legitimacy after the blood has been washed away and the bodies buried.

★ ★ ★

Many agents of influence mourn the passing of the time since they played 'the game'. Some, like Willie Carlin, feel nostalgia about the old days and are glad of the opportunity to discuss memories of their spying exploits. Carlin spent much of his time as a mole inside Sinn Féin, watching, listening, reporting and, occasionally, subtly intervening in paramilitary politics. It seems clear that he was also a vital influence on Martin McGuinness' personal journey from Armalite to ballot box. Other agents of influence, like Síomón, an infiltrator of the borderlands IRA, regaled me with his tales of frustrating operations inside these deadly squads, while 'Tony' reminisced about his time in character helping British authorities apprehend dangerous terrorists. All three men were involved in deception of one kind or another, the ultimate purpose of which was to help neutralise the threat of militant republicanism.

The most successful agents of influence maintain their cover long after the deception has been carried out. Some quietly retire, their secrets disappearing along with them. Less successful agents of influence have had their cover blown, either as the result of a slip-up on their own part or when their secrets were disclosed by their handlers, such as Michael Bettaney, whose prison-house conversion to Irish Republicanism saw him drop enough breadcrumbs to lead back to Willie Carlin and, according to Intelligence historian Nigel West, even Hal Doyne-Ditmas.[8] Intelligence Officers are sworn to secrecy by the Official Secrets Act (1911; 1989), which prevents them from speaking out. Bettaney flaunted his legal obligation because he was lonely and desperate to belong to a new cause. The Official Secrets Act ensures the identities of agents remain hidden, unless the agents choose to avow themselves. In recent years, the Public Records Act (1956) and the Freedom of Information Act (2000) have resulted in the release of MI5 documents containing the names of many Cold War agents to the National Archives. However, in the case of Northern Ireland, few documents have been disclosed.

One former Director General of MI5, Sir Stephen Lander, explained the rationale for withholding information in an article he wrote in the *Intelligence and National Security* journal almost two decades ago: '[O]ur interest in individual members of the Provisional IRA has been ongoing for more than 30 years,' he wrote. Such work 'in some cases goes back to the 1950s. In short, much of our work has long antecedents, knowledge of which is important to success today.' Whereas other government departments release material that may only be of historical interest, MI5 material continues 'to be of value in the day-to-day work of the Service'.[9] It is possible that some agents have been left 'behind enemy lines', so their identities must remain forever hidden.

ACKNOWLEDGEMENTS

As readers of my previous book, *UVF: Behind the Mask*, will know, I do not always opt for the easiest of research assignments. Certainly, *Agents of Influence* involved its fair share of risks, rewards and opportunities.

For many years, I have been intrigued by the world of secret intelligence and covert action. I have primarily been interested in understanding and explaining how counter-terrorism operations helped bring an end to violent conflict in Northern Ireland. This was at the forefront of my mind as I researched and wrote the book you now hold in your hands.

I wish to pay tribute to the late Professor Keith Jeffery, the official historian of the Secret Intelligence Service, who gave me early encouragement in my academic research on the security dimension of the Troubles. Additionally, I would like to thank Professor Michael Goodman, the official historian of the Joint Intelligence Committee, for his more recent advice. Other academic colleagues involved in the study of Intelligence history whose assistance and work I have drawn on include Professor Mark Phythian, Dr Jon Moran, Dr David Strachan-Morris, Dr Stephen Dorril and Dr Rob Dover. They have all been encouraging and supportive and – through their own work – have inspired me and helped me to understand the inner workings of this secret world. None of them bear responsibility for my interpretation of the facts.

Research and writing are solitary pursuits, but they depend on the help, support and intervention of other people. This is especially true of the dangerous and difficult work I have undertaken over the past twenty years. Early in the research for this project, I was told by a former member of the RUC Special Branch that I would face insurmountable challenges on my journey. In fact, he said, 'You probably won't get anywhere close to the answers you're after', especially in relation to meeting former agents. Undoubtedly, this was difficult, but I eventually did meet three such individuals. Willie Carlin, 'Síomón' and 'Tony' are three of the bravest people I have ever met.

Thanks also to Raymond White OBE BEM LLB, for his assistance over the years and for convening several focus groups with his former colleagues. It was during these encounters that I met 'Toby', 'Jack', 'Ronnie' and many others, including 'Jimmy B', Jimmy Nesbitt, MBE, and Roy Cairns, QPM, who are, sadly, no longer with us. These retired police officers greatly enhanced my knowledge of the inner operational workings of RUC Special Branch and CID. For obvious security reasons, it is impossible to thank the many others who helped me with my research, though I do also wish to acknowledge Dr William Matchett, GB and 'Bob' who helped shape some of my ideas. Hopefully the remainder will recognise themselves when they read this book. Lord Maginnis of Drumglass was also generous with his recollections of FT Murray and I wish to thank him for taking the time to speak to me.

I'd also like to take the opportunity to thank other writers, researchers and journalists who have helped along the way. Thanks to Liz Bingham, Ian Cobain, Martin Dillon, Hugh Jordan, Henry McDonald, Dr Anthony McIntyre, the late Lyra McKee, Dr Malachi O'Doherty, Jennifer O'Leary, Richard O'Rawe, Clifford Peeples and Dr Graham Spencer.

At the Royal Military Academy Sandhurst (RMAS), I'd like to thank my Head of Department, Dr Ed Flint, as well as my colleagues, Dr Martin Smith and Dr David Brown, and the team at the RMAS Central Library, John Pearce, Ken Franklin and Mel Bird. Thanks also to the Dean of Academic Studies at RMAS, Brigadier (Ret'd) Ian Thomas, OBE, who supported my research trip to the Brendan Duddy Archive at NUI Galway in October 2019. Outside RMAS, my late friend and mentor Colonel (Ret'd) David Benest, OBE, and friends, Dr Stephen Bloomer, Dr Sean Brennan, Dr Crispin Coates, Dr Paddy Hoey, Chris Johnson, Dr Martin McCleery, Dr Connal Parr, Lieutenant Colonel (Ret'd) Peter McCutcheon, MBE, and Dr Simon Taylor, kept me grounded and honest. Writing books while in a full-time teaching role – especially having lost half my department through bureaucratic inertia – is no easy task. Nevertheless, the past twelve years at Sandhurst have been an honour and a privilege. I'd like to thank my family, who have been there for me through some trying times, particularly James, Barbara, Ryan and Stephanie and, of course, Charlotte.

My publisher Conor Graham has been on hand to talk through ideas and constantly remind me about staying within the word count. He has stuck by me since commissioning *UVF: Behind the Mask* and he deserves my thanks for his patience with *Agents of Influence*. Thanks also to Maeve Convery and Patrick O'Donoghue at Merrion Press and to my editor, Michael Garvey.

While I was researching and writing *Agents of Influence*, I received the devastating news that my close friend Lyra McKee had been murdered by republican terrorists in Derry. We saw each other whenever our schedules permitted and talked all the time. I still miss her dearly. She always encouraged me in my investigative writing and stood by my side when I launched *UVF: Behind the Mask*. Lyra blazed a trail in her own investigative work and was truly a rising star. This book is dedicated to her memory – and her indomitable, inquisitive spirit. As I stood in St Anne's Cathedral in Belfast at Lyra's funeral a few days after her death, I recalled another memorial service honouring fallen reporters in St Bride's Church on Fleet Street, London, on 12 November 2010. The celebrated war reporter Marie Colvin told those gathered:

> Covering a war means going to places torn by chaos, destruction and death, and trying to bear witness. It means trying to find the truth in a sandstorm of propaganda when armies, tribes or terrorists clash. And yes, it means taking risks, not just for yourself but often for the people who work closely with you.

Colvin's words apply in times of fragile peace, as well as times of war, and are all the more poignant given that both Marie Colvin and Lyra McKee were both tragically killed while bearing witness. Colvin's words should also serve to remind us of what Lyra stood for and what she willed others to stand for. I will never forget her.

ENDNOTES

Preface

1 A copy of the Walker Report (declassified in 2018) can be found at the Orwellian-sounding Campaign for the Administration of Justice: https://caj.org.uk/2018/07/02/ruc-walker-report-1980/.

2 The National Archives, Kew (TNA), CJ 4/2903, Report of the Working Party on Force Levels in Northern Ireland, 21 September 1979, annex D – Police Tasks.

3 Intelligence is seen more as an art than a science and so, understandably, there is no agreed-upon, precise definition of the term. This book adheres to the definition proposed by Gill and Phythian: 'Intelligence is the umbrella term referring to the range of activities – from planning and information collection to analysis and dissemination – conducted in secret, and aimed at maintaining or enhancing relative security by providing forewarning of threats or potential threats in a manner that allows for the timely implementation of a preventive policy or strategy, including, where deemed desirable, covert activities'. Peter Gill and Mark Phythian, *Intelligence in an Insecure World*, Second Edition (Cambridge: Polity, 2012), p. 19.

4 Patrick Walker, Report on the Interchange of Intelligence between Special Branch and CID and on the RUC Units Involved, including those in Crime Branch C1(1) (31 March 1980). Archived: https://caj.org.uk/2018/07/02/ruc-walker-report-1980/. Accessed: 23 December 2019.

5 MI5 Officer A, Statement 1 given to the Bloody Sunday Inquiry, 12 April 2000. Publicly accessible at: https://webarchive.nationalarchives.gov.uk/20101017072448/http://report.bloody-sunday-inquiry.org/evidence/K/KA_0002.pdf.

6 Focus group with former senior Special Branch officers, 25 October 2010. See Aaron Edwards, *Defending the Realm? The Politics of Britain's Small Wars since 1945* (Manchester: Manchester University Press, 2012), Chapter 6.

7 Ministry of Defence, *Operation Banner: An Analysis of Military Operations in Northern Ireland*, Army Code 71842 (London: MoD, July 2006), Para 812.

8 Private information, November 2015.

9 Robert Thompson, *Defeating Communist Insurgency: Experiences from Malaya and Vietnam* (London: Chatto & Windus [1966], 1972), p. 85.

10 David McKittrick, 'Setting spy against spy', *The Irish Times*, 24 April 1980.

11 Focus group with several former RUC Special Branch officers, 4 April 2011. Cited in Edwards, *Defending the Realm?*, p. 213.

12 Frank Kitson, *Gangs and Counter-gangs* (London: Barrie and Rockliff, 1960). Many republicans are obsessed with Kitson. While his books were read by some of his contemporaries, he had left Northern Ireland by 1973 and it was subsequent commanders who shaped the intelligence-led apparatus

that would be in place by the early 1980s.

13   "'Have A Go": British Army/MI5 Agent-running Operations in Northern Ireland, 1970–72', *Intelligence and National Security*, 28(2), (2013), pp. 202–229.

14   CLF's Study Period on Army Source Handling and Structures, 24 May 1989. Archived at: https://www.hiainquiry.org/sites/hiainquiry/files/media-files/MI5-Material-Pages-1-to-359-Rev-RO.pdf. Accessed: 1 October 2019.

15   Author interview with Peter, 30 July 2019.

16   Desmond de Silva, *The Report of the Pat Finucane Review. The Rt Hon Sir Desmond de Silva QC, Vol. I* (London: The Stationery Office, 12 December 2012), p. 61.

17   Ibid.

18   Liam Clarke, 'Half of all top IRA men "worked for security services"', *Belfast Telegraph*, 21 December 2011.

19   MoD, *Operation Banner*, Para 818.

20   MI5, 'Covert Human Intelligence Sources': https://www.mi5.gov.uk/covert-human-intelligence-sources.

21   Christopher Andrew, *The Defence of the Realm: The Authorized History of MI5* (London: Allen Lane, 2009).

22   Robert Dover and Michael S. Goodman, 'Lessons Learned: What the History of British Intelligence Can Tell Us about the Future' in Robert Dover and Michael S. Goodman, *Learning from the Secret Past: Cases in British Intelligence History* (Washington, DC: Georgetown University Press, 2011), p. 293.

23   This is true of intelligence agencies around the world. See Amy Zegart and Michael Morell, 'Spies, Lies and Algorithms: Why U.S. Intelligence Agencies Must Adapt or Fail', *Foreign Affairs*, 98(3), (2019), pp. 85–96.

Prologue: In the Zone

1   Kim Philby, *My Silent War: The Autobiography of a Spy* (London: Arrow Books, 2003), p. 201.

2   Anthony McIntyre, 'Who Knew – Who Knows – Who Will Tell?', *The Blanket*, 15 May 2003. Archived at: http://indiamond6.ulib.iupui.edu:81/who.html. Accessed: 9 March 2020.

3   Kiran Sarma, 'Informers and the Battle Against Republican Terrorism: A Review of 30 Years of Conflict', *Police Practice and Research: An International Journal*, 6(2), (2005), pp. 165–180.

4   Angelo M. Codevilla, 'Political Warfare' in Frank R. Barnett and Carnes Lord (eds), *Political Warfare and Psychological Operations: Rethinking the US Approach* (Washington, DC: National Defense University Press, 1989), p. 85.

5   Private information, 2016.

Chapter One

1   House of Commons Debates (Hansard), 2 July 1979, Vol. 969, Col. 932.

2   The soldiers killed in the first explosion were Corporal J.C. Giles, Lance Corporal C.G. Ireland, Privates G.I. Barnes, J.A. Jones, R.D.V. Jones and M. Woods. Privates Paul Burns and T. Caughey were wounded. Paul Burns lost both legs and an arm in the attack. All of those killed and injured were members of 3 Platoon, A Company, 2 PARA.

3   Public Records Office of Northern Ireland (PRONI), DOW/6/1/1/57/26A,

Inquest File relating to the deaths of eighteen soldiers at Narrow Water, 27 August 1979, Sworn Affidavit, dated 27 August 1980.

4. Paul Potts, 'Paras tell of miraculous escapes … and carry on', *Daily Telegraph*, 31 August 1979.

5 Ibid.

6 PRONI, DOW/6/1/1/57/26A, Inquest File relating to the deaths of eighteen soldiers at Narrow Water, 27 August 1979, Sworn Affidavit, dated 27 August 1980.

7 Mike Jackson, 'Gen Sir Mike Jackson relives IRA Paras bombs', *The Daily Telegraph*, 5 September 2007.

8 'Open verdict on soldiers killed at Warrenpoint', *The Guardian*, 9 July 1980.

9 Ibid.

10 Judge Peter Smithwick, *Tribunal of Inquiry into Allegations of Garda Collusion* (Dublin: The Stationary Office, 2013), pp. 138–150.

11 'War is what it is', *An Phoblacht/Republican News*, 1 September 1979.

12 Ibid.

13 Interview with Toby, 5 July 2019. A day before the Narrow Water attack, a squad of IRA members had been intercepted by the RUC as they attempted to smuggle a huge shipment of 850lb of cannabis with a street value of £500,000 from Warrenpoint to Stranraer.

14 Author interview with Roy Cairns, 26 October 2011.

15 Margaret Thatcher, *The Downing Street Years* (London: HarperCollins, 1993), p. 56.

16 TNA, PREM 19/81, No. 10 Note to Cartledge, 27 August 1979.

17 Margaret Thatcher Foundation, Written Statement on Warrenpoint and Mountbatten murders, 27 August 1979. Archived at: https://www.margaretthatcher.org/document/104135.

18 Liddell Hart Centre for Military Archives, King's College London (LHCMA), Ramsbotham Papers, Box 1, Report by Brigadier David Ramsbotham to Major General James Glover, 15 July 1980.

19 TNA, PREM 19/79, No. 10 record of conversation between Margaret Thatcher and Cabinet Ministers, 28 August 1979.

20 Margaret Thatcher, *The Downing Street Years*, p. 57.

21 John Potter, *A Testimony of Courage: The Regimental History of the Ulster Defence Regiment* (Barnsley: Leo Cooper, 2001), p. 217.

22 Ibid.

23 Thatcher, *The Downing Street Years*, p. 57.

24 TNA, PREM 19/817, Outline of additional security arrangements for Northern Ireland.

25 Ibid., Job Description, 17 September 1979.

26 Comments by Killick about his reputation can be found in the Cambridge University British Diplomatic Oral History Programme, 14 February 2002. Archived at: https://www.chu.cam.ac.uk/media/uploads/files/Killick.pdf. Accessed: 10 December 2019.

27 TNA, PREM 19/817, Letter from Sir John Killick to Clive Whitmore, 21 September 1979.

28 Martin Pearce, *Spymaster: The Life of Britain's Most Decorated Cold War Spy and Head of MI6, Sir Maurice Oldfield* (London: Transworld Books, 2016), pp. 20–21; p. 356.

29 Richard Deacon, *C: A Biography of Sir Maurice Oldfield, Head of MI6* (London: Futura Publications, 1984), pp. 210–211.

30 TNA, PREM 19/817, Clive Whitmore, Note for the Record: Appointment of Security Coordinator in Northern Ireland, 9 October 1979.

31 Thatcher, *The Downing Street Years*, p. 57.

32 This description of Oldfield was given by Alec Guinness in a letter to John Le Carré. See Adam Sisman, *John Le Carré: The Biography* (London: Bloomsbury, 2015), p. 404.

33 See Pearce, *Spymaster*, for a full account of Oldfield's career in SIS.

34 TNA, PREM 19/817, Correspondence and Press Release on the appointment of Sir Maurice Oldfield, from the NIO to Cabinet Office, 1 October 1979.

35 In a letter to the *Telegraph* shortly after Oldfield's appointment, Kingsley Amis disputed that Oldfield was a model for M, citing the date of publication of Fleming's novels and his age at that time. *The Daily Telegraph*, 18 October 1979.

36 Sisman, *John Le Carré*, pp. 403–404.

37 'Intelligence in Ulster', *The Daily Telegraph*, 4 October 1979.

38 For more on the unfounded allegations that later surfaced about Oldfield, see Historical Institutional Abuse Inquiry (HIAI), SIS Records, Witness Statement – Supplementary #6, Officer A, dated 8 December 2016. Archived at: https://www.hiainquiry.org/sites/hiainquiry/files/media-files/Secret-Intelligence-Service-MI6-Material-Rev-RO.pdf. MI6 makes it clear that 'SIS has reviewed all the material it holds on its former Chief and has identified no material to indicate that Sir Maurice Oldfield had visited Northern Ireland during his SIS career'. However, this has been disputed by some historians, with Dr Stephen Dorril suggesting that Oldfield had been in Ireland in the mid-1970s to run a particularly tricky intelligence operation. My thanks to Dr Dorril for discussing Oldfield's role with me.

39 Bob Rodwell, 'Security tightens around Oldfield', *The Guardian*, 9 October 1979.

40 Deacon, *C*, pp. 223–224.

41 Aaron Edwards '"A whipping boy if ever there was one"? The British Army and the Politics of Civil–Military Relations in Northern Ireland, 1969–79', *Contemporary British History*, 28(2), (June 2014), pp. 166–189.

42 Edwards, *Defending the Realm?*, p. 207.

43 Pearce, *Spymaster*, p. 386; Peter Wright, *Spycatcher: The Candid Autobiography of a Senior Intelligence Officer* (London: William Heinemann, 1988), pp. 371, 377.

44 Ibid., p. 378.

45 TNA, DEFE 24/2841, Notes of a Meeting on Security Policy at Stormont Castle on Tuesday, 22 March 1977.

46 Pearce, *Spymaster*, p. 384.

Chapter Two

1 Erskine Childers, *The Riddle of the Sands: A Record of Secret Service* (London: Penguin Books, [1903] 1979), p. 144.

2 David McKittrick, Seamus Kelters, Brian Feeney and Chris Thornton, *Lost Lives: The Stories of the Men, Women and Children who Died as a Result of the Northern Ireland Troubles*, Revised and Updated (Edinburgh: Mainstream, 2001), p. 779.

3   Thatcher Foundation CCOPR 174/80, Margaret Thatcher, Airey Neave Memorial Lecture, 3 March 1980. Archived at: https://www.margaretthatcher.org/document/104318.

4   Ibid.

5   House of Commons Debates, 6 March 1980, Vol. 980, Col. 651–652.

6   Thatcher Foundation, Margaret Thatcher letter to Sir Antony Acland, dated 5 March 1980. Archived at: https://www.margaretthatcher.org/document/119787. Accessed: 10 December 2019.

7   Percy Cradock, 'Review of Michael Herman's *Intelligence Power in War and Peace*' in *International Affairs*, 73(4), (October 1997), p. 786.

8   For more on the JIC, see Michael Goodman, *The Official History of the Joint Intelligence Committee*, Volume I (Abingdon: Routledge, 2016).

9   The Rt Hon. the Lord Franks, *Falkland Islands Review* (London: HMSO, January 1983), Annex B.

10 Ibid.

11 Sir Percy Cradock served as British Ambassador to China in the early 1980s and later chaired the JIC in the period 1985–92. He explained that its 'function was, and is, to inform senior ministers and the Chiefs of Staff of situations, mainly abroad, likely to threaten British interests and to provide estimates of those, agreed between all interested departments, and drawing on all relevant material, so that ministers will be alive to what is impending and able to make the best policy responses'. Percy Cradock, *Know Your Enemy: How the Joint Intelligence Committee Saw the World* (London: John Murray, 2002), p. 1.

    One of those who would later attend JIC meetings on a regular basis was Sir David Omand, who wrote: 'The best assessments are forward looking, informed by a sound understanding of the past.' See David Omand, 'Introduction: Learning from the Secret Past' in Dover and Goodman (eds), *Learning from the Secret Past*, p. 2.

12 TNA, CAB 186/30, JIC, The Threat to the Cyprus Sovereign Bases, the Retained Sites and British Personnel Serving in Them, 2 November 1979.

13 'Dubliner held in Germany', *The Irish Times*, 18 February 1980.

14 Malcolm Stuart, 'British officer killed in Germany', *The Guardian*, 18 February 1980.

15 Stephen Cook, 'Colonel's murder: couple released', *The Guardian*, 19 February 1980.

16 Ruth Walker, 'German Crime Gang Aiding IRA Assassins', *Christian Science Monitor*, 13 March 1980.

17 'IRA admits German killing', *The Guardian*, 20 February 1980.

18 'No safe refuge', *An Phoblacht/Republican News*, 23 February 1980.

19 Moloney, Ed, *A Secret History of the IRA*, Revised and Updated Edition (London: Penguin, 2007). p. 178.

20 PRONI, ENV/19/1/2A, Trends in Paramilitary Activities: The Provisional Republican Movement, dated 19 February 1979.

21 Ibid.

22 TNA, CAB 186/30, Joint Intelligence Committee, The Current Threat to the United Kingdom from Terrorism (London: Cabinet Office, March 1980).

23 Mark Urban, *Big Boys' Rules: The Secret Struggle Against the IRA* (London: Faber, 1992), p. 125.

24 Stephen Dorril, *The Silent Conspiracy: Inside the Intelligence Agencies in the 1990s* (London: Mandarin, 1994), p. 195.

25 Ibid., p. 194.

26 Urban, *Big Boys' Rules*, p. 126.

27 Ibid.

28 Ibid., pp. 220–221.

29 Kevin J. Kelley, *The Longest War: Northern Ireland and the IRA* (London: Zed Books, 1982), pp. 311–312.

30 Urban, *Big Boys' Rules*, p. 95.

31 Ibid., pp. 95–96.

32 Raymond Murray, *The SAS in Ireland*, New Revised and Updated Edition (Cork: Mercier Press, 1990), p. 253.

33 'Quiet transfer first as "Stormont KGB" goes into action', *The Lethbridge Herald*, 11 October 1979.

34 TNA, PREM 19/280, Security Coordinator Review of East Tyrone, 2 April 1980.

35 Author interview with Peter, 30 July 2019.

36 Urban, *Big Boys' Rules*, p. 223.

37 McKittrick et al., *Lost Lives*, p. 823.

38 HIAI Special Branch Material, SB50 form, dated 30 April 1980. Archived at: https://www.hiainquiry.org/sites/hiainquiry/files/media-files/RUC-Special-Branch%20Material-Rev2-RO.pdf.

39 David McKittrick, 'Political and security ripple as ex-spy master settles in at Stormont', *The Irish Times*, 17 November 1979.

40 Author interview with Danny Morrison, 1 August 2019.

41 *An Phoblacht/Republican News*, 23 February 1980.

42 Author interview with Danny Morrison, 1 August 2019.

43 McKittrick, 'Political and security ripple'.

44 Ibid.

Chapter Three

1 Harry McCallion, *Killing Zone: A Life in the Paras, the Recces, the SAS and the RUC* (London: Bloomsbury, 1995), p. 151.

2 Conversation with a former member of the PIRA, April 2018.

3 Jack Holland and Susan Phoenix, *Phoenix – Policing the Shadows: The Secret War Against Terrorism in Northern Ireland* (London: Coronet Books, 1996), p. 123.

4 Liam Clarke and Kathryn Johnston, *Martin McGuinness: From Guns to Government* (Edinburgh: Mainstream, 2001), pp. 107–108.

5 Martin Dillon, *Killer in Clowntown: Joe Doherty, the IRA and the Special Relationship* (London: Hutchinson, 1992), p. 68.

6 Ted Oliver, 'Deadly Blunder of SAS: Revealed for the first time: How the IRA chief in extradition row shot down officer', *The Sunday Mail* (Scotland), 9 January 2000. Military historian Tony Geraghty later claimed the SAS had 'no time for the normal reconnaissance'. Tony Geraghty, *Who Dares Wins: The Special Air Service – 1950 to the Gulf War* (London: Time Warner, 2002), p. 255. This was incorrect: Westmacott had briefed Brigadier David Ramsbotham about the operation in the hours before he and his men deployed.

7 Ted Oliver and Alastair McQueen, 'I have this premonition, Sir, that I will be killed', *The Sunday Telegraph*, 9 January 2000.

8 Ibid.

9 *Daily News*, 3 April 1984.

10 Dillon, *Killer in Clowntown*, p. 95.

11 Robin Horsfall, *Fighting Scared: Para, Mercenary, SAS, Bodyguard* (London: Cassell, 2002), p. 160.

12 Correspondence with Robin Horsfall, 30 July 2018.

13 Author interview with Lord Ramsbotham, 12 November 2018.

14 TNA, CJ 4/4837, Extradition of Joe Doherty, International Correspondence, 27 March 1984.

15 Urban, *Big Boys' Rules*, pp. 94–96.

16 McCallion, *Killing Zone*, p. 160.

17 Conversation with a former Special Branch officer, 12 September 2018.

18 Author interview with Tommy Gorman, 23 June 2010.

19 McKittrick et al., *Lost Lives*, p. 825.

20 'M60 Machine Gun creates Havoc', *An Phoblacht/Republican News*, 12 April 1980.

21 This is emphasised in books like *Killing Zone* and *Fighting Scared*.

22 Correspondence with Robin Horsfall, 30 July 2018.

23 Dillon, *Killer in Clowntown*, p. 99.

24 Ibid.

25 Ibid.

26 Ibid.

27 Ibid., p. 103.

28 House of Commons Debates (Hansard), 8 May 1980, Vol. 984, Col. 506.

29 TNA, CJ 4/3742, Note of PUS's conversation with VCGS, 7 December 1979.

30 Ibid.

31 Holland and Phoenix, *Policing the Shadows*, p. 87.

32 Ibid., pp. 84–86; Clarke and Johnston, *Martin McGuinness*, pp. 109–111.

33 LHCMA, Ramsbotham Papers, Box 1, Report by Brigadier David Ramsbotham to Major General James Glover, 15 July 1980.

34 HIAI MI5 Material – Part 1 – CLF's Study Period on Army Source Handling and Structures, minutes dated 16 June 1979. Archived at: https://www.hiainquiry.org/sites/hiainquiry/files/media-files/MI5-Material-Pages-1-to-359-Rev-RO.pdf. Accessed: 15 October 2019.

35 Ibid.

36 Ibid.

37 LHCMA, Ramsbotham Papers, Box 1, Report by Brigadier David Ramsbotham to Major General James Glover, 15 July 1980.

38 HIAI CLF's Study Period on Army Source Handling and Structures. Archived at: https://www.hiainquiry.org/sites/hiainquiry/files/media-files/MI5-Material-Pages-1-to-359-Rev-RO.pdf. Accessed: 15 October 2019.

39 'RUC Threats: One of the Branch said "we are out to get you"', *An Phoblacht/Republican News*, 14 June 1980. These allegations are disputed by RUC officers, who say that a gun would not have been permitted in the interview room. For more information on the allegations surrounding Castlereagh, see Ian Cobain, *Cruel Britannia: A Secret History of Torture* (London: Portobello Books, 2013), Chapters 5 and 6.

40 HIAI CLF's Study Period on Army Source Handling and Structures. Archived at: https://www.hiainquiry.org/sites/hiainquiry/files/media-files/MI5-Material-Pages-1-to-359-Rev-RO.pdf. Accessed: 15 October 2019.

41 Deacon, *C*, p. 247.

Chapter Four

1 TNA, PREM 19/817, Sir Robert

Armstrong to Margaret Thatcher, 14 May 1980.

2   Conversation with former RUC Special Branch officers, November 2015.

3   Dorril, *Silent Conspiracy*, pp. 55–56.

4   Cobain, *Cruel Britannia*, p. 145.

5   Pearce, *Spymaster*, p. 397.

6   Ibid.

7   HIAI Cabinet Officer Material – MI5 Report on Maurice Oldfield. Report was addressed to Sir Robert Armstrong and also includes Detective Inspector Catherall's statement on Sir Maurice Oldfield, dated 31 March 1980. Archived at: https://www.hiainquiry.org/sites/hiainquiry/files/media-files/Cabinet-Office-Material-Rev-RO.pdf. Accessed: 15 October 2019.

8   TNA, PREM 19/817, Letter from Sir Maurice Oldfield to Margaret Thatcher, 25 June 1980.

9   Dorril, *Silent Conspiracy*, p. 55.

10 'Coming home to roost', *An Phoblacht/Republican News*, 17 May 1980.

11 Charles Nevin, 'A spymaster's secret friends pay tribute', *The Daily Telegraph*, 13 May 1981.

12 Author interview with Peter, 30 July 2019.

13 TNA, PREM 19/817, Secret and Personal letter to MT from Sir Robert Armstrong, 14 May 1980.

14 Ibid.

15 'Obituary: Sir Brooks Richards', *The Guardian*, 19 September 2002.

16 'G3' is the administrative name for those from the infantry, cavalry and artillery who tend to lead in front-line Army operations.

17 LHCMA, Ramsbotham Papers, Box 1, Report by Brigadier David Ramsbotham to Major General James Glover, 15 July 1980.

18 Author interview with Lord Ramsbotham, 12 November 2018.

19 LHCMA, Ramsbotham Papers, Report by Brigadier David Ramsbotham to Major General James Glover, 15 July 1980.

20 For more in-depth discussion of the NLF's war in Aden and South Arabia, see Aaron Edwards, *Mad Mitch's Tribal Law: Aden and the End of Empire* (Edinburgh: Mainstream Publishing, 2014).

21 Colonel Tony Jeapes, *SAS: Operation Oman* (London: William Kimber and Co. Limited, 1980), p. 192.

22 TNA, CJ 4/3742, Draft Speaking Notes for Staff College Presentation, 16 November 1979. Creasey's remarks caused a stir in government circles.

23 TNA, CJ 4/3742, Draft Speaking Notes for Staff College Presentation.

24 Author interview with Lord Ramsbotham, 12 November 2018.

25 LHCMA, Ramsbotham Papers, Box 1, Report by Brigadier David Ramsbotham to Major General James Glover, 15 July 1980.

26 'G2' is the administrative term for Army Intelligence.

27 Gerry Bradley, *Insider: Gerry Bradley's Life in the IRA* (Dublin: The O'Brien Press, 2009), pp. 153–154.

28 LHCMA, Ramsbotham Papers, Ramsbotham to Glover, 15 July 1980.

29 Ibid.

30 Dorril, *Silent Conspiracy*, p. 55.

31 Patrick Walker, *Report on the Interchange of Intelligence between Special Branch and C.I.D. and on the R.U.C. Units Involved, including those in Crime Branch C1(1)* (31 March 1980). Archived: https://caj.org.uk/2018/07/02/ruc-walker-report-1980/. Accessed: 23 December 2019.

32 LHCMA, Ramsbotham Papers, Ramsbotham to Glover, 15 July 1980.

33 Ibid.

34 Ibid.

35 McKittrick et al., *Lost Lives*, p. 842.

36 Martin Dillon, *The Dirty War* (London: Arrow Books, 1991), pp. 390–393.

37 Author interview with a former RUC officer, December 2019.

38 Ibid.

39 David McKittrick 'Secret RUC operations leaked to Provisionals', *The Irish Times*, 27 October 1979.

40 Pat Finucane Centre, 'Ronnie Flanagan – A Fact File on the RUC Chief Constable', 4 November 1997. Archived at: https://www.patfinucanecentre.org/policing/ronnie-flanagan-fact-file-ruc-chief-constable. Accessed: 2 January 2020.

41 Dillon, *The Dirty War*, pp. 390–393.

42 Bradley, *Insider*, p. 208.

43 Ibid.

44 William Matchett, *Secret Victory: The Intelligence War that Beat the IRA* (Lisburn: Hiskey Ltd, 2016), p. 94.

45 Ibid., p. 181.

46 Ibid., p. 92.

Chapter Five

1 J.C. Masterman, *The Double-Cross System in the War of 1939 to 1945* (London: Yale University Press, 1972), p. 13.

2 Met Office, Introduction to the Daily Weather Record, 1 October–31 December 1980, Weather and Temperatures for London (Kew). Archived: https://digital.nmla.metoffice.gov.uk/IO_578988d4-0fad-4711-bdaa-1fbb5131bd9d. Accessed: 31 October 2019.

3 Peter Simmonds, 'How it looks from No. 10', *The Sunday Telegraph*, 7 December 1980.

4 Thatcher Foundation, MT Engagement Diary, 5 December 1980. Accessible at: https://www.margaretthatcher.org/document/113655

5 Thatcher Foundation, MT Engagement Diary, 26 November 1980. Accessible at: https://www.margaretthatcher.org/document/113646.

6 Carlin claimed the car was blue, but in his memoirs it is a red Peugeot. Willie Carlin, *Thatcher's Spy: My Life as an MI5 Spy inside Sinn Féin* (Dublin: Merrion Press, 2019), p. 54.

7 Niall Ó Dochartaigh, 'The Role of an Intermediary in Back-Channel Negotiation: Evidence from the Brendan Duddy papers', *Dynamics of Asymmetric Conflict*, 4(3), (October 2011), pp. 214–225; 'Brendan Duddy Obituary', *The Daily Telegraph*, 15 May 2017.

8 Ben MacIntyre, *The Spy and the Traitor: The Greatest Espionage Story of the Cold War* (London: Penguin Books, 2018), p. 168.

9 Author interview with Willie Carlin, 28 September 2018.

10 MI5 contemporaries suggest that Northern Ireland changed Bettaney for the worse, while more sympathetic Marxist voices argue that the place 'changed him for the better'. See Jack Conrad, 'A Man of Contradictions: Michael Bettaney, February 13 1950–August 16 2018', *Weekly Worker*, 6 September 2018. Archived at: https://weeklyworker.co.uk/worker/1217/a-man-of-contradictions/. Accessed: 8 January 2020.

11 MacIntyre, *The Spy and the Traitor*, pp. 168–171.

12 After it was announced that Patrick

Walker's replacement as Director General of MI5 would be his protégée, Stella Rimington, Carlin realised that 'Paula' was, in fact, Rimington. It is probable that Rees-Morgan was John Deverell, head of F5, MI5's Irish Terrorism branch, though Carlin has never revealed the true identities of his handlers. See Duncan Campbell, 'Carry on Spying – and Dying?, *The New Statesmen*, 20 October 1989; Dorril, *Silent Conspiracy*, p. 195.

13 Carlin, *Thatcher's Spy*, p. 56.

14 The Irish Joint Section operated from the 1970s until the mid-1980s and brought together specialists from both MI5 and MI6.

15 MI5 Officer A Statement 2 to the Bloody Sunday Inquiry, dated and signed 16 January 2003. Publicly accessible at the National Archives Inquiries Website: https://webarchive.nationalarchives. gov.uk/20101017072448/http:// report.bloody-sunday-inquiry.org/ evidence/K/KA_0002.pdf.

16 Clarke and Johnson, *Martin McGuinness*, p. 124.

17 TNA, PREM 19/817, Brooks Richards, Coordination of the Security Effort in Northern Ireland: The Way Forward (Belfast: Stormont Castle, 1981).

18 For more on the concept of stovepiping vis-à-vis British Intelligence and Northern Ireland, see Tony Craig, '"You will be responsible to the GOC". Stovepiping and the problem of divergent intelligence gathering networks in Northern Ireland, 1969–1975', *Intelligence and National Security*, 33(2), (2017), pp. 211–226.

19 Named by both Stephen Dorril and Nigel West as the DCI in the early 1980s, David Ranson was also avowed in Stella Rimington's autobiography.

He died in 1992.

20 TNA, PREM 19/817, Richards, Coordination of the Security Effort in Northern Ireland.

21 Ibid.

22 David McKittrick, 'Oldfield's job sets the tongues wagging', *The Irish Times*, 6 October 1979.

23 Murray, *The SAS in Ireland*, p. 256.

24 TNA, CJ 4/4571, GOC's Lecture Notes Belfast Rotary Club Lunch, 6 April 1981.

25 Author interview with Willie Carlin, 28 September 2018; Carlin, *Thatcher's Spy*, p. 58.

26 Author interview with Willie Carlin, 28 September 2018.

27 Ibid.

28 Ibid.

29 The gun used in the murder was later traced to punishment beatings in Derry.

30 Carlin, *Thatcher's Spy*, p. 62.

31 Author interview with Willie Carlin, 28 September 2018.

32 Author interview with Willie Carlin, 3 June 2019.

33 Willie Carlin gave a full account of his background as an MI5 agent to the Saville Inquiry. A transcript can be found here: https://webarchive.nationalarchives. gov.uk/20101017071718/http:/ report.bloody-sunday-inquiry.org/ evidence/K/KC_0005.pdf.

34 NIO, 1 May 1981–5 May 1981. On the day Sands died, there were 1,361 prisoners in the Maze, as well as seventy prisoners in Armagh jail, 636 in the Crumlin Road jail, 197 in Magilligan and 231 young offenders in Hydebank Wood detention centre.

35 Author interview with Willie Carlin, 28 September 2018.

36   A shorter version of the poem is contained in Carlin, *Thatcher's Spy*, pp. 65–66.

37   Author interview with Willie Carlin, 28 September 2018.

38   Carlin, *Thatcher's Spy*, pp. 66–67.

39   Author interview with Willie Carlin, 3 June 2019.

Chapter Six

1   Author interview with Willie Carlin, 3 June 2019.

2   *The Daily Telegraph*, 20 December 1871.

3   'Derry Riots', *The Daily Telegraph*, 18 August 1913.

4   'Trouble in Derry', *The Daily Telegraph*, 21 March 1921.

5   Author interview with Eamonn McCann, 21 December 2007.

6   Wolfe Tone was the leader of the United Irishmen.

7   'Profile: Father James Chesney', *The Irish Times*, 25 August 2010; 'Unionists seek extradition of priest who became IRA bomb maker', *The Irish Times*, 24 September 2019.

8   Margaret M. Scull, 'The Catholic Church and the Hunger Strikes of Terence MacSwiney and Bobby Sands', *Irish Political Studies*, 31(2), (2016), p. 289.

9   Author interview with Willie Carlin, 3 June 2019.

10   'Fógraí bháis: John "Stylo" Curran', *An Phoblacht/Republican News*, 11 October 2007.

11   Author interview with Willie Carlin, 28 September 2018.

12   From a witness statement given by Officer Z to the Bloody Sunday Inquiry, publicly accessible at: https://webarchive.nationalarchives. gov.uk/20101017074406/http:// report.bloody-sunday-inquiry.org/ evidence/K/KZ_0001.pdf.

13   TNA, PREM 19/817, Richards, Coordination of the Security Effort in Northern Ireland.

14   Author interview with Willie Carlin, 3 June 2019.

15   Ibid.

16   See Tony Craig, 'From Backdoors and Back Lanes to Backchannels: Reappraising British Talks with the Provisional IRA, 1970–1974', *Contemporary British History*, 26(1), (2012), pp. 97–117; Tony Craig, 'Laneside, then left a bit? Britain's Secret Political Talks with Loyalist Paramilitaries in Northern Ireland, 1973–1976', *Irish Political Studies*, 29(2), (2014), pp. 298–317.

17   NUI Galway, Brendan Duddy Archive, 434, Michael Oatley to Brendan Duddy, 29 March 1981.

18   According to historian Tom Griffin, David Ranson was a senior MI5 officer at the time of the hunger strikes. He may have been DCI in 1979–81. See Tom Griffin, 'The conspiracy theory of the peace process is a dangerous myth', *Open Democracy*, 27 June 2012. Archived at: https://www.opendemocracy.net/en/ opendemocracyuk/conspiracy-theory- of-peace-process-is-dangerous-myth/. Intelligence historian Nigel West also lists the names of DCI postholders in his *Historical Dictionary of British Intelligence*, Second Edition (Plymouth, Scarecrow Press, 2014), p. 291. In her memoir, former MI5 Director General Stella Rimington said David Ranson had a professional reputation in counter-subversion and counter-terrorism.

19 TNA, PREM 19/499, Situation in Northern Ireland: Force Levels, No. 10 record of conversation (MT-Atkins-Stowe-Lawson-Hermon-Ranson) on the situation in Northern Ireland, 27 May 1981.

20 Ibid.

21 TNA, PREM 19/499, Situation in Northern Ireland: Force Levels, 'The Provisionals: Political Activity – Briefing for the Prime Minister by David Ranson', 16 June 1981.

22 Richard O'Rawe, *Blanketmen: An Untold Story of the H-block Hunger Strike* (Dublin: New Island Books, 2004; 2016), pp. 184–194.

23 Author interview with Danny Morrison, 22 February 2012.

24 TNA, CJ 4/3965, HQNI, GOC's Speaking Notes for the SPM, 22 September 1981.

25 Tommy McKearney, *The Provisional IRA: From Insurrection to Parliament* (London: Pluto Press, 2011), pp. 152–155.

26 Matchett, *Secret Victory*, p. 104.

27 Raymond Gilmour, *Dead Ground: Infiltrating the IRA* (London: Warner Books, 1998), p. 321.

28 My thanks to GB for passing on a transcript of his interviews with former RUC officers.

29 Author interview with Willie Carlin, 31 December 2018.

30 Author interview with Willie Carlin, 28 September 2018.

Chapter Seven

1 HIAI KIN-105219, 'CLF's Study Period on Army Source Handling and Recruitment', 24 May 1979. Archived at: https://www.hiainquiry.org/sites/hiainquiry/files/media-files/MI5-Material-Pages-1-to-359-Rev-RO.pdf. Accessed: 28 October 2019.

2 House of Commons Debates (Hansard), 2 July 1981, Vol. 7, Col. 1056.

3 Ibid. Col. 1057.

4 Greg Harkin, 'MP could have been saved', *Belfast Telegraph*, 11 July 2008.

5 Investigative journalist Lyra McKee interviewed a former member of the RUC Special Branch who said they were detained in a meeting and could not get the information out in time. Lyra McKee, *Angels with Blue Faces* (Belfast: Excalibur Press, 2019), pp. 83–84.

6 PRONI, ANT 6/1/1/30/12A, Coroner's Inquest into the Deaths of Robert Bradford and Kenneth Campbell who died on 14 November 1981.

7 Interview with Witness A for the ULET Legacy Archive, 25 October 2017. Cited with permission.

8 'Bradford shot dead', *Belfast Telegraph*, 14 November 1981.

9 Ibid.

10 Ibid.

11 Hugh Jordan, 'Chief Suspect Bradford Murder: Kenova probe had eyes on "The Hawk"', *Sunday World*, 16 December 2018. According to Jordan, Haughey's fingerprints were found on the grip but he was never charged.

12 Eilis O'Hanlon, 'Joseph Haughey, who has died aged 66, was guilty of many foul deeds … there is little reason to pretend any more that the murder of Mary Travers was not one of them', *Belfast Telegraph*, 14 December 2018.

13 Ibid.

14 Jordan, 'Chief Suspect Bradford Murder'.

15 PRONI, DOW 1/1/B/89/17, John Joseph Haughey, Robert Henry

McCallum and Robert Joseph O'Hanlon – robbery and possession of firearms (Downpatrick County Court, 4 September 1972). Curiously, like many files on republicans, this one remains closed.

16 PRONI, CRCT 3/2/3/70, Joseph Haughey et al. – Murder of Herbert Richard Westmacott and Stephen Magill. The charges also included attempted murder, possession of firearms and ammunition with intent, false imprisonment and belonging to a proscribed organisation. CRCT 3/2/2/288, John Joseph Haughey – Causing an explosion and possession of explosive substances with intent and belonging to a proscribed organisation.

17 Jordan, 'Chief Suspect Bradford Murder'.

18 Cited in Harkin, 'MP could have been saved'.

19 TNA, PREM 19/817, Richards, Coordination of the Security Effort in Northern Ireland, p. 23.

20 McKearney, The Provisional IRA, p. 152.

21 TNA, PREM 19/817, Sir Brooks Richards, Review of the Security Situation in Northern Ireland (Belfast: Stormont Castle, November 1981), p. 3.

22 Ibid., p. 8.

23 Ibid.

24 Ibid., p. 12.

25 PRONI, CRCT 3/2/4/473A, Patrick Pearse O'Neill – Murder of Albert Beacom. Possession of firearms and ammunition with intent. Possession of firearms and ammunition, July 1982.

26 PRONI, CRCT 3/2/4/473A, Patrick Pearse O'Neill – Murder of Albert Beacom. Possession of firearms and ammunition with intent. Possession of firearms and ammunition, July 1982.

27 John Cunningham, 'Close encounters with the Third Force', The Guardian, 26 November 1981.

28 Lord Ernest Hamilton, The Soul of Ulster (New York: E.P. Dutton and Co., 1917), p. 111.

29 Ibid., p. 112.

30 On the IRA border campaign, see Henry Patterson, Ireland's Violent Frontier: The Border and Anglo-Irish Relations During the Troubles (Basingstoke: Palgrave Macmillan, 2013).

31 TNA, CJ 4/3965, Commander NI speaking notes for SPM, 10 December 1981 to 13 January 1982, dated 13 January 1982.

32 Maev-Ann Wren, 'IRA gained in eventful year', The Irish Times, 30 December 1981.

33 Urban, Big Boys' Rules, p. 133.

34 Paul Johnson, 'Naïve recruit who shopped IRA: Paul Johnson examines the career of Christopher Black, the terrorist who became Ulster's most spectacular "supergrass"', The Guardian, 5 August 1983.

35 'Trial told of IRA clubs', The Irish Times, 20 January 1983.

36 Ultimately, thirty-eight people (including five women) were put on trial thanks to Black's allegations.

37 Johnson, 'Naïve recruit who shopped IRA'.

38 Patrick Bishop, 'IRA informer gets immunity', The Observer, 6 December 1981.

39 David Beresford, 'Police success in coping with IRA', The Guardian, 12 December 1981.

40 TNA, CJ 4/4750, Meeting with the GOC at Stormont Castle on 12 January

1982.

41 Ibid.

42 '43 people now held for questioning in North swoops', *The Irish Times*, 8 February 1982.

43 Conversation with a former RUC detective, 5 March 2020.

44 Colin Brady, 'IRA steps up its campaign to find "betrayers"', *The Daily Telegraph*, 8 February 1982.

45 Andrew Pollak, 'Three soldiers die in Belfast ambush', *The Irish Times*, 26 March 1982. It was later seized in an operation mounted by RUC Special Branch in Derry, helped principally by their agent Raymond Gilmour.

46 TNA, CJ 4/3965, CLF Speaking Notes for period 1–25 March 1982, dated 26 March 1982.

Chapter Eight

1 TNA, WO 305/6020, Post Tour Report – 2 RGJ, dated 16 March 1982. Their operational tour of north and west Belfast lasted from 15 November 1981 to 28 March 1982.

2 This is further evidence that the cellular system was not working.

3 TNA, CJ 4/3965, Minutes of the SPM held at 1445hrs on 29 March 1982.

4 Dorril, *Silent Conspiracy*, pp. 204, 484.

5 Doyne-Ditmas' friend John McPhee refers to him as 'Doyne Ditmas of the Box [MI5]' in an article published in *The New Yorker* called 'Season on the Chalk: From Ditchling Beacon to Épernay', published on 4 March 2007.

6 Nigel West, *At Her Majesty's Secret Service: The Chiefs of Britain's Intelligence Agency MI6* (London: Greenhill Books, 2006); Dorril, *Silent Conspiracy*, pp. 484–485. Eulogy for Hal Doyne-Ditmas. Archived at:

http://www.olduppinghamian.co.uk/uploads/media/75ad5cb4d69b4a124ef050fedefc7139f17e3842.pdf. Accessed: 31 October 2019.

7 Andrew, *The Defence of the Realm*, p. 621.

8 Ibid.

9 This description of the role of the DCI and Security Service in Northern Ireland is taken from the Right Honourable Lord MacLean et al., *The Billy Wright Inquiry – Report* (London: The Stationary Office, 14 September 2010), p. 105.

10 Dorril, *Silent Conspiracy*, p. 204.

11 TNA, CJ 4/4571, Vengeful and Long Car Checks.

12 This information is now in the public domain, with documents available at: TNA, CJ 4/4571, Automatic Data Processor for Army Use in Northern Ireland: Project Crucible', dated 25 May 1983. See also Urban, *Big Boys' Rules*, pp. 115–117; Duncan Campbell, 'Led by the Nose', *The Guardian*, 2 November 2000.

13 TNA, CJ 4/4571, Automatic Data Processor for Army Use in Northern Ireland: Project Crucible, dated 25 May 1983.

14 Confirmed in the testimony of Ian Hurst to the Bloody Sunday inquiry on 12 May 2003. Archived at: https://webarchive.nationalarchives.gov.uk/20101017063949/http://report.bloody-sunday-inquiry.org/transcripts/Archive/Ts329.htm. Accessed: 6 January 2020. Also confirmed by Officer Y to the Bloody Sunday Inquiry on 14 May 2003. Archived: https://webarchive.nationalarchives.gov.uk/20101017063635/http://report.bloody-sunday-inquiry.org/

transcripts/Archive/Ts331.htm. Accessed: 8 January 2020.

15 TNA, CJ 4/4571, Automatic Data Processor for Army Use in Northern Ireland: Project Crucible, dated 25 May 1983.

16 Dorril, *Silent Conspiracy*, p. 204.

17 Ibid. See also Donald A. Borrmann, William T. Kvetkas, Charles V. Brown, Michael J. Flatley, and Robert Hunt, *The History of Traffic Analysis: World War 1 to Vietnam* (Fort Meade, MD: NSA, 2013). Archived at: https://www.nsa.gov/Portals/70/documents/about/cryptologic-heritage/historical-figures-publications/publications/misc/traffic_analysis.pdf. Accessed: 11 December 2019.

18 Dorril, *Silent Conspiracy*, p. 204.

19 TNA, CJ 4/4571, Automatic Data Processor for Army Use in Northern Ireland: Project Crucible, dated 25 May 1983.

20 All this information was taken from the Witness Statement of Officer Y to the Bloody Sunday Inquiry. Publicly accessible at: https://webarchive.nationalarchives.gov.uk/20101017065733/http://report.bloody-sunday-inquiry.org/evidence/K/KY_0001.pdf.

21 Confirmed in the testimony of Ian Hurst to the Bloody Sunday inquiry on 12 May 2003. Archived at: https://webarchive.nationalarchives.gov.uk/20101017063949/http://report.bloody-sunday-inquiry.org/transcripts/Archive/Ts329.htm. Accessed: 6 January 2020.

22 Ibid.

23 Ibid.

24 Mark Urban argues that the Crucible system, which replaced Project 3702, was able to do this from 1987. However, documents since released to the author under the FOI Act, together with the testimony of Ian Hurst to the Bloody Sunday Tribunal, suggest that this could be done earlier. See Urban, *Big Boy's Rules*, pp. 116–117; also TNA, CJ 4/4571, Automatic Data Processor for Army Use in Northern Ireland: Project Crucible, dated 25 May 1983.

25 This information was taken from the Witness Statement of Officer Y to the Bloody Sunday Inquiry. Publicly accessible at: https://webarchive.nationalarchives.gov.uk/20101017065733/http://report.bloody-sunday-inquiry.org/evidence/K/KY_0001.pdf.

26 Thatcher, *The Downing Street Years*, p. 179.

27 Royal Hampshire Regiment, 'Fermanagh 1982'. Archived at: https://www.royalhampshireregiment.org/about-the-museum/timeline/fermanagh-1982/. Accessed: 11 December 2019.

28 Airborne Forces Museum (AFM), Intelligence Summary, 3 May to 16 May 1982; TNA, WO 305/5360, Commander's Diary, 1 April 1982 to 30 April 1982.

29 AFM, Secret Op Instruction for 1 PARA, dated May 1982.

30 Ibid.

31 Rory Finegan, 'Targeted killings in Northern Ireland: An analysis of their effectiveness and implications for counter-terrorism policies' (Dublin City University: PhD Thesis, 2014), pp. 139, 271, 274; Matchett, *Secret Victory*, p. 104.

32 Obituary of Philip McDonald in *An Phoblacht/Republican News*, 30 March 2006. Archived at: https://www.anphoblacht.com/contents/15045.

Accessed: 5 November 2019.

33 AFM, INTSUM, 31 May to 13 June 1982.

34 During the On The Run (OTR) scandal, Downey was acquitted in a criminal trial on the Hyde Park bombing in 2014. However, in a civil case hearing, in December 2019, a High Court judge ruled that, given evidence she considered, and 'In the circumstances, it is reasonable to infer that the defendant [Downey] was knowingly involved in the concerted plan to detonate the bomb in Hyde Park specifically targeted at the passing Guard'. See Sarah Jane Young and John Anthony Downey, Hearing Date, 11 & 12 December 2019. Accessible at: https://www.judiciary.uk/wp-content/uploads/2019/12/APPROVED-JUDGMENT-Young-v-Downey-18.12.19.pdf.

35 AFM, INTSUM, 31 May to 13 June 1982.

36 TNA, CJ 4/4750, E.R. Lunn to Paul Buxton, 24 May 1982.

Chapter Nine

1 AFM, INTSUM, 17 September 1982.

2 AFM, INTSUM, 20 July 1982.

3 Andrew, The Defence of the Realm, p. 697.

4 Ibid.

5 Twenty-nine-year-old Paul Kavanagh was later arrested and convicted of the Chelsea Barracks attack. Ed Blanche, 'IRA guerrilla found guilty in bomb trial', Associated Press, 6 March 1985.

6 Andrew Fisher and Margaret van Hattem, 'Eight Soldiers killed in London IRA bombings', Financial Times, 21 July 1982.

7 Tim Pat Coogan, The IRA (London: HarperCollins, 1995), p. 502.

8 Fisher and van Hattem, 'Eight Soldiers killed in London IRA bombings'.

9 Ibid.

10 Author interview with Patrick Mercer, 25 January 2011.

11 Ibid.

12 Ibid.

13 Moloney, Secret History, 215.

14 Author interview with Willie Carlin, 28 September 2018.

15 Ibid.

16 Crumley got 556 votes.

17 Gregory Campbell got 5,305 votes.

18 Author interview with Willie Carlin, 28 September 2018.

19 Author interview with Anthony McIntyre, 20 October 2019.

20 McKittrick et al., Lost Lives, p. 918.

21 Ibid.

22 Ian Cobain, 'Northern Ireland: When Britain Fought Terror with Terror', The Guardian, 9 July 2015.

23 European Court of Human Rights, Case of McKerr v. the United Kingdom: Final Judgement, 4 May 2001. Archived at: https://www.bailii.org/eu/cases/ECHR/2001/329.html. Accessed: 31 March 2020.

24 Ibid.

25 Private information, April 2020.

26 ECHR, Case of McKerr v. the United Kingdom.

27 Ibid.

28 Author interview with Jack, 10 October 2018.

29 Matchett, Secret Victory, p. 104.

30 Ibid.

31 Ibid.

32 Ed Moloney, 'Bessbrook unit the model for RUC covert groups', The Irish Times, 21 January 1985.

33 Author interview with Jack, 2 August 2019.

34   Chief Constable's Report 1980 (dated April 1981), p. 16. My thanks to the PSNI Freedom of Information team for releasing these reports to me.

35   In an article on the appointment of Charles Kelly to preside over disciplinary recommendations for those officers caught up in the so-called 'Shoot to Kill' incidents, *The Guardian* attributed this quote to 'a senior member of the RUC'. I have been told that the words were spoken by Sir John Hermon himself in a briefing to the new unit in 1980. Private information, October 2018. See David Hearst, 'Kelly faces obstinate questions on trail pioneered by Stalker', *The Guardian*, 18 February 1988.

36   Author interview with Jack, 10 October 2018.

37   Lieutenant Colonel A. De P. Gauvain, 'Commanding Officer's Notes', *The Oak Tree: Journal of the 22nd (Cheshire) Regiment*, 67(1), (Summer 1982), p. 32.

38   *Daily Mirror*, 8 December 1982.

39   Ibid.

40   TNA, DEFE 25/532, Northern Ireland Ops and Int, Operational Summary – 1 November–31 December 1982.

41   *Daily Express*, 8 December 1982.

42   *Daily Mirror*, 8 December 1982. According to Willie Carlin, the OC of the Derry Brigade gave permission for one of his volunteers to tip off the RUC about the whereabouts of the INLA man responsible for the Droppin' Well attack. *Thatcher's Spy*, p. 123.

43   McKittrick et al., *Lost Lives*, p. 929.

44   Ibid.

45   Ibid.

46   Ibid. p. 943.

Chapter Ten

1   Louis MacNeice, 'Obituary' (1940), appeared in *Poetry: A Magazine of Verse*, 61(11), (May 1940), p. 61. Archived: https://www.poetryfoundation.org/poetrymagazine/browse?contentId=22599.

2   Other reports suggest that the IRA squad had gone to assassinate a part-time UDR man who worked as a postman in Rostrevor. Private information, August 2019.

3   David Beresford, 'RUC men shot dead', *The Guardian*, 7 January 1983.

4   PRONI, NIO 10/9/8/A, Letter from RUC Central Stores to Police Authority for N Ireland, 29 July 1983.

5   Matchett, *Secret Victory*, p. 209.

6   'NI Commander reaffirms army role', *The Irish Times*, 24 March 1983.

7   Detail provided by Willie Carlin in an interview with the author, 28 September 2018.

8   Description of McGuinness and the Cable Street offices taken from Patrick Bishop, 'A gunman cleans up his act', *The Observer*, 17 April 1983.

9   Interview with Willie Carlin, 28 September 2018.

10   Robert White, *Out of the Ashes: An Oral History of the Provisional Irish Republican Movement* (Dublin: Merrion Press, 2017), p. 198.

11   Ibid.

12   Author interview with Willie Carlin, 28 September 2018.

13   Ibid.

14   TNA, DEFE 25/532, Northern Ireland Ops and Int, Monthly Intelligence Summary: Northern Ireland, dated 22 April 1983.

15   Ibid., dated 21 June 1983.

16   Ibid.

17 PRONI, CENT 1/12//24, D.G. McNeill to Mr Reeve, 7 June 1983.

18 PRONI, CENT 1/12/33, D.G. McNeill, Visit to Londonderry, 16 August 1983, dated 18 August 1983.

19 Author interview with Willie Carlin, 28 September 2018.

20 Private information, 2018.

21 Moloney, *Secret History*, p. 243; United Press International (UPI), 20 October 1983.

22 Author interview with Anthony McIntyre, 20 October 2019.

23 Moloney, *Secret History*, p. 385.

24 Author interview with Colonel (Ret'd) David Benest, 2018.

25 TNA, DEFE 68/842, Report of Escape, dated 23–26 September 1983.

26 Interview with the Provisional IRA leadership in 'The Great Escape from the H-Blocks: Remembering the Past', *An Phoblacht/Republican News*, 25 September 2017. Half of those who escaped subsequently died in various IRA operations.

27 TNA, DEFE 25/532, Northern Ireland Ops and Int, Intelligence Summary as at 1 November 1983.

28 Ibid.

29 TNA, DEFE 25/532, Operational Summary, 1 November–31 December 1983.

30 Author interview with Jimmy B., 26 October 2011.

31 House of Commons Debates (Hansard), 8 December 1983, Vol. 50, Col. 450.

32 This claim, given without evidence, was reported by BBC Northern Ireland in an episode of their series *Spotlight on the Troubles* broadcast on 1 October 2019. Gerry Adams told the *Belfast News Letter* that, 'The claim in the BBC programme, based on an anonymous British source, is untrue.' Much of the intelligence product from this time is obsessed with Adams, even though he has strenuously denied ever being a member of the IRA. See 'Gerry Adams can "leave positive legacy" says sister of murdered unionist lawyer', *Belfast News Letter*, 5 October 2019.

33 TNA, DEFE 25/532, Monthly Intelligence Summary: Northern Ireland, 10 November–22 December, dated 23 December 1983.

34 Ibid. See previous endnote for a disclaimer on these allegations.

35 TNA, DEFE 25/532, Intelligence Summary as at 1 January 1984. Although the murderers were alleged to have been from West Belfast, some police sources claim that the personnel were drawn from an ASU in South Belfast.

36 Aaron Edwards, *UVF: Behind the Mask* (Dublin: Merrion Press, 2017), pp. 166–172.

37 John Horgan and Max Taylor, 'Playing the "Green Card": Financing the Provisional IRA: Part 1', *Terrorism and Political Violence*, 11(2), (1999), p. 10.

38 TNA, PREM 19/1285 f190, Butler Letter, dated 31 January 1984.

39 Moloney, *Secret History*, p. 243.

Chapter Eleven

1 Barbara Day, 'Fiancé at side of dying WPC', *The Times*, 18 April 1984.

2 Alan Hamilton, Stewart Tendler and John Witherow, 'London Embassy Shots Kill Policewoman', *The Times*, 18 April 1984.

3 Author interview with Oliver Miles, 6 November 2018.

4 TNA, PREM 19/1300, 17 April 1984.

5 TNA, PREM 19/1300, Record of a

telephone conversation between the Prime Minister in Lisbon and the Home Secretary in London, 18 April 1984.

6   Ibid.

7   TNA, PREM 19/1300, Coles minute to Margaret Thatcher, 18 April 1984.

8   Author interview with Oliver Miles, 6 November 2018.

9   Author interview with Oliver Miles, 12 June 2013.

10   TNA, FO 973/368, Libya and Irish Terrorism – FCO Background Brief, dated June 1984.

11   Author interview with Oliver Miles, 6 November 2018.

12   Oliver Miles, 'The Arms Dealer's Assistant', *London Review of Books*, 16 October 2012.

13   TNA, FO 973/368, Libya and Irish Terrorism – FCO Background Brief, dated June 1984.

14   PRONI, LOND 6/1/1/22/41A, Coroner's Report on the Death of Richard Quigley, Deposition of Witness, 27 June 1985.

15   PRONI, LOND 6/1/1/22/41A, Coroner's Report on the Death of Richard Quigley, Deposition of Detective Constable, North Region CID, 27 June 1985.

16   PRONI, LOND 6/1/1/22/41A, Coroner's Report on the Death of Richard Quigley, Deposition of Witness, 27 June 1985.

17   Ibid.

18   Edward Scallan, 'Bomb blunder kills IRA man', *Daily Mail*, 23 April 1984; 'IRA man killed in Derry blast', *The Irish Times*, 23 April 1984.

19   TNA, WO 305/5530, Headquarters Northern Ireland, Diary of Events, dated 9 February 1984.

20   TNA, WO 305/5530, Headquarters

Northern Ireland, Operational Summary for the Period 210001Z Feb 84 – 052359Z Mar 84, dated 8 March 1984.

21   McKittrick et al., *Lost Lives*, p. 980.

22   '2 more charged with murder', *The Irish Times*, 8 May 1984. Two weeks later, police had arrested, interrogated and charged two young men from the Bogside area. Nineteen-year-old John Joseph McDevitt, an unemployed grocer from Lisfannon Park, and 17-year-old Christopher James Kyle of Drumcliffe Avenue in the city, both younger than Neil Clarke, were remanded in custody for the soldier's murder. Both of the accused were to serve life sentences for the murder of Clarke. Kyle was charged with throwing the petrol bomb. Both men denied the charges. McDevitt still protests his innocence of the crime and is seeking to clear his name. See https://www.derrynow.com/news/troubles-derry-man-launches-bid-clear-name-murder-british-soldier-1984/268347.

23   'Huge turnout at funeral of IRA man', *Derry Journal*, 27 April 1984.

24   Ibid.

25   TNA, FO 973/368, Libya and Irish Terrorism – FCO Background Brief, dated June 1984.

26   Ibid.

27   Ibid.

28   A decade later, the disgraced Security Service officer David Shayler revealed an alleged conversation he had with someone with knowledge of INFLICTION, claiming that the agent was 'not' an MI5 agent and that he was regarded as a 'bullshitter'. Both claims were revealed by senior MI5 officers in the Saville Inquiry to be untrue. It was also said that Shayler never had access

to top-secret material, certainly not from the Irish agent runners.

29 Evidence by Officer A to Bloody Sunday Inquiry, dated 12 April 2000. Archived at: https://webarchive.nationalarchives.gov.uk/20101017072448/http://report.bloody-sunday-inquiry.org/evidence/K/KA_0002.pdf. Accessed: 31 October 2019.

30 Secret Transcript of a Source Report, Saville Inquiry. Archived at: https://webarchive.nationalarchives.gov.uk/20101017072448/http://report.bloody-sunday-inquiry.org/evidence/K/KA_0002.pdf. Accessed: 31 October 2019.

31 Interview with Willie Carlin, 25 October 2018. The episode is also recounted in Carlin, *Thatcher's Spy*, pp. 107–108.

32 Michael Herman, *Intelligence Power in Peace and War* (Cambridge: Cambridge University Press, 1996), p. 65.

33 Clarke and Johnston, *Martin McGuinness*, p. 147.

34 Greg Harkin and Martin Ingram, *Stakeknife: Britain's Secret Agents in Ireland* (Dublin: O'Brien Press, 2004), p. 120.

35 Clarke and Johnston, *Martin McGuinness*, pp. 147–148.

36 Martin Ingram statement to the Bloody Sunday Inquiry, Letter from WG Byatt, Head of the MoD's Bloody Sunday Inquiry Unit, to W.J. Tate, 8 May 2003. Publicly accessible at: https://webarchive.nationalarchives.gov.uk/20101017074349/http://report.bloody-sunday-inquiry.org/evidence/K/KI_0002.pdf.

37 Harkin and Ingram, *Stakeknife*, p. 117.

38 Carlin, *Thatcher's Spy*, pp. 139–140.

39 Author interview with Willie Carlin,

28 September 2018.

40 Carlin, *Thatcher's Spy*, p. 188.

41 Ibid., p. 187.

42 'Obituary for Michael Bettaney', *The Daily Telegraph*, 18 October 2018; Paul Foot, 'Whitehall Farce', *London Review of Books*, 11(19), (12 October 1989).

43 MacIntyre, *The Spy and the Traitor*, pp. 162–177.

44 The figure was divulged by Margaret Thatcher in a written statement to a question posed in the House of Commons. House of Commons Debates (Hansard), 9 November 1981, Vol. 12, Col. 43. She said it would not be in the public interest to disclose how many other people had confessed to committing espionage but were never convicted for their treasonous crimes.

45 Author interview with Willie Carlin, 28 September 2018.

46 Ibid.

Chapter Twelve

1 TNA, WO 305/5530, HQNI Operational Summary for the Period 30 October to 12 November 1984.

2 TNA, CJ 4/4790, Minutes of a Security Policy Meeting held at Stormont Castle at 3 p.m. on Monday 9 July 1984.

3 Ibid.

4 Ibid.

5 Ibid.

6 The labelling of McGuinness as the 'Provo enigma machine' came from a conversation with a former senior member of the PIRA in December 2019.

7 Clarke and Johnston, *Martin McGuinness*, p. 254.

8 Edwards, *UVF*, p. 71; Kevin Myers, *Watching the Door: Cheating Death in*

1970s Belfast (London: Atlantic Books, 2008), pp. 95–96.

9   Author interview with Willie Carlin, 25 October 2018.

10 Author interview with Síomón, September 2018.

11 Author interview with Toby, 2018.

12 Ian Cobain, 'FBI Informer armed the IRA', *The Daily Telegraph*, 25 June 2000.

13 John Goldman and William Tuohy, 'Tribute to Teamwork: Catch of Year – IRA Arms Seized at Sea', *Los Angeles Times*, 13 January 1985.

14 'Trawler's seizure called major setback for IRA', *The New York Times*, 30 September 1984.

15 Ella O'Dwyer, 'Interview: Martin Ferris – A Life in Struggle', *An Phoblacht/Republican News*, 15 November 2007.

16 Sean O'Callaghan, *The Informer* (London: Bantam Press, 1998), pp. 245–246.

17 PRONI, CENT 3/35A C.R. Budd to Charles Powell, 5 October 1984.

18 Author interview with Willie Carlin, 28 September 2018.

19 Ibid.

20 O'Callaghan, *The Informer*, p. 246.

21 NUI Galway, Brendan Duddy Archive, POL 35/536, 1984.

22 Ibid.

23 Ibid.

24 The police investigation revealed that the bomb may have been placed in the bathroom of room 629 several days before the explosion.

25 Heather Mills, 'Bomb drove tile shards like bullets', *The Daily Telegraph*, 13 May 1986.

26 Heather Mills, 'Don't go plea by Tebbitt in blast rubble', *The Daily Telegraph*, 9 May 1986.

27 Brendan Keenan, 'The Brighton Bombing', *Financial Times*, 13 October 1984.

28 Ibid.

29 TNA, CAB 186/37, Joint Intelligence Committee, The United Kingdom's Intelligence Requirements, 1984–86 – Report by the JIC, approved by Ministers, dated December 1984.

30 Douglas Hurd, *Memoirs* (London: Little, Brown, 2003), p. 301.

31 TNA, WO 305/5530, HQNI Diary of Events, 29 November 1984.

32 TNA, WO 305/5530, Commander's Diary Narrative.

33 Matchett, *Secret Victory*, p. 226.

34 TNA, WO 305/5530, Headquarters Northern Ireland, Operational Summary for the Period 270001Z Nov 84 to 102359Z Dec 84.

35 Carlin, *Thatcher's Spy*, p. 174.

36 Urban, *Big Boys' Rules*, p. 195.

37 Carlin, *Thatcher's Spy*, p. 174.

38 Urban, *Big Boys' Rules*, p. 196.

39 Ian S. Wood, interview with General Sir Bob Richardson, 8 October 2009. My sincere thanks to Ian Wood for making the transcript of his interview with General Richardson available to me.

40 Ibid.

41 Ibid.

42 Ibid.

43 Carlin, *Thatcher's Spy*, pp. 184–189.

Chapter Thirteen

1   My thanks to GB for permission to quote from his extensive interviews with former members of the RUC.

2   Author interview with a former Army Officer, November 2018.

3   Author interview with Peter, 30 July 2019.

4   'Hides' or arms caches were where

terrorists stored their weapons and ammunition. They took many forms. For example, some were constructed under the floorboards of houses, in the cavity walls of shop or community premises, or buried in fields inside barrels or beneath rocky outcrops.

5 Author interview with Peter, 30 July 2019.

6 For an obituary on Frank Murray, MBE, QPM, see 'Francis Thomas Murray, Police Officer; born February 23, 1945, died March 21, 1996', *The Herald* (Scotland), 23 March 1996.

7 Author interview with Jim, 6 October 2018.

8 Chris Ryder, *The RUC: A Force Under Fire* (London: Arrow, 2000), p. 232.

9 Private information, November 2018.

10 Holland and Phoenix, *Policing the Shadows*, p. 289; Jon Moran, 'Evaluating Special Branch and the Use of Informant Intelligence in Northern Ireland', *Intelligence and National Security*, 25(1), (2010), p. 23; Thomas Leahy, *The Intelligence War Against the IRA* (Cambridge: Cambridge University Press, 2020), pp. 5, 167, 186.

11 Author interview with Jim, 6 October 2018.

12 Author interview with Edward, 14 November 2018.

13 Private information, November 2018.

14 Author interview with Jim, 6 October 2018.

15 'Danger money' was slang for the financial incentive paid to officers who risked their lives to recruit and handle agents in the hard loyalist and republican areas.

16 Author interview with Jimmy B., 26 October 2011.

17 Ibid.

18 PRONI, NIO 25/1/76, RUC Reward Scheme Payments to Informants, 17 April 1985.

19 Ibid.

20 Dillon, *The Dirty War*, p. 309.

21 My thanks to Jim for this information.

22 In his evidence to the Smithwick Tribunal in 2013, one former Head of Special Branch in Belfast explained that, 'By and large, the idea was that as much intelligence as possible would be reflected within the SB50, but there would have been occasions when, as I say, it would not just have been as graphic, perhaps, as it could be.' Archived at: http://www. justice.ie/en/JELR/2012-02-07_-_ Smithwick_Tribunal_-_Day_71. pdf/Files/2012-02-07_-_Smithwick_ Tribunal_-_Day_71.pdf. Accessed: 5 April 2020.

23 De Silva, *Pat Finucane Review*, Vol. I, p. 61.

24 Author interview with Fred, 14 November 2018.

25 Author interview with Lord Maginnis of Drumglass, 2 April 2020.

26 A.R. Oppenheimer, *IRA, The Bombs and the Bullets: A History of Deadly Ingenuity* (Dublin: Irish Academic Press, 2009), p. 206.

27 Paul Johnson, 'IRA gunmen fire volleys over coffin of bomber', *The Guardian*, 28 April 1986.

28 Colm Tóibín, *Bad Blood: A Walk Along the Irish Border* (London: Picador, [1987] 2001), p. 142.

29 After McElwain's death, his father supported Sinn Féin President Ruairí Ó Brádaigh on the issue of abstentionism, thereby breaking with Gerry Adams and the Provisional Republican Movement.

30 John Crawley, 'Seamus McElwain

Remembered', *Irish Republican News*, 16 April 2016.

31 Information on Seamus McElwain's exploits as an IRA gunman can be found in 'Vol Seamus McElwaine IRA', YouTube, https://www.youtube.com/watch?v=wf2UsJNNSp8. Accessed: 25 October 2020.

32 Tóibín, *Bad Blood*, pp. 138–139.

33 Ciaran Dowd, 'Revolutionary Guerrilla Warfare in Ireland Today', *An Phoblacht/Republican News*, 17 May 1980.

34 Crawley, 'Seamus McElwain Remembered'.

35 Author interview with Danny Morrison, 22 February 2012.

36 Ibid.

37 Author interview with Sean, 24 March 2009.

38 PRONI, NIO 12/513A, HM Prison Maze – Escape 25 September 1983 – Prisoners at Large on 26 September 1983.

39 Tóibín, *Bad Blood*, p. 143.

40 Urban, *Big Boys' Rules*, p. 218.

41 'Interview: Seán Lynch – From Long Kesh to the District Policing Partnership', *An Phoblacht/Republican News*, 22 May 2008.

42 'IRA: Fighting the Chains of Imperialism, 1916–1986', *Workers Press*, 10 May 1986.

43 Ibid.

44 Matchett, *Secret Victory*, p. 231.

45 J. Bowyer Bell, *The IRA: 1968–2000: Analysis of a Secret Army* (London: Frank Cass, 2000), pp. 249–250.

46 Moloney, *Secret History*, p. 317.

47 Urban, *Big Boys' Rules*, p. 218.

Chapter Fourteen

1 Jeapes, *Operation Oman*, p. 237.

2 Ibid., p. 230.

3 De Silva, *Pat Finucane Review*, Vol. I, p. 72.

4 Ibid.

5 Ibid., p. 112.

6 Author's notes taken at an academic seminar, November 2015.

7 My thanks to GB for permission to quote from his extensive interviews with former members of the RUC. Conversation with former RUC Special Branch officers, November 2015.

8 Mark Brennock, 'Man shot by IRA is buried', *The Irish Times*, 20 August 1986.

9 Ibid.

10 Jim Cusack, 'IRA says man shot dead was an informer', *The Irish Times*, 16 August 1986.

11 Author interview with a former member of the IRA, October 2019.

12 Private information, 2018.

13 Bradley, *Insider*, p. 216.

14 Ibid., p. 217.

15 Nicholas Davies, *Dead Men Talking: Collusion, Cover-Up and Murder in Northern Ireland's Dirty War* (Edinburgh: Mainstream, 2005), p. 160.

16 Helen Shaw, 'Lurgan man killed by IRA', *The Irish Times*, 11 September 1986.

17 Ibid.

18 Author interview with Peter, 30 July 2019.

19 Ibid.

20 Ibid.

21 Author interview with Sean, 24 March 2009.

22 Bradley, *Insider*, p. 219.

23 Dillon, *The Dirty War*, Chapter 17; Holland and Phoenix, *Policing the Shadows*, pp. 106–109; TNA, CJ 4/4871, Cooperation between UVF

and PIRA/INLA, 17 February 1983.

24 Ulidia Legacy & Educational Trust (ULET), *Summary Report into the Murder of John Bingham: The Case for Collusion* (Belfast: ULET, 2017).

25 Justine McCarthy, 'Martin McGuinness in 1986' in Deric Henderson and Ivan Little (eds), *Reporting the Troubles: Journalists Tell Their Stories of the Northern Ireland Conflict* (Belfast: Blackstaff Press, 2018), pp. 98–100.

26 Stephen Collins, '"To leave Sinn Féin is to leave the IRA," Adams told Ard Fheis', *The Irish Times*, 30 December 2016.

27 McKearney, *The Provisional IRA*, p. 159.

28 TNA, DEFE, 25/554, Northern Ireland: General, Major General John MacMillan to Major General Tony Jeapes, 18 March 1987.

29 Royal Hampshire Regiment Museum (RHM), Andrew Freemantle End of Tour Talk (n.d.).

30 RHM, SITREP, 12 April 1987.

31 RHM, Serious Incident 2/87, Mortar Attack on Bessbrook Mill Army Base, Thursday 16 April 1987, dated 19 April.

32 Ibid.

33 RHM, Royal Hampshire Regiment Newsletter, dated 1987.

34 RHM, SITREP, 18 April 1987.

35 RHM, Serious Incident Report 3/87, RCIED and Murder on Main A1 South of Newry Saturday 25 April 1987.

36 House of Commons Debates (Hansard), 27 April 1987, Vol. 115, Col. 21.

37 During their roulement tour between January and June 1987, the Hampshire Regiment had searched 16,342 cars, 238 motorcycles and 5,019 HGVs. They also made extensive use of helicopters in support of their operations, expending some 2.1 million litres of aviation fuel, which was enough to drive the average car 400 times around the earth, and logged a total of 1,420 flying hours. All this speaks to the determination to fulfil the mission as handed down by senior Security Forces commanders responsible for the area.

38 House of Commons Debates (Hansard), 27 April 1987, Vol. 115, Col. 22.

Chapter Fifteen

1 Theodore Roosevelt Center, Dickinson State University, Theodore Roosevelt, 'The Man in the Arena', speech delivered at the Sorbonne, Paris, 23 April 1910. Accessible at: https://www.theodorerooseveltcenter.org/Learn-About-TR/TR-Encyclopedia/Culture-and-Society/Man-in-the-Arena.aspx.

2 Clarke and Johnston, *Martin McGuinness*, pp. 163–164.

3 Holland and Phoenix, *Policing the Shadows*, p. 141; see also Clarke and Johnston, *Martin McGuinness*, p. 164.

4 Thompson, *Defeating Communist Insurgency*, pp. 118–119.

5 Connla Young, 'IRA man tells the inside story of the Loughgall attack and the SAS ambush', *The Irish News*, 8 May 2017.

6 Author interview with Jack, 28 February 2019.

7 James Adams, Robin Morgan and Anthony Bambridge, *Ambush: The War between the SAS and the IRA* (London: Pan Books, 1988), p. 114.

8 Ibid., p. 115.

9 Ibid.

10 Ibid., p. 116.

11 TNA, WO 305/5849, Northern Ireland Post Tour Report: 1st Battalion, The Royal Hampshire Regiment, 25 May to 6 August 1987.

12 Ibid.

13 Ibid.

14 Moloney, *Secret History*, pp. 308, 311; 'State papers: Gerry Adams accused of "setting up" IRA men for slaughter by SAS', *Irish Independent*, 29 December 2017.

15 Police Ombudsman of Northern Ireland (PONI), *Report relating to the Attempted Murder of Gerry Adams on 14 March 1984* (Belfast: PONI, 19 June 2014). Gerry Adams alleged that there was collusion between the British state and the gunmen who tried to assassinate him. This report by the Police Ombudsman found that allegations of collusion could not be substantiated.

16 Author interview with a former UVF Director of Operations, 5 April 2016.

17 MI5 reported that '[i]n order to frustrate the operation the Army had arranged with the RUC that Security Forces activity in the area be stepped up so that the operation would have to be aborted – this was successfully done'. Telegram from MI5's Agent Running Section to HQ, dated 21 May 1987. De Silva, *Pat Finucane Review*, Vol. II, p. 302. MI5 were 'perturbed' by the FRU's decision to push the Adams plan in order to reinforce Nelson's standing in the UFF. MI5 managed to persuade the Army of the 'wider implications' of doing so and the 'longer term view of the case'.

18 Author interview with Jack, 10 October 2018.

19 Author interview with Ronnie, 10 October 2018.

20 Statistics compiled from data in the Sutton Index on the CAIN website. In the period prior to 1994, the UVF/RHC were responsible for 534 deaths (72.6 per cent were Catholic civilians and only 4.3 per cent were republican paramilitaries or political affiliates), while the UDA/UFF killed 406 people (71.4 per cent were Catholic civilians and a smaller number were republicans). Loyalists did not need assistance from the state to target members of the Catholic community, especially in a society that was heavily segregated. For more analysis of loyalist violence, see Rachel Monaghan and Peter Shirlow, 'Forward to the Past? Loyalist Paramilitarism in Northern Ireland Since 1994', *Studies in Conflict & Terrorism*, 34(8), (2011), p. 654.

21 The late political scientist Professor Frank Wright referred to this phenomenon as 'representative violence', which describes how victims were 'chosen because of their individual characteristics; they are attacked because they are identified as representing groups of people'. See Frank Wright, *Northern Ireland: A Comparative Analysis* (Dublin: Gill and Macmillan, 1987), p. 11.

22 Moloney, *Secret History*, pp. 3–4.

23 The full inventory was read out by the Minister for Justice in the Irish Parliament when French authorities shared intelligence on the five Irish men aboard the ship. Dáil Éireann Debates, Vol. 374, No. 11, 5 November 1987.

24 Moloney, *Secret History*, p. 3.

25 Ibid., p. 326.

26 Bob Rodwell, 'IRA's Enniskillen bomb was "triggered by timer"', *The Guardian*, 19 November 1987.

27 Fulton, Kevin *Unsung Hero: How I Saved Dozens of Lives as a Secret Agent Inside the IRA* (London: John Blake, 2006), p. 93.

28 Sixty-eight-year-old Ronnie Hill, a retired headmaster, was so badly injured by the explosion that he remained in a coma until his death on 28 December 2000.

29 *The Irish Times*, 10 November 1987.

30 Moloney, *Secret History*, p. 347.

31 Ibid.

32 'The IRA statement in full', *The Irish Times*, 10 November 1987.

33 'Twisted Logic', *The Irish Times*, 10 November 1987.

34 M.L.R. Smith, *Fighting for Ireland? The Military Strategy of the Irish Republican Movement* (London: Routledge, 1995), p. 178.

35 *The Irish News*, 4 February 1988.

36 Patrick Bishop and Eamonn Mallie, *The Provisional IRA* (London: Corgi Books, 1988), pp. 460–461.

37 Ibid., p. 461.

38 National Archives of Ireland, DFA 2018/28/2799, Record of a meeting between Father John Murphy and Brendan McMahon on 3 February 1988, dated 5 February 1988.

39 Ibid.

40 House of Commons Debates (Hansard), 17 February 1988, Vol. 127, Col. 978.

41 'Soldiers will never defeat the Provos, says British General', *Irish Independent*, 1 March 1988.

42 George Byrne, 'The remaking of Gerry Adams', *Irish Independent*, 4 February 1995.

43 Author interview with Jack, August 2019.

44 Adams et al., *Ambush*, p. 142.

45 Moloney, *Secret History*, pp. 329–331.

46 According to J. Bowyer Bell, the 'C/S [Chief of Staff] and the GHQ were less important in Northern operations' but 'in the case of English and Continental missions this meant direct oversight'. Bowyer Bell, *The IRA*, p. 136.

Chapter Sixteen

1 House of Commons Debates (Hansard), 3 May 1988, Vol. 132, Col. 729.

2 One of the suspected sources inside GHQ was Dennis Donaldson, compromised in the early 1980s and by now an Intelligence Officer in GHQ. Tommy McKearney argued that Donaldson was close to the Republican leadership and would have been able to keep the British 'reasonably well informed of the thinking of the leadership of the senior IRA and Sinn Fein members'. McKearney, *The Provisional IRA*, pp. 142, 173. See also John Mooney, 'Donaldson killer "confesses"', *The Sunday Times*, 6 May 2018. Donaldson's influence, however, is played down by academic Thomas Leahy in *The Intelligence War Against the IRA*, pp. 228–229.

3 This information is taken from Andrew, *The Defence of the Realm*, p. 741.

4 Tony Dawe, Michael Evans, Richard Wigg and Harry Debelius, 'How the Spanish police and SAS kept track of suspects', *The Times*, 8 March 1988.

5 Ibid.

6 White, *Out of the Ashes*, p. 247.

7 Adams et al., *Ambush*, pp. 140–142

8 White, *Out of the Ashes*, p. 247.

9 Mark Hollingsworth and Nick Fielding, *Defending the Realm: Inside MI5 and the War on Terrorism* (London: André

Deutsch, 1999), pp. 74–75.

10   Ibid.

11   Ibid.

12   Andrew, *The Defence of the Realm*, p. 741.

13   All of the information in this section is drawn from: European Court of Human Rights, Case of McCann and Others vs The United Kingdom: Judgement, 27 September 1995. Archived at: http://hudoc.echr.coe.int/eng?i=001-57943. Accessed: 12 March 2020.

14   Ibid.

15   Ibid.

16   Ibid.

17   Ibid.

18   Department of Homeland Security, FEMA: Reference Manual to Mitigate Potential Terrorist Attacks Against Buildings (December 2003), para. 4–1. Archived: https://www.fema.gov/media-library-data/20130726-1455-20490-6222/fema426.pdf. Accessed: 3 December 2019.

19   Andrew, *The Defence of the Realm*, p. 744.

20   This is the argument of experts including Dr Rory Finegan in 'Targeted Killings in Northern Ireland' p. 210.

21   *Associated Press*, 10 March 1988. At the subsequent inquest into their killings, Sinn Féin Director of Publicity Danny Morrison said that the Inquest Court's decision came as 'no surprise given the dependency of the Gibraltarians on Britain and the withholding of information by the Spanish authorities who were involved in the [shoot to kill] conspiracy.'

22   John J. O'Connor, 'Review/Television; An I.R.A. Member, From Several Angles', *The New York Times*, 13 June 1989.

23   *An Phoblacht/Republican News*, 10 March 1988.

24   For more on the dangers posed along the border, see Patrick Mulroe, *Bombs, Bullets and the Border – Policing Ireland's Frontier: Irish Security Policy, 1969–1978* (Dublin: Merrion Press, 2017).

25   Toby Harnden, *Bandit Country: The IRA and South Armagh* (London: Hodder & Stoughton, 1999), Chapter 1.

26   RHM, Andrew Freemantle End of Tour Talk.

27   Ibid.

28   Author interview with Síomón, October 2018.

29   RUC Special Branch knowledge of the IRA in the borderlands was extensive, including numbers, age profiles and MO, as one former Branch officer, Witness 62, told the Smithwick Tribunal. Archived at: http://www.justice.ie/en/JELR/2011-11-08_-_Smithwick_Tribunal_-_Day_51.pdf/Files/2011-11-08_-_Smithwick_Tribunal_-_Day_51.pdf. Accessed: 2 April 2020.

30   AFM, 1 PARA Intelligence Summary, dated 1988.

31   Author interview with Síomón, October 2018.

32   Ibid.

33   AFM Brigadier C.G.C. Vyvyan to CO, 1 PARA, 20 June 1988.

34   Ibid.

35   Ibid.

36   Tony Geraghty, *The Irish War: The Hidden Conflict between the IRA and British Intelligence* (London: HarperCollins, 1998), pp. 158–159.

37   See Chapter 5; for more on

framework patrolling, see also Aaron Edwards, "'Acting with Restraint and Courtesy, Despite Provocation?" Army Operations in Belfast During the Northern Ireland "'Troubles'" 1969–2007' in Gregory Fremont-Barnes (ed.), *A History of Modern Urban Operations* (Basingstoke: Palgrave Macmillan, 2020), pp. 287–319.

38 *The Globe and Laurel*, Vol. 96, No. 1 (May/June 1988), p. 134.

39 Richard Norton-Taylor, 'Armagh watchtowers go', *The Guardian*, 4 April 2006.

40 *The Globe and Laurel*, Vol. 96, No. 1 (May/June 1988), p. 134.

41 Ibid., p. 136.

42 Bowyer Bell, *The IRA*, p. 246.

43 Cross Examination of Witness 27 at the Smithwick Tribunal, 8 September 2011, pp. 133–134. Accessible at: http://www.justice.ie/en/JELR/2011-09-08_-_Smithwick_Tribunal_-_Day_30.pdf/Files/2011-09-08_-_Smithwick_Tribunal_-_Day_30.pdf.

44 Interview with a former IRA volunteer, October 2018.

45 Ibid.

46 AFM, 1 PARA Serious Incident Report 27 July 1988, dated 10 August 1988.

47 Private information, 2018.

48 AFM, INTSUM, 17–23 July 1988.

49 Author interview with a former IRA volunteer, October 2018.

50 AFM, 1 PARA Serious Incident Report 1/88, Explosion at Killeen, Saturday, 23 July 1988.

51 PRONI, NIO 8/3/4A, Semtex, Letter from Chief Superintendent A.J. Anderson to W.G. Cleland, 22 August 1988. An internal report on the explosive suggested that Semtex was attractive to the PIRA because it was 'pliable, safe to handle, and with very little smell', making it 'attractive to terrorist organisations and a headache to Security Forces'. Ibid., Governor IV to Chief Inspector Rudovich, RUC Headquarters, 21 March 1988.

52 Ronald Faux, David Sapsted and Tony Dawe, '£100,000 for IRA informers – Action on Northern Ireland violence', *The Times*, 29 August 1988.

53 Peter Taylor, *Provos: The IRA and Sinn Féin* (London: Bloomsbury, 1998), Chapter 1.

54 Harnden, *Bandit Country*, pp. 258, 267.

55 TNA, HO 325/866, PIRA Activities in Europe, MI5 Report, dated 2 September 1988.

56 Ibid.

Chapter Seventeen

1 Martin Cowley 'Selling Derry's image in the US', *The Irish Times*, 23 January 1988.

2 Templegrove Action Research Limited, Third Public Discussion: The Changing Population Balance and Protestant Drift, Derry Central Library, 13 April 1995.

3 Statistics taken from the Sutton Deaths Index, archived at: https://cain.ulster.ac.uk/sutton/.

4 Patrick Nolan, 'Unemployment providing "recruits for paramilitaries"', *The Irish Times*, 13 April 1988.

5 Padraig O'Morain, 'Fair employment head says changes substantial', *The Irish Times*, 2 August 1988.

6 Helen Shaw, 'IRA armour-piercing grenade poses new threat', *The Irish Times*, 27 January 1988.

7 Martin Cowley, 'More bombs on the way, IRA warns', *The Irish Times*, 25 August 1988.

8 Clarke and Johnston, *Martin McGuinness*, p. 183.

9 Ibid.

10 Paddy Flood was abducted by the Nutting Squad in May 1990 and held captive for many weeks before being executed. His body was discovered on a lonely border road on 25 July 1990. The IRA claimed that he was an informer, a view given credence in Kevin Toolis' otherwise excellent book *Rebel Hearts: Journeys within the IRA's Soul* (London: Picador, 1995), Chapter 4. However, this allegation has never been proven. Other sources spoken to by the author suggest that Paddy Flood simply talked too much about his terrorist involvement and that this 'loose talk' was intercepted by the Security Forces. Private information, 2011.

11 Northern Ireland Retired Police Officers' Association, *The Good Neighbour Bombing* (October 2013), p. 20.

12 Ibid.

13 Ibid.

14 *The Irish News*, 31 August 2018. An eight-year investigation by the Police Ombudsman concluded that the responsibility for the deaths of Eugene Dalton, Sheila Lewis and Gerard Curran rested 'with those who planted the bomb'. However, it was also concluded that 'whilst I cannot be certain the police knew there was a bomb specifically at 38 Kildrum Gardens, there is strong evidence that the police had sufficient information and intelligence to identify the location of the bomb'. Importantly, the Ombudsman's Report is devoid of context, which means that it is impossible to establish, with any real accuracy, why the decisions were taken by the police officers at the time. See PONI, *Statutory Report: Relating to the Complaints by the Relatives of a Victim in Respect of the events surrounding the bombing and murders at 38 Kildrum Gardens, Derry/Londonderry, on 31 August 1988* (Belfast: PONI, 10 July 2013).

15 TNA, HO 325/866, IRA Activities in Great Britain, Peter Bell to Ivor Roberts, 'Gripping the IRA', 5 October 1988.

16 TNA, HO 325/866, IRA Activities in Great Britain, Ivor Roberts to Peter Bell, 'Gripping the IRA', 12 October 1988.

17 Moloney, *Secret History*, pp. 331–332.

18 Terry Kirby, 'Dealer aided IRA bombs campaign', *The Independent*, 1 May 1990.

19 Malcolm Pithers, 'Police try to quash Semtex rumours', *The Independent*, 10 March 1989.

20 Smithwick, *Tribunal of Inquiry*, p. 68.

21 Ibid., p. 1.

22 Ibid., p. 24.

23 Harnden, *Bandit Country*, pp. 157–158.

24 Smithwick, *Tribunal of Inquiry*, pp. 55–56.

25 Harnden, *Bandit Country*, pp. 198–199.

26 Owen Bowcott, 'IRA says murdered man was a police informer', *The Guardian*, 19 July 1989.

27 'No clues in McAnulty kidnap', *The Irish Times*, 18 July 1989.

28 'McAnulty murder may be linked to protection racket', *The Irish Times*, 19 July 1989.

29 'The murder of John McAnulty', *The Irish Times*, 19 July 1989.

30 Jim Cusack, 'McAnulty "refused

to pay protection'", *The Irish Times*, 19 July 1989. Relatives and associates of McAnulty denied that he was shot dead for being an informer – rather, they claimed, it was because he refused to pay protection money.

31 'Extracts from interview in relation to SF talks', *The Irish Times*, 4 November 1989.

32 Ibid.

33 Ibid.

34 *The Times*, 5 November 1989.

35 Author interview with Síomón, August 2019.

36 Mark Urban, 'The secret war of Ulster's SB spooks and IRA touts', *The Independent*, 5 August 1989.

Chapter Eighteen

1 Author interview with Anthony McIntyre, 20 October 2019.

2 Author interview with Síomón, October 2018.

3 Ed Moloney, *Voices from the Grave: Two Men's War in Ireland* (London: Faber, 2010), p. 280.

4 According to his Death Certificate, John Joseph Magee died in Dundalk on 1 November 1994. He was 65.

5 Author interview with Anthony McIntyre, 20 October 2019.

6 From information on John Joseph Magee's Death Certificate.

7 Author interview with Síomón, October 2018.

8 Ibid.

9 Ibid.

10 IRA *Green Book* reproduced in Dillon, *The Dirty War*, pp. 487–488.

11 Author interview with Anthony McIntyre, 20 October 2019.

12 Ibid.

13 Moloney, *Voices from the Grave*, p. 276.

14 Author interview with Anthony McIntyre, 20 October 2019.

15 Ibid.

16 Ibid.

17 Danny Morrison, 'Dirty Fighting', *The Guardian*, 13 January 2009.

18 Owen Bowcott, 'Informer "pleaded for life"', *The Guardian*, 21 February 1991.

19 Gerry Moriarty, 'Conviction for falsely holding informer quashed', *The Irish Times*, 25 October 2008; see also 'Intelligence war that left undercover agent in no man's land', *The Guardian*, 9 May 1991.

20 'Intelligence war that left undercover agent in no man's land', The Guardian, 9 May 1991.

21 Dillon, *The Dirty War*, p. 318.

22 Ibid., p. 325.

23 'Seven for trial in murder conspiracy case', *The Irish Times*, 19 January 1991.

24 Owen Bowcott, 'Sinn Féin trial witness admits lying', *The Guardian*, 27 February 1991. The police did not comment on Lynch's allegations in open court and it would be eighteen years before an appeal court judge quashed the convictions.

25 Author interview with former PIRA commander Tommy Gorman, 23 June 2010.

26 Bradley, *Insider*, p. 222.

27 Private information, 2016.

28 McKittrick et al., *Lost Lives*, p. 1135; Harkin and Ingram, *Stakeknife*, p. 230.

29 Harkin and Ingram, *Stakeknife*, p. 228.

30 John Wilsey, *The Ulster Tales: A Tribute to those who Served, 1969–2000* (Barnsley: Pen & Sword, 2011) p. 122.

31 Ibid., p. 109.

32 Ibid.

33 PRONI, NIO 10/9/13A, John Blelloch,

Defeating Terrorism, dated 23 January 1990, p. 1.

34 Ibid., p. 18.

35 PRONI, NIO 10/9/13A, Blelloch to Ken Bloomfield and Permanent Secretaries, dated 2 March 1990.

36 Ibid.

37 Ibid.

38 Ibid.

39 Peter R. Neumann, 'British Government Strategy in Northern Ireland, 1969–98: An Evolutionary Analysis' (King's College London: PhD Thesis, 2002), p. 376.

Chapter Nineteen

1 Author interview with Jimmy B., 26 October 2011.

2 NUI Galway, Brendan Duddy Archive, POL 35/227, General – MO [Michael Oatley] + 1990/91.

3 Ibid.

4 Ibid.

5 NUI Galway, Brendan Duddy Archive, POL 35/590(2), General – MO [Michael Oatley] + 1990/91.

6 *An Phoblacht/Republican News*, 22 February 1990.

7 In his statement in *Setting the Record Straight* (Sinn Féin, 5 January 1994), McGuinness suggests that it was mid-1990 when 'the British government representative intimated that he wished to open up a line of communication once again'. Accessible at: https://www.sinnfein.ie/files/2009/Settingrecordstraight.pdf.

8 In *Setting the Record Straight*, McGuinness says he was sent on a 'listening brief' and that the meeting lasted for 'three hours and discussed the general political and the current state of British policy and Anglo–Irish

relations. In keeping with my brief, I said very little and was noncommittal on all aspects of republican policy.'

9 NUI Galway, Brendan Duddy Archive, POL 35/227, General MO and 1990/91, transcript of reflections by BD on 1 August 1999.

10 Ibid.

11 Ibid.

12 Eamonn Mallie and David McKittrick, *The Fight for Peace* (London: Heinemann, 1996), p. 105.

13 NUI Galway, Brendan Duddy Archive, POL 35/227, General MO and 1990/91, transcript of reflections by BD on 1 August 1999.

14 Ibid.

15 Author interview with Danny Morrison, 23 November 2010.

16 *An Phoblacht/Republican News*, January 1991.

17 NUI Galway, Brendan Duddy Archive, POL 35/227, General MO and 1990/91, transcript of reflections by BD on 1 August 1999.

18 Frank Lloyd, 'Sir Colville Deverell – Obituary', *The Independent*, 23 December 1995.

19 For the now-disclosed papers on the Schulze case see TNA, J 82/4345, Reinhard Schulze and Sonja Schulze: offences under section 1(1)(c) of the Official Secrets Act 1911 and section 5(1) of the Forgery and Counterfeiting Act 1981. Despite an FOI request to access the CAB 318/16, 17, 22–23, and twenty-seven files on the Bettaney case retained by the Cabinet Office, the request was refused under Section 23(1), Section 40(2) and Section 41(1).

20 De Silva, *Pat Finucane Review*, Vol. II, Minutes of a meeting between Secretary of State for Defence, DCI, ACOS G2, GS Sec 2, 26 September

1990.

21 De Silva, *Pat Finucane Review*, Vol. II, Secret minutes of a meeting between MI5 and the Secretary of State for Defence, 26 September 1990.

22 Ibid., Top-secret report by ACOS G2 to GOC (no date, poss. 1990).

23 Ibid.

24 Ibid. Tom King to Paddy Mayhew, 3 October 1990, pp. 229–232.

25 Sir Michael Quinlan, 'The Future of Covert Intelligence' in Harold Shukman (ed.), *Agents for Change: Intelligence Services in the 21st Century* (London: St Ermin's Press, 2000), p. 68.

26 Ibid.

27 PRONI, NIO 10/9/13A, letter from P.N. Bell to Mr Ledlie, 11 December 1990.

28 Neumann, 'British Government Strategy', p. 375.

29 Ibid.

30 House of Commons Debates (Hansard), 8 May 1992, Vol. 207, Col. 297–298.

31 'Security Chiefs must stand by their men', *The Sunday Telegraph*, 9 February 1992.

32 Author interview with Danny Morrison, 23 November 2010.

33 NUI Galway, Brendan Duddy Archive, POL 35/272, Fred to Duddy, 18 February 1992.

34 Ibid., POL 35/241, Reply to Adams, 18 February 1992.

35 Ibid., POL 35/227, General MO and 1990/91, Communique from the Republican Movement to the British, dated 22 June 1992.

36 Author interview with Johnny Adair, 17 January 2016.

37 Ibid.

38 These statistics were calculated using two sources, the Sutton Index of Deaths on the CAIN website and also McKittrick et al., *Lost Lives*, pp. 1494–1495.

39 Edwards, *Behind the Mask*, p. 226.

40 Holland and Phoenix, *Policing the Shadows*, pp. 188–189.

41 Author interview with Sean, 24 March 2009.

Chapter Twenty

1 NUI Galway, Brendan Duddy Archive, POL 35/540, Brendan Duddy to Martin McGuinness, dated 2 June 1993. Duddy gave himself the codename 'Roadrunner'. McGuinness' codename was 'Penguin'.

2 Author interview with General Sir Roger Wheeler, from Edwards, *Defending the Realm?* pp. 195–196.

3 Ibid.

4 Ibid.

5 Author interview with General Sir Roger Wheeler, 28 January 2011. As a sign of the quality of his security sources, Intelligence historian Stephen Dorril first revealed the existence of the PEC in his ground-breaking book, *The Silent Conspiracy*, shortly after the formation of the PEC. 'The new proposal, while sensible,' argued Dorril, 'hardly seems a step forward but rather a nostalgic retreat to the period in Malaya when Templer had complete control over security powers with almost dictatorial powers,' p. 205.

6 General David Richards, *Taking Command: The Autobiography* (London: Headline, 2014), p. 78.

7 Ibid., p. 80.

8 Ibid.,

9 Ibid., p. 81.

10 Ibid., p. 80.

11 Ibid., p. 77.

12 Leahy, *The Intelligence War Against the IRA*, p. 209; see also Owen Bennett-Jones, 'What Fred Did', *London Review of Books*, 37(2), (2015), p. 209.

13 NUI Galway, Brendan Duddy Archive, POL 35/283 (1), 'Handwritten note marked Monday 10 May 11pm Walter, June, Star, Tax'.

14 Ibid.

15 NUI Galway, Brendan Duddy Archive, POL 35/283(13). As the note was written in 1993, the 'plane crash' referred to may have been the Mull of Kintyre disaster of 2 June 1994. The only woman on-board the aircraft was MI5 officer Anne Catherine James.

16 Graham Spencer (ed.), *The British and Peace in Northern Ireland: The Process and Practice of Reaching Agreement* (Cambridge: Cambridge University Press, 2015), p. 129.

17 Ibid., p. 80.

18 Ibid.

19 Ibid.

20 Ibid.

21 Niall Ó Dochartaigh, 'The Longest Negotiation: British Policy, IRA Strategy and the Making of the Northern Ireland Peace Settlement', *Political Studies*, 63(1), (2015), p. 218.

22 Paul Kingsley, *Londonderry Revisited: A Loyalist Analysis of the Civil Rights Controversy* (Belfast: Belfast Publications, 1989), p. 237. My thanks to Professor Henry Patterson for pointing me in the direction of this book.

23 George Orwell, *The Lion and the Unicorn: Socialism and the English Genius* (London: Secker and Warburg, 1962), p. 29.

24 Kingsley, *Londonderry Revisited*, p. 249.

25 NUI Galway, Brendan Duddy Archive, POL35/340, Brendan Duddy to 'Elizabeth', dated 28 February 1994. It is unclear who Elizabeth was, but Duddy's candidness in terms of his secret work and news about his family suggests she was a close friend.

26 Author interview with Danny Morrison, 23 November 2010.

27 Conversation with a former member of the PIRA, April 2018.

28 Urban, Mark, *UK Eyes Alpha: The Inside Story of British Intelligence* (London: Faber, 1996). pp. 270, 272, 276.

29 Author interview with Jimmy B., 26 October 2011.

30 De Silva, *Pat Finucane Review*, Vol. I, p. 183.

31 De Silva, *Pat Finucane Review*, Vol. II, Report on Brian Nelson by J.C.B. Fitzsimmons, ACC E Department, dated 29 January 1991, p. 234.

32 Deverell and Fitzsimmons were contemporaries in their respective services. To mark the occasion of their retirement, the Army organised a helicopter ride to Scotland in early June 1994. Due to bad weather conditions, the Chinook aircraft crashed, killing all twenty-nine people on-board, including the Chief of G2 at HQNI, and the CO of the FRU, now rebranded JSU, thus wiping out the entire top tier of the three Intelligence agencies in Northern Ireland.

33 Conversation with a former member of the RUC Special Branch, 5 June 2019.

34 Author interview with Jimmy B., 26 October 2011.

35 Matchett, *Secret Victory*, p. 234.

36 Anthony McIntyre, 'The Funeral of Brendan Hughes: Setting the Record Straight', *The Blanket*, 28 September

2008. Archived at: http://indiamond6. ulib.iupui.edu:81/AMDARK3.html. Accessed: 6 April 2020.

37 Author interview with Danny Morrison, 23 November 2010.

38 Kevin Bean, 'The Economic and Social War Against Violence: British Social and Economic Strategy and the Evolution of Provisionalism' in Aaron Edwards and Stephen Bloomer (eds), *Transforming the Peace Process in Northern Ireland: From Terrorism to Democratic Politics* (Dublin: Irish Academic Press, 2008), p. 164.

39 Anthony McIntyre, 'Of Myths and Men: Dissent within Republicanism and Loyalism' in Edwards and Bloomer, *Transforming the Peace Process in Northern Ireland*, p. 122.

40 The Billy Wright Inquiry Oral Hearings – Hearing: 28 January 2008, day 24. Archived at: https:// webarchive.nationalarchives.gov. uk/20101210144932/http://www. billywrightinquiry.org/transcripts/ hearing-day/24/. Accessed: 30 September 2019.

41 Sir Michael Morland, *The Rosemary Nelson Inquiry Report* (London: HMSO, 2011), p. 243. Archived at: https://assets.publishing.service. gov.uk/government/uploads/ system/uploads/attachment_data/ file/247461/0947.pdf. Accessed: 6 April 2020.

42 The Billy Wright Inquiry Oral Hearings – Hearing: 30 January 2008, Day 26. Archived at: https:// webarchive.nationalarchives.gov. uk/20101210144932/http://www. billywrightinquiry.org/transcripts/ hearing-day/26/. Accessed: 2 April 2020.

43 Hollingsworth and Fielding, *Defending*

the *Realm*, p. 162.

44 Author interview with Tony, June 2019.

Chapter Twenty-One

1 The Billy Wright Inquiry Oral Hearings – Hearing: 10 March 2009, Day 136. Archived at: https:// webarchive.nationalarchives.gov. uk/20101210145512/http://www. billywrightinquiry.org/transcripts/ hearing-day/136/. Accessed: 4 April 2020.

2 Stephen Oldfield, 'Steve smiled and then there was a crash. He dropped by the side of the car', *Daily Mail*, 14 February 1997.

3 Jim Cusack, 'Hardliners may be in control of IRA', *The Irish Times*, 8 February 1997.

4 PONI, *Report into a complaint from Rita and John Restorick regarding the circumstances of the murder of their son, Lance Bombardier Stephen Restorick on 12th February 1997* (Belfast: PONI, 2006), p. 22. Archived at: https:// cain.ulster.ac.uk/victims/docs/group/ police_ombudsman/restorick_131206. pdf. Accessed: 31 March 2020.

5 Ibid.

6 Author interview with Colonel David Benest, 11 September 2019.

7 Ibid.

8 Ibid.

9 Private information, 2019.

10 British and Irish Legal Information Institute, HM Court of Appeal in Northern Ireland, The Queen v Michael Colm Caraher and Bernard Michael McGinn, 29 September 2000. Archived at: https://www.bailii.org/nie/ cases/NICA/2000/35.html. Accessed 4 April 2020.

11 Nicholas Watt, 'Terrorists raise the stakes as Adams hints at Labour hope', *The Times*, 31 March 1997.

12 Author interview with Danny Morrison, 23 November 2010.

13 IRA Statement, 19 July 1997. Accessible at: https://cain.ulster.ac.uk/events/peace/docs/ira19797.htm.

14 Author interview with Anthony McIntyre, 20 October 2019.

15 Leahy, *The Intelligence War Against the IRA*, p. 236.

16 Ibid., p. 126; see also Malachi O'Doherty's review of Leahy's book, *Flawed Strategy*, in *The Sunday Times*, 5 April 2020.

17 Author interview with Bob, June 2019.

18 Author interview with Peter, December 2017.

19 Author interview with Anthony McIntyre, 20 October 2019.

20 Author interview with Danny Morrison, 23 November 2010.

21 Matchett, *Secret Victory*, p. 100.

22 Liam Clarke, 'Half of all top IRA men "worked for security services"', *Belfast Telegraph*, 21 December 2011.

Epilogue: Collecting People

1 House of Lords Debates (Hansard), 9 December 1993, vol. 550, Col. 1059.

2 De Silva, *Pat Finucane Review*, Vol. I, p. 68.

3 Matchett, *Secret Victory*, p. 238.

4 Author telephone interview with Lord Maginnis of Drumglass, 2 April 2020.

5 For instance, in the wake of the publication of the Police Ombudsman's Report on its investigation, Operation Ballast, in January 2007, which resulted in many people connected with loyalism being placed in danger and several men being sentenced to death by the UVF.

6 Author interview with Willie Carlin, June 2019.

7 Ibid.

8 Nigel West, 'Ulster Espionage: A Review of Thatcher's Spy by Willie Carlin', *International Journal of Intelligence and Counter-Intelligence*, published online February 2020. Archived at: https://www.tandfonline.com/doi/abs/10.1080/08850607.2019.1690353. Following his release from prison, Bettaney wrote extensively for the *Weekly Worker* under the nom de plume Michael Malkin. This article shows his close sympathies for Irish republicanism and his hatred for British imperialism: Michael Malkin, 'Ireland: Wilderness of Mirrors', *Weekly Worker*, 21 May 2003. https://weeklyworker.co.uk/worker/481/ireland-wilderness-of-mirrors/.

9 Stephen Lander, 'British Intelligence in the Twentieth Century', *Intelligence and National Security*, 17(1), (2002), p. 10.

BIBLIOGRAPHY

Newspapers and Journals

An Phoblacht/Republican News
Associated Press
Belfast News Letter
Belfast Telegraph
Daily Express
Daily Mail
Daily Mirror
Daily News
The Daily Telegraph
Derry Journal
Financial Times
The Guardian
The Herald (Scotland)
The Independent
Irish Independent
The Irish News
The Irish Times
The Lethbridge Herald
Los Angeles Times
The New York Times
The Oak Tree: Journal of the 22nd (Cheshire) Regiment
The Observer
The Sunday Mail (Scotland)
The Sunday Telegraph
The Sunday Times
Sunday World
The Times
Workers Press
Weekly Worker

Archives

Airborne Forces Museum (AFM)
Brendan Duddy Archive, National University of Ireland (NUI), Galway
British Diplomatic Oral History Archives, Cambridge University
Cheshire Regiment Archives, Chester
Liddell Hart Centre for Military Archives, King's College London (LHCMA)

Margaret Thatcher Foundation, Cambridge University
National Archives Ireland, Dublin
Public Records Office of Northern Ireland, Belfast (PRONI)
Royal Hampshire Regiment Museum, Winchester (RHM)
Ruairí Ó Brádaigh Archive, National University of Ireland, Galway
The National Archives, London (TNA)

Government Documents and Reports

de Silva, Sir Desmond, *The Report of the Pat Finucane Review – The Rt Hon. Sir Desmond de Silva QC*, Volumes I–II (London: The Stationery Office, 2012).
The Rt Hon. the Lord Franks, *Falkland Islands Review* (London: HMSO, January 1983).
Hart, Sir Anthony, *Historical Institutional Abuse Inquiry Report* (Belfast: The Inquiry into Historical Institutional Abuse 1922 to 1995 and The Executive Office, 2017).
The Rt Hon. the Lord MacLean, Professor Andrew Coyle CMG, the Right Reverend John Oliver, *The Billy Wright Inquiry – Report* (London: The Stationary Office, 2010).
Ministry of Defence, *Operation Banner: An Analysis of Military Operations in Northern Ireland*, Army Code 71842 (London: MoD, July 2006).
Morland, Sir Michael, *The Rosemary Nelson Inquiry Report* (London: HMSO, 2011).
Police Ombudsman of Northern Ireland (PONI), *Report into a complaint from Rita and John Restorick regarding the circumstances of the murder of their son, Lance Bombardier Stephen Restorick on 12 February 1997* (Belfast: PONI, 2006).
PONI, *Report relating to the Attempted Murder of Gerry Adams on 14 March 1984* (Belfast: PONI, 2014).
PONI, Statutory *Report relating to the Complaints by the Relatives of a Victim in Respect of the events surrounding the bombing and murders at 38 Kildrum Gardens, Derry/Londonderry, on 31 August 1988* (Belfast: PONI, 2013).
RUC, *Chief Constable's Annual Reports, 1980–89* (Belfast: RUC, various dates).
The Rt Hon. the Lord Saville of Newdigate, the Hon. William Hoyt OC and the Hon. John Toohey AC, *Report of the Bloody Sunday Inquiry*, Volumes 1–10 (London: The Stationary Office, 2010).
Smithwick, Judge Peter, *Tribunal of Inquiry into Allegations of Garda Collusion* (Dublin: The Stationary Office, 2013).
US Department of Homeland Security, *FEMA: Reference Manual to Mitigate Potential Terrorist Attacks Against Buildings* (December 2003).
Walker, Patrick, *Report on the Interchange of Intelligence between Special Branch and C.I.D. and on the R.U.C. Units Involved, including those in Crime Branch C1(1)* (1980).

Memoirs and First-hand Accounts

Adams, Gerry, *The Politics of Irish Freedom* (Dublin: Brandon, 1986).
Bradford, Norah, *A Sword Bathed in Heaven* (London: HarperCollins, 1984).
Bradley, Gerry, *Insider: Gerry Bradley's Life in the IRA* (Dublin: The O'Brien Press, 2009).
Brown, Johnston, *Into the Dark: 30 Years in the RUC* (Dublin: Gill and Macmillan, 2005).

Carlin, Willie, *Thatcher's Spy: My Life as an MI5 Spy inside Sinn Féin* (Dublin: Merrion Press, 2019).

Clarke, George, *Border Crossing: True Stories of the RUC Special Branch, the Garda Special Branch and the IRA Moles* (Dublin: Gill and Macmillan, 2009).

Collins, Eamon, with Mick McGovern, *Killing Rage* (London: Granta, 1997).

Craig, Paddy, *Undercover Cop: One Man's True Story of Undercover Policing in Ireland, the UK and Europe* (London: Gill and Macmillan, 2008).

Devlin, Paddy, *Straight Left: An Autobiography* (Belfast: Blackstaff Press, 1993).

Fulton, Kevin, *Unsung Hero: How I Saved Dozens of Lives as a Secret Agent Inside the IRA* (London: John Blake, 2006).

Gilmour, Raymond, *Dead Ground: Infiltrating the IRA* (London: Warner Books, 1998).

Holland, Jack, and Susan Phoenix, *Phoenix – Policing the Shadows: The Secret War Against Terrorism in Northern Ireland* (London: Coronet Books, 1996).

Horsfall, Robin, *Fighting Scared: Para, Mercenary, SAS, Bodyguard* (London: Cassell, 2002).

Hurd, Douglas, *Memoirs* (London: Little, Brown, 2003).

Jeapes, Colonel Tony, *SAS: Operation Oman* (London: William Kimber and Co. Limited, 1980).

Lewis, Rob, *Fishers of Men: The Gripping True Story of a British Army Undercover Agent in Northern Ireland* (London: John Blake, 1999).

McCallion, Harry, *Killing Zone: A Life in the Paras, the Recces, the SAS and the RUC* (London: Bloomsbury, 1995).

Masterman, J.C., *The Double-Cross System in the War of 1939 to 1945* (London: Yale University Press, 1972).

Myers, Kevin, *Watching the Door: Cheating Death in 1970s Belfast* (London: Atlantic Books, 2006).

O'Callaghan, Sean, *The Informer* (London: Bantam Press, 1998).

O'Doherty, Malachi, *Belfast 1972: The Telling Year* (Dublin: Gill and Macmillan, 2007).

Philby, Kim, *My Silent War: The Autobiography of a Spy* (London: Arrow Books, 2003).

Richards, David, *Taking Command: The Autobiography* (London: Headline, 2014).

Simpson, Alan, *Murder Madness: True Crimes of the Troubles* (Dublin: Gill and Macmillan, 1999).

Stalker, John, *Stalker: Ireland, 'Shoot to Kill' and the 'Affair'* (London: Penguin, 1988).

Thatcher, Margaret, *The Downing Street Years* (London: HarperCollins, 1993).

Tóibín, Colm, *Bad Blood: A Walk Along the Irish Border* (London: Picador, [1987] 2001).

Books and Articles

Ackerman, Gary A., 'The Provisional Irish Republican Army and the Development of Mortars', *Journal of Strategic Security*, 9(1), (2016), pp. 12–34.

Adams, James, Robin Morgan, and Anthony Bambridge, *Ambush: The War between the SAS and the IRA* (London: Pan Books, 1988).

Al-Gaddafi, Muammar, *The Green Book* (Tripoli : Public Establishment for Publishing, Advertising and Distribution [n.d.])

Alonso, Rogelio, *The IRA and Armed Struggle* (Abingdon: Routledge, 2007).

Andrew, Christopher, *The Defence of the Realm: The Authorized History of MI5* (London: Allen Lane, 2009).

Andrew, Christopher, *The Secret World: A History of Intelligence* (London: Yale University Press, 2018).

Bean, Kevin, 'The Economic and Social War Against Violence: British Social and Economic Strategy and the Evolution of Provisionalism' in Aaron Edwards and Stephen Bloomer (eds), *Transforming the Peace Process in Northern Ireland: From Terrorism to Democratic Politics* (Dublin: Irish Academic Press, 2008), pp. 163–174.

Bean, Kevin, *The New Departure: Recent Developments in Irish Republican Ideology and Strategy*, Occasional Papers in Irish Studies, 6 (Liverpool: Institute of Irish Studies, October 1994).

Bennett-Jones, Owen, 'What Fred Did', *London Review of Books*, 37(2), (2015), pp. 3–6.

Beresford-Ellis, David, *Ten Dead Men: Story of the 1981 Irish Hunger Strike* (London: HarperCollins, 1994).

Bew, John, Martyn Frampton and Inigo Gurruchaga, *Talking to Terrorists: Making Peace in Northern Ireland and the Basque Country* (London: Hurst, 2009).

Bew, Paul, and Gordon Gillespie, *Northern Ireland: A Chronology of the Troubles 1968–1999* (Dublin: Gill and Macmillan, 1999).

Bishop, Patrick, and Eamonn Mallie, *The Provisional IRA* (London: Corgi Books, 1988).

Borrmann, Donald A., William T. Kvetkas, Charles V. Brown, Michael J. Flatley and Robert Hunt, *The History of Traffic Analysis: World War 1 to Vietnam* (Fort Meade, MD: NSA, 2013). Archived at: https://www.nsa.gov/Portals/70/documents/about/cryptologic-heritage/historical-figures-publications/publications/misc/traffic_analysis.pdf. Accessed: 11 December 2019.

Bowyer Bell, J. *The IRA: 1968–2000: Analysis of a Secret Army* (London: Frank Cass, 2000).

Bowyer Bell, J. *The Secret Army: The IRA, 1916–1979* (Dublin: Poolbeg, 1970; revised edition, 1989).

Burton, Frank, *The Politics of Legitimacy: Struggles in a Belfast Community* (London: Routledge and Kegan Paul, 1978).

Charters, David, '"Have A Go": British Army/MI5 Agent-running Operations in Northern Ireland, 1970–72', *Intelligence and National Security*, 28(2), (2013), pp. 202–229.

Charters, David, 'Professionalizing clandestine military intelligence in Northern Ireland: creating the Special Reconnaissance Unit', *Intelligence and National Security*, 33(1), (2018), pp. 130–138.

Childers, Erskine, *The Riddle of the Sands: A Record of Secret Service* (London: Penguin, [1903] 2011).

Clarke, Liam, and Kathryn Johnston, *Martin McGuinness: From Guns to Government* (Edinburgh: Mainstream, 2001).

Cobain, Ian, *Anatomy of a Killing: Life and Death on a Divided Island* (London: Granta, 2020).

Cobain, Ian, *Cruel Britannia: A Secret History of Torture* (London: Portobello Books, 2013).

Codevilla, Angelo M., 'Political Warfare' in Frank R. Barnett and Carnes Lord (eds), *Political Warfare and Psychological Operations: Rethinking the US Approach* (Washington, DC: National Defense University Press, 1989), pp. 77–101.

Coogan, Tim Pat, *The IRA*, Completely Revised New Edition (London: HarperCollins, 1995).

Cormac, Rory, *Disrupt and Deny: Spies, Special Forces and the Secret Pursuit of British Foreign Policy* (Oxford: Oxford University Press, 2018).

Cox, Michael, 'Bringing in the "International": the IRA Ceasefire and the End of the Cold War', *International Affairs*, 73(4), (1997), pp. 671–693.

Cradock, Percy, *Know Your Enemy: How the Joint Intelligence Committee Saw the World* (London: John Murray, 2002).

Cradock, Percy, 'Review of Michael Herman's *Intelligence Power in War and Peace*', *International Affairs*, 73(4), (October 1997), pp. 785–787.

Craig, Tony, 'From Backdoors and Back Lanes to Backchannels: Reappraising British Talks with the Provisional IRA, 1970–1974', *Contemporary British History*, 26(1), (2012), pp. 97–117.

Craig, Tony, 'Laneside, then left a bit? Britain's Secret Political Talks with Loyalist Paramilitaries in Northern Ireland, 1973–1976', *Irish Political Studies*, 29(2), (2014), pp. 298–317.

Craig, Tony, '"You will be responsible to the GOC". Stovepiping and the problem of divergent intelligence gathering networks in Northern Ireland, 1969–1975', *Intelligence and National Security*, 33(2), (2017), pp. 211–226.

Davies, Nicholas, *Dead Men Talking: Collusion, Cover-Up and Murder in Northern Ireland's Dirty War* (Edinburgh: Mainstream, 2005).

Deacon, Richard, *C: A Biography of Sir Maurice Oldfield, Head of MI6* (London: Futura Publications, 1984).

Dillon, Martin, *Killer in Clowntown: Joe Doherty, the IRA and the Special Relationship* (London: Hutchinson, 1992).

Dillon, Martin, *The Dirty War* (London: Arrow Books, 1991)

Dixon, Paul, 'Guns First, Talks Later: Neoconservatives and the Northern Ireland Peace Process', *The Journal of Imperial and Commonwealth History*, 39(4), (November 2011), pp. 649–676.

Dorril, Stephen, *The Silent Conspiracy: Inside the Intelligence Agencies in the 1990s* (London: Mandarin, 1994).

Dover, Robert, and Michael S. Goodman, *Learning from the Secret Past: Cases in British Intelligence History* (Washington, DC: Georgetown University Press, 2011).

Duffy, Angela, *Informers in 20th Century Ireland: The Costs of Betrayal* (Jefferson, NC: McFarland, 2018).

Edwards, Aaron, '"Acting with Restraint and Courtesy, Despite Provocation?" Army Operations in Belfast During the Northern Ireland "Troubles", 1969–2007' in Gregory Fremont-Barnes (ed.), *A History of Modern Urban Operations* (Basingstoke: Palgrave Macmillan, 2020), pp. 287–319.

Edwards, Aaron, 'Beating the Retreat on a Contested Past? The British Army and the Politics of Commemoration in Northern Ireland' in J. Smyth (ed.), *Remembering the Troubles: Contesting the Recent Past in Northern Ireland* (Notre Dame, IN: University of Notre Dame Press, 2017), pp. 77–95.

Edwards, Aaron, 'British Security Policy and the Sunningdale Agreement: The Consequences of Using Force to Combat Terrorism in a Liberal Democracy' in D.

McCann and C. McGrattan (eds), *Sunningdale, the Ulster Workers' Council Strike and the Struggle for Democracy in Northern Ireland* (Manchester: Manchester University Press, 2017), pp. 87–99.

Edwards, Aaron, *Defending the Realm? The Politics of Britain's Small Wars since 1945* (Manchester: Manchester University Press, 2012).

Edwards, Aaron, 'Deterrence, Coercion and Brute Force in Asymmetric Conflict: The Role of the Military Instrument in Resolving the Northern Ireland "Troubles"', *Dynamics of Asymmetric Conflict*, 4(3), (2011), pp. 226–241.

Edwards, Aaron, *Mad Mitch's Tribal Law: Aden and the End of Empire* (Edinburgh: Mainstream Publishing, 2014).

Edwards, Aaron, 'Misapplying Lessons Learned? Analysing the Utility of British Counter-insurgency Strategy in Northern Ireland, 1971–76', *Small Wars and Insurgencies*, 21(2), (2010), pp. 303–330.

Edwards, Aaron, *The Northern Ireland Troubles: Operation Banner, 1969–2007* (Oxford: Osprey, 2011).

Edwards, Aaron, 'Practice without Principles? Northern Ireland and the Struggle against the Provisional IRA, 1969–2007' in Gregory Fremont-Barnes (ed.), *A History of Counter-insurgency: Volume 2 – From Cyprus to Afghanistan, 1955 to the 21st Century* (Santa Barbara, CA: Praeger, 2015), pp. 255–276.

Edwards, Aaron, 'The Provisional IRA and the Elusive Concept of Winning' in Matthias Strohn (ed.), *Winning Wars: The Enduring Nature and Changing Character of Victory from Antiquity to the 21st Century* (London: Casemate, 2020), pp. 229–242.

Edwards, Aaron, *UVF: Behind the Mask* (Dublin: Merrion Press, 2017).

Edwards, Aaron, 'When Terrorism as Strategy Fails: Dissident Irish Republicans and the Threat to British Security', *Studies in Conflict & Terrorism*, 34(4), (2011), pp. 318–336.

Edwards, Aaron, '"A whipping boy if ever there was one"? The British Army and the Politics of Civil–Military Relations in Northern Ireland, 1969–79', *Contemporary British History*, 28(2), (June 2014), pp. 166–189.

Edwards, Aaron, and Cillian McGrattan, *The Northern Ireland Conflict: A Beginner's Guide* (Oxford: Oneworld Publications, 2010).

Edwards, Aaron, and Cillian McGrattan, 'Terroristic Narratives: On the (Re) Invention of Peace in Northern Ireland', *Terrorism and Political Violence*, 23(3), (2011), pp. 357–376.

Edwards, Aaron, and Stephen Bloomer (eds), *Transforming the Peace Process in Northern Ireland: From Terrorism to Democratic Politics* (Dublin: Irish Academic Press, 2008).

English, Richard, *Armed Struggle: A History of the IRA* (London: Pan Macmillan, 2003).

English, Richard, *Does Terrorism Work? A History* (Oxford: Oxford University Press, 2016).

English, Richard, *Terrorism: How to Respond* (Oxford: Oxford University Press, 2009).

Evelegh, Robin, *Peace-keeping in a Democratic Society: The Lessons of Northern Ireland* (London: Hurst, 1978).

Finn, Daniel, *One Man's Terrorist? A Political History of the IRA* (London: Verso, 2019).

Foot, Paul, 'Whitehall Farce', *London Review of Books*, 11(19), (12 October 1989).

Fukuyama, Francis, *The End of History and the Last Man* (London: Hamish Hamilton, 1992).

Gauvain, Lieutenant Colonel A. De P., 'Commanding Officer's Notes', *The Oak Tree: Journal of the 22nd (Cheshire) Regiment*, 67(1), (Summer 1982).

Geraghty, Tony, *The Irish War: The Hidden Conflict between the IRA and British Intelligence* (London: HarperCollins, 1998).

Geraghty, Tony, *Who Dares Wins: The Special Air Service – 1950 to the Gulf War* (London: Time Warner, 2002).

Gill, Peter, and Mark Phythian, *Intelligence in an Insecure World*, Second Edition (Cambridge: Polity, 2012).

Goodman, Michael, *The Official History of the Joint Intelligence Committee*, Volume I (Abingdon: Routledge, 2016).

Gray, Colin S., 'Irregular Warfare: One Nature, Many Characters', *Strategic Studies Quarterly*, 1(2), (2007), pp. 35–57.

Gray, Colin S., *Tactical Operations for Strategic Effect: The Challenge of Currency Conversion*, Special Report for the Joint Special Operations University (Tampa, FL: JSOU, November 2015).

Grossman, Lt Col Dave, *On Killing: The Psychological Cost of Learning to Kill in War and Society* (New York: Little, Brown, 1995).

Hamilton, Lord Ernest, *The Soul of Ulster* (New York: E.P. Dutton and Co., 1917).

Hanley, Brian, and Scott Millar, *The Lost Revolution: The Story of the Official IRA and the Workers' Party* (Dublin: Penguin Ireland, 2009).

Harkin, Greg, and Martin Ingram, *Stakeknife: Britain's Secret Agents in Ireland* (Dublin: O'Brien Press, 2004).

Harnden, Toby, *Bandit Country: The IRA and South Armagh* (London: Hodder & Stoughton, 2000).

Hennessey, Thomas, *Hunger Strike: Margaret Thatcher's Battle with the IRA, 1980–1981* (Dublin: Irish Academic Press, 2014).

Hennessey, Thomas, *The Northern Ireland Peace Process: Ending the Troubles?* (Dublin: Gill and Macmillan, 1999).

Hennessy, Peter (ed.), *The New Protective State: Government, Intelligence and Terrorism* (London: Continuum, 2007).

Herman, Michael, *Intelligence Power in Peace and War* (Cambridge: Cambridge University Press, 1996).

Hollingsworth, Mark, and Nick Fielding, *Defending the Realm: Inside MI5 and the War on Terrorism* (London: André Deutsch, 2003).

Horgan, John, and Max Taylor, 'Playing the "Green Card": Financing the Provisional IRA: Part 1', *Terrorism and Political Violence*, 11(2), (1999), pp. 1–38.

Howard, Michael, *The Causes of War* (London: Counterpoint, 1983).

Jeffery, Keith, 'Intelligence and Counter-insurgency Operations: Some Reflections on the British Experience', *Intelligence and National Security*, 2(1), (1987), pp. 117–149.

Jeffery, Keith, *MI6: The History of the Secret Intelligence Service, 1909–1949* (London: Bloomsbury, 2010).

Jordan, Hugh, *Milestones to Murder: Defining Moments in Ulster's Terror War* (Edinburgh: Mainstream, 2002).

Kelley, Kevin J., *The Longest War: Northern Ireland and the IRA* (London: Zed Books, 1982).

Kingsley, Paul, *Londonderry Revisited: A Loyalist Analysis of the Civil Rights Controversy* (Belfast: Belfast Publications, 1989).

Kitson, Frank, *Gangs and Counter-gangs* (London: Barrie and Rockliff, 1960).

Lander, Stephen, 'British Intelligence in the Twentieth Century', *Intelligence and National Security*, 17(1), (2002), pp. 7–20.

Leahy, Thomas, *The Intelligence War Against the IRA* (Cambridge: Cambridge University Press, 2020).

MacIntyre, Ben, *The Spy and the Traitor: The Greatest Espionage Story of the Cold War* (London: Penguin Books, 2018).

McAuley, James W., Catherine McGlynn and Jonathan Tonge, 'Conflict Resolution in Asymmetric and Symmetric Situations: Northern Ireland as a Case Study', *Dynamics of Asymmetric Conflict*, 1(1), (2008), pp. 88–102.

McCarthy, Justine, 'Martin McGuinness in 1986' in Deric Henderson and Ivan Little (eds), *Reporting the Troubles: Journalists Tell Their Stories of the Northern Ireland Conflict* (Belfast: Blackstaff Press, 2018), pp. 98–100.

McCleery, Martin J., *Operation Demetrius and its Aftermath: A New History of the Use of Internment without Trial in Northern Ireland, 1971–75* (Manchester: Manchester University Press, 2015).

McCleery, Martin J., and Aaron Edwards, 'The 1988 Murders of Corporal David Howes and Corporal Derek Wood: A Micro-Dynamic Analysis of Political Violence during the Northern Ireland Conflict', *Critical Military Studies*, 5(2), (2017), pp. 131–149.

McDonald, Henry, *Gunsmoke and Mirrors: How Sinn Féin Dress Up Defeat as Victory* (Dublin: Gill and Macmillan, 2008).

McGarry, J., and B. O'Leary, *Explaining Northern Ireland* (Oxford: Blackwell, 1995).

McIntyre Anthony, 'The Funeral of Brendan Hughes: Setting the Record Straight', *The Blanket*, 28 September 2008.

McIntyre Anthony, 'Of Myths and Men: Dissent within Republicanism and Loyalism' in Aaron Edwards and Stephen Bloomer (eds), *Transforming the Peace Process in Northern Ireland: From Terrorism to Democratic Politics* (Dublin: Irish Academic Press, 2008).

McIntyre, Anthony, 'Who Knew – Who Knows – Who Will Tell?', *The Blanket*, 15 May 2003.

McKearney, Tommy, *The Provisional IRA: From Insurrection to Parliament* (London: Pluto Press, 2011).

McKee, Lyra, *Angels with Blue Faces* (Belfast: Excalibur Press, 2019).

McKittrick, David, Seamus Kelters, Brian Feeney and Chris Thornton, *Lost Lives: The Stories of the Men, Women and Children who Died as a Result of the Northern Ireland Troubles*, Revised and Updated (Edinburgh: Mainstream, 2001).

Mallie, Eamonn, and David McKittrick, *The Fight for Peace* (London: Heinemann, 1996).

Matchett, William, *Secret Victory: The Intelligence War that Beat the IRA* (Lisburn: Hiskey Ltd, 2016).

Moloney, Ed, *A Secret History of the IRA*, Revised and Updated Edition (London: Penguin, 2007).

Moloney, Ed, *Voices from the Grave: Two Men's War in Ireland* (London: Faber, 2010).

Monaghan, Rachel, and Peter Shirlow, 'Forward to the Past? Loyalist Paramilitarism in Northern Ireland Since 1994', *Studies in Conflict & Terrorism*, 34(8), (2011), pp. 649–665.

Moran, Jon, 'Evaluating Special Branch and the Use of Informant Intelligence in Northern Ireland', *Intelligence and National Security*, 25(1), (2010), pp. 1–23.

Moran, Jon, *From Northern Ireland to Afghanistan: British Military Intelligence Operations, Ethics and Human Rights* (Farnham: Ashgate, 2013).

Moran, Jon, *Policing the Peace in Northern Ireland: Politics, Crime and Security After the Belfast Agreement* (Manchester: Manchester University Press, 2008).

Morrison, John F., *The Origins and Rise of Dissident Irish Republicanism: The Role and Impact of Organizational Splits* (London: Bloomsbury Academic, 2013).

Mulroe, Patrick, *Bombs, Bullets and the Border – Policing Ireland's Frontier: Irish Security Policy, 1969–1978* (Dublin: Merrion Press, 2017).

Mumford, Andrew, 'Covert Peacemaking: Clandestine Negotiations and Backchannels with the Provisional IRA during the Early "Troubles", 1972–76', *Journal of Imperial and Commonwealth History*, 39(4), pp. 633–648.

Murray, Raymond, *The SAS in Ireland*, New Revised and Updated Edition (Cork: Mercier Press, 1990).

Neumann, Peter R., *Britain's Long War: British Strategy in the Northern Ireland Conflict 1969–98* (Basingstoke: Palgrave Macmillan, 2004).

Newbery, Samantha, *Interrogation, Intelligence and Security: Controversial British Techniques* (Manchester: Manchester University Press, 2015).

Northern Ireland Retired Police Officers' Association, *The Good Neighbour Bombing* (October 2013).

Ó Dochartaigh, Niall, *From Civil Rights to Armalites: Derry and the Birth of the Irish Troubles* (Cork: Cork University Press, 1997).

Ó Dochartaigh, Niall, 'The Longest Negotiation: British Policy, IRA Strategy and the Making of the Northern Ireland Peace Settlement', *Political Studies*, 63(1), (2015), pp. 202–220.

Ó Dochartaigh, Niall, 'The Role of an Intermediary in Back-Channel Negotiation: Evidence from the Brendan Duddy Papers', *Dynamics of Asymmetric Conflict*, 4(3), (October 2011), pp. 214–225.

O'Doherty, Malachi, *Gerry Adams: An Unauthorised Biography* (London: Faber, 2017).

O'Doherty, Malachi, *The Trouble with Guns: Republican Strategy and the Provisional IRA* (Belfast: Blackstaff Press, 1998).

Omand, David, 'Introduction: Learning from the Secret Past' in Robert Dover and Michael Goodman (eds), *Learning from the Secret Past: Cases in British Intelligence History* (Washington, DC: Georgetown University Press, 2011).

Oppenheimer, Andrew R., *IRA, The Bombs and the Bullets: A History of Deadly Ingenuity* (Dublin: Irish Academic Press, 2009).

O'Rawe, Richard, *Afterlives: The Hunger Strike and the Secret Offer that Changed Irish History* (Dublin: Lilliput Press, 2010).

O'Rawe, Richard, *Blanketmen: An Untold Story of the H-block Hunger Strike* (Dublin: New Island Books, 2004; 2016).

Orwell, George, *The Lion and the Unicorn: Socialism and the English Genius* (London: Secker and Warburg, 1962).

Parr, Connal, *Inventing the Myth: Political Passions and the Ulster Protestant Imagination* (Oxford: Oxford University Press, 2017).

Patterson, Henry, *Ireland Since 1939* (Dublin: Penguin Ireland, 2006).

Patterson, Henry, *Ireland's Violent Frontier: The Border and Anglo–Irish Relations During the Troubles* (Basingstoke: Palgrave Macmillan, 2013).

Patterson, Henry, *The Politics of Illusion: A Political History of the IRA* (London: Serif, 1997).

Pearce, Martin, *Spymaster: The Life of Britain's Most Decorated Cold War Spy and Head of MI6, Sir Maurice Oldfield* (London: Transworld Books, 2016).

Potter, John, *A Testimony of Courage: The Regimental History of the Ulster Defence Regiment* (Barnsley: Leo Cooper, 2001).

Quinlan, Michael, 'The Future of Covert Intelligence' in Harold Shukman (ed.), *Agents for Change: Intelligence Services in the 21st Century* (London: St Ermin's Press, 2000), pp. 61–71.

Ross, F. Stuart, *Smashing H-Block: The Rise and Fall of the Popular Campaign against Criminalization, 1976–1982* (Liverpool: Liverpool University Press, 2011).

Rowan, Brian, *An Armed Peace: Life and Death after the Ceasefires* (Edinburgh: Mainstream, 2003).

Rowan, Brian, *Behind the Lines: The Story of the IRA and Loyalist Ceasefires* (Belfast: Blackstaff Press, 1995).

Ruane, Joseph, and Jennifer Todd, *The Dynamics of Conflict in Northern Ireland: Power, Conflict and Emancipation* (Cambridge: Cambridge University Press, 1996).

Ryder, Chris, *The RUC: A Force Under Fire* (London: Arrow, 2000).

Ryder, Chris, *The Ulster Defence Regiment: An Instrument of Peace?* (London: Metheun, 1991).

Sanders, Andrew, *Inside the IRA: Dissident Republicans and the War for Legitimacy* (Edinburgh: Edinburgh University Press, 2011).

Sanders, Andrew, and Ian S. Wood, *Times of Troubles: Britain's War in Northern Ireland* (Edinburgh: Edinburgh University Press, 2012).

Sarma, Kiran, 'Informers and the Battle Against Republican Terrorism: A Review of 30 Years of Conflict', *Police Practice and Research: An International Journal*, 6(2), (2005), pp. 165–180.

Scull, Margaret M., 'The Catholic Church and the Hunger Strikes of Terence MacSwiney and Bobby Sands', *Irish Political Studies*, 31(2), (2016), pp. 282–299.

Shanahan, Timothy, *The Provisional Irish Republican Army and the Morality of Terrorism* (Edinburgh: Edinburgh University Press, 2009).

Sisman, Adam, *John Le Carré: The Biography* (London: Bloomsbury, 2015).

Smith, M.L.R., *Fighting for Ireland? The Military Strategy of the Irish Republican Movement* (London: Routledge, 1995).

Spencer, Graham (ed.), *The British and Peace in Northern Ireland: The Process and Practice of Reaching Agreement* (Cambridge: Cambridge University Press, 2015).

Stewart, Brian T.W., and Samantha Newbery, *Why Spy? The Art of Intelligence* (London: Hurst, 2015).

Taber, Robert, *The War of the Flea: A Study of Guerrilla Warfare Theory and Practice* (London: Paladin, 1970).

Taylor, Max, *The Fanatics: A Behavioural Approach to Political Violence* (London: Brassey's, 1991).

Taylor, Peter, *Beating the Terrorists? Interrogation in Omagh, Gough and Castlereagh* (London: Penguin, 1980).

Taylor, Peter, *Brits: The War Against the IRA* (London: Bloomsbury, 2001).

Taylor, Peter, *Loyalists* (London: Bloomsbury, 1999).

Taylor, Peter, *Provos: The IRA and Sinn Féin* (London: Bloomsbury, 1998).

Thompson, Robert, *Defeating Communist Insurgency: Experiences from Malaya and Vietnam* (London: Chatto & Windus, [1966], 1972).

Tonge, Jonathan, Peter Shirlow and James McAuley, 'So Why Did the Guns Fall Silent? How Interplay, not Stalemate, Explains the Northern Ireland Peace Process', *Irish Political Studies*, 26(1), (2011), pp. 1–18.

Toolis, Kevin, *Rebel Hearts: Journeys within the IRA's Soul* (London: Picador, 1995).

Urban, Mark, *Big Boys' Rules: The Secret Struggle Against the IRA* (London: Faber, 1992).

Urban, Mark, *UK Eyes Alpha: The Inside Story of British Intelligence* (London: Faber, 1996).

West, Nigel, *At Her Majesty's Secret Service: The Chiefs of Britain's Intelligence Agency MI6* (London: Greenhill Books, 2006).

West, Nigel, *Historical Dictionary of British Intelligence*, Second Edition (Plymouth, Scarecrow Press, 2014).

West, Nigel, 'Ulster Espionage: A Review of *Thatcher's Spy* by Willie Carlin', *International Journal of Intelligence and Counter-Intelligence*, published online, February 2020.

White, Robert, *Out of the Ashes: An Oral History of the Provisional Irish Republican Movement* (Dublin: Merrion Press, 2017).

Wilsey, John, *The Ulster Tales: A Tribute to those who Served, 1969–2000* (Barnsley: Pen & Sword, 2011).

Woodford, Isabel, and M.L.R. Smith, 'The Political Economy of the Provos: Inside the Finances of the Provisional IRA – A Revision', *Studies in Conflict & Terrorism*, 41(3), (2018), pp. 213–240.

Wright, Frank, *Northern Ireland: A Comparative Analysis* (Dublin: Gill and Macmillan, 1992).

Zegart, Amy, and Michael Morell, 'Spies, Lies and Algorithms: Why U.S. Intelligence Agencies Must Adapt or Fail', *Foreign Affairs*, 98(3), (2019), pp. 85–96.

PhD Theses

Dudai, Ron, 'The IRA and the shadow of the informer: Punishment, governance, and dealing with the past' (Queen's University Belfast: PhD Thesis, 2013).

Finegan, Rory, 'Targeted killings in Northern Ireland: An analysis of their effectiveness and implications for counter-terrorism policies' (Dublin City University: PhD Thesis, 2014).

Hurley, Timothy, '"No ordinary campaign": The British government's search for a security strategy during the Northern Ireland conflict, 1972–94' (King's College London: PhD Thesis, 2018).

Leahy, Thomas, 'Informers, agents, the IRA and British counter-insurgency strategy during the Northern Ireland Troubles, 1969 to 1998' (King's College London: PhD Thesis, 2015).

Matchett, William, 'The RUC Special Branch: How effective was it at defeating an insurgency?' (Ulster University: PhD Thesis, 2014).

Neumann, Peter R., 'British government strategy in Northern Ireland, 1969–98: An evolutionary analysis' (King's College London: PhD Thesis, 2002).

INDEX